The Dynamic Landscape

Design, Ecology and Management of Naturalistic Urban Planting

Edited by Nigel Dunnett and James Hitchmough

Taylor & Francis
Taylor & Francis Group
LONDON AND NEW YORK

First published 2004 by Spon Press

This paperback edition published 2008 by Taylor & Francis
2 Park Square, Milton Park, Abingdon, OX14 4RN

Simultaneously published in the USA and Canada
by Taylor & Francis
270 Madison Avenue, New York, NY 10016

Taylor & Francis is an imprint of the Taylor & Francis Group, an informa business

Typeset in Univers by Ninety Seven Plus
Printed and bound in India by Replika Press Pvt. Ltd.

British Library Cataloguing in Publication Data
A catalogue record for this book is available from the British Library

Library of Congress Cataloging in Publication Data
The dynamic landscape : naturalistic planting in an urban context /
[edited by] Nigel Dunnett and James Hitchmough
p. cm.
Includes bibliographical references and index.
1. Landscape gardening. I. Dunnett, Nigel. II. Hitchmough, James.
SB473. D95 2003
721'.5–dc21 2003010782

ISBN13: 978-0-415-43810-0 (pbk)
ISBN13: 978-0-415-25620-9 (hbk)

Contents

Illustration credits

Anna Jorgensen
Figures 11.4, 11.7, 11.11–11.13
Darrel Morrison
Figures 5.1–5.11
Hein Koningen
Figure 10.1
James Hitchmough
Figures 2.16–2.18, 6.1–21, 9.1–9.15, 11.9
Jan Woudstra
Figures 2.10, 2.11, 2.15, 2.22
Nigel Dunnett
Figures 1.1–1.15, 9.1–9.15, 11.1–11.3, 11.5, 11.6, 11.8 and 11.10
Noel Kingsbury
Figures 4.1, 4.9
Roland Gustavsson
Figures 7.1–7.22
Wolfram Kircher
Figures 8.2–8.5, 8.7–8.10, 8.12–8.13, 8.15, 8.17–8.19, 8.22–8.23, 8.25–8.28

Chapter 1

Introduction to naturalistic planting in urban landscapes

James Hitchmough and Nigel Dunnett

Although this book is potentially relevant to many urban contexts, it is most strongly aimed at the 'public' and 'semi-public' landscape. Some of these landscapes are public parks of one sort or another. The remainder are a difficult-to-characterise mix of spaces around public housing, commercial developments and institutions, car parks, left-over spaces from development, structure plantings of massed trees and shrubs, and strips along paths, roads and other corridors. Taken as a whole, these often very ordinary places are the landscapes we are most familiar with and which inform, and perhaps even shape, our attitudes to the world around us. In combination with private gardens, these urban spaces are also the landscapes where we have most of our first-hand experiences of 'nature'. The design form of these landscapes is as diverse as their physical size, location and history. Examples of planting styles inspired by or derived from the picturesque, the gardenesque, the garden city, the modern movement, the municipal engineer, the ecological and, latterly, the community involvement style can all be found. Irrespective of how we now judge the aesthetic merits of the planting styles associated with these movements, in their day all were founded on the principle of being pleasing (as well as functional) to their creators and to the public at large.

Over the past couple of decades in Britain and other Western countries, the ongoing decline of public landscape maintenance, the realisation that funding will never again reach the levels of the nineteenth century or even early twentieth century, and the arrival of new social and environmental movements, has initiated a search for 'new' planting styles to help re-envigorate public landscapes. Views differ on what these might be, however the consensus is that these plantings should have relatively low-maintenance costs, be as sustainable as possible, taxonomically diverse, demonstrate marked seasonal change, and support as much wildlife as possible. These requirements fly in the face of traditional horticultural wisdom, which rightly argues that maintenance costs are generally proportional to planting complexity. We argue in this book that the only possible way to escape this restriction is to move away from wholesale reliance on traditional horticulturally-based plantings. By 'horticultural', we refer to plantings composed primarily of exotic species and cultivars, organised in culturally informed arrangements, rather than as ecologically-based plant communities, and managed relatively intensively to reduce competition between planted stock and spontaneously invading weeds, and to instead develop plantings that exploit ecological *as well as* horticultural processes and understanding (Figure 1.1).

It is reasonable to ask at this point whether the notion of maintaining a degree of quality in urban public planting should really be a point of concern – does urban horticulture, as represented in the diverse plantings of a well-maintained public park, for example, any longer have relevance to the general urban dweller? What is the benefit of introducing and maintaining ornamental or amenity vegetation in urban areas? Setting aside the purely functional roles of spatial subdivision and screening, and the obvious benefit of aesthetic delight, urban landscape plantings may become increasingly important to the health of the city environment and of those who live within it. With ever greater emphasis on the 'compact city' and higher densities of building in urban areas, good quality green spaces take on a special recreational, social and environmental role. There is mounting evidence that environmental quality is one of the factors that has a direct affect on the health and well-being of people in urban areas. This goes much further than a simple feeling of uplift at the sight of colourful flowering vegetation. In a wide-ranging study of urban green spaces in England, Dunnett *et al.* (2002) found that the quality of green spaces and their maintenance is likely to be viewed by local residents as one of the main indicators of general neighbourhood quality. There are therefore compelling arguments to be made that urban public planting has an important role to play in the general quality of life of people living in towns and cities, and this is before we even consider the benefits to wildlife and the functioning of a city's ecological networks. It is all very well to

1.1
'Horticultural' landscape vegetation: (a) blocks of evergreen shrubs, mechanically cut on a regular basis to maintain an artificial geometric shape, combined with mown grass and widely spaced trees. A very common and unfortunate contemporary approach to public landscape planting; and (b) seasonal bedding – still regarded by many as the epitome of the craft of public horticulture. The extensive and vibrant colour of such bedding is achieved as a result of significant financial, labour and resource inputs

1.2
Direct-sown annual meadow 10 weeks after sowing in a Sheffield housing estate. Mixed native-exotic meadows provide high-impact, long-lasting colour and receive high public support

make general statements like this about what is desirable, however the real challenge is how can these benefits be achieved in reality? And in particular, how can we both uphold the quality of plantings where they exist already, but equally importantly, how can we extend the benefits of good urban plantings to those areas where they have been lost or may never have existed in the first place. It is hoped that this book provides some possible answers. Before going on to discuss the principles behind a more ecological approach to urban planting, it is first important to consider the social implications – what do people generally like to see in their surroundings and can an ecologically-informed approach provide this?

Public plantings – the social dimension

The nature conservation movement has seized upon the inability to adequately fund the maintenance of traditional horticulturally based plantings as an opportunity to increase the use of native 'habitat' plantings in urban landscapes. This has occurred to a considerable degree over the past 20 years in Britain, mirroring what had happened much earlier in some other European countries. This has been a very positive development, the most obvious product of which has been substantial areas of young woodlands, which, although rather ecologically depauperate, should enrich with time. This movement has not, however, been able to fully address the latent needs left unfulfilled by the decline of traditional horticultural planting. To do this, it is necessary to understand the reasons why these horticultural styles developed in urban public landscapes in the first instance.

In Britain, even at the height of the most ascetic planting traditions of the eighteenth-century English Landscape movement, highly colourful planting persisted within Pleasure Grounds (Laird 1999). People continued to pursue the horticultural exaggeration or 'improvement' of the nature they knew in the countryside. However abstracted, planting in private gardens nearly always demonstrates this exaggeration of nature; a latent desire for colour and drama appears to be an important part of the human psyche. This desire might be seen as a form of decadence, of wanting more than nature can offer, but why should this be considered to be regressive? Most lay people intuitively make judgements on the semi-natural vegetation around them on the basis of appearance, and always value some bits more than others, often because they are more colourful (Figure 1.2). If we are honest about it, and for a moment strip away learnt notions of ecological value, design values of rhythm and unity, and remove it from its context as part of scenery, on most days of the year semi-natural vegetation is often visually rather mundane. For individual people, this common, passive response to semi-natural vegetation can be papered over by taking on-board additional value systems that suppress or redefine these visceral aesthetic feelings. By doing this, tall rank grassland goes from being untidy and dull to a worthy vegetation involving a dramatic play of pulsating stems against the light, as well as being an important habitat for small mammals. Dullness or subtlety becomes reinterpreted as a virtue. There is merit in this reinterpretation, but we should not lose sight of how these values come together if we are not to be blind to other people's perceptions. As a cultural institution, one of the key roles of the garden is in effect to gather together the plants, and the communities drawn from semi-natural vegetation, that are the most appealing to humans (Figure 1.3).

It is interesting that in Germany, the Netherlands and North America, the idea of nature-like, ecological planting was well founded by the end of the nineteenth century, and was vigorously pursued by landscape architects who were as strongly influenced by aesthetic as well as ecological and cultural outcomes. Art and design traditions would be invoked to package nature to look good and, by doing so, more urban people would be able to embrace it. These ideas are discussed in greater detail by Jan Woudstra in Chapter 2. Awareness of these foreign traditions was limited in Britain, and even when present, became lost or perhaps obscured towards the end of the twentieth century in the enthusiasm to embrace a more literal 'native' urban nature. In this later habitat restoration inspired movement, art and culture, and aesthetics play little

1.3
Spontaneous urban vegetation. An important habitat resource, yes, but is it appreciated as such by the general public?

1.4
Ponds and lakes in urban parks offer great potential for dramatic planting; Parc Andre Malreaux, Paris

or no conscious part, putting back what has been lost being the key measure of success.

Although in Britain many of the urban Wildlife Trusts maintain a very liberal perspective on conservation, grounded in social awareness, overall habitat restoration is a conservative rather than a creative discipline, sometimes motivated by rigid moral assumptions about what is right. Proponents adhere to the philosophy that if you put back the species that were there before humans destroyed them, the aesthetics will sort themselves out. In any case, with such moral authority on your side, there is no need to consider whether such vegetation positively enriches the lives of the public. This philosophy is less troublesome to apply *in toto* in rural landscapes that are less subject to intense public scrutiny but is sometimes problematic in urban landscapes founded on different cultural assumptions. Whilst they share many common goals, these two traditions of using nature-like landscapes in urban landscapes are sometimes difficult to reconcile in practice.

This impasse is perhaps the ideal place to tackle exactly where a book about how to design and manage ecologically informed, nature-like planting fits in practice and philosophy. Books written by a collective of authors are often awkward in that it is often impossible for everyone to sign up to the same principles. The idea that unites all of the contributors of *The Dynamic Landscape* is that, in urban contexts, designed, nature-like vegetation must be strongly informed by aesthetic principles if it is to be understood and valued by the public at large (Figure 1.4).

This prompts the question that Anna Jorgensen explores in detail in Chapter 11: what do we know about how the public appreciate nature-like vegetation? Do people actually like this type of vegetation, and if so why and if not why not? There is a tendency for all professional groups and disciplines to believe that their perceptions of worth and beauty are intrinsically valid, and that those who hold different views are at best poorly informed. Such attitudes are particularly strongly held within nature conservation, where attitudes are increasingly shaped by a sense of a moral outrage. Aesthetic perceptions and preferences do however differ enormously between individuals, peer groups and cultures, with truths being relative rather than absolute. If it were not for this psychological quirk our species would have no need for landscape architects and related disciplines to exist. We would happily live surrounded by whatever vegetation sprouted spontaneously from the soil. Our own experience of some of the ecologically-based vegetation we have created is that, to many lay observers, until it flowers and, in some cases, even when flowering, it is indistinguishable from weed communities! On the other hand, it is interesting how readily some aesthetic preferences change, through experience and learning. These values are not fixed and this process can be readily observed, for example, as landscape design students progress from the first to final year.

There has been much research on landscape perception and preference in rural situations. Most people seem to like 'natural scenes' in a rural context, however it is unsound to try to apply this verbatim to urban spaces. There has been little work at the level of individual plant communities. Culture, context and familiarity seem to be very important, but, in general, the disorderly appearance of nature-like landscapes seems to be challenging in many urban situations. This suggests that nature-like vegetation which is not designed to make it clear that it is meant to be there and is cared for, may not be widely valued. It is certainly naïve to imagine that 100 m^2 of vegetation 'lifted out' of a semi-natural landscape scene will be perceived in the same way when placed in an urban context. In most cases, the transformation will only be successful where the scene is ordered in some way, the viewer provided with cues, or the visual intensity exaggerated by design, as previously mentioned.

Given our strong concern for the aesthetics of landscape, this book adopts a pluralistic approach to nature-like planting. The authors suggest that it is possible to identify at least three broad strands within nature-like planting, which, to some degree, are encompassed by the authors within this text. A more detailed exploration of these strands is provided in the context of practice by Noel Kingsbury in Chapter 3. The first of these, and probably the least relevant to this text, is the *habitat restoration* landscape. As commonly practised, this involves trying to establish, or failing that, guessing what species might have occupied the site in the past, then locating seed of these, preferably from local, extant populations. Reinforcing biodiversity, and essentially not adding anything as either species or sub-populations that might not have existed on the site, is uppermost. The core values of this activity are nature conservation *per se* and, with the exception of overall planning issues, design plays a very limited role. Habitat restoration projects of this type are most frequently associated with parcels of land that retain some semblance of natural character, whether in urban or rural locations. Frequently, this type of planting is used to create connections to link surviving fragments of semi-natural vegetation, to improve the movement of plants and animals and, more importantly, their genes, and create the opportunity for the development of viable populations.

Habitat restoration is an important form of practice. However, as it is based on the assumption that such works are an indisputable good, it sometimes generates social and political tensions when applied to highly urbanised landscapes. Despite being a highly conservative approach to the use of native plants, habitat restoration can be despised by the arch puritans of the environmental movement, especially those operating within the frameworks constructed by philosophers such as Katz (2000), who argue that the very act of creating a facsimile simultaneously devalues it. Some of this unease, together with fears about the commodification of nature, have led to less interventionist forms of habitat restoration, where management is used to create the conditions to kick start the redevelopment of plant communities by natural colonisation. This seems a very elegant and attractive approach, but is potentially very long term and, in the case of species that are poorly dispersed, a supremely optimistic practice.

The second strand in creating nature-like plantings is the *creative conservation* landscape style. This involves a less rigidly defined approach because it is often impossible to know exactly what once occupied a site; practice is therefore inevitably conjectural. Even where prior plant composition is known with some certainty, this merely provides a snapshot of an arbitrary point in time, before and after which plant composition would be different. The problem of timescale and the fact that the conditions on urban sites in particular will generally be very different in the present than in the past, undermines the rigid right or wrong presumptions associated with a pure habitat restoration approach. The creative conservation style is, in essence, a process that leads to some, as yet undefined, future product, the precise nature of which is shaped by the combination of site and management. The conservation charity Landlife, based in Liverpool, is the most articulate proponent of this approach in the UK. As a result of these considerations, native species that are associated with similar environmental conditions as those that prevail on the site to be worked upon are selected. Seed or plant material is obtained from native plant nurseries within the geographical region, for example, in our case the UK. The rationale for doing this is that there is little evidence (see Wilkinson 2001) that the genes of more local populations will be better fitted to the changed site conditions and, in any case, natural selection will sort things out. Fears of out-breeding depression, reducing the fitness of extant local populations of species (Keller *et al*. 2000), are often overemphasised (Luijten *et al*. 2002), especially in urban situations where such populations may be absent or effectively quarantined by surrounding urban development. The visual characteristics of the vegetation that is produced will often be recognised within this approach to be important in gaining community and political support. This style is based on a number of key principles: plants must be ecologically well fitted to where they are to grow; they must function as a plant community rather than as individual species; change in plantings is inevitable and must be allowed for; and management practices need to be informed by ecological as well as horticultural understanding. Darrel Morrison discusses this approach in greater detail in Chapter 5 (Figure 1.5).

The third approach involves the application of human agency to create nature-like communities of species that could never have 'naturally' occurred on the sites but which may, given its current conditions, be well fitted to it. This *anthropogenic landscape* approach may be seen as an abomination by those who pursue habitat restoration, and even creative conservation landscape approaches, because it involves the synthesis of novel plant communities that have never before existed and that cannot be found in any flora. This practice has been an unconscious trait in human beings for millennia, indirectly through hunter gathering and latterly through low-intensity agriculture, creating along the

way plant communities that we now consider to have high nature conservation value, for example cornfield annuals. It has reached its zenith in the spontaneously occurring and planted vegetation of cities. Anthropogenic plant communities are based on exactly the same ecological processes as habitat restoration and creative conservation landscape styles, although this is obscured by the use of species that are not native to the site. It involves the assemblage of species that possess evidence of fitness for a particular environment that are then subjected to the combination of low-intensity management and natural selection (Figure 1.6).

The anthropogenic landscape approach is strongly influenced by aesthetic concerns, but also recognises that some of the species we want to have in the community will fail and disappear. Change in the composition of this type of vegetation across time is an inevitable fact and, even when dealing with entirely non-native plant communities, clearly distinguishes this approach from horticultural plant communities. Given the aesthetic perspectives of managers and the public however, it is inevitable that managing change will not be value neutral but will be focused, where possible, to favour the retention of some species at the expense of others.

This text is mainly concerned with creative conservation and anthropogenic nature-like vegetation. As soon as one begins to discuss ecological principles in the creation of vegetation that does not follow a pure habitat restoration approach, a raft of issues arise. Is it possible to reconcile the creative conservation landscape and, in particularly, the anthropogenic landscape style with current urban environmental dialogues on issues such as sustainability, biodiversity and developing local character? Is it ethical, at a time of clear evidence of massive human impact on the environment, to create new plant communities that are not the same in terms of species and sub-specific

1.5
'Creative Conservation' – a flowering meadow and wetland landscape around a new commercial development in Germany

1.6
'Anthropogenic' naturalistic vegetation – a naturalistic mix of herbaceous perennials and shrubs, but composed predominantly of non-native species, Henry Doubleday Research Association Headquarters, Ryton

genetic variation as those that may once have occupied what is now an urban site? The remainder of this chapter attempts to address these issues and to steer a course through a debate that is at times heavily confused through the adoption, in the urban context, of ideas developed primarily for use in nature conservation in the rural environment.

What is an ecologically-informed approach to urban planting?

The concept of ecologically-based plantings is unfortunately a very slippery one, and one that is open to wide interpretation. The urban environment, characterised by altered climate and water relations, damaged soils, skeletal and man-made substrates, a specialised flora of native and non-native species, and a strong cultural context, means that taking a purist ecological line is untenable. Indeed, many core principles that have come to be associated with an ecological approach to designed vegetation can be seen to be full of contradictions when applied in the urban situation. For the remainder of this chapter we will consider how a number of ideas that are considered important to the application of the term 'ecological' to designed vegetation relate to the urban context. These include the origin of component species and issues revolving around native and non-native species, biodiversity, the use of chemicals in establishment, the structure and appearance of vegetation, and the promotion of ecological processes.

Biodiversity – native species, non-native species and provenance

Native species are typically seen as being inherently ecological, whereas exotic species are not, unless considered in the context of the country they hail from, in which case they immediately become ecological! Whilst superficially the idea that all urban space available for planting should be filled with communities of native species to counterbalance loss elsewhere is attractive, we argue that in an urban context this is just unworkable. Such vegetation simply would not meet the purpose of the inhabitants in many situations. In any case, irrespective of calamities elsewhere, cities and civilisation are not about remaking the world as it once was. Instead they are about transforming it, and shaping new realities. Given the mobility and cultural evolution of *Homo sapiens*, the dominant species in this habitat, it is inevitable that these landscapes will support spontaneous non-native species that exploit new ecological niches more effectively than the original native inhabitants. This idea of transformation has also been applied to the plant and animal communities of cities by Gilbert (1989) and others, leading to the development of the scientific discipline *urban ecology*. Philosophical interpretations of urban ecology have differed greatly. Some ecologists and conservationists persist in seeing urban ecology as dealing with native species that survive, plus alien species, and in doing so suggest that urban species essentially form a degenerate version of adjacent rural ecosystems. This view is unwittingly derived at least in part from romantic nineteenth-century views of industrialisation and urbanisation as being synonymous with social and moral corruption. Others, and particularly those able to construct a more culturally based perspective, for example McIntyre *et al.* (2000), see the anthropogenic jumble of urban plant assemblages as being of intrinsic worth. Why should, for example, nature-like plant communities brought into effect by intentional (or unintentional) human agency be ecologically and aesthetically intrinsically less valuable than those that result from random combinations of chance events? In biological terms they may be demonstrably less or more valuable, depending on their architecture and the species present, whilst in most cases being more aesthetically pleasing due to having been so designed. Why is human agency so bad when it was unconsciously or consciously employed in the past to help create semi-natural vegetation, such as meadows, steppe, prairie and various woodland communities that we now cherish as 'nature'? To escape significant human agency one has to return to the Pleistocene.

Even within urban ecology circles that embrace these latter notions, researchers have shied away from including cultivated garden vegetation in the concept, on the basis that it does not arise spontaneously and that its composition is directly influenced by people, and therefore lies outside of ecology.

For both philosophical and pragmatic perspectives, this situation is difficult to defend. In many industrial and post-industrial countries, in excess of 75% of the population lives in towns and cities (90% in the UK and the Netherlands), and a greater percentage of urban areas are covered with gardens as opposed to spontaneously occurring plant communities. Thompson *et al.* (2003) have recently published a description of gardens and their plant communities as habitats; a significant step to correcting this historical bias. To return to the original question on the ethics of using non-native species in urban landscapes, for the combinations of factors referred to above, the authors of this chapter reject the notion that it is unethical to depart from a purely habitat restoration approach in developing urban vegetation.

Instead, we propose that there are opportunities in urban areas to make greater use of native and non-native species in naturalistic plant communities. In proposing this we recognise that these types of plant communities are not suitable for all planting environments, nor indeed are they necessarily intrinsically more worthy than more conventional, horticultural types of urban vegetation. Decisions on which is most appropriate need to be based on an understanding of the site and on the social, political and biological context. What this means in practice is that the outcome of the decision-making process will vary between practitioners in different countries in response to local conditions and issues. In Britain for example, and in some other European countries, there is a widespread, and highly intellectualised culture associated with the cultivation of non-native species. In parallel with this, Britain has a very small native flora, which may, in turn, be a factor that has encouraged interest in non-native plants in gardens. Given this combination, it is easy to see why, for example, the use of non-native plants in naturalistic plant communities might seem appropriate in some urban settings (Figure 1.7). The authors' interest in anthropogenic plant communities is not driven by a preference for non-native over native species, but rather the desire to be able to effectively utilise visual and functional characteristics that are absent in the native flora (Figure 1.8).

In countries with very rich floras, and a relatively restricted tradition of sophisticated gardening, such as the USA, the impetus to use non-native species is likely to be greatly reduced. Countries such as Germany lie halfway between these two poles, and this is reflected in a clear split between the use of native and non-native species in practice, as discussed by Noel Kingsbury in Chapter 3. In most cases, the creation of completely anthropogenic plant communities will be a response to a particular set of needs, often associated with the users of a building or facility. As a result, most anthropogenic plant communities are likely to be less commonly used and to cover a smaller area of ground than 'native', nature-like communities, which will generally form the vegetative backcloth. These issues are discussed in greater detail by James Hitchmough for herbaceous vegetation in Chapter 6, and by Roland Gustavsson for woody vegetation in Chapter 7 (Figure 1.9).

We have previously argued that in urban situations it is often difficult to sustain the view that

1.7
Naturalistic sown meadow in an urban park, Sheffield. By not including grasses in the meadow mix, the flowering impact is heightened dramatically

1.8
The full zonation of wetland planting, from wet woodland through to submerged aquatics promotes both visual and biological diversity

1.9
The interior quality of a woodland varies greatly according to tree species, arrangements, densities, composition and ground treatment. How often are the many aesthetic possibilities considered in urban woodland design?

seed and other propagules of native plants used in these landscapes *must be* derived from a local population. A pragmatic reason for adopting this position is that in many situations it is difficult to locate local populations to act as a seed source. More important, however, is the fact that where extant populations of, say, common native species – for example, oak trees – are present, this does not mean they represent a 'local population' in a genetic sense. In many cases, they are likely to represent a combination of genes from planted oaks derived over the centuries from non-local and foreign seed, intermixed with genuinely local genotypes. Most urban sites are heavily transformed, particularly in terms of soil conditions and climate, and the assumption that original genotypes will be better fitted than non-local genotypes is inherently too unreliable to be a defining objective of practice. Natural selection results in local populations that are well enough fitted but no more than this, non-local genotypes may be equally well fitted (Gould 1997). Sackville-Hamilton (2001) has argued that we have a duty to use only local populations because our governments have signed up to the Bio-diversity

1.10
Sown native-exotic annual meadow along an urban highway, Gloucester. A very different approach to standard landscape treatments that, as well as providing visual interest, also supports biodiversity

Convention and this must be interpreted to mean every last bit of genetic variation must be conserved *in toto*. This is clearly impractical and indeed nonsensical in many urban contexts, and flies in the face of the reality of ongoing evolution of plant populations in response to environmental and cultural change. It is perhaps telling that some of the most vociferous supporters of using only local genotypes work in the least urbanised regions of the UK.

In the light of the biodiversity debate, can a cogent argument be made for using non-native plants in naturalistic plantings in urban places? The rational arguments against using non-native plants are often contradictory. Non-native species are claimed to be inevitably poorly fitted, and need cosseting and therefore cannot be sustainable. Non-native species are also however claimed to be invasive! Some non-native species are poorly fitted, and can only persist when competition with other plants and herbivores is carefully controlled, as in gardens. These species are of little value in naturalistic plant communities, however there are other species that are perfectly robust, even in the face of competition, but without being invasive, that are well suited to anthropogenic plant communities. Invasiveness is not a property of which geopolitical region a plant hails from, but is based on the possession of certain biological traits, such as high seed production, effective seed dispersal, capacity for vegetative spread, low palatability to herbivores and so on. There are invasive natives and there are invasive aliens. Most, if not all, of the non-native species that are likely to be used in nature-like plant communities will already have been cultivated in urban and rural gardens and parks for many years, in some cases for centuries, particularly in Europe. The widespread practice of dumping garden waste on roadsides and other places has provided abundant opportunity for the naturalisation of these species, yet only a very small percentage of the cultivated decorative flora has taken advantage of this. In Britain, for example, the commercially available cultivated decorative flora is in excess of 70,000 taxa, only a tiny percentage of which are extensively naturalised (Clement and Foster 1994) and fewer still have anywhere near the adverse ecological impact of invasive natives. The authors' work on deliberately attempting to naturalise non-native herbaceous plants in purpose-sown native meadow vegetation in urban parks has demonstrated just how difficult it is to establish even well-fitted species in the grassy vegetation that dominates the British landscape (Hitchmough and Woudstra 1999; Hitchmough 2000). This is not, however, the situation in some other countries, and practice needs to reflect this.

Against the risks of naturalisation have to be set the cultural meaning and richness that many urban people derive from such plants. This is especially so in a country like Britain where the cultivation of decorative plants is one of the most widespread and important recreational activities.

It is also important to take into account the habitat that non-native species provide for fauna in towns and cities, and how these plants are important in developing a positive empathy with the natural world beyond the garden. As with native species, non-native species differ in their value as a habitat or foraging resource, but it is clear that they are very important for nature conservation in urban landscapes, as can be gauged for invertebrates by the work of Owen (1991). It is important to recognise that many users of non-native plant materials are equally passionate about native plants inside and outside their gardens. The relationship is not a mutually exclusive one, what is favoured at a point in time varies according to the urban-rural context. Issues of naturalisation and attitudes to non-native plants are heavily grounded in human culture and, once again, can only be discussed sensibly within the context of that culture, and therefore often the nation state.

Can the use of non-native species be considered to be sustainable? Sustainability is a difficult issue to address in terms of right and wrong because major elements within the sustainability model, for example, ecological, economic and social values, are sometimes at odds with one another. In addition, the component factors exist as a continuum of possible responses, and most importantly we read our own bias into sustainability. Within local authority planning departments there is anectodal evidence that sustainability is nearly always equated only with native plants. This is a convenient but often false assumption when applied as a universal truth. Plants that are likely to be most sustainable in a biological sense are those that are likely to be able to reproduce *in situ*, and thereby perpetuate themselves through subsequent sexual or clonal generations and undergo evolutionary change. Such plants may be native but they might also be exotics. In many cases, with both native and exotic species persistence will depend on human intervention to create the required conditions for regeneration and the growth of adults. Much of the native vegetation that the public regards as highly desirable, for example hay meadows and heathland, only persist in the longer term because of management. There are many situations in which we may, for a variety of ecological or cultural reasons, not want to use exotic species but this does not mean that they cannot be sustainable. Species that are too enthusiastically sustainable through profligate reproduction cross the line and are judged undesirable. Often we desire species that occupy the mid ground.

Within landscape practice our view of sustainability is often skewed to elevate biological above other categories of sustainability. Plant communities that are successful in terms of biological sustainability may score poorly in terms of social sustainability. The latter may, for example, be promoted more successfully with many lay people by plant communities that represent a compromise between what is ecological and what they are familiar with and value, for example the form and colour of a particular flower.

From a biological perspective, the degree of fitness for the environment as found is likely to be a better measure of likely sustainability than the origin of the species. Very often a key factor in this is the inherent productivity of a species (the capacity to produce vegetative growth to compete for resources with adjacent plants) in relation to the productivity of the environment it is expected to grow in. This is particularly marked for herbaceous plant communities which have fewer opportunities to distribute their canopies in space to avoid competition. On highly fertile productive sites, species that are not themselves highly productive are rapidly competitively displaced by other planted or spontaneously occurring species of higher productivity. This happens irrespective of where they originate from or what other cultural labels they bear. These ideas are explored further by Nigel Dunnett in Chapter 4.

As with nearly all of the ideas in this chapter, sustainability is subject to ongoing cultural reinterpretation in response to local conditions. In North America, relatively few people pursue the care of the vegetation in their 'yard' as an engrossing, intellectually rewarding recreation; it is maintenance and little more. As a result, there is a huge garden and lawn care industry with much routine garden-care work undertaken by contractors. Many of these employ a very prescriptive approach to plant care; pests and diseases are to be eliminated when found, irrespective of the damage they cause, and plants are to be watered and fertilised, irrespective of whether this is required or not. Against such a backcloth of resource consumption, it is not surprising that native plants should be seen as more sustainable by virtue of not requiring such care in the wild. The point is, however, cultivated non-natives do not necessarily require such care either, except when these are poorly fitted and inappropriately used in a particular location. Sustainability thus becomes an artefact of cultural perceptions rather than biological reality.

One of the most frequently made arguments concerning the use of native species is that they support a wider biodiversity. Native plant species generally appear to support a wider range of invertebrates than, for example, do non-native species, and in some cases planting that mimics the structure of naturally occurring arrangements may increase habitat value for some organisms, particularly birds. Exotic species will also, however, support some species, and in some cases more species than some native species. Many invertebrates in particular may not distinguish between vegetation that mimics natural arrangements and that which does not.

Management, sustainability and resource inputs

Another measure of 'ecological' might involve the degree to which 'non-natural' approaches are used to manage vegetation. Hence, the Organic Movement see cultivated vegetation which is hand weeded or mulched with decomposing organic debris, and with pests controlled by plant synthesised pesticides, such as pyrethrum, as more ecological than that in which pests and weeds are managed by factory synthesised organic (i.e. carbon based) chemicals. The underlying rationale for this view is the value judgement that, irrespective of actual toxicity, the latter are intrinsically bad and must have a greater negative effect on non-target fauna. Again, this perspective is problematic: does native vegetation in a National Nature Research managed by English Nature become less ecological because herbicides are used to control some problem weed species, despite the fact that on all other counts it is a model of 'ecological-ness'? Conversely, do exotic species planted in a conventional garden become more ecological when managed by organic husbandry?

Sustainability has also been subject to highly selective interpretation from within the environmental movement. For example, some would argue that it is unsustainable to use any sort of organic chemical in vegetation management because such materials are synthesised in a factory. As the lives of most people in industrial and post-industrial cultures are, and will continue to be, heavily dependent on anthropogenic organic molecules, is this a sensible measure of sustainability? A more useful measure might be to contrast how much fossil-fuel derived energy is required for synthesis in comparison with alternative means of undertaking the task. The situation becomes even more complex when toxicological concepts are considered. It has been put to the authors that it is better to use rhubarb leaves (a potent source of oxalic acid) to control weeds than a herbicide such as glyphosate because, despite similar toxicity, the former is naturally occurring. Putting weed-control efficacy to one side for a moment, no fossil-fuel energy has been used by the rhubarb in producing the oxalic acid, but are natural toxins more sustainable than anthropogenic toxins? Is it better to control weeds by burning propane gas in a flame gun or to use a far less energy intensive herbicide, or an even less energy intensive person with a trowel who may have to be transported regularly to the site in a diesel-fuelled vehicle? The latter may be very energy intensive but valuable in terms of social and economic sustainability, if funds are available to pay the wages. In North America, spring burning is a standard technique for managing prairie vegetation, and is seen as good because it is a 'natural' and highly effective form of management with a long history of use by aboriginal Americans. Yet, in terms of current environmental dialogues, it is undesirable in terms of CO_2 emissions?

In highly urbanised societies, discussion of sustainability in relation to vegetation management is never too far away from romantic sepia images of contented agricultural-horticultural workers cultivating the earth, in perfect harmony with the land. Surely all one has to do to be sustainable is to reconnect with this halcyon past. Many urban people enjoy cultivating plants as a recreation, however relatively few seem to want to hand-weed urban plantings all day as a full-time job for low wages. Even if these people existed, there are not the funds to pay them. Hein Koningen discusses the implications of changes in the aspirations of staff for the management of naturalistic vegetation in Chapter 10. In some situations, however, with the increasing involvement of local communities in urban green space management, and given some initial training and ongoing support where required, it may be possible for volunteers to successfully direct the development of naturalistic landscape plantings through occasional intensive maintenance days. In many naturalistic plantings, for example, woodland edges or prairie type vegetation, annual maintenance can be compressed into a couple of days in spring, cutting down the previous year's growth and manually removing undesirable colonists (Figures 1.11 and 1.12). Access to sufficient skilled labour would largely negate the need to use herbicides and other techniques that may be seen as undesirable.

We all want to be as sustainable as possible, but the problem is in agreeing what are the limits to what is sustainable and what is not? Can you be not very sustainable on one aspect and then very sustainable in another and come out overall with an acceptable sustainability 'score', or does one transgression place you outside the sustainability project? We are sure all of the authors in this book have struggled with these ideas, although given that they come from a variety of disciplines and traditions they will no doubt have come to different positions.

Most nature-like vegetation is potentially highly sustainable biologically in that it is intended to persist and regenerate *in situ* given appropriate management, and is expected to grow without additional inputs of water and nutrients, pest and disease control. Its complex structure and taxonomical diversity provides habitat opportunities for many other organisms, and if it is attractive and appropriate to its context it may be embraced by local people, thus fostering its social and economic sustainability. The sustainability score for nature-like vegetation will, however, fluctuate across time, as more or less management is required. Economic and biological sustainability is likely to be lowest during establishment and at critical points in long-term management, due to the need to manage to temporarily eliminate or reduce populations of weeds and some herbivores that may compete with, and lead to the decline of, the vegetation. To put this into perspective, these inputs are far greater with vegetation based on traditional horticultural principles of *comparable taxonomic diversity*. The only vegetation that is free of these sorts of inputs is that which spontaneously occurs and is in the process of turning into something else, plus monocultures of densely leafy long-lived evergreen shrubs. Whilst of value in specific situations, neither of these types of plant community can meet the needs of twenty-first-century green space, referred to at the beginning of this chapter.

1.11
North American prairie vegetation created through sowing in a trial plot in Sheffield. Creating colourful herbaceous vegetation through seeding is both cost-effective and promotes a spontaneous visual effect

Management will generally be most sustainable where plant communities are designed from the outset to be managed primarily by simple non-selective techniques that are applied to all the plants in a community, as discussed by James Hitchmough in Chapter 6. This has often been the philosophy behind the creative conservation landscape style, but has been conspicuously absent from many continental European examples of anthropogenic plant communities. These have been maintained by the traditional horticultural technique of intensive hand-weeding; they look but do not necessarily function ecologically. In the absence of clear information to the contrary, people seem to perceive that plants arranged to mimic the structural and spatial arrangements found in naturally occurring vegetation are more 'ecological' than those that are not. From these spatial arrangements the concept of 'nature-like' or 'naturalistic' vegetation is born. In most cases, of course, a more nature-like structure is likely to support a wider range of species and be more open to dynamic processes. However, Noel Kingsbury, in Chapter 3, raises the possibility that more formal planting styles can also have ecological characteristics.

Local character

Increasingly interwoven with the sustainability project is the idea that notions of place and local character should, where possible, inform the design of planting. This can also operate at a variety of scales and levels.

- Planting may simply replicate the vegetation that is found around the site. This habitat restoration approach is most common in rural landscapes where planting is used as background low-key 'filler'.
- Alternatively, planting can reflect the arrangement and patterns of vegetation found around a site, whilst at the same time involve different species. For example, until sown prairie vegetation flowers it looks perfectly in character with European native shrubs and trees, and will be perceived by the general public to be native. When in flower it is far more distinctive, however due to its complex, naturalistic, spatial patterns it continues to remain within the ubiquitous character created by tall swards of native species, such as nettles, rosebay willowherb and meadowsweet.
- Finally, vegetation may respond to ecological processes in the local environment at a more subtle level and sometimes in ways that are invisible to the lay observer, for example on a site with wet, poorly drained soils, and species that tolerate these conditions but which are not native to the site might be used to supplement those that are native. The same might be true for dry sites,

1.12
Coppicing is a valuable woodland edge maintenance-technique. Here, a mix of the North American species, *Rhus typhina* and *Rudbeckia fulgida* var. *deamii*, are coppiced and cut back each winter, in a planting at RHS Harlow Carr, Harrogate

or shady sites, or highly alkaline or infertile soils. With vegetation it is possible to respond to local character far more subtlely than is generally seen with built form.

Responding to local character is often a sensible principle to follow, however should it always be a goal of urban practice (Figure 1.13)? Can one be over sensitive to context to the point that plantings are just too dull to the public? In some cases, plantings should aim to stop people in their tracks irrespective of local character notions.

Process

The final, least obvious but perhaps most immutable criterion for what constitutes 'ecological' is that the vegetation is subject to, and able to respond to, ecological processes and, in particular, natural selection, the key agent of evolutionary change. Ecological processes include factors such as regeneration, competition, death and decay, and nutrient recycling. In traditionally cultivated vegetation, irrespective of origin, spatial arrangement and husbandry, we grossly inhibit these processes. These processes are not tied to national origin, they are blind and completely value neutral, although as human beings we are intensely interested in making our own value judgements on the outcomes. That ecological worth may be more tied up in notions of process rather than a product is an unsettling idea, as it undermines the foundations of many of our values, which are grounded in commodities, a perspective in time and the current boundaries of the nation state. Ultimately, the semantics of what 'ecological' means are pointless as it is impossible to separate perspectives from cultural relativism. All we can do is attempt to gain acceptance that it is a broad church, especially in urban contexts.

Thus far the discussion in this chapter has tried to establish some of the principles that underpin the creation and management of naturalistic planting design. This type of planting is, however, still relatively rare in most countries, even where some of the philosophical background is long established, as for example in Germany. What are some of the factors that are restricting the popularity of this style? This question is pondered in greater detail by Noel Kingsbury in chapter three, however in Germany it appears that insufficient knowledge of plants and their requirements, plus the costs of detailing complex naturalistic plantings, and the funds and skills needed for a selective maintenance regime, limit the practical application of this style. Many of these limitations are less evident in the less horticultural, anthropogenic planting style, however this type of vegetation is still attractive enough to be valued by the public. The authors see this style as more practical for more general landscape application, especially given that in Britain and many other countries, vegetation management skills in urban green space have often declined, placing considerable limitations on what can be achieved. To operate in this environment requires the development of new knowledge on: plant establishment and, in particular, planting and sowing mixes for a range of different site conditions; plant tolerance of less closely regulated competition; the long-term dynamics of plant communities; and, finally, how this knowledge can be used to create and manage this type of vegetation within landscape practice. We hope that this book will contribute to developing and propagating this knowledge.

1.13
Vegetation with a strong local character such as this Scottish Birch forest may form the basis of plantings that reflect the arrangement and patterns of vegetation around a site, but is it always possible to do this in an urban environment?

Summary and conclusions

In putting forward these arguments we are not suggesting that all urban green spaces should be treated in the same way and incorporate the same approaches to landscape planting. Instead, we are proposing that if quality is to be maintained and the benefits of landscape planting are to be extended

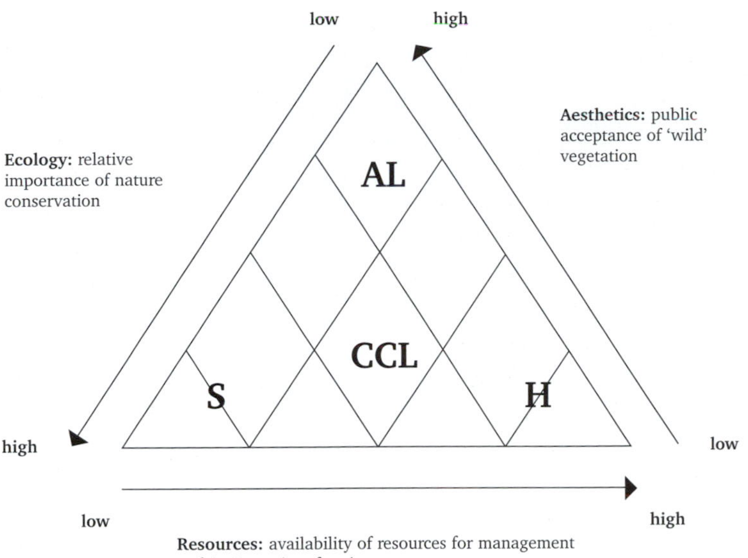

1.14

Model describing the relationship between three factors: availability of resources for management (——), public acceptance of 'wild vegetation' (- - - -) and the importance of nature conservation (........) that determine the potential character of amenity plantings. Key to vegetation types: S = spontaneous vegetation; H = horticultural vegetation; CCL = creative conservation landscape; AL = anthropogenic landscape

then radical solutions may have to be considered that involve a more ecologically-informed basis for the use of plants in designed landscapes. In this chapter we have sought to provide a vision for what an ecological approach might mean in the urban context. Perhaps above all we have stressed the importance of the social and cultural dimension – that plantings must be publicly acceptable, as well as environmentally sound, if they are also to be sustainable in the long term. We have also stressed the utmost importance of the promotion of the ecological *process* as the basis of a dynamic and self-sustaining landscape, rather than a rigid concentration on native species lists. Within this framework, however, there is a wide spectrum of planting styles, as will be evident from reading this book, ranging from evocations and distillations of native plant communities and landscapes through to highly abstracted plantings that, although nature-like, may bear no resemblance to any natural vegetation.

So, how might this all fit within the network of urban green spaces? In order to maximise value in plantings, the appropriate style must match with available resources and the degree to which 'wildness' might be publicly acceptable. It is possible to recognise three major factors that determine the type of amenity planting in any given urban area. Firstly, the availability of resources for management (such as maintenance budgets, and the level of knowledge of those responsible for maintenance) will be critical determinants of what is possible. Secondly, the cultural context will determine the degree of public acceptance of 'wildness' in vegetation on, or within, any given site. These factors are related to aesthetics and include public preference for colour or tidyness, the character of a site (for example, whether it is an historic landscape) and the use of the site (whether, for example, it is primarily sports-based, recreational or horticultural). And the third determinant is the relative importance of nature conservation (either actually through site designation or perceived through the attitudes of major users). This factor determines, to a large extent, whether species content should be predominantly native or mixed and also, to some extent, the structure and appearance of the vegetation (i.e. a high nature conservation value can mitigate against a relatively neglected appearance).

Figure 1.14 shows a hypothetical model that integrates these three strands and shows the types of vegetation possible under different relative combinations of these three determinants. The internal grid lines follow bands of low, moderate and high values for each factor leading from each appropriate side of the triangle. It is possible to locate different combinations of resource availablity, importance of ecology and public acceptance of naturalistic plantings within the triangle, using these gridlines. For example, under a combination of relatively high resource availability, low public acceptance of wild vegetation and a relatively low requirement for nature conservation, standard horticultural plantings (H) are a potential solution. Such situations may include city centre parks or conventional commercial landscapes. Where available maintenance resources are non-existent,

1.15
Colourful, flower-rich spontaneous vegetation on a brown-field site in Sheffield, featuring Goat's Rue (galega officinalis). Can designed and enhanced naturalistic herbaceous vegetation that captures some of this visual spectacle, become an important part of the urban landscape?

and wild vegetation is acceptable and justified for nature conservation, spontaneous vegetation (S) will be tolerated. Such situations may include the banks of urban rivers, canals, railways and roads, or, in a more managed state, areas of tall grassland and woodland in urban parks (Figure 1.15). Certainly in the UK, the horticultural and the spontaneous are the two extremes of vegetation, and the majority of sites are left somewhere in the middle, with little beyond standard trees, mown grass and shrub mass. The great value of the vegetation types described in this book, the ecologically-based creative conservation landscape (CCL) and anthropogenic landscape (AL), is that they fill this middle ground, providing new opportunities where resources are restricted. However, the model indicates that the benefit of reduced resource consumption is not enough on its own. There must also be a shift in public attitudes away from formal horticultural styles. This shift can either be achieved by aesthetic enhancement and moderation of the characteristics of truly spontaneous vegetation, as described throughout this book, and/or through demonstrable wildlife benefit. Indeed, it is the experience of the authors, and of many others working in this field, that one of the best ways to 'sell' anthropogenic and native nature-like plantings is that

1.16
Robust sculpture helps increase the aesthetic appeal of spontaneous urban vegetation (birch woodland and grassland) in the Natur Park Südgelände in Berlin

they will increase visible wildlife, mainly birds and butterflies. So, again we come back to the fundamental importance of public support.

The differing relative importance of aesthetics (as defined above), resources and ecology can form the basis of a vegetation strategy within a single site, or can inform the dominant planting approaches between sites throughout an urban area. We believe that to achieve a wider application of naturalistic vegetation, in all its forms, in towns and cities we need to begin championing the visual and aesthetic benefits of urban nature as well as the conservation and biodiversity benefits. The authors anticipate that the rest of this book will begin to provide a theoretical and practical basis for designers and managers to create rewarding urban landscapes that meet the real challenges discussed in this chapter.

References

-- Clement, E. J. and Foster, M. C. (1994). *Alien Plants of the British Isles*. Botanical Society of the British Isles, London.

-- Dunnett, N. P., Swanwick, C. and Woolley, H. E. (2002). *Improving Urban Parks, Play Areas and Green Spaces*. Department of Transport, Local Government and the Regions, HMSO, London.

-- Gilbert O. L. (1989). *The Ecology of Urban Habitats*. Chapman and Hall, London.

-- Gould, S. J. (1997). An Evolutionary Perspective on strengths, fallacies, and confusions in the concept of native plants. In Wolschke-Bulmahn, J. (ed.) *Nature and Ideology, Natural Garden Design in the Twentieth Century*. Dumbarton Oaks, Washington, DC, pp. 11–19.

-- Hitchmough, J. D. (2000). Establishment of cultivated herbaceous perennials in purpose-sown native wildflower meadows in south-west Scotland. *Landscape and Urban Planning*, **51**, 37–51.

-- Hitchmough, J. D. and Woudstra, J. (1999). The ecology of exotic herbaceous perennials grown in managed, native grass vegetation in urban landscapes. *Landscape and Urban Planning*, **45**, 107–121.

-- Katz, E. (2000). Ecological Restoration: Technology and Artificial Nature. In Gobster, P. H. and Hull, R. B. (eds) *Restoring Nature, Perspectives from the Social Sciences and Humanities*. Island Press, Washington, DC.

-- Keller, M., Kollmann, J. and Edwards, P. J. (2000). Genetic introgression from distant provenances reduces fitness in local weed populations. *Journal of Applied Ecology*, **37**, No. 4, 647–659.

-- Laird, M. (1999). *The Flowering of the Landscape Garden: English Pleasure Grounds 1720–1800.* University of Pennsylvania Press, Philadelphia.

-- Luijten, S. H., Kery, M., Osstermeijer, J. G. B. and Den Nijs, H. J. C. M. (2002). Demographic consequences of inbreeding and outbreeding in *Arnica montana*: a field experiment. *Journal of Ecology*, **90**, 593–603.

-- McIntyre, N. E., Knowles-Yanez, K. and Hope, D. (2000). Urban ecology as an interdisciplinary field: differences in the use of 'urban' between the social and natural sciences. *Urban Ecosystems*, **4**, No. 1, 5–24.

-- Owen, J. (1991). *The Ecology of a Garden, the first fifteen years*. Cambridge University Press, Cambridge.

-- Sackville Hamilton, N. R. (2001). Is local provenance important in habitat creation? A reply. *Journal of Applied Ecology*, **38**, 1374–1376.

-- Thompson, K. Austin, K. C., Smith, R. M. Warren, P. H. , Angola, P. and Gaston, K. J. (2003) Urban domesic gardens (1), Putting small scale plant diversity in context. *Journal of Vegetation Science*, **14**, 1, 71–78.

-- Wilkinson, D. M. (2001). Is local provenance important in habitat creation? *Journal of Applied Ecology*, **38**, 1371–1373.

Chapter 2

The changing nature of ecology: a history of ecological planting (1800–1980)

Jan Woudstra

Man's philosophical view of nature has altered across different historical periods and political movements, and this has been reflected in the way that plants are used. Ecological ideas and principles, although not necessarily referred to as such at the time, have been applied in landscape and garden design much longer than is generally appreciated. Two main applications of ecological ideas can be traced over the last 200 years or so: the *plant geographic* approach that aims to recreate representative examples of specific vegetation types from around the world (or their essential character); and the *physiognomic* approach that aims for natural character, patterns and functioning in vegetation, but without particular regard to the geographic origin of the component species.

Whilst gardens have always been recognised as a creation of art and nature, seventeenth-century gardens, for example, are nowadays perceived as highly artificial. Yet in their heyday, designers were perceived as assisting nature. This can be illustrated with the example of the gardens at Versailles. A now famous account by Le Duc de Saint-Simon, written after the death of its designer André le Nôtre, noted: 'His only thought was to aid nature and reveal beauty at as low a cost as possible' (Norton 1980: 59). It is clear that clipped hedges, avenues and parterres de broderie were being perceived as nature perfected.

Over the next half-century after Le Nôtre's death in 1700, the perception and view of nature gradually changed. Reference was now made to the pictorial quality of nature, with certain painters depicting the

2.1
Enlightenment supported a new vision of nature – here Rousseau's novel *Julie ou la Nouvelle Héloïse* (1761) is enacted in a garden (Rousseau 1767: plate 1)

distinctive moods of the natural world, with, for example, Claude Lorrain representing the beautiful scenes of nature, and Salvator Rosa the terrible and the sublime (Jacques 1983: 59). Yet the practice of gardening that represented these various moods adhered by and large to the predominant model of graduated shrubberies and flowerbeds, and clumps and masses of trees (Laird 1999). This clearly illustrated a divergence between the ideal and the practice, which already became perceived as such by the end of the eighteenth century, when the planting of parks was considered to be too neat, and ended in the Picturesque debate in Great Britain. This, in turn, stimulated a new manner of planting design – picturesque planting – in the early nineteenth-century, and which became the predominant ideal for planting proposals in public parks (Legate 2000).

In England, enlightened thinkers, such as Alexander Pope, Joseph Addison and Anthony Shaftesbury, supported this new aesthetic vision of nature. In France, Jean-Jacques Rousseau in his novel *Julie ou la Nouvelle Héloïse* (1761) depicts a vivid picture of a garden of trees, of which the irregularity was an attempt to imitate nature as closely as possible. Nature gardens avoided architectural decoration and attempted to create an ideal Elysium, one which would represent pure nature (Figure 2.1). Johann Wolfgang Goethe's novel *Die Leiden des jungen Werthers* (1774) was influenced by Rousseau's work and similarly envisaged the Elysian Fields, which led him and others to imagine nature in the form of a park. This new ideal led people to reasses ever increasing human interventions in a different light as representing a break in the harmony with nature. The German philosopher and natural historian Alexander von Humboldt, who was connected with Goethe, found inspiration in far away countries where he studied nature and wrote about it in order to inspire a higher pleasure (Hermand 1997).

Humboldt assessed nature by means of a scientific methodology and by inspired analyses. This specifically encouraged a new understanding of the world's vegetation and inspired a new practice of planting parks and gardens, related to the arrangements in nature. Referred to as plant geographical or phytogeographical planting, this gradually grew into ecological planting, becoming more sophisticated with advancing knowledge. Whilst the politics of the ecological movement have been well-explored, this has not been the case for the practice of ecological planting. This chapter explores these scientific approaches, and how traditions were handed on and developed from one generation to the next. It concentrates on scientific rather than artistic approaches and excludes vegetation created in what would now be interpreted as being in a nature-like or ecological manner, as for example grassy swards enriched with – often exotic – perennials, the so-called 'enamelled mead'. These meads represent an ancient horticultural practice, which precedes ecological thinking and are the subject of a publication by Woudstra and Hitchmough (2000). This chapter does not aim to be all inclusive but concentrates on some of the main trends in five countries, where this type of planting has had a profound influence on landscape design and management, and which, at some time, has been considered exemplary.

The two strands: plant geography and physiognomy

On his return from South America, Alexander von Humboldt (1769–1859) wrote his *Essai sur la géographie des plantes* (1805)/*Ideen zu einer Geographie der Pflanzen* (1807). Within this he observed that there was a similarity between the vegetation within the different geographical zones at comparable latitudes around the earth and also that the flora at high altitudes on a mountain was similar to that which occurred at low altitude in the high latitudes of the arctic. Both of the latter floras had adapted to the cold and he concluded that vegetation zones around the earth were determined by temperature and rainfall, and that plants within each zone all possessed similar adaptations to the conditions (Bowler 1992: 273). Deserts, seas and mountain ranges determine geographical boundaries, and Humboldt noted that the separation of Africa and South America must have taken place before the development of living organisms, as hardly a single plant of one continent was found in the other.

In 1822, the British garden author John Claudius Loudon summarised the findings by Humboldt, and acknowledged their importance, referring to 'Botanical geography, or the knowledge of the places where the plants grow (*habitationes plantarum*) and the causes which influence their distribution over the globe ….' (Loudon 1822: 124, 242). In his garden tours through Europe he included a visit to the botanic garden in Berlin where he observed that this 'is one of the few gardens in which the arrangement of the plants is according to their native *habitations*' (Loudon 1822: 45). He however fails to make the connection with Humboldt's writings and does not include this as an option in his planting advice for botanical gardens, until slightly later. For these he proposes 'systematic or methodical planting', which is concerned with contemporary scientific classification according to the system of Jussieu or Linnaeus 'as a foundation, and combining at the same time a due attention to gradation of heights', which shows a concern for contemporary aesthetic tradition (Loudon 1822: 915, 1191).

The botanist Karl Ludwig Willdenow first inspired Humboldt in botany in 1788 (Kelner 1963: 9[1]), and has therefore been referred to as the 'grandfather of botanical geography' (Hyams and MacQuitty 1969). As Professor Willdenow he took over the botanic garden in Berlin in 1801, after a period of neglect, and converted this into a flourishing institution (Wendland 1979: 186). Through mediation by Alexander von Humboldt, he was able in 1807 to obtain an additional grant for maintenance via the French administrator whilst retaining the existing allowance from the Academy. By the time of his death in 1812, the garden had substantially altered (Figures 2.2. and 2.3), and his gardener, Friedrich Otto, continued the improvements, later with Professor Heinrich Friedrich Link who was appointed to replace Willdenow in 1815 (Loudon 1822: 45). The Berlin botanic garden differed from others in that it no longer contained any order beds, the classical feature for systematic or methodological planting as found in other botanical gardens. Willdenow established this through his friendship with Humboldt, with the garden displaying features of the 'landscape' style, but details as to the exact arrangement and groupings are not known. Humboldt later acknowledged that the path of his entire career had been due to the Berlin botanic garden, which implanted in his mind 'the seeds of an irresistible desire to undertake distant travels'.[2]

Whilst this landscape style became fashionable in botanical gardens elsewhere shortly afterwards, as for example Loudon with the Birmingham Botanical Garden (1831, which still contained areas of order beds), and the Derby Arboretum (1839), and Robert Marnock at the Sheffield Botanic Garden (1834), the arrangement followed aesthetic rather than scientific, phytogeographical principles. In 1835, Loudon had first promoted the idea of 'scientific gardens' in his famous essay 'On the laying out public gardens and promenades'. A total of 12 categories of scientific gardens are included, including *'Zoological', 'Botanical', 'Horticultural'* and *'Agricultural Gardens', 'Arboretums', 'Herbacetums', 'Plantariums'*, but also *'British Floras*, or gardens of British Plants …', *'Local Floras*, or assemblages of the plants of the neighbourhood, district or province …', *'Geographical Gardens*, in which plants, either hardy or exotic, or both, are arranged according to their native countries', and *'Geological*

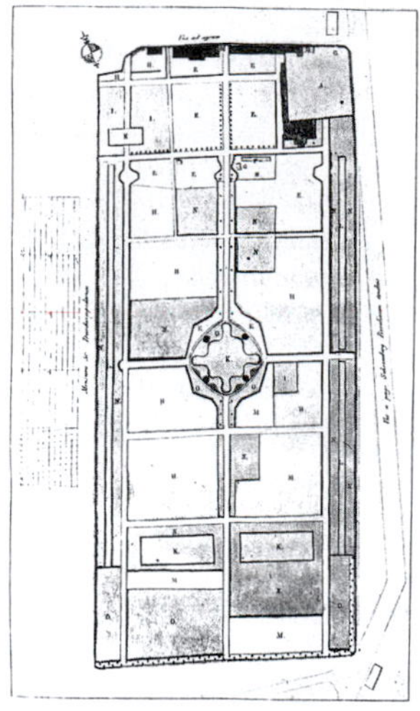

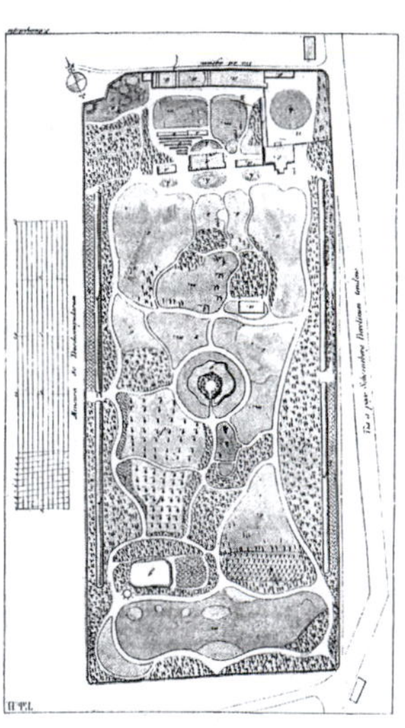

2.2
Survey of the Berlin botanical garden in 1801 – prior to alterations by Carl Ludwig Willdenow (Heinrich Friedrich Link *Hortus regius botanicus berolinensis* (1827)

2.3
Survey of the Berlin botanical garden in 1812 – indicates the changes of the intervening years, when orderbeds were removed and the layout was modified in a more naturalistic landscape style layout (Heinrich Friedrich Link *Hortus regius botanicus berolinensis* (1827)

Gardens, in which hardy plants are arranged according to the soils in which they thrive best'. A garden of plants that are natives of the British Isles had to be 'both interesting and instructive', and Loudon suggested a number of possibilities of arrangement, 'either methodical, geographical, geological, or topographical'. Topographical meant the 'placing of plants of each county in a group by themselves'. This varied from a *Local Flora,* i.e. 'a collection of the plants indigenous to a particular locality' only in the extent (Loudon 1835).

Similar ideas had been mooted a few years earlier by Joseph Paxton, the head gardener to the Duke of Devonshire at Chatsworth, who had promoted a new national garden, a zoological garden arranged according to the different quarters of the globe. He suggested that quarters might again be divided in the different states located in them 'and thus, in connexion with Zoology and Botany, would be given practical acquaintance with Geography'. The plants were proposed to be planted according to the 'Natural Arrangement' within these, i.e. presumably planted according to the Linnaean system (Paxton 1831).

The first landscape designer who appears to have published the relevance of Humboldt's discoveries as part of a coherent theory was Gustav Meyer in his *Lehrbuch der schönen Gartenkunst* (1860), which acknowledges Humboldt's influence (Meyer 1860: 163) and includes lists of plants arranged according to their native countries, habitats and soil conditions (Meyer 1860: 171–177). In this he also includes the term 'plant physiognomy' for which he quotes from Humboldt and Zollinger, and he lists the main plant shapes relating to adaptation to different environmental conditions (Meyer 1860: 158). Meyer thus incorporated his ideas in his proposals, including the design of the (and his) third public park in Berlin, the Humboldthain, founded to memorise the hundredth anniversary of the birthday of Humboldt in 1869. This park included an area for cultivation of plants and education, and a small area for botanical education. The planting of the larger area of the park was noted for a scientific approach, which 'not only included all our native woody plants, but also those from other countries, especially North America and Siberia, which without protection resist our climate and can be recommended for their beauty'. There was substantial planting of allees, including one with various exotics, which enabled landowners to increase their knowledge in selecting appropriate trees for their properties. Meyer also 'composed plant geographical groups which provided a notion of the vegetation and physiognomy of other countries'.[3]

Meyer was not the only landscape designer to be influenced by Humboldt's treatises; from 1857–1860 Eduard Petzold executed an arboretum at Muskau, which was arranged both scientifically and artistically, and incorporated a geographical section where the woody plants were arranged according to their countries of origin (Schmidt 1984). Humboldt's influence was not restricted to Germany, however, as several of his books were translated. The American landscape gardener Andrew Jackson Downing showed an awareness of Humboldt's writings, quoting from *Cosmos* in an 1849 essay entitled 'The philosophy of rural life'. Here he compared the differences in approach between the people of north and south Europe, and Humboldt was recognised to be the 'only writer who has ever attempted to account for this striking distinction of national taste of gardening …'. Appealing presumably to an audience of north European émigrés, he quoted that 'certain races of mankind are … deficient in their perception of natural beauty; that northern nations possess the love of nature much more than those in the south …' (Downing 1853: 102).[4]

Origin of ecological science

The word '*Oekologie*' was coined by Ernst Haeckel (1834–1919) in his *Generelle Morphologie* (1866). A scientist and later politician, he rejected religion with its traditional mind-body split and replaced this with a holistic view of the world, a belief that the real world could only be properly understood 'by experience and pure reason'. This he referred to as Monism, which became a political movement. This is the context in which he conceived the word '*oekology*', as the science of relations between organisms and their environment. It looked at organisms in context, their lifecycle, their environment and their place in the cycle of energy use. The word had overtones of the Greek word '*oekonomie*'; '*oekos*' used by Aristotle to mean the proper functioning of a household unit, which was further developed by the Monists.[5]

Whilst it signifies a shift to a contextual, holistic biology, Haeckel did not fully develop ecology, which was carried out especially by plant geographers, emerging as a distinct science during the 1890s. In 1896, Oscar Drude of the Dresden Botanical Gardens published *Deutschlands Pflanzengeographie,* a plant geography of Germany, which refined the Humboldtian approach and showed how local factors, such as hills and rivers, combined with the overall climate of a region to determine the actual distribution of plants. The relative abundance of each species in an area was depicted with a ranking system, ranging from 'social' to 'scarce' (Bowler 1992: 370). Another group of scientists saw physiology as a starting point for ecology. The interaction between the plant as a living organism and its environment determined whether or not a particular species could live in a certain area. Different levels of moisture, heat, light, etc. further

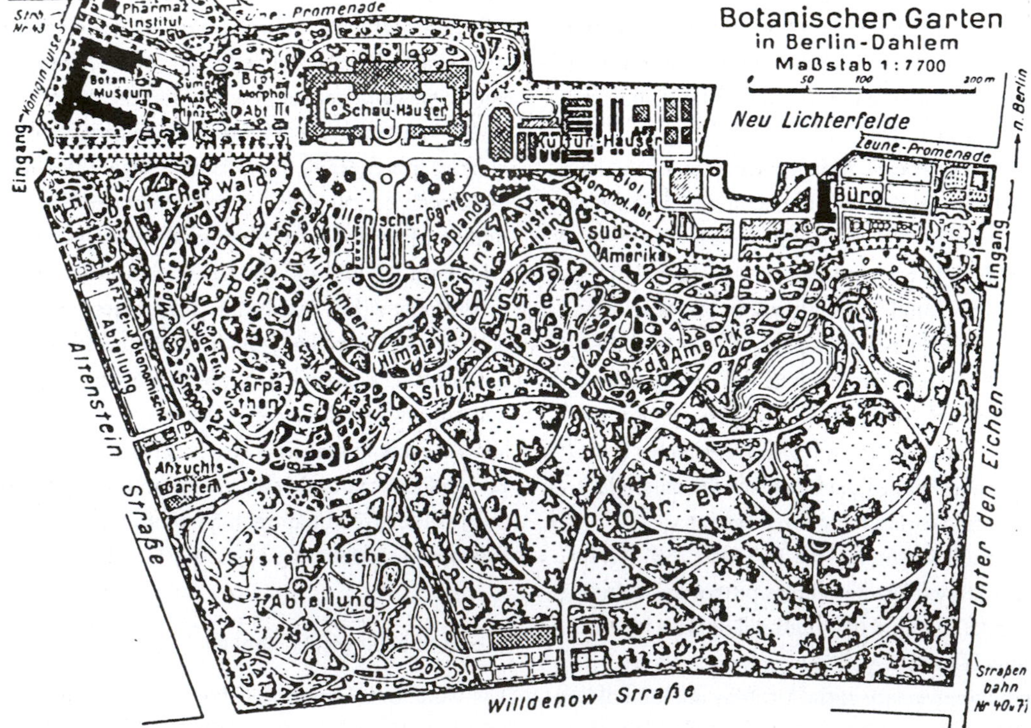

2.4
In 1897 the new botanical garden in Berlin-Dahlem was arranged according to plant geography, supervised by Adolf Engler and Ignatz Urban

affected whether or not a species flourished. Whilst some of this was well known, in the 1890s the field of study was further extended to include how plants coped with different environmental factors. This was greatly stimulated by research in exotic locations, and particularly the Buitenzorg botanical laboratory in Java, the studies of which were quoted in landscape treatises as early as 1860.[6]

The Danish plant physiologist Eugenius Warming was particularly influential with his book entitled *Oecology of Plants: an Introduction to the Study of Plant Communities* (1909), which was the first attempt to publish 'on Oecological Plant-geography' (Warming 1909: 3). The ecological approach was developed as an alternative to both pure physiology and the sterile emphasis on classification of many field naturalists. He introduced the term 'community', and communities as 'the essential foundations of oecological phytogeography' which were linked together through various interactions, such as symbiosis and parasitism (Warming 1909: 91).

In both the USA and Great Britain, Warming's approach influenced pioneering plant ecologists. In his study of changing vegetation along the shores of Lake Michigan, Henry Chandler Cowles of the University of Chicago argued that local factors, such as the lake, influenced vegetation cover. In Lincoln, Nebraska professor Charles Edwin Bessey of the State University, concerned with conservation, intended to study the grasslands of the prairie before they were completely ploughed up. Two of his students, Frederic E. Clements and Roscoe Pound, inspired by Drude's book, published *Phyto-geography of Nebraska* (1898), which became a standard text for American botany, whilst Clements' *Research Methods in Ecology* (1905) was the first textbook to describe a new method of surveying techniques used for this survey, by using small quadrats and surveying every plant within that (Bowler 1992: 373).

In Britain, the new ecology was championed by Arthur G. Tansley, who, in 1904, had set up a Committee for the Survey and Study of British Vegetation, which later published *Types of British Vegetation* (1911). The first society devoted to ecology was the British Ecological Society, founded in 1913 (Bowler 1992: 377). This limited historical overview shows how a new science evolved and became more complicated and involved additional aspects which were considered in time, acquiring more appropriate methodologies and terminology along the way.

Ecological gardening

William Robinson is often considered as an early applier of ecological ideas, especially in connection with his publication *The Wild Garden* (1870). This, however, deals with the naturalisation of hardy exotic plants in grassy swards and was no more than a revival and modernisation of an old gardening practice (Woudstra and Hitchmough 2000). Whilst also including a chapter on British plants, there is no evidence of phytogeographical or ecological principles being used, and the distribution of planting is based on pictorial or aesthetic criteria only. Similarly in Germany, Hermann Jäger suggested naturalisation of perennials and bulbs in woodland or in grass swards, but again this does not seem to have been based on scientific principles. He noted that 'the only rule was to copy nature' by which he meant the general appearance of nature (Jäger 1877: 422).

Germany

Owing to a lack of space, the Berlin Royal Botanic Garden was moved to Dahlem in 1897. Adolf Engler, the then director, and Ignatz Urban, his deputy, oversaw this move (Figure 2.4). Engler was a keen proponent of plant geography, and there was an emphasis on this type of arrangement for large parts of the garden. Both the arrangement and intent of the underlying geography is clear, with an Italian garden on the far side of an Alpine garden (Lack 2001: I, 132). The ambitious plant geographical section covered 23 ha and followed the latest scientific knowledge on vegetation, distinguishing the Pyrenees, the Alps, the Apennine and Balkan Peninsulas, the Caucasus, the Himalayas and the Appalachians.[7] The greenhouses and conservatories were also arranged according to plant geographical principles and represented South Africa, Australia and the Mediteranean. Like his publications *Natürlichen Pflanzenfamilien* (1887–1915), *Das Pflanzenreich* (1900–1937) and *Die Vegetation der Erde* (1896–1923), the garden set new standards in the display according to phytogeographical principles (Hyams and MacQuitty 1969: 80).

The German landscape designer and teacher Willy Lange started to teach at the Royal Horticultural College Berlin-Dahlem after its move from Wildpark-Potsdam in 1903, when the new Berlin-Dahlem botanic garden first (and unofficially) opened to the public. He therefore was fully aware of the Humboldtian heritage of phytogeography and physiognomy, and he used this as a basis for his theories. However, he was also firmly rooted in the German tradition of Prince Hermann von Pückler Muskau and Hermann Jäger, who had anticipated much of the later ecological science 'intuitively', and he noted that he had 'inherited Gustav Meyer', meaning the application of scientific techniques (Lange 1927: 2). Before his teaching appointment, Lange had, after a busy period as a horticulturist, withdrawn from public life by living in a secluded woodland area for a seven-year period, which gave him time to reflect on society and the ability to study art, art history, nature and cultural history. At this time he also published numerous articles with racist overtones that were later adopted by National Socialists (Wolschke-Bulmahn and Groening 2001). His landscape theories were therefore complex and charged, but they were similarly extremely popular and influential. His main textbook, *Gartengestaltung der Neuzeit* (1907) was published in five editions with a total of 22,000 copies and was widely read, particularly in the Nordic countries (Wimmer 1989).

The principles as set out in his *Gartengestaltung der Neuzeit* adopted plant geographical principles and discussed the 'composition of plant communities in the garden according to nature motifs' (Lange 1919: 175), discussing 'nature gardens' and 'biological garden design' (Lange 1919: 27). Lange saw the purpose of a biologically designed garden not as imitating nature but as advancing the intent of nature. He noted that since the description of communities in the German nature tradition was an artificial task, one might as well take this one step further (Lange 1919: 163). Thus, Lange returned to a reinterpretation of the old Humboldt theories. So, whilst he followed the latest developments in the various sciences, particularly ecology, he settled on the physiognomy of plants as the basis for their final selection. The expression of the plant's external characteristics in habitat and living conditions was proposed as a determining factor in plant selection. With sufficient knowledge of the external characteristics, the designer would be able to determine the correct position in a design for each species. It is this aspect for which Lange was later most attacked by academic ecologists as this did not match recent advances in botanical-ecological knowledge.[8] Physiognomy is a potentially useful contribution to assessing plant compatibility and fitness of specific environments, for example plants with small sparse leaves are often slow growing, sun-demanding species. To make this interpretation does, however, require extensive knowledge of plants, and in some cases the external appearance of a plant does not give an accurate picture of its requirements. Whilst claiming he based his planting schemes on scientific principles, Lange allowed aesthetic considerations to take precedent by supplementing native species for exotics where this was desired (Figure 2.5).

2.5
Planting principles on the observations of the composition of natural communities by Willy Lange in his *Gartenpläne* (1927) described this 'as the form of planting after the pattern of molehill tunnels', whereby symbols for individual species were interconnected with lines (Lange 1927)

Zeichenerklärung
zu nebenstehender Abbildung.

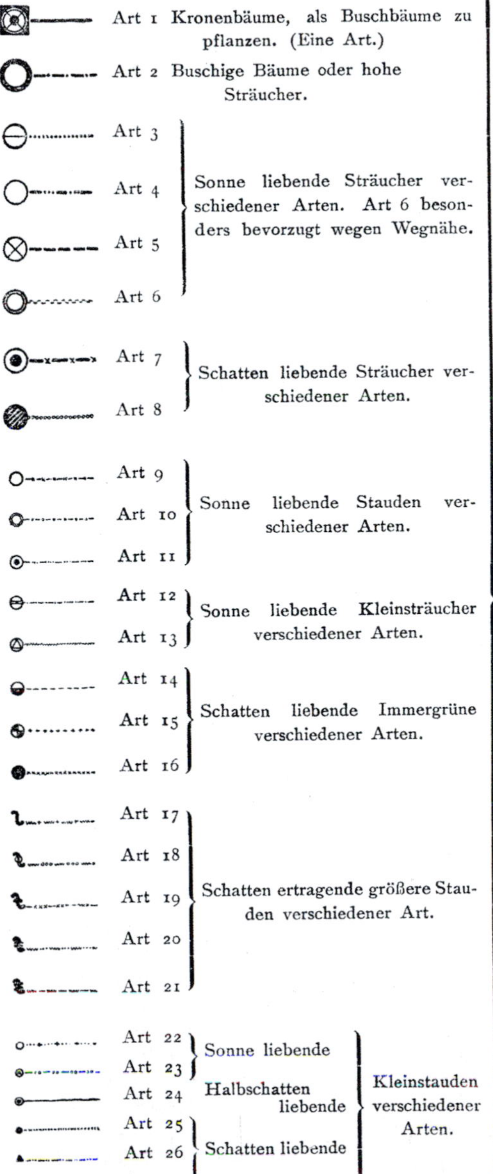

Form der Pflanzung
nach Art der Maulwurfsgänge.

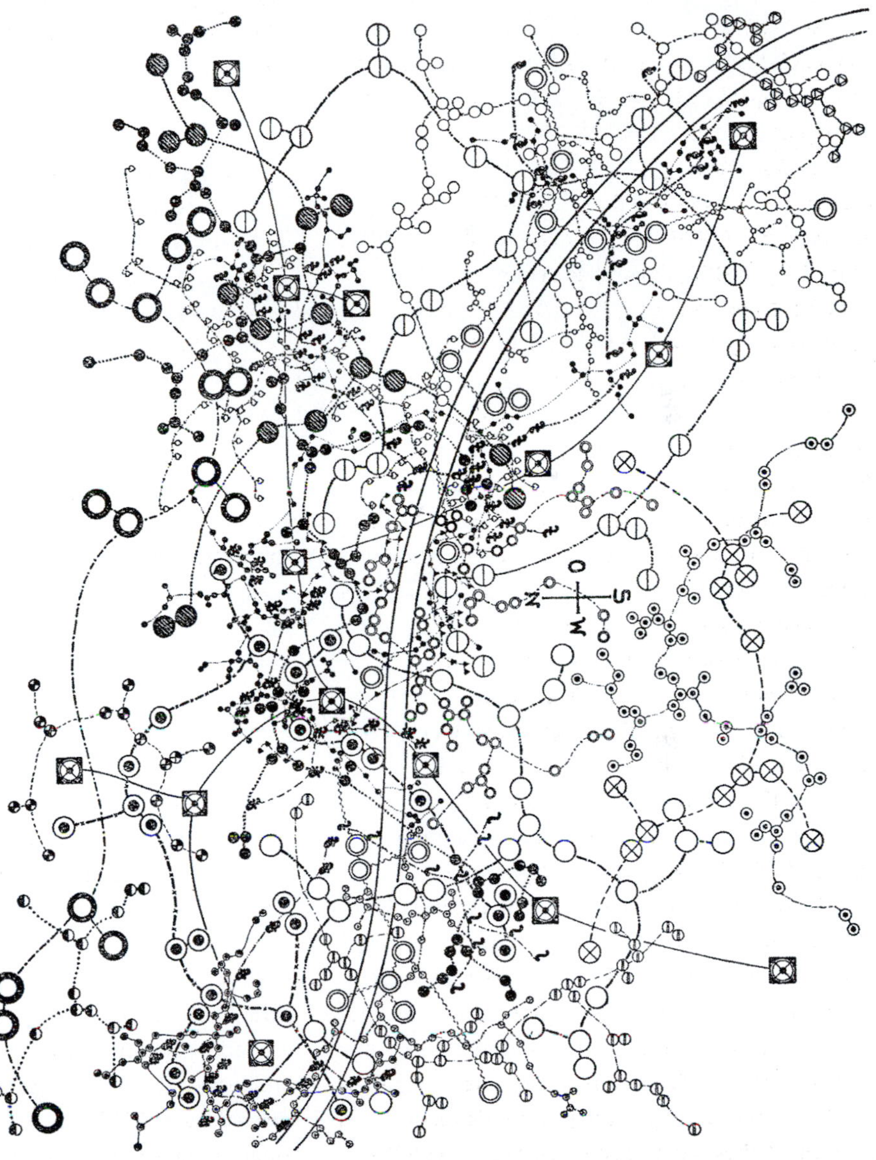

Abb. 25. Naturliche Pflanzengesellschaft physiognomischer Zusammengehörigkeit in künstlerischer Steigerung.

2.6
Willy Lange's planting was according to physiognomic principles, which assessed the external characteristics of plants and not ecological principles. Thus, an illustration of an arrangement in Lange's own garden included native junipers set over a carpet of *Sedum spurium* (Lange 1919: plate 14)

Lange highlighted his principles with the example of his own garden in Wannsee. Contemporary colour photos illustrate native plant associations with a naturalistic character, but where certain plants have been replaced with those with a similar physiognomy but which are exotic. One illustration shows native pine trees and junipers in a carpet of non-native *Sedum spurium* dotted with crocus (Lange 1919: plate 14) (Figure 2.6).

An early example of the application of ecology was the 1913 proposal for a 2 ha public square in Charlottenburg to the west of Berlin. It was conceived by Erwin Barth, who had been at the Wildpark-Potsdam Royal Horticultural College from 1900–1902 and had returned to Berlin-Dahlem to take his head gardener's exam. He was therefore well aware of the possibilities of the application of plant geography and is likely to have been familiar with Lange's writings. In 1913, as Director of Parks of Berlin-Charlottenburg, he took the opportunity to implement this for a people's park (Volkspark) named Sachsenplatz, a public square of approximately 2 ha. The site was a former gravel pit with a depth of 14 m and was to form a space for both children's play and relaxation for adults, with attractive planting. It was to include a

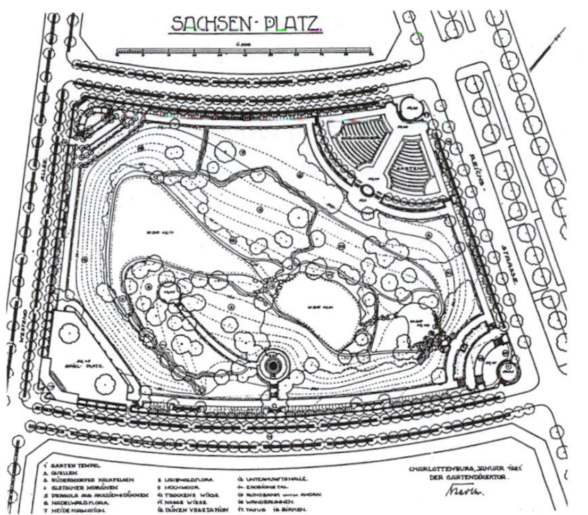

2.7
The Sachsenplatz, Berlin, was laid out by Erwin Barth in 1913 on the site of an old gravel pit which contained the 'natural vegetation types and geological formations' of the Brandenburg area (*Der Gartenkunst*, XV; 14 (1913))

2.8
Sachsenplatz was renamed Brixplatz after the Second World War, but still retains much of the original layout

demonstration garden and the intention here was to represent the 'natural vegetation types and geological formations' of the Brandenburg area (Figure 2.7).

Planting was to take place 'according to ecological principles'. The square was surrounded with field maple hedges aligned with birch trees, from which there are good views to the centre of the site. At the corners were seating and play areas and a 'biological garden' at the north side next to the main entrance. This was to serve as a school garden for the instruction of pupils and to show some well-known flowers and economic crops. A second path at a 2 to 3 m lower level than the first circular one wound around the site, and provided the opportunity for close contact with nature 'to view the individual plants and vegetation exhibits in greater detail' from numerous sitting areas. The focal point of the site was formed by three ponds in the centre of the site, around which various habitats were recreated; a Rüdersdorf limestone quarry next to the uppermost pond, with denser native waterside vegetation along the other ponds. Also represented were moist and dry meadows, different types of coniferous and broad-leaved woodland, and dunes and heathland. The plants used for the planting of the square were collected for the purpose by Erwin Barth and his colleagues, who also introduced related fauna into the square, which by 1931 was highly regarded (Barth 1980) (Figure 2.8).

After 1933 the new National Socialist government with its 'Blood and Soil' ideology assumed a close relationship between the Nordic race and the land. This brought natural landscape design to the forefront of the political agenda, which flourished as a result. At its most extreme, this involved landscape architects, such as Heinrich Wiepking-Jürgensmann, in devising policies for the new territories, the occupied lands (Poland and also the Soviet Union), which were to be Germanised once the existing population had been removed. Alwin Seifert was responsible for the landscape aspects relating to the new German motorways, the achievements of which were also part of the National Socialist propaganda.

Seifert's motto was 'the landscape is the eternal foundation of our being', which meant that 'we, the human beings are characterised by their constructions in the natural environment in which we live and grow up' (Schneider 1935). From this emerged a coherent design theory with the concept of indigenous garden art (bodenständiger

Gartenkunst), *bodenständig* being defined as: 'In a garden every native plant which achieves the full extent of its beauty and which is in artistic and biological harmony with its immediate and wider environment is *"bodenständig".'* This was closely connected with *Landschaftsverbundenheit*, landscape harmony or connected to the landscape, which were two of the catch phrases of the landscape profession during the Nazi era (Seifert 1939). Thus, the native landscape and its flora were to serve as the model for the landscape design of motorways. Exotic plants had to be avoided for the conservation of the German countryside (Heimatschutz) and the conservation of nature (Naturschutz). Movements with similar objectives were recognised in the US, where the Ministry of Agriculture published landscape guidelines. The English Roads Beautifying Association recommendation in favour of the planting of ornamental plants, such as Japanese cherries, was explained as a result of the English landscape already being more strongly intermingled with *Ausländer,* 'foreigners' (i.e. foreign species), than the German landscape (Schneider 1935).

The attitude of avoiding exotics in the German landscape came to be likened with that of avoiding foreigners in German society, in order to retain the purity of the Nordic race, and which ultimately validated the deportation and extermination of Jews and gypsies. This connection between native and exotic plants, and between the indigenous and foreign population, came to be represented by Willy Lange, who over time had included more and more racist remarks in his garden writings. These were further developed by Hans Hasler, a student of Lange's, which the latter referred to as a 'graft' of himself (Lange 1922: viii). Hasler extended Lange's theories to embrace Nazi philosophy in his *Deutsche Gartenkunst* (1939).

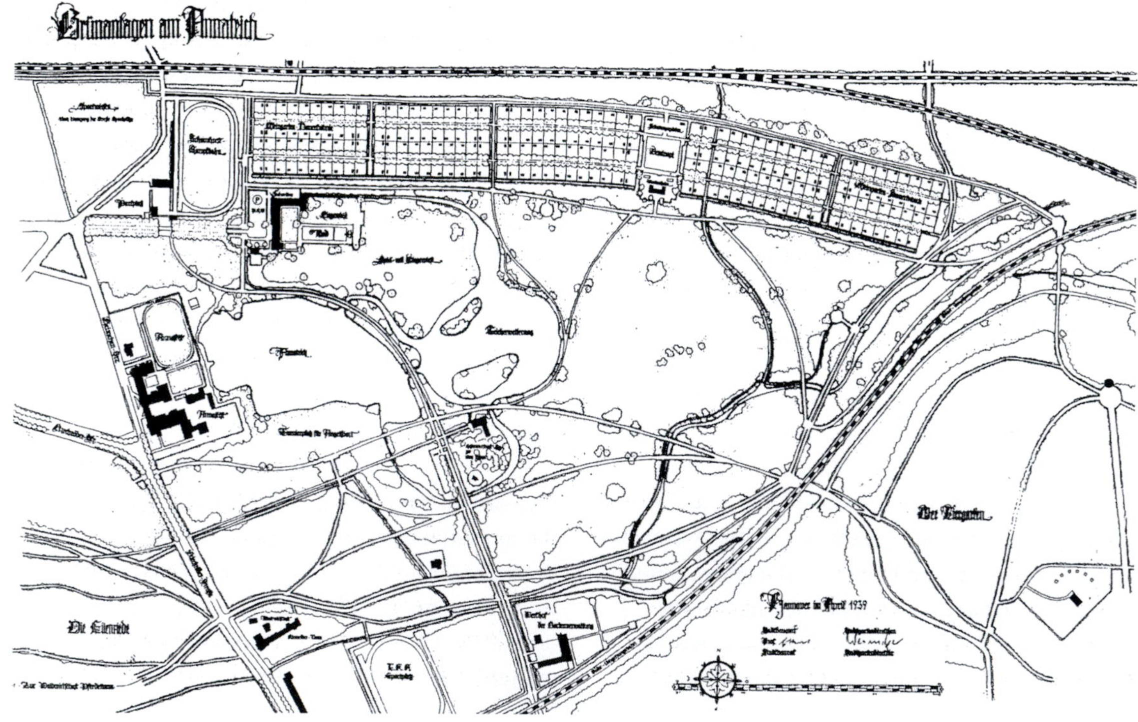

2.9
The early layout plan of the Hermann Löns Park in Hanover was conceived in association with Reinhold Tüxen, who emphasised the meaning of plant sociology to landscape designers (Wernicke 1941)

2.10
The Hermann Löns Park consists of a large naturalistic area, but it also contains an athletics track, allotment and a swimming pool

An approach related to Lange's was that of the nurseryman Karl Foerster. In 1930, he wrote about the garden of Berthold Körting, to provide evidence for the validity of his theories on planting design. Foerster noted how the starting point and the basis for new ideas in garden art is 'always tremendous travel experiences'. He believed that Körting's travels to Africa and Russia, and the experience of nature in these regions, had expanded the framework of customary German feelings for nature and gardens, and had forced him to search for new, innovative symbolic expressions (Foerster 1930). This is rather similar to remarks made by Humboldt a century earlier. During the Nazi period, Foerster and his circle would speak of 'world gardens' and even dedicated a book series to this.[9]

A more scientific approach towards ecological planting was developed by Reinhold Tüxen from Hanover, who wrote about 'the meaning of plant sociology for landscape culture', influenced by the methodology developed by the Swiss botanist Josias Braun-Blanquet who had surveyed vegetation by means of representative quadrats, in which each species was identified. Thus, tables of associations between species were created which were given names and which were classified in a similar manner as the species themselves. This approach was followed by Tüxen for northwest Germany, characterising each plant association of the region. This was thought to be of importance in 'offering clear possibilities for application', as long as the basics of plant sociology were known (Tüxen 1939). This work enabled landscape architects to compose naturalistic vegetation types adapted to soil and weather conditions of the region. This approach found immediate uptake and resulted in publications such as Louis Kniese's *Die Pflanzensociologie in der Landschafts- und Gartengestaltung* (Plant sociology in landscape and garden design (1942)), which translated ecological data into more practical advice (Kniese 1942).

At the time of the publication of his article, Tüxen was already involved with a practical application at the Annateich/Hermann Löns Park in Hanover (Wernicke 1941). Based on a number of prize winning entries for a 1936 competition, a final scheme was devised by the Hanover Parks Department in association with H. Klüppenberg, the first-prize winner. The final scheme envisaged a meadow landscape as a contrast to surrounding woodlands, and contained an athletics track, allotments and a swimming pool along the northern and western edge respectively (Wernicke 1936). By the 1940s, the Head of Parks, Hermann Wernicke, was able to report on the progress of the establishment of the park, noting that it had been designed according to plant sociological principles. Professor Tüxen had surveyed the original vegetation and had advised on the design for the park (Klaffke 1985), which had then been re-named after Hermann Löns, one of the popular folkish authors who had romanticised about the native landscape, particularly the north German heath (Figures 2.9 and 2.10).

In post-war Germany, plant sociology and plant physiognomy continued to be discussed critically, without the political connotations it had had during the Nazi era, and during the 1960s it gradually disappeared from public consciousness (Schiller 1959; Roemer 1963). By the end of the 1970s, however, a new group of people generated the idea of the eco-garden, without knowledge of the achievements of the previous generations. Yet some of the main advances in planting design were made by others who did not work in a purely ecological manner but were inspired by it. This is part of a long pedigree, commencing with landscape designers associated with the nurseryman Foerster starting in the late 1920s at the so-called Bornim School, especially Herta Hammerbacher (Hottenträger 1992).

Like their contemporaries, the emphasis was on the use of perennials in naturalistic groupings. The middle-American prairie or the Eurasian steppe had been taken as an example by various gardeners,[10] and after the Second World War by Professor Richard Hansen. Hansen, who in 1948 set up the Institut für Stauden, Gehölze un angewandte Pflanzensociologie (Institute for perennials, shrubs and applied plant sociology) in Weihenstephan, explored how different plants could be associated together in stylised vegetation types. The overall aim was to search for labour-efficient plant associations, particularly for use in public green space. Hansen, in association with Friedrich Stahl, ultimately summarised the results in *Perennials and their Garden Habitats*, first published in Germany in 1981 and translated into English in 1993. On the flyleaf it was noted that: 'Until recently, gardeners have paid little attention to the ecological requirements of perennials when planting them in parks and gardens. This book describes a new way of using perennials in parks and gardens based on ecological rather the purely aesthetic principles …'. It is interesting to establish that even after almost two centuries of experimentation, ecological planting can still be described as new, which suggests that it had never been part of mainstream practice.

The Netherlands[11]

Naturalistic planting design in the Netherlands derived from a different need. By the end of the nineteenth century prevalent landscape design was still firmly rooted in the landscape style, which with Leonard A. Springer (1855–1940), the best-known landscape architect of the period as a proponent, continued well into the twentieth century. Springer had argued that nature could not be imitated, and that the natural style was a compromise between nature and art, which as a result was artful and therefore included exotics. Artful nature had to be well-maintained, well-arranged, neat and tidy (Greenen and Roeleveld 1982: 116). Another group of landscape designers, represented by the 'nature style', responded against the artificiality in gardens; they were against cultivated varieties of plants and against traditional pruning regimes, preferring a more natural appearance instead. This was achieved through an emphasis on planting, which was to be established prior to laying out walks. This movement coincided with the popularisation of nature, which started in the late nineteenth century under the auspices of Jacobus P. Thijsse and Eli Heimans, two schoolteachers. They promoted a popular scientific approach to the study of local nature.

They aimed to increase awareness of nature and its conservation by means of education. Besides publications this was done with gardens such as Thijsse's Hof, Bloemendaal, founded in 1925 to raise

2.11
Jacobus P. Thijsse promoted conservation by means of education. The educational garden at Thijsse's Hof, Bloemendaal, recreated a vegetation with all the species of dune flora growing in the area

a general concern about the Dutch dunes, their flora and fauna. Designed by Springer at the initiation of Thijsse and planted by Cees Sipkes, it attempted to include all the species of the dune flora referred to as growing in the region by F. W. van Eeden in 1886. During the Second World War this sort of garden was referred to as an instructive park, emphasising its educational importance, but since the war these types of parks have been referred to as *heemparks*, with 'heem' representing environment, yard or home. These were defined as areas in which landscape architecture was conducted with the assistance of wild flora. They were as labour intensive as ordinary parks (Figure 2.11).

Thijsse's Hof gradually found a following with other such parks throughout the country. An early example was De Heimanshof in Vierhouten, named after Thijsse's late partner, and designed by Springer's nephew, the landscape architect G. Bleeker in 1935. It incorporated the flora of De Veluwe. More ambitious was the Scientific Garden in the Zuiderpark in the Hague, designed by A. J. de Gorter- ter Pelkwijk between 1933 and 1935, which aimed to include the various Dutch plant communities, and was intended for primary school education. The best known examples, however, are those designed as part of a park system for Amstelveen, De Braak and Westelijk Bovenland (later renamed Jac. P. Thijssepark) in 1939 and 1940, respectively. These were designed by C. P. Broerse, with the assistance of J. Landwehr.

The popular appeal of native plants was clear; Thijsse had suggested they might be used in the garden (Thijsse 1926: 90). J. M. van den Houten in his *Wilde Planten en hare Toepassing in onze Tuinen* (Native plants and their application in our gardens, 1935) discussed the ancient history of cultivation of native plants in gardens and organised his descriptions according to the various plant communities. The basic distinctions in this publication that was intended for the popular market was to differentiate two soil types – rich in nutrients and poor in nutrients – with seven types of communities – arable land, natural meadows, woodland, peat bogs versus dunes, heathland and moorland. Yet the author realised that not many private gardens would be able to include phytogeographical plantings, but that plant lovers might include a small section within the garden for native flora, with hints on how to create the right conditions for a number of vegetation types. There was practical information on collecting plants and on the limited number of nurseries specialising in native plant material.

During the 1920s the debate about a new garden style had moved away from romantic and aesthetic notions, and had become more scientifically based. The curator of the Amsterdam Hortus Botanicus, A. J. van Laren, introduced the concept of phytogeographical planting. In 1907 he had argued that the terminology of 'nature style' was unsuitable and had suggested such alternatives as 'landscape-like' and 'free-form layout'. He had used the term 'nature groupings' to describe various habitats that might be created in the garden, such as a bog garden, rockery, pond and woodland edge. In 1930 he promoted phytogeographic plant groupings as a 'new and more correct principle for the planting of parks, green spaces and gardens'. This meant that plants would be arranged by their countries of origin and according to the natural plant communities or associations. Whilst the Arboretum of Tervueren near Brussels was quoted as an example of such planting, it is clear that German examples and the long pedigree of plant geography were either not known by Van Laren or he may not have felt the necessity to acknowledge these (Van Laren 1907, 1927, 1929).

During the 1930s, the proposals for a new city park for Amsterdam focused discussions on the layout and design of public parks. The proposed planting of the Amsterdam bos was to be designed according to phytogeographical principles, and the planting was intended to satisfy both demands for nature conservation and an arboretum. Whilst doing so, Thijsse had criticised the term 'phytogeographical' as used by Van Laren, as this would not be generally understood, and suggested that 'plant sociological' might be added in order to explain the principles. In this instance 'phytogeographical' was not just used to denote plants from a particular region, but different countries were represented with certain plant communities or specific habitats (Thijsse 1934).

As a result of the limited availability of scientific and practical information, the uptake of this type of planting was restricted to large parks, such as the Zuiderpark in the Hague, implemented between 1921 and 1936 according to designs by landscape architect D. F. Tersteeg and P. Westbroek (Pannekoek and Schipper 1944). The confusion in terminology is evident in their standard textbook for landscape architecture *Tuinen* (Gardens). They recognised five different ways of grouping plants in the garden, three of which relate to various ecological approaches. They distinguish 'grouping according to plant communities', for example heath and woodland vegetation, dune flora, peat and moorland vegetation. There is 'phytogeographical planting', considered only suitable for larger gardens and parks, and 'groupings of wild plants', which differed from the former in scale. The other two types of planting were 'systematic groupings of plants', plants arranged according to family groupings, and the most common type 'mixed aesthetically and physiologically correct grouping', where due care and attention for the condition of the garden, its soil, and to form a harmonic whole (Pannekoek and Schipper 1944: II, 85–94).

In his inaugural lecture, 'The problem of plant grouping', on becoming a reader in landscape design, J. T. P. Bijhouwer, who had previously completed his PhD on a geobotanic study of the dunes in Bergen, added to this planting. He discussed two types of planting: one based on physiognomy as devised by Willy Lange, and another system devised by Hartogh Heys van Zouteveen. This did not arrange plants according to their external character, but selected those that occur in the temperate zone in similar plant communities (Bijhouwer 1939). As a result of the confusion over the terminology, 'phytogeographical' was gradually being phased out and was only occasionally used, such as by the townplanner Piet Verhagen who wrote about creating a phytogeographical garden (Verhagen 1945). By the 1950s the term 'plant sociology' was widely used.[12]

Research into phytogeography focused around the various botanical gardens, with a Laboratory for Plant Taxonomy and Geography established in Wageningen in 1930. Practically oriented research was encouraged by Bijhouwer, who in his inaugural lecture of 1939 had suggested that:

> Everywhere where an area is of such character and size that a visitor would experience this as landscape, a landscape architect would be sensible to adapt the choice of species to the constraints of the terrain, and to the existing natural vegetation. This also has enormous practical advantages – the plants will grow successfully, without the necessity of extensive soil improvements.
>
> One of the points, perhaps one of the few, with which critical Dutchmen all agree, is the value of landscape beauty, commonly natural beauty. What that is concerned we have a common asset, that also today is part of our civilisation as a community. If we manage to analyse the grouping of plants, if in this way we will come to a further solution, then this will already produce an expression of our common cultural inheritance. So in any case this should be part of a style.

To arrive to a fully comprehensive style, which links to our Dutch landscape appreciation, I believe that a better understanding and a more intense observation of our cultural landscapes will be necessary.

(Van Leeuwen and Doing Kraft 1959: 7–9)

It is clear that Bijhouwer saw the basis of a new landscape style in a deeper understanding of the existing landscape. Thus, increased knowledge of vegetation types was desirable; there were practical and economic advantages when these were applied to native species. It was particularly Victor Westhoff, first Director of the Laboratory, who took on the responsibility for the classification of the vegetation in the Netherlands (Westhoff *et al.* 1942). His successor, H. Doing Kraft, translated this into guidelines for forestry and landscape planning with Van Leeuwen in *Landschap en Beplanting in Nederland: Richtlijnen voor de Soortenkeuze bij Beplantingen op Vegetatiekundige Grondslag* (Landscape and planting in the Netherlands: guidelines for the species choice with plantations based on plant ecology (1959)). This used the plant geographical districts of the Netherlands as devised by J. L. van Soest in 1929 as a basis (Van Leeuwen and Doing Kraft 1959: 55) and provided detailed advice concerning plant communities and their composition for practical application (Figure 2.12). Whilst they were understood to be only a starting point, they were already in use with the Landscape section of the State Forestry Service prior to their publication, mainly concentrating on woody plants.

These guidelines were not intended for gardens and parks, as such an approach would lead to the impoverishment of such places, as exotic plants have for centuries made a valuable contribution to the richness of gardens. Knowledge might even be extended to non-native plant communities drawn from exotic locations. 'Equipped with this knowledge and with his creative abilities the park and garden architect would be able to compose plantings, which are justified both scientifically and aesthetically.' A further disclaimer finished the introduction to the guidelines, which stated that as an artist the desire to group plants according to whatever order was totally left to the garden architect. The most important part of the guidelines consisted of a table of plants found in the 12 Dutch woodland types, as defined in Heukels and Van Oostroom's *Flora van Nederland* (1956), which then enabled the designer to make appropriate selection for the region. It was noted that there were objections from the science world to planting schemes based on ecological principles, as copying of the 'natural' vegetation types would be confusing for further plant

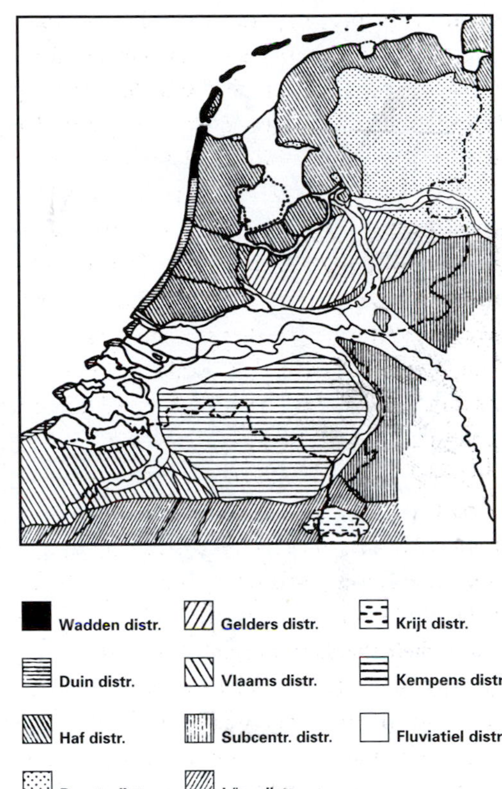

2.12
A division of the Netherlands in plant geographical districts produced by J. L. van Soest in 1929 – later became the basis for guidelines for forestry and landscape planning (Heukels 1976)

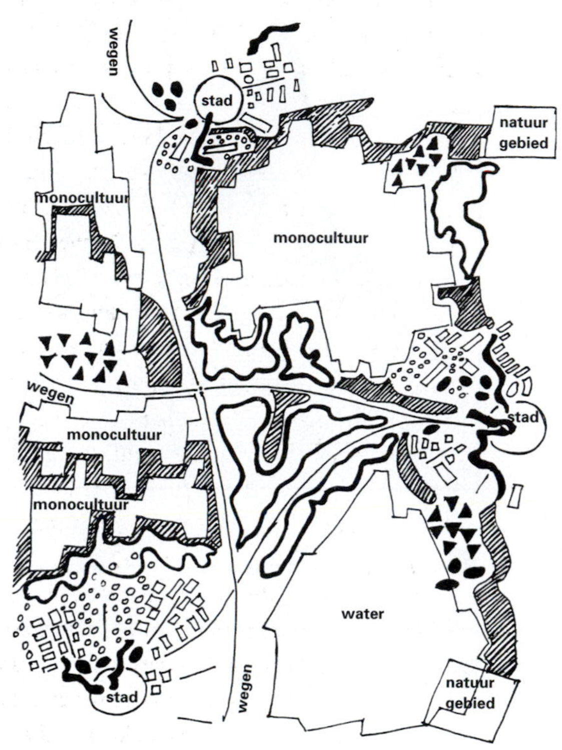

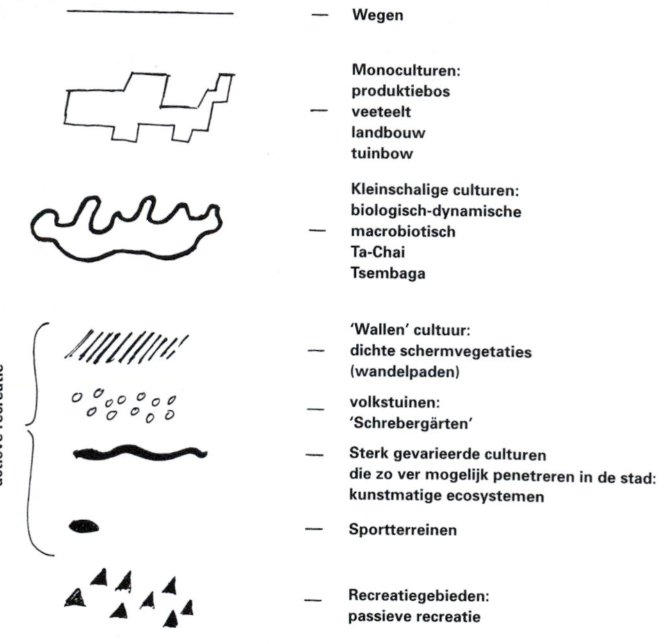

2.13
Louis le Roy saw the city (*stad*) as being surrounded by alternative small scale cultures in a network of artificial ecosystems, allotments and artificial dry wall systems with footpaths into the countryside (Le Roy 1973: 184–185)

geographic research. The authors did not consider this to be a sufficiently important counter-argument against well-adapted planting schemes (Van Leeuwen and Doing Kraft 1959: 55).

Ger Londo of the governmental Department for Management of Nature extended the ideas, bridging the gap left between the ecologically appropriate woodland vegetations and the labour-intensive *heemparks*. The latter had been the subject of a book by J. Landwehr and Cees Sipkes, entitled *Wildeplantentuinen* (Native plant gardens, 1973), which contained many years of experience in laying out and maintaining *heemparks*. Londo's publication *Natuurtuinen enparken: Aanleg en Onderhoud* (Nature gardens and parks: layout and maintenance (1977)) was concerned with the development of natural vegetation in which all plants belonging to it are included, without the necessity for intensive weeding as with *heemparks*. This book provided a practical manual as to how to establish environments with more or less natural plantings with native species. There was no necessity for weeding and planting, and the maintenance was much less intensive with, for example, a mowing regime of once or twice annually. These nature gardens were simple to establish and cheap to maintain (Londo 1977), but less finely detailed than traditional *heemparks*.

From the late 1960s the artist and teacher Louis le Roy reacted to what he saw as an unacceptably *laissez-faire* contemporary attitudes and policies to the environment, and the risks posed by man-made

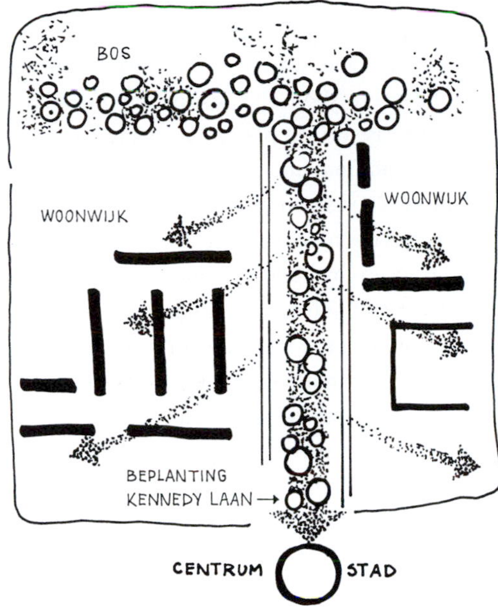

2.14
In Le Roy's vision, nature would invade the housing areas (Le Roy 1973: 190)

pollution and pesticides. He maintained that the historic development of nature and culture were to be considered as a continuity, and that any severance in space or time might cause an ecological calamity. He saw the function of cities as providing oases in which human beings would be able to express their creativity, rather than in specially created recreation areas. Emerging from the city would be alternative small-scale food cultures in a network of artificial ecosystems, allotments and artificial wall systems with footpaths into the countryside. Thus, surrounding monoculture agriculture would be enclosed by these interconnecting systems leading from city to city (Figure 2.13).

Le Roy proposed that the management of vegetation should aim for and encourage a relatively stable climax situation, which in most cases would be some form of woodland, with some pruning being the only maintenance; there should be no soil cultivation (Figure 2.14). Planting was to take place with any species, by applying the Darwinian approach of the survival of the fittest. His book *Natuur Uitschakelen; Natuur Inschakelen* (Turn off nature; turn on nature, 1973) motivated a whole generation of enthusiasts. Yet his projects, such as the Kennedylaan at Heerenveen in the Netherlands, all fell foul of the fact that success was dependent on relinquishing power to a counter-culture and authorities were reluctant to do so (Le Roy 1973) (Figure 2.15). Le Roy was not always thanked for his approach by nature conservationists, as he did not remain true to the existing vegetation, but they did acknowledge him for being able to arouse a new generation and get them to think about ecology on a larger scale. Nowadays, the nature gardens of Londo, the gardens following the principles of Le Roy, and the Thijsse type heemgardens are all included in a guide to 170 sites throughout the Netherlands (Leufgen and Van Lier 1992).

During the 1980s, the environmental debate was dominated by changes in the rural landscape, with concern about farming, its overproduction and continued mechanisation. A design competition held in 1986 addressed these issues by looking at the river valleys of the Rhine and Meuse. The characteristics of the valleys meant that the area is subject to pressures from gravel and clay extraction, and that efficient large-scale agriculture was not possible on often small and irregular plots. Despite the rich soil, agriculture was therefore not economical and a complete reassessment was

2.15
Most of Le Roy's projects, such as the Kennedylaan in Heerenveen, fell foul of the fact that success was dependent on relinquishing power to a counter-culture and local authorities were reluctant to do so

required. The winning entry to this competition addressed the various issues through a very careful historical, social and ecological analysis, and was adopted and given the project name 'Stork'. This plan aimed to create a new interaction between the natural dynamics of a river system, the resulting visual expression and the land use. The plan was both philosophically and economically appealing, and gained immediate and widespread publicity because it provided a framework for the management of rivers, nature, agriculture and the extraction of minerals. On a practical level with regard to vegetation, it meant that instead of planting whole areas, the area would be given over to natural processes to encourage natural regeneration. Traditional low-intensity management practices, for example grazing, were used to encourage a rich mosaic of grassland, copses and woodlands. This project represented one of the first holistic large-scale applications of ecological ideas to the repair of a large-scale cultural landscape (De Bruin *et al.* 1987).

USA

Although the great nineteenth-century American landscape gardener Andrew Jackson Downing was aware of Alexander von Humboldt, he does not appear to have applied his theories in his design proposals, nor did he discuss them in *The Theory and Practice of Landscape Gardening* (1859). Although the name Humboldt occurs occasionally, as in Humboldt Park, Chicago, it is unclear whether his theories on plant geography made any impact in the USA. The Humboldtian legacy is therefore not noticeable until the return of Frank A. Waugh to the US. Waugh had studied at the Royal Horticultural College Berlin-Dahlem with Willy Lange and was clearly inspired by the latter's theories, which he popularised as a Professor at the Massachusetts State Agricultural College and adapted to an American context in such publications as *The Natural Style in Landscape Gardening* (1917) (Wolschke-Bulmahn 1997: 2).

In the USA there was, as in European countries, a general concern about the destruction of wild flora, in this case driven partly by advances in technology, and fundamental changes in the way people lived. The vast industrial expansion in the second half of the nineteenth century had created enormous wealth by 1900. Conspicuous consumption and unbridled materialism was seen to be undermining the morality of the country. At the same time, immigration escalated with unprecedented numbers of poor, less educated, and more culturally diverse incomers, which threatened national identities and values. Clayton observed that until then the interaction with nature had assured physical, moral and spiritual well-being, and nature had been considered such a powerful force of good that a return to nature was popularly accepted as an antidote for the various social upheavals. This was represented by calls for the conservation of wild flowers and wild gardening, which flourished as popular topics from the 1890s until the end of the First World War (Clayton 1997).

The same issues led to landscape architects desiring to establish a distinctive American style. Ossian Cole Simonds (1855) and Jens Jensen (1860–1951) both experimented with native flora and developed a garden style which, from 1915, came to be referred to as the 'prairie style'. This name was coined by Wilhelm Miller in a publication entitled *The Prairie Spirit in Landscape Gardening* (1915), which featured Simonds and Jensen's work. The prairie style was defined as 'an American mode of design based upon the practical needs of the Middle-Western people and characterised by preservation of typical Western scenery, by restoration of local color, and by repetition of the horizontal line of land or sky, which is the strongest feature of prairie scenery'.[13]

Whilst the emphasis of the prairie style was on

the use of indigenous plants, Jensen normally also used non-native plants in his designs, but would include small sections with native themes, particularly his ‘prairie rivers’ in Humboldt Park (1907) and Columbus Park, Chicago (1917), celebrated by Miller as the prairie-style water garden. Like Simonds, Jensen did not propose restorations of prairie landscapes, but as they considered their gardens to be art, intended instead to provide idealised images of the prairie. Only in late works, such as the Lincoln Memorial, Springfield, Illinois (1936), did Jensen concentrate purely on native plants, which were grouped in ecological associations as they might be found in the wild. Here he anticipated natural succession, with his design serving as a framework only for a mosaic that would develop in time (Grese 1995). It is remarkable that such approaches did not occur before this time, as he had learned about ecology from the plant ecologist Cowles much earlier. Jensen contacted Cowles after the publication of ‘The ecological relations of the vegetation of the sand dunes of Lake Michigan’ in the *Botanical Gazette* (1899), which became a classic reference. Soon after they explored various local vegetation types together (Grese 1992). Cowles was a charter member of The Friends of Our Native Landscape, a conservation organisation founded by Jensen in 1913 (Vernon 1995). By the 1930s, Jensen’s attitudes may have derived from other sources, specifically Germany, as the phraseology and rhetoric in his writings is similar to Nazi landscape architects of the period and there were publications about and by him in German contemporary magazines (Domer 1997). Similarly, Miller’s writings gained a strong ideological stance in which he strove to promote ‘a natural “American” landscape design aesthetic’.[14]

Frank A. Waugh on his return from Germany in 1910 had proposed to use the word ecological to translate Lange’s biological-physiognomical method, and suggested that the nearest in approach was Warren H. Manning of Boston. Unlike Lange or Miller, Manning did not have a strong ideology, but favoured a more pragmatic approach. Manning initially considered ‘nature gardens’ or wild gardens in which the existing conditions were carefully surveyed, then eliminated material that was out of place. New plants were positioned where they appeared to grow naturally. Such an approach demanded a profound understanding of site conditions and knowledge of plants, as well as a ‘close sympathy with nature’. Manning recommended native plants because of the ease of availability, transplanting and growing; and the fact that they were inexpensive. He was not dogmatic about the use of native plants however, but recommended cultivated species which might add floral value and, in doing so, he noted that ‘the spirit of the wild garden is essentially cosmopolitan’ (Karson 1997).

From the late 1920s, however, ecological principles can be seen to be more generally applied by other landscape architects. In their book *American Plants for American Gardens*, Edith A. Roberts and Elsa Rehmann (1929), a plant ecologist and a landscape architect respectively, promoted the use of native American plants in groupings based on natural plant communities. The text provided underlying ecological concepts and also recommended lists of native plant species for use in landscape designs (Tishler 1989). The landscape architect H. Stuart Ortloff refers to Roberts and Rehmann, and summarises the ecological knowledge a few years later when he writes:

> A better understanding of plant ecology opens up many new fields of endeavor, and allows us to correct many old mistakes that have endangered the success of our gardens. It is one of the guides to the selection of plants particularly suited for use in naturalistic plantings. If we are trying to catch the spirit of Nature in our work it is obviously important that we follow her

The renewed interest in native plantings encouraged professional interest and in the 1970s professionals re-emerged with so-called 'natural landscape restoration concepts', with Jensen and Roberts and Rehman as the main references. Darrel G. Morrison was one of the main proponents of this movement who demonstrated the 'ecological and aesthetic potential of plant community restorations'. His projects were related mainly to corporate and residential sites in Wisconsin. Morrison maintained that:

> The art of restoring natural lands implies first an understanding of the natural landscape and native communities of a region; then an ability to simplify and stylize without losing the aesthetic essence of these complex systems in a designed environment; and knowledge of plant propagation and establishment techniques. Finally, it requires an understanding that natural landscapes, particularly restored natural landscapes, require intelligent management to perpetuate dynamic natural character whilst maintaining designed spatial configurations.
>
> (Morrison 1989: 190)

Morrison's 'restored' landscapes, therefore, were still only an interpretation of native landscapes, like that of previous generations, but he had access to more extensive ecological information.

John Curtis and Henry Greene who, in 1934, started experimentation at the University of Wisconsin, Madison, with re-establishing prairie plant communities, undertook a much more exacting approach (Figure 2.17). They were led in their concern by the disappearance of the prairie and by despoliation of the land, a cause taken up by Aldo Leopold, who had joined the University in 1933 as Professor in Wildlife Management. Leopold's posthumous *Sand County Almanac* (1949) was a plea for the development of a land ethic, which prevented the desecration of the soil and disappearance of the wilderness. A co-founder of the Wilderness Society, he spent years single-handedly trying to restore a parcel of farmland he had acquired (Sand County) to its natural habitat (Grese 1992: 155, 237, 272). Leopold became the spiritual leader of the restoration ecology movement, which saw ecological restoration as a technique for basic research (Jordan *et al.* 1987: 3). The emphasis here was to create the pre-existing plant communities previously destroyed with genetically identical plants. His writings and approach have since

2.17
The Greene Prairie at the University of Wisconsin arboretum, Madison, re-established lost plant communities

2.18
Lorrie Otto has spent years fighting against the American lawn and promoting more naturalistically planted front yards, here an example in Milwaukee

2.19
William Robinson drew his inspiration from the wild and promoted naturalisation and natural groupings of hardy exotic plants (Robinson 1894: 101)

sparked several other generations of environmentalists to undertake similar ecological restoration projects, but seem more or less to have by-passed the landscape architecture profession. One well-known environmentalist is Lorrie Otto who took the plight into the community, fighting against the American lawn and promoting 'naturally landscaped frontyards' (Figure 2.18). She had converted her own garden in Bayside, Wisconsin, to native plantings in 1955. Her example had a great following, particularly from the Wild Ones, a native plant educational group, which promoted the Otto cause.

Great Britain

Pre-Second World War British landscape design was dominated by the writings of Gertrude Jekyll and William Robinson, with a horticultural and artistic emphasis, rather than an ecological one. Yet much of their inspiration for plants and planting arrangement came from wildflowers of the British countryside. The Reverend C. A. Johns' *Flowers of the Field* (1851) had been a Victorian classic which had drawn attention to botany, popularised it, and encouraged gardeners to reappreciate wildflowers. Robinson's *The Wild Garden* (1870) summed up this development and gave a new impetus to the expression. This book was concerned with the naturalisation and natural grouping of hardy exotic plants, and concentrated on examples of a wide range of habitats; on hardy bulbs in grass; on ditches, lanes, copses and hedgerows; on brookside, water and bog gardens; and on walls and rocks. In these, inspiration was drawn from examples in the wild, with suggestions on establishment in a similar setting within the garden (Robinson 1894) (Figure 2.19).

Gertrude Jekyll, a former artist turned gardener, expressed the process even more eloquently. She discussed 'the enjoyment of beauty of a pictorial kind' and trying to make 'a beautiful garden picture'. She noted that 'I had the advantage in earlier life of some amount of training in [the] appreciation of the fine arts, and this, working upon an inborn feeling of reverent devotion to things of the highest beauty in the works of God, has helped me to an understanding of their divinely-inspired interpretations by the noblest of men, into those forms that we know of works of fine art'. Thus, she concluded: 'And so it comes about that those of us who feel and understand in this way do not exactly attempt to imitate Nature in our gardens, but try to become well acquainted with her moods and ways, and then discriminate in our borrowing, and so interpret her methods as best we may to the making of our garden pictures' (Jekyll 1914: 196). This is a very similar approach to that taken by previous generations of designers working in the landscape style, with Jekyll planting in informal drifts rather than in more formal blocks, or planting in the old-fashioned mixed or mingled manner (Figure 2.20).

The artistic approach dominated in Great Britain, and there are only a few references that suggest knowledge and application of Humboldt's plant geography. One notable example is Patrick Geddes, the Scottish biologist and planner, who in his proposals for Pittencrieff Park, Dunfermline, recommended the rock garden to be further developed, both 'evolutionary and geologically', which included the 'geographical distribution of our different plant types' (Geddes 1904: 59, 115, 118). Geddes's proposals, however, remained unexecuted and were read by town planners rather than horticulturalists and garden designers, and therefore appear to have had limited impact.

New trends in planting occurred in Britain, but none of them appears to be derived from ecological research. The Road Beautifying Association in its advice on roadside planting, for example, recorded two different schools of thought, one 'that only trees which are indigenous to the British soil should be planted' and the other that 'it is perfectly good taste to make use of beautiful trees and shrubs, no matter what the country of their origin, provided they grow

2.20
Getrude Jekyll suggested an artistic approach in order to make garden pictures – one of the examples included in her *Colour Schemes for the Flower Garden* (1925), and includes an example of the alteration of the formal planting of a heath garden, showing the drifts instead of blocks

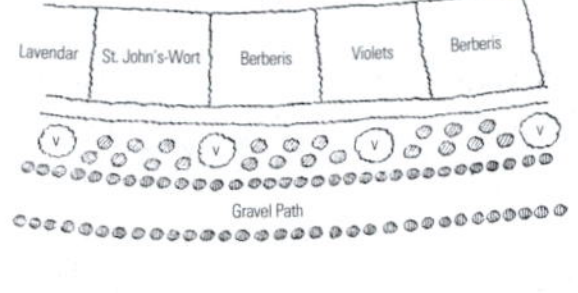

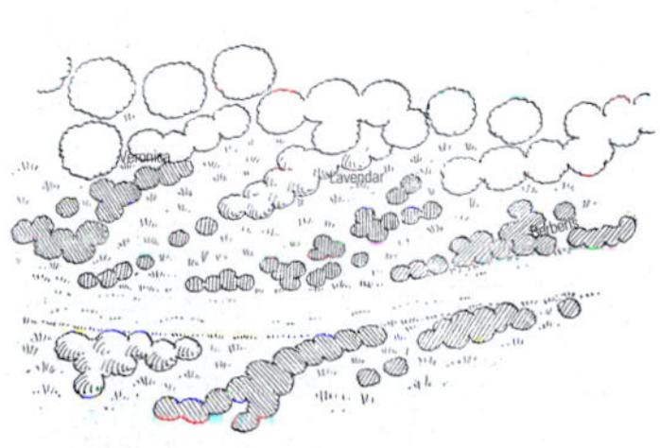

A Wild Heath Garden
Upper Figure: As First Planted
Lower Figure: After Alteration

well …' (Road Beautifying Association 1930). This was in contrast to the German tradition as observed by Christopher Tunnard in 1935, who noted that German designers 'based their principles on natural oecological development …'. He contrasted their planting of roads which conformed 'to the general principle of natural planning' and endeavoured 'to retain the character of the district in which the work is being carried out' with the British approach. In Germany 'one seldom sees avenue planting in any form outside the towns and the white ribbon of a trunk road is not, as is often the case with by-pass in this country, merely accentuated throughout its length by soldier-like lines of one particular species of ornamental tree. The planting is instead made compatible with both countryside and road, now swelling over the brow of the hill and running close to the carriage-way, now receding to allow for wide views over a plain level, now evergreen, now deciduous, according to the exigencies of the site …' (Tunnard 1937).

None of this appears to have influenced Tunnard himself and he did not refer to this in his *Gardens in the Modern Landscape* (1938), which reproduces a planting scheme dependent on purely aesthetic principles (Tunnard 1938: 118–124).

The appearance of Arthur G. Tansley's *The British Islands and Their Vegetation* (1939) made a significant impact on landscape architects. Landscape architect Sylvia Crowe considered that 'there is no better guide to the principles of natural planting than an examination of the diagrams of natural associations in Tansley's *The British Islands and Their Vegetation* – coupled with first-hand observation' (Crowe 1956: 76). Her colleague Brenda Colvin similarly used Tansley's book as a reference and explained the concept of community, the study of which she considered 'of vital interest to the landscape designer if he appreciates the native character of our landscape'. She noted that it was all too easy to introduce foreign plants, and that these should not be spread recklessly over the countryside, but concentrated to parks, gardens and towns. She proposed keeping the countryside to the natural plant groups, with which she did not mean just 'true' native species, but included others 'which have established themselves as party of that landscape and are able to hold their own as members of one or other of the native plant associations' (Colvin 1948: 65*ff*, 143).

There appears to have been a general consensus within the post-war generation of landscape architects about the application of ecological principles as a basis for planting design in the countryside. Another example of this is Brian Hackett, who argued that planting design could 'be helped by studying the arrangement of the various members of the native plant community and simplifying the patterns identified so that they form a source of inspiration upon which the planting plan is built-up with some variation in the species' (Hackett 1971: 102). This shows expanding degrees of sophistication and creativity in the application of ecological principles, or an acknowledgement that completely accurate reinterpretations were not possible. There is also a general acknowledgement that the purist adherence to native, as opposed to exotic, species would lead to an impoverishment of the British landscape and was not a feasible option.

All landscape architects of this period strongly perceive the countryside as a source of food production (its continued need for this was confirmed by the Second World War) and national identity. This was best expressed by Brenda Colvin, who in this was clearly influenced by Sir George Stapledon, and is not dissimilar from German Nazi philosophy (Stapledon 1935: 1). She noted: 'The land has always been the reserve and origin also of healthy human stock: the solid base of the population contributing to sturdy heredity through the interchange between town and country populations, and to health through provision of good fresh food' (Colvin 1948: 175). This was, of course, best represented by an appropriate setting of a

2.21
The William Curtis Ecological Park near Tower Bridge was founded in 1977, but has now been built over. It was designed by Lyndis Cole, who had been inspired by Dutch examples

landscape with vegetation of a 'native' appearance. Throughout her career, Colvin was to stress the importance of ecological planting for reasons of conservation, appearance, diversity and economy (Colvin 1977: 10*ff*).

After he had promoted 'an ecological approach to design' (Hackett 1962–63), Hackett's ideas on planting policies in landscape plans reflected the ideas of his predecessors with respect to the selection of plants and attitude to non-native species (Hackett 1971),[15] and were later included in his *Planting Design* (1979). He distinguishes two ways in which ecology might serve as a basis for planting design. The first manner is to base any planting proposals on a survey of the natural vegetation of the area and, where absent, on conjectural analysis. The second manner refers to establishing a vegetation by means of traditional maintenance techniques, which is said to 'accept the principles underlying the existence of the flora and fauna in a habitat and to use these principles for design purposes whilst introducing man as a new and possibly dominant factor – from either the aesthetic or use points of view, or both'. Another approach selects plants not necessarily based on ecological principles but 'in accordance with the soil, climate, aspect and other relevant environmental determinants, and for their appearance, in the knowledge that if competition from other plants is removed as a result of maintenance techniques, success is likely' (Hackett 1979: 80).

Hackett proceeds to explain the relevance of the latest scientific information relating to ecological principles; of biotic communities, habitat provision, food webs and dominant species. The methodology recommended is the survey of patterns of the local native vegetation, the analysis of which may then be used as a basis for planting designs (Hackett 1979: 80–87). The methodology suggested is similar to what was recommended by the German Willy Lange in 1922. The examples listed by Hackett however relate to woodland landscapes rather than a garden setting, or urban contexts.

Whilst ecological planting was mainly pursued in the countryside and land reclamation schemes, another group of landscape architects and ecologists pursued the urban context. From the late 1960s onwards, these stressed the importance of nature and the natural environment for the quality of life. Inspired by German, Dutch and Swedish examples, ecological concepts slowly permeated into the work and policies of urban landscape designers.[16] One of the most outspoken activists proposing the relevance of ecology in towns was Max Nicholson, the Director General of the Nature Conservancy, who believed in 'ecology and conservation as a scientific basis of landscape design' (Nicholson 1965). Upon his retirement in 1966, he founded the Land Use Consultants in order to undertake environmental projects with an emphasis on the creation of naturalistic landscapes. One of the pioneering schemes with which the firm became involved was a massive reclamation programme in the Potteries and Stoke-on-Trent, for which they designed Central Forest Park, Hanley. It included Dutch inspired approaches to encouraging native vegetation and regeneration, whilst accepting the quarried topography of the site and utilising this to create a number of spaces with different functions (Aldous and Clouston 1979: 91). In 1979, Nicholson was instrumental in the formation of the Ecological Parks Trust, later renamed the Trust for Urban Ecology, which aimed to manage the William Curtis Ecological Park, near Tower Bridge and founded in 1977, and other urban nature reserves. The designer of this park was Lyndis Cole of the Land Use Consultants who had been inspired by Dutch examples (Woudstra 1985) (Figure 2.21).

At around the same time, another group of landscape architects was involved in developing a landscape strategy and detailed planting at Warrington New Town, based on ecological principles. Their aims were to establish a nature-like planting which was cost effective to establish and maintain, robust but did not appear contrived, and was structurally diverse. It also had to form a replacement for former semi-natural habitats in their locality. Planting took place primarily with native species with mixes prescribed in percentages and planted in irregular groups, with guidance on minimum and maximum numbers per group (Beckett and Parker 1990). The emphasis was on native trees (and shrubs), the area of which had declined as a result of modern agricultural practice and Dutch elm disease. A working party of the Botanical Society of the British Isles, which included the landscape architect Allan R. Ruff, set out to make ecological information more available in order to promote the appropriate use of native woody plants. This culminated in the publication *Planting Native Trees and Shrubs* (1979), edited by Kenneth and Gillian Beckett.

Sweden

In the eighteenth century, Carl von Linné (Linnaeus) had given natural history research a fresh impetus and had provided a new perspective on nature, with Uppsala University as the centre. Botanical research remained important and one of his later successors as professor in botany, Rutger Sernander (1866–1944), wrote his thesis about the development of vegetation in Gotland in 1894 (Warming 1909). From the 1910s, Sernander performed an important position in the reform of landscape design by criticising traditional parks. In his criticisms he reinforced the late nineteenth-century conception of the 'nature-loving Swede' (Hillmo *et al.* no date) by arguing in favour of parks more in keeping with the existing landscape rather than schemes imported from outside. In 1918 he had criticised St Erik's Park in Stockholm for the lack of respect to natural features on the site, which deprive future citizens 'of existing natural values that cannot be recreated'. He thus promoted projects which included features of the local landscape with plant material more sympathetic to the existing characteristics of the site (Andersson 1993). In doing this, Sernander merely expressed contemporary concerns and took an approach which had already been acknowledged in the design competition for the new South Cemetery in 1915, the later Woodland Cemetery, Enskede. An early ecological garden that well displays the mood of the times was that at Vasaparken, Uppsala, also referred to as the biological park or school park, as it was intended for educational purposes. It was laid out in 1911 around the newly established Biological Museum and there were areas representing the flora of the three main plant geographical districts of Sweden: Götaland (south), Svaeland (middle) and Norrland (north) (Adrén and Lagerwall 1997: 170). In 1926, Sernander published *Stockholms Natur* (Stockholm's nature), which was intended as a masterplan of future park development for Greater

Stockholm and for nature reserves within the boundaries in the city (Bucht 1997: 85).

By the 1930s, there had been a general adoption of the above principles by Swedish landscape architects, who expressed their theory and principles as follows:

> The utilitarian style has strongly influenced the construction of domestic buildings; they are often asymmetrically planned, have large windows exposed to the sun, and, if possible, are sufficiently free from screening to permit of distant views.
>
> Ordinarily, the garden is planned in such a way as to form a direct relationship with the house, access from one to the other being everywhere facilitated. The garden thus becomes a part of the dwelling. Its arrangement is decided more for the activities of the people – especially of children – than for flowers. It allows for seats and benches resting on pavement areas which relate to the house, and lawns as extensive as possible, though not always mown. Paths and walks are reduced to the minimum and often consist only of stepping stones between which grass or creeping plants are allowed to grow, thus conserving a homogeneity between the units of the plan. Pools for the children are much appreciated and, when possible, they are made deep enough to allow for bathing. In general, trees are not numerous in these gardens; most people prefer to have flowering shrubs. Even [when] herbaceous plants are used they have a definite part of the plan devoted for their culture, and need not, as formerly, be confined to the conventional flower bed. There is little room in gardens now for the bedding plants which for so many years have enjoyed such a wide vogue.
>
> The utilitarian style of building has exercised a profound influence on gardens, which it appears to be ridding of conscious symmetrical planning. The arrangement of gardens is freer and more mobile than formerly. One does not look for axial construction and the monumental planning of former styles, which could never be prevented from looking severe, above all when close to the house, the hard lines of which can be softened by subtle plant arrangements. One strives to create a contrast between the disciplined outlines of terrace walls, paved spaces, pools, etc., and a free and luxuriant vegetation designed to produce a happy decorative effect and to give the impression that it is the work of nature or of chance. It is pleasant to leave an existing gnarled pine in a paved courtyard the aspect of which is otherwise strictly architectural, or to arrange matters so that trees with heads of interesting shapes appear to detach themselves from the smooth walls of the house, their rigidity being softened by the foliage. It is admissible that between the paving stones of courtyard space should be left for isolated plants to give the impression that they have grown there spontaneously.[17]

Tunnard (1937) noted that Swedish designers preferred 'to group their plants in simple natural arrangements rather than confine them to severe geometrical patterns'.

Post-war Swedish planting design was widely regarded as exemplary (Haywood and Booth 1954), with Frank Clark noting that the 'free planting of flowers and shrubs follows the teachings of our own William Robinson so closely that it must be more than a mere coincidence' (Clark 1947). George Chadwick similarly detected the influence of Robinson and Jekyll, describing 'the use of Petasites and rhubarbs for foliage effect, the naturalising of tulips in the long grass in Humlegarden, the cow the development of scientific understanding.

As a result, as with other landscape design styles, it is possible to distinguish distinct types of ecological planting in different eras. In 1935, the landscape architect Marjorie Cautley observed:

> In nature plants are grouped according to ecology, or adaptability to their environment. In landscape work, plant groups seem to depend upon fashions and styles. It is often possible to ascertain the decade in which a garden was laid out by the type of plants that were in vogue at the time.
>
> (Cautley 1935: 200)

This clearly is also the case with various types of ecological planting, where there are distinct developments and changes of emphasis, with nowadays a greater emphasis on artistic outcomes (particularly where these principles are applied to garden plantings), whereas historically ecological principles were mainly thought of in connection with a scientific approach. However, aesthetic considerations have always had a special significance, often aiming to challenge perceived notions of what garden planting is supposed to look like. Scientific approaches remain the dominant emphasis in larger-scale work, with the latest projects concerned primarily about restarting natural processes, and natural recolonisation. In time, even this will be shown to have a period feel. This is even more evident for the whole series of artistic approaches stimulated by the ecological ideal that developed in the later decades of the twentieth century.

Acknowledgements

The author would like to thank the following people who have supplied information used in the preparation of this chapter: Erika Schmidt, John Glenn, Nigel Temple, James Hitchmough, David Jacques, Clas Florgård, Clemens Wimmer, Andrea Koenecke and Susanne Gerulat.

References

- Adrén, H. and Lagerwall, M. (1997). *Parker and Trädgårdar i Sverige (Parks and Gardens in Sweden).* Lunds Offset, Lund.
- Aldous, T. and Clouston, B. (1979). *Landscape by Design.* Heinemann, London.
- Andersson, T. (1993). Erik Glemme and the Stockholm Park System. In Treib, M. (ed.) *Modern Landscape Architecture: a Critical Review.* MIT, Cambridge, Massachusetts.
- Barth, J. (1980). Erwin Barth's Sachsenplatz in Berlin. *Garten und Landschaft,* No. 11, 931–936.
- Beckett, K. and Beckett, G. (1979). *Planting Native Trees and Shrubs*. Jarrold, Norwich.
- Beckett, P. and Parker, D. (1990). The use and management of plant species native to Britain. In Clouston, B. (ed.) *Landscape Design with Plants.* Heinemann Newnes, Oxford.
- Bijhouwer, J. T. P. (1939). *Het Vraagstuk der Plantengroepeering: Rede uitgesproken bij de Aanvaarding van het Ambt van Lector aan de Landbouwhoogeschool te Wageningen of 30 November 1939.* Veenman, Wageningen.
- Bowler, P. (1992). *The Fontana History of the Environmental Sciences.* Fontana, London.
- Bruin, D. de, Hamhuis, D., Nieuwenhuijze, L. van, Overmars, W., Sijmons, D. and Vera, F. (1987). *Ooievaar: De Toekomst van het Rivierengebied.* Stichting Gelderse Milieufederatie, Arnhem.
- Bucht, E. (1997). *Public Parks in Sweden 1860–1960: The Planning and Design Discourse.* Swedish University of Agricultural Sciences, Alnarp.
- Cautley, M. (1935) *Garden Design.*
- Chadwick, G. F. (1966). *The Park and the Town.* Architectural Press, London.
- Clark, H. F. (1947). Space between buildings: the landscaping of Stockholm's parks. *The Architectural Review,* **102**, 190.
- Clayton, V.T. (1997). Wild gardening and the popular American magazine, 1890–1918. In Wolschke-Bulmahn, J. (ed.) *Nature and Ideology: Natural Garden Design of the Twentieth Century.* Dumbarton Oaks, Washington DC.
- Colvin, B. (1948). *Land and Landscape.* John Murray, London.
- Colvin, B. (1977). Trees in the countryside. In Clouston, B. (ed.) *Landscape Design with Plants.* Heinemann, Oxford.

- Colvin, B., Ledeboer, J. and Clark, H. F. (1952). The International Federation of Landscape Architects and the Stockholm Conference. *Journal of the Institute of Landscape Architects,* No. 25, 10–12.
- Crowe, S. (1956). *Tomorrow's Landscape.* The Architectural Press, London.
- Domer, D. (1997). *Alfred Caldwell: The Life and Work of a Prairie School Landscape Architect.* John Hopkins, Baltimore.
- Downing, A. J. (1853). *Rural Essays.* Putnam, New York.
- Eckbo, G. (1950). *Landscape for Living.* Architectural Record, Los Angeles.
- Florgård, C. (1981). *Att anlägga mager mark och växtlighet – 13 exempel.* Statens råd för byggnadsforskning. Stockholm.
- Foerster, K. (1930). Neue Wege der Gartenkunst: Berthold Körtings Vermächtnis. *Gartenschönheit,* **11**, 203–207.
- Geddes, P. (1904). *City Development: A Study of Parks, Gardens, and Culture – Institutes.* Saint George Press, Birmingham.
- Greenen, G. and Roeleveld, G (1982). *Leonard A.Springer: Beschrijving en documentatie van zijn beroepspraktijk.* Vakgroep Landschapsarchitectuur Landbouwhogeschool, Wageningen.
- Grese, R. (1992). *Jens Jensen: Maker of Natural Parks and Gardens.* John Hopkins, Baltimore.
- Grese, R. (1995). The prairie gardens of O. C. Simonds and Jens Jensen. In O'Malley, T. and Treib, M. (eds) *Regional Garden Design in the United States.* Dumbarton Oaks, Washington, DC.
- Groening, G. and Wolschke-Bulmahn, J. (1989). Changes in the philosophy of garden architecture in the 20th century and their impact upon the social and spatial environment. *Journal of Garden History,* **9**, 53–70.
- Hackett, B. (1962–63). Ecological approach to design. *Landscape Architecture,* **53**, 123–126.
- Hackett, B. (1971). *Landscape Planning.* Oriel Press, Newcastle upon Tyne.
- Hackett, B. (1979). *Planting Design.* Spon, London.
- Hansen, R. and Stahl, F. (1993). *Perennials and their Garden Habitats.* Cambridge University Press, Cambridge.
- Haywood, S. and Booth, K. (1954). Planting design. *Journal of the Institute of Landscape Architects,* No. 29, 6.
- Hermand, J. (1997). Rousseau, Goethe, Humboldt: their influence on later advocates of the nature garden. In Wolschke-Bulmahn, J. (eds) *Nature and Ideology: Natural Garden Design in the Twentieth Century.* Dumbarton Oaks, Washington, DC.
- Hillmo, T., Lohm, U. and Bateld, K. (no date). Swedish national report. In *Nature, Environment, Landscape: European Attitudes and Discourses 1920–1970 (ECQUA Working Paper Number 1).* Co-ordinating Centre, Department of Geography, Royal Holloway, Egham, Surrey, pp. 56–95.
- Hottenträger, G. (1992). New flowers-new gardens: residential gardens designed by Karl Foerster, Hermann Mattern and Herta Hammerbacher (1928–c.1943). *Journal of Garden History,* **12**, 207–227.
- Houten, J. M. van den (1935). *Wilde Planten en hare Toepassing in onze Tuinen.* W.L. & J. Brusse, Rotterdam.
- Hyams, E. and MacQuitty, W. (1969). *Great Botanical Gardens of the World.* Thomas Nelson, London.
- Jacques, D. (1983). *Georgian Gardens.* B. T. Batsford, London.
- Jäger, H. (1877). *Lehrbuch der Gartenkunst.* Hugo Voigt, Berlin.
- Jekyll, G. (1914). *Wood and Garden: Notes on Thoughts, Practical and Critical, of a Working Amateur.* Longmans, London.
- Johnson, L. and Lees, C. (1988). *Wildflowers across America.* National Wildflower Research Center, New York.
- Jordan III, W. R., Gilpin, M. E. and Aber, J. D. (1987). *Restoration Ecology: A Synthetic Approach to Ecological Research.* Cambridge University Press, Cambridge.
- Karson, R. (1997). Warren H. Manning: pragmatist in the wild garden. In Wolschke-Bulmahn, J. (ed.) *Nature and Ideology: Natural Garden Design of the Twentieth Century.* Dumbarton Oaks, Washington, DC.
- Kelner, L. (1963). *Alexander von Humboldt.* Oxford University Press, London.
- Kenfield, W. (1966). *The Wild Gardener in the Wild Landscape: The Art of Naturalistic Landscaping.* Hafner, London.
- Klaffke, K. (1985). Hermann Löns Park in Hanover. *Garten und Landschaft,* **7**, 17–22.
- Kniese, L. (1942). *Die Pflanzensoziologie in der Landschafts- und Gartengestaltung.* Bechtold, Wiesbaden.
- Lack, H. W. (2001). Berlin-Dahlem, Botanischer Garten, Dahlem, Berlin, Germany. In Shoemaker, C. A. (ed.) *Chicago Botanic Garden Encyclopedia of Gardens: History and Design* (3 volumes). Fitzroy Dearborn, Chicago and London. Volume I, pp. 132–134.
- Laird, M. (1999). *The Flowering of the Landscape Garden.* University of Pennsylvania Press, Philadelphia.
- Lange, W. (1919). *Gartengestaltung der Neuzeit.* J. J. Weber, Leipzig.
- Lange, W. (1922). *Gartenbilder.* J. J. Weber, Leipzig.
- Lange, W. (1927). *Gartenpläne.* J. J. Weber, Leipzig.
- Laren, A. J. van (1907). Het aanleggen van natuurlijke plantengroepjes. *Onze Tuinen,* **2**, 563–565, 595–597.
- Laren, A. J. van (1927). De nieuwe tuin. *Onze Tuinen,* **22**, 97–100, 113–116, 145–147, 161–163, 177–179, 193–195, 209–211, 253–255.
- Laren, A. J. van (1929). *Phytogeografische plantengroepeering als element in de tuinkunst.* Onze Tuinen, Amsterdam.
- Leeuwen, C. van and Doing Kraft, H. (1959). *Landschap en Beplanting in Nederland: Richtlijnen voor de Soortenkeuze bij Beplantingen op*

Vegetatiekundige Grondslag. H. Veenman, Wageningen.

-- Legate, K. (2000). Shrubbery planting (1830–1900). In Woudstra, J. and Fieldhouse, K. (eds) *The Regeneration of Public Parks.* E. & F. N. Spon, London.

-- Leufgen, W. and Lier, M. van (1992). *Oase Heemtuingids: Wegwijzer for nature rich gardens and parks in Nederland en Vlaanderen.* Landelijke Werkgroep Heem – en Natuurtuinen, Zuidbroek.

-- Londo, G. (1977). *Natuurtuinen en – parken: Aanleg en Onderhoud.* Thieme, Zutphen.

-- Loudon, J. C. (1822). *An Encyclopaedia of Gardening.* Longman, Hurst, Rees, Orme and Brown, London.

-- Loudon, J. C. (1835). Remarks on laying out public gardens and promenades. *The Gardener's Magazine,* **I**, 644–669.

-- McHarg, I. L. (1966–67). An ecological method for landscape architecture. *Landscape Architecture,* **57**, 105–107.

-- McHarg, I. L. (1969). *Design with Nature.* Falcon Press, Philadelphia.

-- Meyer, G. (1860). *Lehrbuch der schönen Gartenkunst.* Riegel, Berlin.

-- Miller, W. (1915). *The Prairie Spirit in Landscape Gardening: What the People of Illinois have Done and can Do toward Designing and Planting Public and Private Grounds for Efficiency and Beauty.* University of Illinois, Urbana.

-- Morrison, D. (1989). Restored natural landscapes. In Tishler, W. H. (ed.) *American Landscape Architecture: Designers and Places.* The Preservation Press, Washington, DC.

-- Nicholson, E. M. (1965). Ecology and conservation as a scientific basis of landscape design. *Journal of the Institute of Landscape Architects*, No. 69, 10–12.

-- Norton, L. (1980). *Saint-Simon at Versailles.* BCA, London.

-- Oostroom, S.J.van (ed). Heukels- Van Oostroom 1975. *Flora van Nederland,* (Wolters-Noordhof, Groningen.)

-- Ortloff, H. S. (1933). *Informal Gardens: The Naturalistic Style.* Macmillan, New York.

-- Pannekoek, P. J and Schipper, J, J. (1944). *Tuinen.* Kosmos, Amsterdam.

-- Paxton, J. (1831). Ideas on forming a new garden, in the neighbourhood of London, for the collective purposes of the Zoological, Horticultural, and Medico-Botanic Societies. *Horticultural Register and General Magazine,* **1**, 171–177.

-- Road Beautifying Association (1930). *Roadside Planting.* Country Life, London.

-- Robinson, F. B. (1940). *Planting Design.* Whittlesey, New York.

-- Robinson, W. (1894). *The Wild Garden: or the Naturalization and Natural Grouping of Hardy Exotic Plants with a Chapter on the Garden of British Flowers.* The Scolar Press, London.

-- Roemer, L. (1963). Gedanken zu einer ökologischen Ordnung der Gartenpflanzen. In Buchwald, K., Lendholt, W. and Meyer, K. (eds) *Beiträge zur Landespflege: Festschrift für Heinrich Friedrich Wiepking,* Volume1. Ulmer, Stuttgart.

-- Roy, L. Le (1973). *Natuur Uitschakelen: Natuur Inschakelen.* Ankh-Hermes, Deventer.

-- Schiller, H. (1959). *Die verwendung der Pflanzen in Garten und Park.* Paul Parey, Berlin and Hamburg.

-- Schmidt, E. (1984). *'Abwechselung im Geschmack', Raumbildung und Pflanzenverwendung beim Stadtparkentwurf Deutschland 19. Jahrhundert.* Institut für Grünplanung und Gartenarchitektur, Hanover.

-- Schneider, C. (1935). Reichsautobahnen und Landschaftsgestaltung. *Gartenschönheit,* **16**, 98–101.

-- Seifert, A. (1939). Von bodenständiger Gartenkunst. *Gartenschönheit,* **20**, 2–3.

-- Sewell Cautley, M. (1935). *Garden Design: The Principles of Abstract Design as Applied to Landscape Composition.* Dodd, Mead & Co.

-- Smyth, B. (1987). *City Wildspace.* Hilary Shipman, London.

-- Stapledon, R. G. (1935). *The Land Now and To-morrow*. Faber and Faber, London.

-- Stuart, H. (1933). *Informal Gardens: The Naturalistic Style.* MacMillan, New York.

-- Thijsse, J. P. (1926). *De Bloemen in onzen Tuin.* Verkade, Alkmaar.

-- Thijsse, J. P. (1934). Natuurhistorische tentoonstelling. *De Groene Amsterdammer*, 7.

-- Tishler, W. (1989). *American Landscape Architecture: Designers and Places.* The Preservation Press, Washington, DC.

-- Tunnard, C. (1937). Landscape design at the Paris International Congress: What other countries are doing. *Landscape and Garden,* Summer, 78–83.

-- Tunnard, C. (1938). *Gardens in the Modern Landscape.* The Architectural Press, London.

-- Tüxen, R. (1939). Die Bedeutung der Pflanzensociologie für die Landeskultur. *Die Gartenkunst,* **52**, 59–61.

-- Verhagen, P. (1945). *Het Geluk van den Tuin.* G. W. Breughel, Amsterdam.

-- Vernon, C. (1995). Wilhelm Miller and *The Prairie Spirit in Landscape Gardening.* In O'Malley, T. and Treib, M. (eds) *Regional Garden Design in the United States.* Dumbarton Oaks, Washington, DC.

-- Warming, E. (1909). *Oecology of Plants: an Introduction to the Study of Plant Communities.* Clarendon, Oxford.

-- Wendland, F. (1979). *Berlin Gärten und Parke von der Gründung der Stadt bis zum ausgehenden neunzehnten Jahrhundert.* Propylaen, Frankfurt am Main.

-- Wernicke, H. (1936). Wettbewerb Annateich Hanover. *Gartenkunst,* **49**, 177–182.
-- Wernicke, H. (1941). Der Hermann-Löns-Park in Hanover: Eine Parkschöpfung auf pflanzensociologischer Grundlage. *Gartenkunst,* **54**, 1–12.
-- Westhoff, V., Dijk, J. W. and Passchier, H. (1942). *Overzicht der Plantengemeenschappen in Nederland.* G. W. Breughel, Amsterdam.
-- Wimmer, C. (1989). *Geschichte der Gartentheorie.* Wissenschaftliche Buchgesellschaft, Darmstadt.
-- Wit, T. de (1942). Het arbeidsveld van den Stockholmer plantsoenendienst. *Bouwkunding Weekblad,* **63**, 348–356.
-- Wolschke-Bulmahn, J. (ed.) (1997). *Nature and Ideology: Natural Garden Design in the Twentieth Century.* Dumbarton Oaks, Washington, DC.
-- Wolschke-Bulmahn, J. and Groening, G. (2001). Lange, Willy 1864–1941: German garden writer, garden theorist, and landscape architect. In Shoemaker, C. A. (ed.) *Chicago Botanic Garden Encyclopedia of Gardens: History and Design.* Fitzroy Dearborn, Chicago.
-- Woudstra, J. (1985). Living and learning. *GC & HTJ,* 26 July, 26.
-- Woudstra, J. (1997). Jacobus P. Thijsse's influence on Dutch landscape architecture. In Wolschke-Bulmahn, J. (ed.) *Nature and Ideology: Natural Garden Design in the Twentieth Century.* Dumbarton Oaks, Washington, DC, pp. 155–185.
-- Woudstra, J. and Hitchmough, J. (2000). The enamelled mead: history and practice of exotic perennials grown in grassy swards. *Landscape Research*, **25**, No. 1, 29–47.

1 This quotes a letter from Humboldt to the Swiss geographer Pictet and suggests 1788 as a date of the former's acquaintance with Willdenow.

2 Quote from *Cosmos* Part I, §ii, included in Albert Forbes Sieveking, *The Praise of Gardens: an Epitome of the Literature of the Garden-Art* (1899: p.232).

3 From *Wochenzeitschrift des Vereins zur Beförderung … für Gärtnerei und Pflanzkunde*, p.13 (1870), p.339 included in Erika Schmidt, *'Abwechselung im Geschmack', Raumbildung und Pflanzenverwendung beim Stadtparkentwurf Deutschland 19. Jahrhundert (Beiträge zur räumlichen Planung Vol.7)* (Hanover: Institut für Grünplanung und Gartenarchitektur, 1984), p.123, n.487 (author's translation).

4 There was an American edition of *Cosmos* (New York: Harper, 1849), translated by E. C. Otte.

5 See for the political connection with ecology: Anna Bramwell in *Ecology in the 20th Century: A History* (New Haven and London: Yale, 1989), pp.39–55.

6 Gustav Meyer, *Lehrbuch der schönen Gartenkunst*, p.158 quotes H. Zollinger, *Ueber Pflanzenphiognomik im Allgemeinen und diejenige der Insel Java insbesondere* (1855).

7 Warming, *Ecology of Plants*, p.381 lists Adolf Engler's publication on his alpine garden: 'Die Pflanzenformationen und die Pflanzengeographische Gliederung der Alpenkette erläutert an der Alpenanlage des neuen königlichen botanischen Gartens zu Dahlem - Steglitz bei Berlin', *Notizblatt der Königlichen Botanischen Garten Berlin,* 3: 7 (1901).

8 See, for example, Hans Schiller, *Die Verwendung der Pflanzen in Garten und Park* (Berlin und Hamburg: Paul Parey, 1959), p.66 and J. T. P. Bijhouwer, 'Plantensociologie en tuinarchitectuur', *De Boomkwekerij,* 6 (1951), p.67.

9 Humboldt, *Kosmos* I, p.87 also refers to Weltgarten even though this had a different meaning; Karl Foerster published the first volume in a book series entitled 'Der Weltgarten' with the Verlag der Gartenschönheit.

10 See Jan Woudstra and James Hitchmough (2000), 'The enamelled mead: history and practice of exotic perennials grown in grassy swards', *Landscape Research,* 25, No. 1, pp.29–47 (pp.42–43).

11 For a more comprehensive account on this section, see Jan Woudstra, 'Jacobus P. Thijsse's influence on Dutch landscape architecture', in Joachim Wolschke-Bulmahn, *Nature and Ideology: Natural Garden Design in the Twentieth Century* (Washington DC: Dumbarton Oaks, 1997), pp.155–185.

12 As for example in J. T. P. Bijhouwer, 'Plantensociologie en tuinarchitectuur' *De Boomkwekerij* 6 (1951), p.67.

13 Quoted from *The Architectural Record* 40: 6 (1916) in Robert E. Grese 'The prairie gardens of O. C. Simonds and Jens Jensen', in Therese O'Malley and Marc Treib's *Regional Garden Design in the United States* (Washington DC: Dumbarton Oaks, 1995), pp.99–123.

14 Wilhelm Miller's *The Prairie Spirit in Landscape Gardening* (1915) has been reprinted with an introduction by Christopher Vernon in Therese O'Malley and Marc Treib (eds) *Regional Garden Design in the United States* (Washington DC: Dumbarton Oaks, 1995).

15 Some of the ideas had already been mooted by Hackett in 1955: Brian Hacket, 'The influence of ecology on choice of plant material: a method for rationalizing plant use in landscape design', *Landscape Architecture,* 45 (1954–55), pp.12–17.

16 See: Ian C. Laurie, *Nature in Cities: The Natural Environment in the Design and Development of Urban Green Space* (New York: John Wiley, 1979) and Allan R. Ruff, *Holland and the Ecological Landscape* (Stockport: Deanwater, 1979).

17 Original statement at the International Congress of Garden Architects, Paris (1937), read by Sven A. Hermelin, and quoted from Christopher Tunnard, *Gardens in the Modern Landscape* (London: Architectural Press, 1938), pp.77–78.

18 On this topic see Eivor Bucht, *Public Parks in Sweden 1860–1960: The Planning and Design Discourse* (Alnarp: Swedish University of Agricultural Sciences, 1997).

19 See, for example, *Journal of the Institute of Landscape Architects*, 14 (1948), p.4.

Chapter 3

Contemporary overview of naturalistic planting design

Noel Kingsbury

Introduction

This chapter provides an overview of contemporary approaches to the use of plants in designed landscapes that are described as being 'ecological', 'natural' or 'naturalistic', or are said to operate or be inspired by the principles that lie behind these words. Needless to say, definitions of 'ecological' vary widely: commercial pressures, fashion-consciousness and a simple desire to be on a bandwagon are major factors in the labelling of practices and philosophies in the horticultural and landscape industries. It is emphatically not the task here to sort sheep from goats, but to develop a framework that describes a variety of practices and opinions from which others may draw their own conclusions. In compiling this chapter, the author undertook personal interviews with a very wide range of practitioners who are actively involved in this area across Europe and the US. This does not pretend to be an exhaustive list of everyone active in the field, but it does give a representative flavour of what is being undertaken. What emerges is a clustering of different working practices and philosophies, each cluster defined by an adherence to a particular aspect of the desire to relate to nature. On occasion the use of the words 'ecological' and 'naturalistic' can be seen to be ambiguous, with certain practices being described as, or perceived to be, in some way 'ecological' when others would deny that this is the case. The importance of developing a framework is that it enables those interested in the field to gain an impression of the variety, flexibility and adaptability of different approaches. It is also useful for gaining an insight into possible conflicts, and in highlighting areas where more research is needed.

Developing a model to describe current practice

These clusters of philosophy and practice can be represented on a gradient to describe the relationship between art and nature in garden and landscape design. The 'nature' end might be indistinguishable by the casual observer from the creation of 'semi-natural habitats', developing dynamically with a minimum of human intervention. The other extreme is represented by what could be termed 'art', the use of plants to supply colour or purely sculptural effects. This approach is almost completely dependent upon frequent and intensive interventions by human agency for its intended effect, and owes little to the inspiration of the natural world. The formality of the Baroque tradition as exemplified by André Le Nôtre would be a classic example.

Our interest is obviously at the 'natural' end of this gradient. The centre might be characterised most usefully by the 'Twentieth-Century English School', the Jekyll and Sackville-West influenced style which so consumately mixes clipped formality with cottage-garden insousiance. The problems of defining when the 'natural' or the 'ecological' stops and the 'informal' starts are legion, and are not helped by the difference in the usage of 'natural' and 'naturalistic' in the jargons of British and American English practitioners and commentators. Semantics plays a role here, as North Americans tend to interpret 'natural' and 'naturalistic' much more widely and loosely than do users of British English; 'natural' planting styles in North America cover any 'informal' style, i.e. where there is no geometrical layout or clipping and training of woody species (Lovejoy 1998).

Taking the gradient concept further, a useful way of looking at the broad range of ecological planting might be through a grid, which not only takes account of both the 'nature/art' equation on one axis but also of another key question in the field, that of the use of locally native plants, on another axis. Whilst this is a much more contested issue in some countries than others, its consideration does help to separate out a disparate variety of planting styles and to make sense of a complex set of philosophies (Figure 3.1).

Positions on the 'nature/art' axis can be defined in relation to the characteristics of natural plant communities:

- the degree of taxonomic diversity in a planted area (i.e. a monoculture versus plantings of many species)
- the degree allowed for dynamism or spatial mobility of a taxa over time (as opposed to the removal of any plant that spreads to a place not chosen by the designer)
- the repetition of taxa across an area
- the intermingling of taxa (as opposed to the planting of monocultural units).

Six positions can be defined as follows.

1 *Formality* – where highly artistic, often geometric, criteria control precise plant placing, often accompanied by clipping and training. This position is not included in Figure 3.1.
2 *Mass planting* – where monocultural blocks of a limited number of taxa of wide ecological amplitude are the defining characteristic.
3 *Conventional informal planting* – no intended visual relationship to natural plant communities; individuals or small groups are placed in positions, from which they are not generally expected to move.
4 *Stylised nature* – a planting with an aesthetic that is recognisably inspired by wild plant

	Static ----->	--------->	**Dynamic** -->		
	Dominant horticultural influence	Strong horticultural influence	Horticultural and ecological influence	Strong ecological influence	Dominant ecological influence
Role of natives					
Native species only		Conventional garden design with natives (a)	Species selected for visual impact e.g. Amstelveen (b)	Colour-schemed wildflower plantings (b)	Prairies, meadows and other wildflower habitats (f)
Mixture of natives and non-natives			'Lebensbereich' German parks style (d)	Native/exotic biotopes e.g. Hitchmough & Dunnett (c)	Woodland with some non-native tree species
No particular emphasis on natives, but plants with a naturalistic aesthetic used, ie, no doubles or variegation.	Mass perennial planting e.g. much Oehme and Van Sweden commercial work	'Informal' garden plantings e.g. Piet Oudolf	'Lebensbereich' German parks style (d)	Botanic Gardens 'biogeographic planting' (e)	
Horticultural aesthetic i.e. Includes double flowers, variegation etc.	Conventional landscape design	Conventional garden design			
	Mass planting	**Informal planting**	**Stylised nature**	**Biotope planting**	**Habitat restoration**

3.1
The relationship between art and nature in garden and landscape design. Letters in parenthesis refer to categories described on page 61

communities but which is designed for visual effect, often with plants located individually by the designer. A high level of dynamism in the ongoing development of this planting, for example self-seeding, is allowed. Intensive maintenance.

5 *Biotope planting* – a plant community with all the dynamism of wild habitat and clearly resembling natural habitats in terms of its structure, but whose species mix is chosen for an aesthetic effect, as well as their ecological suitability for the conditions at the site. Maintenance is generally extensive (i.e. with minimal input).

6 *Habitat restoration* – where the aim is to create something as close as possible to a 'wild' habitat, at either a climax or relatively stable sub-climax community. Maintenance is generally extensive.

In Figure 3.1, these positions are classified into three groupings: those that are strongly influenced by ecological principles and aesthetics ('Biotype planting' and 'Habitat restoration'), those that are strongly influenced by more traditional horticultural aesthetics ('Mass planting and 'Informal planting'), and those that are highly influenced by both horticultural and ecological ideals ('Stylised nature'). There is a tendency for levels of maintenance to tend to become lower as one moves from mass planting through to habitat restoration, although mass planting is frequently an exception in that the plants selected are generally selected to be ultra-low maintenance. Maintenance increases with the increase in the 'unnatural' nature of the planting, but a further reason is an aesthetic one; the more 'naturalistic' plantings are better able to visually 'carry' unwanted weedy species, as they are less prominent (Hitchmough 1995a).

The 'native species contents' axis can be defined by the following stops on a gradient.

1 The use of only plants that are 'native', defined with reference to a region of greater or lesser size (often a nation state, arguably an inappropriate way of doing so).
2 A mixture of natives and non-native 'exotics', often with the former preponderant.
3 The inclusion of species 'exotics' and cultivars of wild origin, but all of which maintain the proportions of wild plants.
4 The inclusion of taxa which are essentially horticultural and ornamental, such as complex hybrids, cultivars with variegated foliage or double flowers, etc.

Referring to Figure 3.1, the area represented by the bottom-left corner covers conventional horticultural and landscape planting design. There are, however, a certain number of practitioners whose work clearly belongs here, such as Piet Oudolf and the Oehme Van Sweden Partnership. They do not use native plants and cannot be said to be ecological, but employ certain naturalistic aesthetic elements in their work, and are seen by many as belonging to the ecological camp. Perhaps most importantly, their work is widely seen as being part of 'ecological design' as a cultural phenomenon. This work is covered on the section 'Evolving nature'.

The top area (a) of Figure 3.1 refers to an artistic, and not particularly ecological use of native plants, rarely seen, but possibly increasingly important in areas where there are strong pressures to use native material, such as the US. This is covered later in the section 'Native flora as an artistic medium'. Habitat restoration is not really the subject of this account, but it can have an important role in designed environments, discussed in the section 'Habitat restoration and beyond'. Plant communities may be modelled on nature, but with a greater or lesser design input; these are covered by (b) in Figure 3.1 and in the section 'New native plant communities'. The introduction of non-native elements into native dominated plant communities (c) is the subject of the section 'Biotype planting – adding exotics to native vegetation', whilst the creation of nature-inspired, but still quite 'artificial' plant communities, such as the German *Lebensbereich* style (d) is the subject of the section 'Stylised nature – German Lebensbereich plantings and others'. As can be expected, many practices do not fit neatly into these boxes. One reason for this is that one practice or location may include several different approaches to planting design that grade into each other. The plantings in the parks of Amstelveen in the Netherlands are a good example, varying between pure habitat restoration on the one hand and an 'artistically driven' management of native species on the other.

'Biogeographic' planting (e) is a highly specific form of ecological planting design, and largely falls outside the scope of this text. A relatively recent trend in botanical garden design, it aims at as complete a representation of a natural plant community as possible, so, for example, the visitor might move from recreated Ukrainian steppe to Anatolian meadow to Caucasian forest in a hundred metres. The Botanic Garden at Bayreuth University, established in 1975, is a fine example, where each area leaves the visitor with a powerful impression of having landed somewhere completely different (Köhlein 1992).

Finally, it is worth mentioning one further form of ecological 'planting', that also belongs on this grid shown in Figure 3.1, sharing (f) with habitat restoration. This is that of 'spontaneous' vegetation development, where post-industrial areas develop their own vegetation through natural processes, and where a design decision may be made to keep the resulting vegetation. Allowing land to support a series of successional communities in urban areas often results in a very distinctive mixture of native and introduced species. Whilst the value of wildlife to such areas is widely appreciated, their aesthetic value rarely is. Austrian landscape architect Cordula Loidl-Reisch is one of the more articulate proponents of the aesthetics of this process of growing wild – *Verwilderung.* Her writing, however, reflects a perspective that is philosophical and theoretical rather than practically orientated (Loidl-Reisch 1986, 1989).

In this chapter we will review the various strands of contemporary ecologically-informed planting design. We will start at the predominantly ecological end of the spectrum (i.e. to the right hand of Figure 3.1) and will finish at the strongly horticulturally-influenced end of the gradient (i.e. the left hand). At each point we will consider relevant philosophical and practical issues that currently dominate the application of ecological ideas in designed landscape and garden plantings.

3.2
The trial grounds at Weihenstephan, at Freising near Munich, are home to extensive collections of perennials but which are arranged in a naturalistic style, key plants being repeated to create a sense of rhythm. Mauve *Salvia verticillata* and deep yellow *Achillea filipendulina* are prominent here (July)

Habitat restoration and beyond: designing a visual aesthetic into native plant communities

The creation of natural habitats, using native species, in urban areas is itself a statement about art, design and philosophy, and is characteristic only of those cultures that have become most intensely urbanised and which display a desire to renegotiate their relationship to nature. The areas which are restored can vary considerably in size, from large parks and campus-type locations down to roadsides, community 'pocket' parks and small private gardens. They are, especially the smaller ones, often highly managed, in order to maintain plant succession at that point which is seen as most desirable. The definition of desirability is largely to do with what is seen by the public as their idea of nature, which has both advantages and disadvantages. Even quite small areas can have considerable educational value for the public and can help to provide a psychological linkage between urban areas and surrounding rural ones (Thompson 2000).

Habitat restoration is a movement with considerable support in the US, UK, Scandinavia, the Netherlands and in German-speaking countries. It does not seem to be anywhere near as popular in the Latin-speaking cultures of Europe, which must reflect the widely different attitudes to nature that are manifested in the traditional garden art of these cultures, which leans heavily towards the sculptural use of plants. Habitat restoration characteristically involves the almost exclusive use of plants native to the state or the region involved, with this being particularly stressed in the US. Generally, the movement is also characterised by the following.

- The identification of stereotype plant communities to be 'put back'. In Britain, these are based upon the National Vegetation Classification.
- The ready availability of native plant seed, often as mixtures and plants, to both professionals and amateurs. Commercial marketing may, however, result in inappropriate species mixtures and techniques being widely distributed.
- A steadily increasing number of landscape and garden design professionals working in the field.
- The media, for example television programmes, books, websites and magazine articles orientated towards this field, with a heavy emphasis on educating amateurs.
- A definite orientation towards grassroots community politics, with native plantings often being part of projects such as community centres, schools, city farms, etc.

However, another common characteristic is the distinct lack of an artistic element in this field. Habitats are basically treated as a kind of filler, to be poured into the space available. This must contribute to occasional conflict with members of the public who may perceive this product as scruffy or inappropriate landscaping. As Hirschmann-Woodward notes, in a major study of the relationship between people and landscape, 'many ecological designs have also been critiqued for not accomodating people's need for order, meaning and beauty' (Woodward 1997). Indeed, she and others might argue that 'filler' landscaping like this is not really ecological as it leaves humans out of the ecological equation; 'Ecological design recognises complex relationships between people, the land and a place. It shapes decisions that may affect both positive site function and positive human response to that site' (Woodward 1997: 201).

The solution may lie in designing or 'stylising' native landscape plantings so that they become meaningful and visually pleasing elements of the landscape. There are three main ways in which this can be done, as follows.

1 The selection of plant communities on the basis of their visual appeal to the public, and adapting the environment to suit them.
2 The use of different kinds of plant community

as large-scale sculptural material.

3 The altering of the species mix so as to create a more visually appealing plant community.

The first two aim to work with 'whole' plant communities, assemblages of species that would occur in nature, the third involves changes to this assemblage, and it is perhaps more appropriate to discuss it in the next section.

Selective use of visually attractive plant communities

Given that the natural environment of urban areas is often so altered and degraded, there is arguably little rationale behind being too fixed in our notions of what vegetation community is appropriate for particular locations. Particular communities are recognised as having an aesthetic that is more appreciated than others, which may lead to situations where attempts are made to establish these communities in places where they would not have occurred prior to human settlement, and to undertake various environmental alterations in order to assist this process. Although the wholesale import or export of soil in order to further the establishment of a particular 'wild' plant community is arguably 'un-ecological', it is a fact of life, one that brings nature and pleasure to a great many people who might not otherwise experience it, and, in some cases, may result in a higher level of biodiversity of both plants and animals.

The choice of habitat selected for restoration in urban and peri-urban areas is arguably a highly anthropocentric one. The public are most appreciative of habitats that are visually pleasing, hence the emphasis in northwest Europe on meadow creation (a semi-natural rather than natural habitat) and in much of the US on prairies, itself a semi-natural vegetation (even in states that never had any 'natural' prairie). Fortunately, these are habitats that display considerable biodiversity. The 'deep ecologist' would probably argue for woodland restoration as the only valid habitat to be restored in many cases. Woodland is, however, generally created by tree planting programmes that pay little or no attention to the ground layer. There is a tendency for new woodland to be treated as glorified forestry, with little regard for the experience of what actually goes on there – a case of not being able to see the trees for the wood. Woodland edge habitats, very rich in biodiversity, have fared a little better, but perhaps largely through default, as the 'green cement' of conventional landscape practice is substituted with blocks of native species. The results may increase biodiversity and introduce nature to the city, but could produce better results on both counts if more attention were paid to their structure, species composition and maintenance (Figure 3.3).

In northern Europe, the floras that combine the greatest public appeal, the greatest floral diversity, with a relatively stable long-term prospect, are those of hay meadows and limestone grasslands. Both establish and are maintained most easily on relatively poor soils, or even waste industrial material, making them a financially attractive possibility, and ideal for urban situations.

Criticism is sometimes heard that the use of seed mixtures over large areas can result in a certain uniformity with species more or less randomly, with little of the ebb and flow of species that gives wild grasslands much of their character (Kendle 2001). Such randomness may also cause more competitive species to suppress less-competitive ones, as was found by Tregay in randomly-planted woodland. However, Julie Toll, one of Britain's most high-profile garden designers, who makes considerable use of native meadows, does not think this is a problem, believing that 'nature eventually sorts itself out', with species finding their own microhabitats over time, although she sometimes enhances particular areas with plugs of particular species, often those combine decorative value with slow germination, for example *Primula veris* (Toll 2001).

3.3
Fertile woodland-edge situations using largely natives of Central Europe can be very effective in early summer and, if competitive species are used, there is little management beyond a late summer mowing – *Alchemilla mollis, Geranium pretense*, a *Symphytum* spp. and *Ranunculus acris* 'Flore Pleno' in the Westpark (June)

Sculpting the landscape with native plant communities

Another approach to enhancing visual appeal operates on a large scale, and essentially contrasts the closed and opaque nature of woody planting against the openness of grass/forb communities, such as the meadow or prairie. The landscape is shaped by using plant communities to guide the eyes and legs (or even wheels) of the human user through it, and so to help contribute layers of meaning to the landscape. It is not surprising that psychological theories of landscape have had a role to play in the development of many practitioners' work in this area.

It is, of course, possible to sculpt landscape very successfully from a visual point of view by using remarkably few species. 'Capability' Brown did so in the eighteenth century, with far-reaching consequences for landscape art. Yet his landscapes were an idealisation and a pastiche relying on a few tree species, the occasional lake and much grazed grassland. The ecology of a Brownian landscape can be very poor and still look lovely. The same can be said of much modern landscaping; trees and grass can be pleasing, but ecologically impoverished, lacking both biodiversity and the zones of transition that are a vital part of a genuinely living landscape. Thus, ecological design practice would aim to include these vital (in both meanings of the word) elements.

Of the large number of people and practices currently working with native plants in the US, it is those who have most clearly understood the human role in the wider landscape who have made the most impact on the market and on their peers. Darrel Morrison, Professor of the School of Environmental Design at the University of Georgia, who also works as a freelance consultant, is an example. For him 'each design should reflect and reveal the local landscape character' so that regional diversity should be celebrated (Morrison 2001). Building on the work of Jens Jensen, Morrison stresses how native plant communities must be used in ways that have meaning for people, for example he states that 'a central theme is that the overall spatial composition has spaces that move like rivers' which allow the viewer to position themselves meaningfully in the landscape. However, he sees conventional landscape practice as being 'extremely oversimplified' and that 'plant distribution must have some relationship to natural distribution patterns'. He regards the key to his own design work as being 'the weaving drift' where a group of plants of one species trails off at the edges, blurring with a group of the next (Morrison 2001). Morrison points out that the complexities begin at ground level, as different light intensities in the shade of the trees result in a complex of different species-mixes in the grass and forb layer. Savannah, then, offers both the clear visual articulation that human users like and feel happy with, and the rich possibilities for biodiversity. For him, layering, the vertical distribution of plants', which produces plantings that are not only visually rich but, through creating a variety of habitats, can support a wealth of wildlife, is a key element (Morrison 2001) (Figure 3.4).

In Europe, German landscape architect Hans Luz, has developed the concept of 'stops' (*Stationenkonzept)*, a strategy that can help give meaning to a wide variety of different landscapes. The idea is 'to create intensive designs at consciously chosen spots within larger, extensively designed spaces'. These extensively designed areas may well be areas of semi-natural vegetation. Depending upon the context, Luz sees the 'stops' including traditional landscape elements such as dry-stone walls, arbours, sculptures or more intensive planting (Luz 1996). Native plant communities have a vital role to play in the creation of zones of transition between 'nature' and 'culture'. It is standard practice for more formal garden or landscape areas to be near buildings and wilder ones to be further away. Long grass or wildflower meadow/prairie are both highly effective at blurring the boundaries between cultivation and rural landscapes, whilst woodland is even more so.

Ecological design principles are nearly always linked with 'organic' amoeboid shapes, but as Lisa Diedrich, in a discussion of the new Riem landscape park near Munich, points out, 'the animals in these meadows could not care less whether they are crawling over straight or crooked edges'. With its almost Versailles-like scale and formality, albeit a very contemporary brand of formality, Riem 'refutes any notion that these (ecological aspirations) can only be satisfied in conjunction with winding paths and amorphous frog ponds'. Areas of meadow, woodland and hedgerow are repeated in strict linear swathes to 'organise the shapeless Riem gravel plain' (Diedrich 2002). This could be the first of many formally designed ecological designs.

Developing an 'ecological aesthetic': altering native species mixes for visual appeal

Many of the US practitioners in the field are eloquent in their articulation of the need to sell ecological planting to the public by making it as attractive as possible, 'we must seduce people into loving the landscape' as Carol Franklin, a senior associate of Andropogon Associates puts it (Franklin 2001a). In particular, 'homeowners' must be 'provided with an elegant and sensual alternative to the usual nursery fare' (Franklin 2001b). Andropogon have established a reputation as being one of the foremost practices at integrating ecological plantings based on native species with relevent aesthetic, historical and social aspects. Franklin describes this as developing an 'ecological aesthetic'. Developing a plan for a particular site begins with relating the basic concept of the design to the bioregion, and then bringing together an accurate listing of local species in the light of an artistic appreciation of the locality. Planting is designed to include 'prototypical relationships of plant to plant or plant to place', including 'wonderful quirky or especially evocative relationships' (Franklin 2001b). Public projects involve community involvement where possible, and linking to the historical design and use of the site where appropriate (McKormick 1991). Established in 1975, Andropogon work throughout the eastern US, and more recently has undertaken a number of projects in Japan. Wetland restoration, or creation, as in the case of stormwater detention systems, is a speciality.

Certain plant communities lend themselves more than others to an aesthetic interpretation. The native flora of the British Isles is one with relatively few possibilities, largely as a result of being rather limited, which gives the designer a very restricted palette, especially for environments that favour competitive species. Others have not only diversity but floras with major aesthetic appeal. A good example might be the desert of the south-western US, where landscape architect Steve Martino has made a major impact in and around the city of Phoenix, Arizona, 'I had to convince people not just to accept but to pay for weeds' but that now 'the desert is seen as a place of value' (Martino 2001). Trees, shrubs and succulent species have strong sculptural appeal, whilst the ground level flora of annuals and short-lived perennials can be spectacular in flower.

Woodland: creative management

Tree-planting schemes are the most widely carried out form of habitat restoration. Native species are generally preferred, with the use of stock raised from local-provenance a relatively recent concern (Flora Locale 2001). As noted above, however, there is often remarkably little insight into either the aesthetic or the ecological aspects of woodland planting in the landscape. As Tregay notes, 'room-like' open spaces, such as glades, have been 'very seldom developed in constructed parks of the last thirty years' (Tregay and Gustavsson 1983). Tregay, working in an area of Warrington New Town in Lancashire, England, developed a sophisticated strategy for enhancing the aesthetic and ecological qualities of woodland.

Paramount was developing a sense of place by relating the new landscape to the site with the development of a diversity of microhabitats playing a major role, for example with narrow 'fingers' of planting penetrating into housing areas, 'little more than broad free-growing hedges, widening in places to scrubby thickets, with an open canopy of light shade-casting trees' (Tregay and Gustavsson 1983: 25).

Tregay criticises the common run of tree planting where transplants are put in at even spacing, 'resulting in a degree of uniformity rarely

3.4
Naturalistic perennial planting on a roof garden at Moorgate Crofts Business Park, Rotherham, UK. Perennials and grasses from hot dry habitats, including *Galium verum, Stipa tenuissima, Salvia nemerosa,* and *Stachys byzantina,* are well adapted to the harsh conditions on this roof terrace

seen in nature ... the elements of surprise, fun, uniqueness, unpredictability and even weirdness, which can be seen in nature' (Tregay and Gustavsson 1983: 72). In order to overcome this, he proposes a variety of imaginative techniques: planting to create multi-stemmed trees, grouping of *Corylus avellana* whips to simulate old coppice, the massing of *Fraxinus excelsior* and *Betula* spp. to look like natural regeneration, the variation of plant spacing throughout the plantations, loose-edge planting at the edges, and the pegging of occasional transplants at angles to encourage variation in form (Tregay and Gustavsson 1983: 73–74).

Crucial to the development of a genuinely naturalistic aesthetic and associated biodiversity is management, with varying densities of thinning, coppicing and the retention of interestingly shaped trees, the aim being the development of a rich variety of tree and shrub combinations, glades and a patchwork of differing light intensities at the forest floor level. Interestingly, Tregay discovered that randomly mixed tree plantings created problems of succession as early as the third year after planting. Extensive thinning was vital to preserve slower growing species, such as *Quercus robur* and *Ilex aquifolium*. The conclusion drawn was that the random mix was too dependent upon management, and that slower-growing species needed to be grouped within a matrix of nurse species (such as *Alnus glutinosa* and *Betula* spp.) (Tregay and Gustavsson 1983).

Gustavsson stresses the importance of creativity in woodland planting, and suggests the use of 'dominating themes and sub-themes' and 'linkage', so, for example, a walker through woodland might come across oak and lime, then notice a shift to oak and maple, and then oak and hornbeam. There should be an underlying feeling of uniformity, but this should be tempered by underlying variations and sub-themes in the species mix, 'if you come 50 times you should still be able to still see new aspects, not just a tourist landscape' (Gustavsson 2000). Gustavsson also does not exclude the use of some non-native tree species included for ornamental reasons.

In *'Det nya landskapet'*, Gustavsson (1994) discusses a range of possibilities for the planting of woodland that offer options based on aesthetic, ecological and functional criteria. Woodland planted with shade-tolerant species in the centre and more light-demanding ones on the outside 'reinforces the centuries-old feeling that forests become denser the further into them one ventures', yet is not particularly effective as screening or windbreak. More dense planting on the outside though 'provides greater durability against outside forces' and 'provides an opportunity to include surprises', and 'gives the illusion of leaving the city behind'. He goes on to discuss zoning in forests to provide different areas for varying recreational, ecological or economic purposes. He recognises the importance of transition zones, and how they can be varied: from sharp to diffuse, with the latter useful for inducing a feeling of being in true countryside, whilst linking species can be used to play down the prominence of a boundary (Gustavsson 1994).

Gustavsson believes tree planting to be too dominated by the use of features that are immediately apparent in individual trees, such as leaf colour or bark texture. The architectural use of trees, and their articulation through space is limited to the thinking about their external appearance, 'I want to stress how it is possible to articulate the *interior* of tree plantings', he says, 'the woodland concept has not been used much' (Gustavsson 2002a). This, perhaps, is not surprising given how little the ground layer is considered in most tree-planting schemes.

It should be clear that management is a very creative process, indeed part of the *design* process. Gustavsson stresses how design should not be limited to the establishment phase, and that it is 'a crucial part of good management'. As an illustration, he discusses how many urban woodlands in Europe are suffering from 'teenager problems', as there is a lack of 'active and creative management' (Gustavsson 2002b). He puts into words what many practitioners involved in tree planting feel all over the world, that trees are planted and then left with little aftercare, or if there is aftercare, it is purely technical.

There seems to be a general lack of what could be called a 'holistic' approach to large-scale tree planting (i.e. considering the whole woodland: trees *and* ground layer), with part of the problem possibly arising from the fact that it is difficult to install a ground layer that needs shade in a young forest that offers none. Andropogon, who do address the problem perhaps more comprehensively than any other practice, favour using a mix of tree sizes, including some semi-mature stock which does offer immediate shade. The costs, however, can be considerable. Carol Franklin stresses how 'every square inch has to be filled', otherwise invasive (often non-native) weeds will take over. The practice favour using native species that are aggressive but 'well down the successional line', for example *Aster divaricatus*, which will compete with invading weeds. In lower-budget projects, the practice favour covering the ground with leaf litter and twigs (which help mycorrhiza establish). 'Critical islands' of slower growing woodland floor species can be planted, which will then hopefully allow propagules to spread into all areas (Franklin 2002).

New native plant communities

Altering the species composition of a plant community to make it more visually appealing is one way to make native plants more exciting to a public whose appreciation of ecology often goes no further than getting a nice warm buzz from hearing the word. It is an approach that is most advanced in the US, although a long-standing and bold statement of the possibilities can be seen in the parks of Amstelveen, a suburb of Amsterdam, in the Netherlands. In Britain, the planting of rhododendrons and other exotic shrubs in native woodland is a nineteenth-century example of this style.

It is theoretically possible to 'tweak' a wide range of native herbaceous plant communities for artistic effect, which may include the following:

- leaving out less visually appealing elements
- shifting the balance from grasses to more decorative forbs
- leaving out taller elements
- concentrating on species that will be decorative for one particular season
- concentrating on forbs with particular coloured flowers, or elements with other particular aesthetic qualities
- aiming at a 'minimalist' effect by reducing visual complexity, usually achieved by reducing the number of species
- creating combinations of species that, although native to the same region, might not occur together in nature.

A good example that combined several of these approaches was a planting carried out for an area in front of the General Mills corporate headquarters in Minneapolis, Minnesota, in 1982. The landscape architect in overall charge of the project, Michael van Valkenburgh, described how 'we got this idea of an embracing grove of trees with an abstraction of a short-grass prairie on the inside' (Gillette 1994). The tree species used was *Betula nigra*, which is not normally found in conjunction with short grass prairie. Matthew Urbanski, a colleague of van Valkanburgh described how 'it comes out of the garden tradition … It's using some natural planted forms – the grove and the prairie in a compositional way'. Two native grasses – *Schizachrium scoparium* and *Sporobolus heterolepis,* and a sedge, *Carex pensylvanica* – were used to create a knee-high 'grassland'. The sedge flourishes in shade, an advantage as the trees grew. A limited number of forbs were also included: *Asclepias tuberosa, Liatris aspera* and *Lupinus perennis.* The artifice of the planting was further advanced by being dissected by very straight granite paths.

Leading specialists, Prairie Restorations, were charged with developing the prairie. Prairie Restorations' Ron Bowen argues for as much diversity as possible, as 'we believe it equates with stability, so the more diversity, the fewer problems'. However, he accepts that in 'half' the plantings that his company carry out 'we are designing for aesthetic effect', particularly with areas smaller than an acre, 'which can't really be called a prairie', the proportion of forbs to grass is increased from the 'natural' 20:80 ratio to 'typically 50:50 or even 80:20' (Bowen 2001).

The number of species used for even really authentic habitat restoration schemes may still be substantially lower than what would be found in natural examples of the habitat, as Bowen points out when he states that 'a plant community may have 200 species, of those only a third may be (commercially) available, and of these we may well end up planting only a third, as the others may be uninteresting, noxious or invasive' (Bowen 2001). It therefore follows that further restricting the palette for aesthetic reasons may restrict the ability of an authentic plant community to develop.

How far one can tinker with native plant communities before damaging their integrity, and, hence, their stability is a question of major importance. Neil Diboll of Prairie Nursery is definite that there comes a point when reducing species diversity in a habitat can create problems. Citing the prairie, he states that certain species do not appear to do as well in the long-term when deprived of their normal companions, for example *Baptisia lactea* sets seed only very poorly in the absence of grasses. Problems may also occur as the prairie negotiates succession; short-lived species may die out and not be replaced, or one species may dominate in the absence of competition (Diboll 2001).

Diboll does, however, have considerable latitude over the appearance of a prairie; 'I have the bias of an ecologists training … I am not a gardener, it's too much like hard work … but we have gardening with seed mixes' (Diboll 2001). The company's seed mixes are generally skewed towards forbs, in addition to which they can custom mix seeds for particular effects, such as for colour, season or height. Forbs used for these effects often include species of *Liatris, Echinacea, Coreopsis, Rudbeckia, Asclepias* and *Aster*. Potentially invasive forbs, such as *Rudbeckia hirta* and some *Solidago* species, are minimised however. Diboll is confident that 'our custom design mixes do not compromise the ecological integrity of the project' (Diboll 2001).

Broadly speaking, there are two types of naturally occurring prairie, the more drought-tolerant western short-grass prairie and the eastern tall-grass prairie. In cultivated situations, these two variations can be used for different landscape effects; short-grass prairie is particularly useful for surrounding buildings or for small spaces, tall-grass for larger areas or to act as a background (Diboll 1998). Areas can be planted so that there are different concentrations of decorative forbs, or where the forbs are kept constant and the grasses change, which creates particularly attractive autumn scenes when the grasses change colour and produce mature seed heads. So long as good species diversity is maintained, these aesthetically determined compositions can be very successful in the long term and they are not even particularly 'unnatural', as one of the fascinating aspects of wild prairie is just how much species-composition changes from area to area. These changes, says Diboll, 'are best experienced through walking along trails, the pattern of which can be changed from year to year' (Diboll 2001).

Stylised 'natural' plant communities can also be interpreted as fulfilling another set of criteria in addition to the 'ecological' or the 'aesthetic', cultural and historical. Meadows are not, of course, 'natural' but a semi-natural habitat that is the result of traditional agricultural management, as is much European woodland, most obviously in the case of coppice and much of the American prairie may have been human influenced too. Creating areas of such habitat can thus also be seen as developing a link between the present modern landscape and the history and culture of the area. Continuity, memory and local distinctiveness can therefore all be emphasised.

The parks at Amstelveen

The Amsterdam suburb of Amstelveen was built during the 1930s along with a number of public parks, most centred around a number of waterways that wind their way through the peaty acidic soil. During the period from 1941 and 1972, garden designer and city architect Chris P. Broerse was involved in creating a series of plantings that were aimed at overcoming the problems presented by soil conditions which were inimical to the development of a conventional garden or landscape flora. Native plants of acidic and wetland soils were used in a pioneering planting scheme (King 1997). The 'heemparks' at Amstelveen have since become famous for their presentation of native flora to the public, particularly under the skilled management of Hein Koningen, senior advisor to the Parks Department (now retired).

The plantings at Amstelveen include areas of straightforward habitat restoration, such as wildflower meadows, dry meadow vegetation in the sandy rubble along the central reservations of roads, and woodland edge planting along roadsides. However, in higher visibility areas, especially in areas where there is considerable foot traffic, a more intensive planting style is used. Particularly in shaded areas, monocultural blocks of groundcover species, such as *Asperula odorata* are used, interspersed very often with taller forbs or ferns. In more open spaces there are areas of mixed wildflower forbs, but with grasses more or less absent. For example, in early June a combination of wet meadow species, *Lychnis flos-cuculi, Silene dioicia, Sanguisorba officianalis* and *Geranium pratense*, makes a highly ornamental display. King comments that 'this parody of natural beauty is highly artificial and can only be sustained by high levels of skilled labour' (King 1997). Hand weeding by gangs of park staff is very much a feature of life in the heemparks.

What is special about Amstelveen, however, is the way in which although there are areas of a highly selected vegetation, there is an engagement with natural processes that allows for constant change in the detail of the plantings, which is quite distinct to the rigid maintaining of an original plan that is normally seen in ornamental herbaceous vegetation management, yet is also quite different to the completely extensive approach to the maintainance of restored natural plant communities. Koningen stresses how the original plan is only a starting point for a process of natural development, as species spread by seed or stolons die out, are predated upon or overrun by other plants. Maintenance tasks include the hand weeding of undesirable species or invasively spreading desired ones, hoeing, planting and the transplanting of desired species, and tree pruning. The level of intervention required is closely related to the competitiveness of the plant species. Areas that feature species which are uncompetitive and need open conditions, such as *Drosera* and *Gentiana* spp., need frequent attention, whereas those that are composed of more competitve vegetation, for example *Persicaria bistorta* and *Caltha palustris*, need much less. Plant groupings are assembled very much on the basis of putting species together that have similar competitiveness (King 1997; Koningen 1997, 2001).

As the *heemparks* are quite heavily wooded in parts, the ground layer vegetation is in a constant state of flux, as trees grow or occasionally fall down or are removed. Whilst their natural shape is preserved, pruning and thinning are necessary to maintain the patchwork of light and shade which allows the development of a gradation from one microhabitat to another, over both space and time. This effect is also a vital part of the heemparks' charm for visitors (King 1997; Koningen 1997, 2001).[1]

Key to success here is the craft tradition of vegetation management, built up over many years, with specialised Parks Department staff responsible and whose training involves the development of a creative, almost artistic sensibility, as well as a high level of horticultural skill. Koningen reckons it 'takes 5–6 years to form a fully skilled *heempark*-worker' (Koningen 1995).

Spontaneous vegetation and its creative management

A common feature of urban and post-industrial environments is the rich but often rather chaotic looking vegetation that arises after the demolition of existing structures. Public perception is likely to see this only as 'weedy', whereas, with time, unique and complex habitats can develop. Landscape and ecology practitioners in Germany have led the way in trying to encourage a more positive perception of this 'spontaneous' vegetation (Figure 3.5).

3.5
Self-sowing of *Verbascum nigrum* can be relied upon to create spectacular effects. This planting at the Klenzepark, Ingoistadt, is on an occasionally dry but fertile soil, and includes crimson *Knautia macedonica*, an extremely useful plant for this style of planting because of its long flowering season and vivid colour (July)

Soils underlying such areas are highly atypical, owing to the presence of large quantities of material derived from buildings or industrial processes. The plant communities that develop inevitably reflect this (Heintz *et al.* 1999). Kühn points out that conventional plant community concepts do not necessarily work in the city, with its distinct climate and soils, and that the ruderal plants that thrive are seen as untidy, whereas in fact they may have a history that should be valued, many being former medicinal herbs or garden plants. 'They could have their place in a new post-industrial urban aesthetic' (Kühn 2000).

Given the level of biodiversity and often the visual beauty of the succession communities of post-industrial wasteland, to say nothing of the apparent ease with which they colonise what would be extremely difficult places to 'restore' in any conventional sense, it would make sense if society made a more positive evaluation of them. As Luken points out, 'the unwillingness – or inability – of ecologists to successfully incorporate the human species in ecological theory has by default devalued ecological processes associated with human activity' (Luken 1997). Conflicts over how ecologists should react to these plantings have been exemplified by the disagreements over buddleia, according to Kühn; a splendid butterfly plant or an invasive alien? (Kühn 1999).

There are two approaches to the use of 'post-industrial vegetation'. One is to manage what comes up by itself, so that the chaos of dereliction may be turned to ecological, functional and aesthetic advantage as part of a new landscape, the other is to learn from these natural test-beds in the creation of attractive but robust new plant mixtures for urban areas. Environmental concerns and the closing down of a lot of old industries have led to the development of a number of projects in northern

Germany that imaginatively make the most of successional wasteland plant communities. Succession is regarded as a key concept in these environments, with a number of possibilities for management: allowing succession to run its course from ruderal to woody communities, halting the succession at a particular stage, perhaps by mowing to eliminate woody plant seedlings, thus maintaining a herbaceous vegetation and, finally, undertaking steps to put the succession process back to an earlier stage, for example by rotovating to maintain annuals and other pioneer vegetation (Eckhardt *et al.* 1999).

Two projects provide successful examples of these processes, as well showing how it is possible to give meaning to what might have been regarded as complete wastelands. The Harbour-Island in Saarbrücken, in Saarland, was developed in the1980s from an old dockside and industrial area, aiming to convey a 'dream of nature' in a park with a defined geometrical/architectural character. The ruins of old industrial installations were preserved, with spontaneous vegetation (a mixture of native ruderals and garden escapes, such as buddleia and mahonia) allowed a place alongside the development of new areas of planted native meadow species and contrasted with more ordered conventional planting. Staff were given special training in the techniques of steering the succession vegetation appropriately (Latz 1987: 42; Rupp 1991: 102–110).

The old marshalling yards near Tempelfhof station in Berlin were abandoned in 1952, turning into a habitat rich in fauna and flora, including some endangered species. The area was given to the city and in 1995 plans, financially supported by the Foundation for the Protection of Nature, were made for its development as a public park, Natur-Park Südgelände. The public can explore it by following paths running on old railway lines or on raised walkways, appreciating contemporary artworks along the way. The park motto is 'Dynamism and Constancy', which expresses the desire to manage the various succession communities according to aesthetic and ecological criteria. Management plays an important role in ensuring that a variety of succession stages are present, for example by ensuring that woodland glades do not close up or grasslands disappear. One paper written about the park notes that 'what landscape architect could design such a place, riven with memories of the railways, filled with woodland, groves and flower-filled glades' (Knoll *et al.* 1997).[2]

Kühn's research at the Technical University of Berlin is one of the few projects currently looking at the creation of viable plant communities based on spontaneous vegetation. With a focus on drought and heat-tolerant species, he has established test plots to evaluate the progress of two different groups of plants for different soil nitrogen levels. The aesthetic criteria used for selection are structure, texture and flowering intensity and duration. Grasses and forbs from North America, continental Europe and Mediterranean Europe are included (Kühn 2000: 11).

Biotope planting – adding exotics to native vegetation

The idea of adding spice to pre-existing native vegetation is an old one, and was the core idea of William Robinson's (1870) 'The Wild Garden' (Robinson 1870). Whilst some in the 'nativist' lobby may find the idea appalling, it is a recognition that local floras do not always have the aesthetic appeal that we might want, and can be visually enhanced by the strategic addition of species whose impact or length of seasonal interest generates public interest and support. This type of planting tends to be based upon recognisable native structural plant community types (biotopes), such as meadows and woodlands (and, therefore, has a philosophical connection to native landscapes), but may be considerably altered in terms of its species composition to include non-natives from similar habitats in different regions of the world. Of course, a full consideration of context is vital here. Those who advocate the inclusion of exotics in native-type vegetations generally do so in relation to urban parks and private gardens and not in the open countryside or ecologically-sensitive sites.

Strictly speaking, this style of planting is the most commonly practised of 'ecological' approaches. Every native woodland that is underplanted with exotics in a garden or park is essentially a replacement of one, or two, layers of native vegetation in a multi-layered native-dominated community. This 'woodland garden' has been much developed in Britain and in the US, although the number of practitioners who are conscious of the possibilities of creating a genuinely self-sustaining plant community remains limited. Attempts at the naturalisation of exotics in open, non-woodland, habitats have been much fewer, as the problems of establishment are much greater. Nevertheless, this is arguably a key area in the development of a planting style for new public landscapes. Before proceeding further, however, we must examine the arguments for and against the inclusion of non-natives in ecological/naturalistic plantings a little further (see also Chapter 1).

Native versus exotic – a key debate

Key to an understanding of the range of planting styles that can be described as ecological is the variety of attitudes to the use of native plants. The intensity of the debate between those who restrict themselves to native-only plantings and those who use non-natives ('exotics') varies considerably from country to country, with considerable implications for the resulting landscapes. Not surprisingly, there is a strong link between a habitat restoration style and the exclusive use of natives. This is seen most clearly in the US, where sections of the garden and landscape industry are now heavily engaged in the promotion of 'native' or 'wildflower' planting. However, little of the literature or other media forms, such as websites, addresses questions of design, either from a functional or aesthetic perspective.

What is so marked about the situation in the US is the tone taken by some of the proponents of native plants, which strongly asserts the morality of using them and their strict definition of 'ecological planting' as meaning 'natives-only'. Consequently, the use of non-natives is seen as somehow unethical, and certainly 'unecological' (Druse 2001). A consequence of this is the reaction of those more pragmatic gardeners who wish to explore a naturalistic style using exotic elements. On several occasions the author has heard the expression 'native Nazis' being used by the latter to describe the former.

Typical of a pragmatic approach to ecological planting design is that of C. 'Cole' Burrell, who argues that 'there is no point in using a native if it can't perpetuate itself'. He is adamant that 'our eco-systems are so trashed, that if I can rebuild any ecological structure then we must be doing some good'. 'Non-natives', he says, 'can do much to expand the season for wildlife … But I do try to limit using non-native berrying plants as these can be carried a long way by birds, and some of our worst invasive species have been berry bearing shrubs' (Burrell 2001). Part of the issue is what precisely constitutes a native. It seems to be a fact of life that our conception of geography is currently dictated by the nation-state and its boundaries, which are nearly always utterly arbitrary as far as nature is concerned. The increasing popularity of 'native' plants in the US has meant that, in the words of Rick Darke, 'a lot of native plants are used way beyond their region … for example *Echinacea purpurea* … a prairie plant … is being sold in Delaware as a native, but Delaware has never had any prairie' (Darke 2001). The marketing ploy of selling 'meadows in a can' in the US has also meant the widespread commerial distribution of 'mixes for broad geographical regions (that) may not be adapted for a particular situation' (Bartels 1992: 74).

Darrel Morrison defines a native as 'a plant present in a region prior to white settlement', although he recognises that 'native Americans distributed plants too' (Morrison 2001). However, Neil Diboll, a leading prairie restoration specialist and proprietor of Wisconsin-based Prairie Nursery, states that 'I am not a purist, human beings are part of the ecology … and have always been implementors of plant distribution', and is happy to implement the occasional prairie scheme in the Eastern states. 'The only issue', he says, 'is if there could be an ecological problem from an invasive species or the polluting of a local gene pool of an isolated population' (Diboll 2001).

Given its island status, definitions of native are easy to make in the UK, or might initially seem so. The island's long history of human impact on the landscape has arguably made the opposing of 'natural' versus 'cultural' quite pointless, and in what is arguably one of the more successful of multi-cultural societies, the political overtones of a natives-only policy may sometimes seem offensive. Kendle and Rose's discussion of the arguments from a variety of standpoints are as good a summary on the current status of the debate as can be found, and their conclusions reflect a classically British pragmatism (Kendle and Rose 2000: 19–31). In Germany this debate does not appear particularly strongly. One reason for this is simply that two categories of ecological planting are clearly recognised, with each having clearly demarcated roles. Habitat restoration involving only native plants is used for both rural locations and many urban locations as a matter of course, and sometimes by legal requirement (Kendle and Forbes 1997). But in high-visibility public parks and other clearly designed public locations, another genre may be used to create a high-visual impact, the Hansen *Lebensbereich* style, with its intimate blending of native and non-native.

There is additionally considerable interest in natives among private gardeners, if we are to judge by the number of books on the subject, for example Witt (Reinhard 1994), but relatively little published material on the *Lebensbereich* style. Additionally, one must suppose that proponents of native-only planting (*pace* Ken Druse, see above) might want to keep their voices low, given the Nazi regime's enthusiasm for native-only plantings. Gert Gröning, in a paper on the ideological aspects of German nature gardening, notes that 'in the late 1980s and early 1990s, books on nature gardens appeared in which more radical positions … were mildly rejected' (Gröning 1997), although he does quote from the Swiss U. Schwartz, who declared in a horticultural journal that 'a weed is what is foreign. I count all cultivars as weeds' (Gröning 1997). In practical terms, there does seem to be a clear split between habitat restoration and the more 'horticultural' *Lebensbereich* school of ecological planting design which is much less extensive (discussed below). The latter always involves nursery-grown plants, whereas the former is nearly always reliant on seed, supplied by specialist wildflower seed companies. Landscape architect Uschi Gräfen reported that 'a problem here is that when you buy native plants from a nursery they may not be the wild forms, but horticultural forms. It is very difficult to get (true) wild forms as plants' (Gräfen 2001). In Sweden, like Britain, invasive non-native species have had a relatively limited ecological impact and there has apparently been little debate in this area (Hammer 2000).

Steve Martino, practising in the US southwest desert, is quite adamant that in many cases he is producing 'contrived native plantings … people have to be around them' so that not only does he use the occasional non-native, especially South African aloe species, but that cultivars have an important part to play in many of the locations he designs for, especially those of high visibility. Colleagues in the nursery trade actively search for new forms in the wild 'which would make better cultivars for cultivation', listing the usual aesthetic and horticultural criterias as well as those with thornless varieties as an important factor among naturally defensive arid-zone plants (Martino 2001).

Morrison, however, is sceptical about using cultivars; 'in urban areas, there is a validity to using cultural heritage rather than just native plants, and for using cultivars. But there is a risk in over-embellishing … I hardly ever specify a cultivar in a design' (Morrison 2001). Cultivars of wild origin, as opposed to hybrids, or doubles, are more acceptable, although he is concerned that their use may restrict the gene pool and, therefore, the ability of a plant community containing them to reproduce and adapt effectively over time.

Woodland gardens

British woodland gardens are often extensive and largely feature flowering shrubs beneath a canopy of native trees, with oak (*Quercus robur, Q.petraea)* being favoured for its compatability with a rich ground and shrub layer. The ground layer can become quite rich and sometimes quite visually exciting, but almost by default, as management practices such as strimming to remove brambles (*Rubus fruticosus)* tend to favour its development. Bluebells (*Endymion non-scriptus)* are particularly favoured by this practice and are much appreciated when they develop into large colonies. In areas with a rich natural flora, a diverse wildflower community can result, with different combinations of moisture and light resulting in a patchwork of different wild plant combinations (Kingsbury 1994: 104).

With shade and additional stresses, such as competition for moisture and nutrients from the trees, aggressive weedy species and pasture grasses are largely eliminated from woodland, making it much easier to naturalise non-native species than in the open. Colourful drifts of geophytes and clumps of slow-growing woodland forbs are a feature of many British woodland gardens. The dormancy period of geophytes is a particular boon for management as it allows the chemical control of weeds during this time. A glyphosate-based herbicide applied during mid to late summer eliminates weeds, and also has the side-effect of stimulating an attractive growth of moss, which then acts as an increasing deterrent to the germination of unwanted seedlings (Hickson 1994).

The reduction of the competitive weed flora should also theoretically allow for greater reproduction through seed of shade-tolerant perennials. This may happen but is very dependent upon the rate of seed production and seedling growth, which can be limited for many woodland perennials. Species with a more ruderal character are most successful at naturalising under these conditions, with some Himalayan primula species (for example *Primula florindae, P.denticulata, P.japonica, P.bulleyana, P.pulverulenta*) forming spectacular colonies in moist shade in some gardens, with extensive hybrid swarms also occurring (Kingsbury 2000). The patchy growth of grass in light shade may also result in the naturalising of a colourful flora. A number of large historic gardens feature combinations of spring-flowering *Cyclamen coum, Galanthus nivalis* and *Primula vulgaris* (the latter two native), along with autumn flowering *Cyclamen hederifolium* and *C. repandum* growing in mown turf, for example Dartingon Hall and Greenways Garden, both in Devon, and Painswick Roccoco Garden, Gloucestershire.

In truth, the spread of native wildflowers or of non-native herbaceous species in woodland gardens is nearly always incidental to the main function of the garden; the cultivation of showy non-native shrubs, with rhododendrons being the centrepiece of many such gardens.

The Pacific northwest, with a similar maritime climate to that of the western British Isles and the northwest of the Iberian peninsula, is an area where there is considerable potential for integrating native and non-native woodland vegetation, despite the fact that there are well-founded concerns over the naturalisation of aggressive species of alien plants. The area is characterised by a very dynamic interest in horticulture and a strong horticultural industry, the climate lending itself to the cultivation of plants from an exceptionally wide range of origins. Lovejoy, in a book aimed at the amateur garden market, notes several woodland gardens where natives and non-natives are grown side by side, with some naturalisation of the latter, and she observes the process of 'editing' that goes on where native woodland and garden vegetation meet. She echoes many others when she states that 'most (native-only gardens) are more earnest than beautiful, and for many years, artful garden makers looked askance at the natural movement, finding it limited in palette and intention' (Lovejoy 1998). However, gardens that blend native and non-native species are more likely to be driven by a strong design ethic, and she states that '(northwest naturalistic gardens) owe a strong debt to Zen tea and sand gardens, both of which emphasise the spare and the sculptural' (Lovejoy 1998).

Woodland edges

Woodland edge habitats offer a variety of ecological niches both spatially and over time. The addition of flowering perennials to the strip that abuts woodland is a feature that adds considerably to its aesthetic value, whilst the development of a ground layer amidst shrubby vegetation could make a considerable difference to the appearance of large areas of public green space. Native vegetation is sometimes used in Germany and the Netherlands in this situation, whilst in Britain occasional use is made of both native species and non-natives (Figure 3.6). Of the latter, forms of *Geranium x oxonianum* are the most widely used, its practically evergreen habit and vigorous nature making it ideal. In addition, its seasonal growth pattern, whereby stems tend to 'collapse' after flowering to be replaced by new growth from the centre, makes it ideal for literally smothering surrounding weedy vegetation. Its long season of growth makes it ideal for use in maritime climates with a long growing season.

Coppicing

One of the most creative styles of woodland edge habitat is potentially afforded by coppicing, whereby trees and shrubs are cut down to ground level on a regular basis. Traditional coppicing, as practised in northwest Europe, works on a cycle of around 25 years, with the ground-layer vegetation changing over this period from a combination of relatively short-lived herbaceous species, such as *Digitalis purpurea* and *Silene dioicia* in the early open stages of the coppice cycle to more shade-tolerant species in the later, more closed, phase. The latter, for example *Primula vulgaris*, often survive the open phase and the late, very shady, phase of the coppice, but not making anything like optimal growth.

Nigel Dunnett has proposed that coppicing has great potential as a creative management tool for gardens and public green space, with areas cut on a rotation basis, resulting in 'coppice shrubbery'. The foliage of many tree species is larger and more luxuriant in the years following 'stooling' or cutting back, whilst the pattern of microhabitats that develops on the ground creates the potential for the cultivation of a wide range of herbaceous species (Dunnett 1995: 144). Dunnett has established an experimental plot at Harlow Carr Gardens (now

RHS Harlow Carr) in Harrogate, Yorkshire, which has been running since 1997, using a mixture of native and non-native species.

The 'marginal garden'

One of the most inspired and determined efforts at creating a garden that relies on a matrix of native vegetation and exotics is the 'marginal garden' of Professor Geoffrey Dutton in the Scottish Highlands. At an altitude of 275 m at 57 degrees of latitude, the climate is indeed 'marginal' for any kind of cultivation. The term, however, also describes the degree of horticultural intervention made and, as such, is an important pointer towards a philosophy of management that could have much wider implications than simply its application to a very severe environment. Dutton also describes his role as 'marginal', in that very limited time has meant that he has become a 'curator' of the land (Dutton 1997).

Hardy woody plants form a screen against the worst of the weather and provide a framework for the garden. Native plants predominate, with a limited number of non-natives used, which can be relied upon to survive both the severe climate and the low level of intervention. The overall feel is that of not quite knowing whether one is in a garden or not. Some clipping of shrubs and mowing of paths, however, illustrates intention and design, 'a path astonishingly transforms confused ground into comprehensible order' (Dutton 1997: 178).

Whilst the introduction of woody non-natives into a minimally maintained woodland-dominated habitat is common, the use of herbaceous species is much less so. Dutton has managed to naturalise several robust species, such as *Aconitum* spp., *Aruncus dioicus* and *Ranunculus aconitifolius*. Early season perennials, such as *Doronicum* spp., are paired with ferns or *Rodgersia* spp., which serve to shade out weedy native species later in the season (Dutton 1997).

Such minimalist interventions in the landscape, with the introduction of a very limited ornamental species, which need the minimum of care, is one possible way in which certain public landscapes could be inexpensively enhanced and managed. Situations that might be suitable include extensive areas of neglected urban parkland, where habitats are often dominated by coarse weedy perennials and succession communities where invasive woody exotics (e.g. *Acer pseudoplatanus*) dominate.

Flowering meadows

Building upon the ideas espoused by Robinson (1870), James Hitchmough started a programme of research in 1994 aimed at assessing the feasibility of establishing mixed native-exotic meadows, i.e. a sown matrix of native grasses and forbs but with added interest from planted exotic forbs, chiefly mainland European and Asian species. British wildflower meadows are a problematic element for managed landscapes because of the poverty of the British wildflower flora, its short season of interest (very few flower reliably after July) and the strong link between the most aesthetically pleasing and most floristically diverse, flora and shallow alkaline soils. A native-exotic meadow cut as hay in later summer/early autumn could be an exciting and colourful low-maintenance alternative to mown grass, or relatively unattractive and species-poor rank grassland, in urban public spaces. Reduced maintenance is a very powerful incentive for the development of this genre, with hay meadows taking at least 12 times less time to maintain than traditional rose borders or 10 times less time than conventional herbaceous ground cover (Hitchmough 1994). The initial work on these meadows was concerned with wet grasslands and the establishment of exotic species by planting. More recent work has focused on the creation of both wet and dry meadows in which both native and exotic species are established by sowing. Successful examples of the native-exotic meadows created by sowing and planting can be seen at RHS Harlow Carr.

Instead of using turf-forming meadow grasses as a matrix, it is possible instead to use clump or tussock forming ones, which creates a dramatically different and very striking visual effect, with taller forbs emerging from a sea of grasses (Hitchmough 1995b). In theory, the danger of weed incursion (the bane of large-scale herbaceous plantings in Britain) should be reduced because of the dominance of the tussock grasses, but there is very little evidence yet for this. A well-known example that demonstrates the possible potential is that created by Piet Oudolf at Bury Court in Bentley, Hampshire.

Annuals

Ecologically inspired annual plantings have a more recent history than those that use perennials. Yet they have enormous potential and, ironically, large-scale projects may sometimes give better value for money than perennials. Their potential lies with their visual impact and ease of growth. The general public like and, to some extent, expect bright colour from public plantings, which annuals are able to provide. Their rapid establishment from seed and low cost per unit area make them a highly attractive option for managers of open space.

The trialling of annuals and the development of nature-inspired seed mixes was started in the 1980s in the Netherlands by Rob Leopold and Dick van der Burg. They produced a range of seed mixtures based around a number of colour schemes which have proved popular with the general public but which have made little impact yet with managers of public spaces. Quite separately, Nigel Dunnett at the University of Sheffield started trials in the late 1990s, aiming at producing seed mixes that could be used by local government open space managers; a project that has got off to a very successful start with sales having started in 2000.

Dunnett stresses the importance of simplicity in creating the seed mixes, with a maximum of 10 species per mix. A number of the species chosen need to have a reputation for both reliability and a long season of flower, for example *Argemone mexicana, Linum grandiflorum* 'Rubrum' and *Eschscholzia californica.* Other species can be included for a spectacular but shorter burst of colour, for example *Phacelia tanacetifolia*, or for late colour, for example *Rudbeckia hirta.* 'Emergents' or taller, more architectural species, add another dimension, for example ornamental grasses or species with attractive seed heads, such as *Nicandra physaloides.* Variations in the overall effect can be created by sowing different mixtures in bands based on differing heights, flowering times or colours. Biennials or short-lived perennials can also be included if the planting is to be left for more than one year, in which case they will flower alongside those annuals which are able to re-sow in the second spring (Dunnett 1999).

Stylised nature – German Lebensbereich plantings and others

One of the most varied planting styles that fulfils our criteria of being ecological involves the use of plants that are not necessarily native to the area but are chosen on the basis of a close match between their ecological needs and a careful analysis of the conditions prevailing at the planting site. Such plantings also possess what could loosely be termed a 'naturalistic aesthetic'. Practitioners in this area are aiming for an effect with a strong visual appeal for the public – colour, length of seasonal interest, structure, etc. – but also with an awareness of the potential value of the planting for local wildlife.

It could be argued that this is what a large number of landscape and horticultural professionals, and a greater number of private gardeners, are doing anyway. There has been a steady rise in what could loosely be called 'environmental awareness' over many years, resulting in a number of developments

3.6
A woodland glade in Sheffield Botanical Gardens. This woodland edge habitat has been filled with *Echinacea purpurea, Rudbeckia fulgida* var. *deamii* and *Aster macrophyllus*

that are making many much more 'ecological' in their approach:

- more closely matching the perceived ecological demands of plants to the ecology of the site – garden writer Beth Chatto has been instrumental in this respect, at least in the English-speaking world (Chatto 1978, 1982)
- a greater awareness of the role of managed landscapes in supporting faunal diversity – Chris Baines' (1984) writings in the UK and Sara Stein's (1993) in the US have played major roles here
- a growing number of 'organic' practitioners.

The most articulate, self-consciously 'ecological' practitioners have been concerned mostly with the role of herbaceous plants in public space, with plants chosen arranged in a way that is radically different to that of conventional planting styles, and very much inspired by the way that they would grow in natural plant communities.

The use of plants from a wide range of countries of origin is very much closer to the traditional horticultural mainstream than many of the approaches discussed in this chapter. Not surprisingly, the role this planting style plays is almost entirely for relatively small areas of high visibility: frequently used areas of public parks and private gardens that may or may not be open to the public. As high-visibility plantings, there is often a considerable investment in plants and design costs, which limits their size. Their visibility, and the need to protect the original investment, also means that there is a readiness on the part of owners to put more into maintenance than in more extensive plantings. In some cases, there is also more need for maintenance, particularly in the face of weed infiltration. This greater need for maintenance also indicates that these planting schemes are very often less ecologically stable than those which rely heavily on native plant communities. Nevertheless, new developments with seed-sown plantings point towards a future where initial costs can be dramatically reduced and where a more extensive and lower-cost maintenance regime can be implemented.

The Lebensbereich style

Of all the ecological planting styles, the work that has been done in Germany by Professor Richard Hansen and his followers represents perhaps the most sophisticated balancing point between nature and art, and one that carries very little ideological baggage or preconceived ideas about what is natural (Kühn 1999). It also has an immense amount of research work behind it, mostly carried out over several decades at the University of Weihenstephan in Freising in Bavaria and which is summarised in an invaluable reference book (Hansen and Stahl). *Lebensbereich* means 'living space' and refers to the close matching between the ecological conditions of the site and the ecological preferences of the species used, which is crucial to the success of the planting schemes carried out. The results are undoubtedly spectacular in visual terms, with sweeping masses of perennials flowering in flushes from spring through to autumn. Walking around public spaces planted up in this style leaves no doubt as to the public appreciation of, and enthusiasm for, its exuberance and vitality.

However, the visitor to Germany soon notices a paradox – there are few examples of *Lebensbereich* planting to be seen. Almost all the extensive areas are to be seen in parks which were originally laid out as garden shows, either for a state (*Landesgartenschau)* or for the country as a whole (*Bundesgartenschau),* with the best examples nearly all being in southern Germany. Occasionally, areas planted with perennials, and obviously inspired by Hansen, are seen in public spaces that have no *Gartenschau* history, and even more occasionally in projects carried out by landscape architects for commercial clients. In a country where public green space is highly valued and new developments are well-resourced, there are obviously factors that have militated against a more widespread adoption of this style. There follows an evaluation of the current status of *Lebensbereich* planting, a look at the direction into which it is heading, and an examination of the work of one of its most skilled practitioners. Practitioners in other countries will then be considered.

The sheer scope and detail of Hansen's body of work may be one factor that militates against its wider use. Cassian Schmidt, current Director of the Hermanshof garden (see below), was one of several practitioners interviewed who suggested that landscape architects are reluctant to implement *Lebensbereich*-style plantings because their training has not given them enough knowledge and confidence to design what are relatively complex planting styles (Schmidt 2001). Urs Walser, former Director of the Hermanshof garden, stresses that design is not a one-off event – 'designing of a planting is ideally a process … the best situation is when one can continue to develop a planting, making changes, developing nuances, making additions, taking some plants away and always making further corrections. This happens when one can look after plantings over many years'. He notes that 'plantings are frequently made and their further development can hardly be influenced – this is a difficult situation' (Walser 1998).

Much of the research into plantings for public space now being carried out is aimed at developing plant communities that can be easily installed and maintained by less-knowledgeable personnel. These may be simpler, less flexible, and less creative than those of Hansen or Walser, but they offer the possibility of a more widely accessible working method. The level of publicly funded research effort going into this work is certainly unique. Additional to these issues concerning the willingness of practitioners to develop complex perennial-based plantings is a financial issue. Landscape architects are paid on the basis of a fee of 10–15% of the total construction cost, which militates against projects with a time-consuming design input (Schönfeld 2001a).

Inspired by Hansen, a small number of dedicated and skilled landscape architects and others have carried on his work. Of these, Urs Walser has achieved fame as the Director (1983–1998) of Sichtungsgarten Hermanshof, in Weinheim in the Rhine valley, before moving on to become Professor of Planting Design and Urban Vegetation at the Technical University of Dresden. He has designed several major perennial plantings for Federal Garden Shows, one of which is now a major feature in the Killesberg Park in Stuttgart. The Hermanshof garden is a showcase of the best of the modern German planting style, aimed at displaying possibilities for both professionals and amateurs. Its plantings can be seen to form a gradient, from those that are strongly naturalistic, using almost entirely European natives, to several which are still strongly habitat-based but more eclectic and with a higher aesthetic/design element, to very colourful and artistic summer plantings.

Walser was a student of Hansen, whose field trips into Alpine and other wild habitats were his inspiration (Walser 1998). His aim has been to build on Hansen's work, giving a greater role to aesthetic criteria (Walser 1994). Indeed, he has said that 'it would be false if there was the impression that the ecological influence dominated my plantings. Of prime importance are the aesthetic influences of texture, structure and flower colour in the plant selection' (Walser 1998). 'The room for manoeuvre in gardens and parks is surely greater than in nature' he says. 'The attempt to realise the garden as arcadia determines an important part of the cultural history of gardens and clearly makes a distinction with ecological planting. The artificiality of planting is a central idea and can be creatively developed in different directions: artistic with a more or less strong ecological connection' (Walser 1998).

Walser continues to make use of the clear distinction that Hansen made between 'wild' and 'border' perennials; the former being species or wild-origin cultivars that could be used in lower maintenance, more naturalistic plantings, the latter, species, cultivars or hybrids that need more intensive cultivation in conventional borders (Hansen and Stahl 1993). Public spaces have clear zones, ranging from very decorative through to naturalistic, and the plant combinations he has worked on clearly reflect this, and yet even the most 'decorative' at Hermanshof, which feature annuals and bedded-out half-hardy species, have the repetition and intermingling characteristic of natural plant communities, which gives them a strikingly contemporary aesthetic.

Walser states: 'For me it is important to take the knowledge of plant community systems and place them in a horticultural form. I have a strong picture in my mind of outstanding plant communities. I study the descriptions of natural plant communities, and have gained much basic knowledge from the scientific literature'. Yet he stresses how 'the transferring of plants from a natural habitat to a cultural one in a completely different context is not a copy, rather an abstraction' (Walser 1998). There is validity to using plants that combine together in nature, but he stresses that 'I do not claim that plant communities must be placed together in a narrow geographical sense, but they should originate from a similar biosphere (*Lebensraum*). It is senseless to say that here I plant short-grass prairie plants in a dry zone and there east European steppe plants, and never mix the two together … my experience does not support the idea that plantings entirely from close geographical origins thrive better. Plants from similar habitats with similar ecological conditions can obviously be combined without taking consideration of their geographical origins … we always notice that plants are more tolerant and adaptable than we expect' (Walser 1998). As well as using the knowledge of a plant's natural habitat in designing planting combinations, Walser stresses the need to be aware of its cultural habitat (*Kulturstandort*), i.e. its placing within the garden as an aesthetic construct.

In selecting plants, Walser is particularly interested in looking at species that are the dominant ones within natural communities, which he then tries out to see how adaptable and gardenworthy they are. When designing plantings though, he emphasises that it is important to have taxa that look good over a long season, the theme plants (Leitpflanzen) of Hansen, for example *Salvia nemorosa*, whose colourful flowers are succeeded by seed heads with good structure (Walser 1998). Walser describes how he is 'very interested in the gradient of vitality of plants in different environments', however he recognises that the immense number of plants in cultivation creates its own problems. Exploiting ecological tolerances allows the designer of plantings to bring many different species together but, at the same time, there is a temptation to play safe and 'to limit the selection to those that one knows will thrive, be long-lasting and are simple to maintain', which will vary from region to region (Walser 1998). But there are also dangers in going in the other direction, 'yucca and astilbe may offer interesting contrasts of form and texture, but I could never place them next to one another' because, although their ecological amplitudes might overlap in cultivation, knowledge of their greatly different origins creates a feeling of inauthenticity (Walser quoted in King (1997)).

Heiner Luz is another practioner, who, like Walser, has created highly decorative plantings for garden shows and public spaces (e.g. IGA 1993, Stuttgart and LGA 2000 Memmingen). He stresses that design must be given 'equal rights' with ecological/phytosociological principles. Too much diversity can lead to 'visual chaos', harmony demands an application of the 'less is more' principle. In any case, he stresses that we know from phytosociology that habitats are dominated by only a limited number of species, which gives them a quality of visual 'impressiveness' (Luz 2002: 16–21).

Lebensbereich practitioners recognise that the development of the planting over time involves a limited succession, with short-lived, essentially ruderal ornamental species, eventually being displaced by longer-lived ones. Hans Simon describes the importance of having some rapidly developing species to prevent unwanted weedy vegetation establishing a foothold (Simon 1990: 10). He also describes how the growth habits of perennials can be utilised by the designer in the ongoing development of a planting, for example species with long stolons can fill in the spaces between tuft-forming species. He also stresses the importance of keeping the ground covered as much as possible with perennial growth (Simon 1990). The implication is that this reduces the infiltration of weed seedlings.

Mixed perennial planting

Dr Walter Korb, at the Bavarian Institute for Viniculture and Horticulture (*Bayerische Landesanstalt für Weinbau and Gartenbau at Veitshöchheim*), has begun to develop a simplified version of the *Lebensbereich* perennial style which is designed to be used by relatively inexperienced practitioners – '*Staudenmischpflanzung*' (Schönfeld 2002). The idea is that by having a plant list, with specified numbers of plants and planting distances, it is possible to create an attractive planting without involving a plan or a designer (and their attendant fees) to specify the location of each plant. Needless to say, the plant mixture needs to be carefully worked out, so that all taxa used are of equivalent competitiveness. Exact plant positions end up by being pretty much random. Discussing experimental work which involved assessing the growth and visual appearance of a number of plant selections and monocultures, Philipp Schönfeld, who has managed the work since 1994, describes how 'the perennials must find their own place in the plant-community. In our (trial) areas we have seen that a strong dynamic develops, which still has not come to an equilibrium after eight years. The area covered by individual taxa is constantly changing. The short-lived species, which are included for a fast effect in the first year, soon disappear. The ground cover ones fight for a place, spread and form small intertwined areas' (Schönfeld 2001a).

The 'mixed planting' idea would appear to have great potential and could prove very attractive to open space managers with limited budgets. However, there are a number of drawbacks that apply to any standardised mixture. One is that there is a point at which popularity becomes a cliché, the repetition of the same mixture many times over different geographical regions is something that ecological design has set itself against. The other is that, without the subtle grouping and intermingling of taxa or the creation of drifts (e.g. in Darrel Morrison's work, see Chapter 5), a definite visual element is possibly lacking, particularly with regard to the more architectural plants.

A variety of planting combinations have been trialled at the Veitshöchheim Institute, with one particular one being launched publicly in 2000 after trialling in a number of other trial gardens (see '*Silbersommer*' in the section 'Steppe planting' below) (Schönfeld 2000). The '*Silbersommer*' (silver summer) mixture is aimed at landscape architects, local government and other open space managers. Its trialling and launch has been carried out by the Local Government Planting Management Group (*Arbeitskreis Pflanzungverwendung*) under the wing of the German Perennial Growers Association (*Bundes Deutscher Staudengärtner*).

Steppe planting

The most successful *Lebensbereich* plantings, in terms of their public impact, have been those for dry habitats, the so-called 'steppe' plantings. Their inspiration is the highly distinctive, species-rich, and attractive flora of relatively low-nutrient soils that develop over limestone or sandstone in East-Central and Eastern Europe. Native species are combined with hardy taxa from Mediterranean maquis and garrigue-type environments, many of which have attractive evergreen grey foliage, as well as some from drier prairie habitats in North America. A spectacular early summer display of flowers is followed by further flushes of flower, with the latter part of the season dominated by the development of attractive grass-seed heads. The suitability of such a flora for urban areas with little quality soil and large quantities of calcareous rubble is obvious.

The steppe planting at the Westpark in Munich, originally laid out for the International Garden Show in 1983, has become particularly well known (Figures 3.7 and 3.8). Laid out by Rosmarie Weisse and Barbara Lange, a number of different habitats are created, yet it is the steppe area which has been the most successful in terms of public approval and in the long-term maintenance of a high number of species. Closely following the Hansen model of plant grouping through the application of the aesthetic quality of their 'sociability' (Hansen 1993: 39–46), the planting aims at the loose intermingling of taxa, some as isolated specimens and others in groups (Weisse 1994; Kingsbury and Von Schoenaich 1995).

Steppe-type plantings continue to reappear at German garden shows (which then become permanent parks), and it seems to be a style whose practical and aesthetic possibilities continue to inspire designers. The 2001 Federal Garden Show at Potsdam, for example, featured a number of raised beds with plantings submitted by different landscape practices around the theme of grey foliage.

'*Silbersommer*', the first of what may well be several mixed perennial planting 'formulas' to be developed by German researchers, is clearly derived from the plant selection used in steppe plantings. It aims to provide a long season of colour and interest with a naturalistic aesthetic, relying on flowers, leaf shape, colour and texture, and overall plant form. The plant selection is broken down into four categories based on aesthetic and practical criteria:

- solitary perennials – grasses such as *Festuca mairei* and architectural perennials like *Verbascum bombyciferum* (10% of selection)
- group perennials – species that form clumps, for example *Knautia macedonica* and *Achillea filipendulina* (40–50%)
- ground cover – low carpeters such as *Thymus pulegioides* (40–50%)
- scatter plants – i.e. bulbs for spring interest, crocus, muscari and tulipa species (Schmidt 2000; Schönfeld 2001b).

Given the practicality of the steppe style for urban environments, where tolerance to drought and other stresses may be of considerable importance, and the undoubted appeal of many of the species from this kind of habitat, there is no doubt that there is still much potential work to be done on species selection. Plenk, for example, draws attention to the richness and diversity of the Central European Pannonian flora, whose ability to survive hot, dry, poor soils, makes it eminently suitable for urban situations (Plenk 1999).

British approaches

The *Lebensbereich* style has had some influence over practitioners outside Germany, and this could well grow as knowledge of Hansen's work and the spectacular park plantings becomes more widespread. Additionally, there are practitioners, often working on a small or local scale, who have evolved a broadly similar approach, whose work is characterised by its natural inspiration, an awareness of the importance of matching plants to site, and a desire to design plantings that reflect a more naturalistic aesthetic with regard to plant groupings. The interest that Walser has in making use of the full ecological amplitude in combining plants in the garden has particularly great potential in Britain. As Plenk notes, the 'distinctive pragmatism of British gardens, a product of climate and species-poor and limited natural environment offers few models for ecological planting, but the combination of native and exotic by no means excludes an ecologically orientated planting design' (Plenk 1998). The maritime British climate, which makes it possible to grow plants from a wide variety of different origins, is a factor that makes the development of a truly adventurous version of ecological planting highly likely.

The author's own work tries to use the principles established by Hansen in an English concept, for both private clients and for an institutional client at Cowley Manor in Gloucestershire (Figures 3.9–3.11). The maritime west of England climate is favourable to the growth of a wide variety of aggressive perennial weeds, particularly evergreen grasses, which makes the growing of winter-dormant perennials more problematic than in more continental climates. Soil fertility, moisture and light levels are generally high, so plant selection has been based on robust perennials from moist habitats (mostly Eurasian) and North American prairie species. The inclusion of some locally native species is important in order to make a reference to local habitats but, at the same time, the inspiration of wild-plant communities in Central Europe and North America is vital. Kingsbury states that it is important to challenge the orthodoxy of the English garden style that limits perennials to relatively narrow borders and which has never really explored the possibilities of intermingling plants in a naturalistic way (Maguire 1998; Kingsbury 1998a, 1998b).

'Gravel gardens' are an increasingly important part of the British horticultural scene, partly because the layer of gravel mulch greatly reduces the amount of weed-seed germination that occurs and, thus, the level of maintenance. Beth Chatto, arguably the 'grandmother' of ecologically-inspired British gardening, was a pioneer in developing and promoting the gravel garden, as she was in making the British garden public more aware of the relationship between plants (particularly perennials) and their environment. However, neither hers nor any others that the author is aware of, use plants with a naturalistic design philosophy. The design possibilities of the 'ecological gravel garden' might be attractive were it not for the fact that gravel extraction has a negative impact (at least in the short term) on the British countryside.

On a heavy soil in an area with high rainfall and a maritime climate, Keith Wiley, Head Gardener at The Garden House, Buckland Monachorum in Devon, has created a spectacular garden based on a series of different ecologically-inspired plant communities. Wiley is an articulate exponent of the importance of those in the horticultural and landscape professions learning from natural plant communities. Some of his plantings involve annuals (see below) but most involve perennials and shrubs. Self-seeding, for example of the short-lived South American *Verbena bonariensis* or the South African dierama species, is encouraged to provide spontaneous 'foundation' plants that create a sense of unity to link several very disparate areas. This is an important aspect of what Wiley refers to as 'diversity with a strong theme' (Wiley 2001).

Wiley describes his design approach as being 'the repetition of a small number of species providing a framework ... in informal groups with outlying singletons'. Further species are added to fill in the gaps between these and space is allowed for self-sowing, which is a vital part of the whole concept (Wiley 2000). The freedom allowed for self-

3.7
The steppe area of Munich's Westpark has become the best-known example of contemporary German *Lebensbereich* planting design. During June, *Iris germanica* hybrids are the main feature along with a variety of ornamental grasses and other drought-tolerant species. The alternation of tall, clump-forming and very low-growing species is a notable feature (June)

3.8
Other areas of the Westpark receive less management. This area, with a very free-draining soil, includes several species which maintain themselves through self-sowing, including a *Verbascum* spp., *Oenothera fruticosa* and *Dipsacus fullonum*, as well as long-lived *Echinops ritro* (July)

seeding, and the advantage this gives to short-lived species, many of which are brightly coloured, gives The Garden House an exuberant, indeed almost playful, atmosphere. A similar approach has been adopted by James Hitchmough to create North American prairie plant communities by sowing, supplemented by the planting of species that cannot be established by seeding. A large-scale example can be seen at the Eden Project in St Austell, Cornwall.

Self-sowing is also a key to the management of Bolton Percy Cemetery, a very successful naturalistic planting that has received relatively little publicity. Roger Brook, a professional horticulturalist, has managed a 0.4 ha cemetery for 25 years, almost entirely through the use of glyphosate-based herbicide, for four hours per 100 m^2 per year. Plants are introduced but there is no overall design. By eliminating competitive grasses and other unwanted species, the ground is left open for colonisation by ornamental species, either through seed or vegetative means. As there is a minimum of 'design', the plant distribution is achieved largely through ecological processes (Dunnett 2000).

The same conclusions that Hansen came to have also been reached by British nurseryman Peter Thompson, whose book *The Self-Sustaining Garden* (Thompson 1997) is an approach to planting design that attempts to present an essentially ecological approach to the general gardening public. His key concept is that of the 'matrix', a largely self-sustaining plant community whose members are chosen to reflect the ecology of the site and which are compatable with each other. He stresses the different layers of vegetation that should occupy space and the dimension of time, recognising the dynamic nature of plantings. Aiming at an amateur audience who have more time to devote to their plantings than money – and time – pressed local government or commercial bodies; his maintenance regime includes a number of practices which would be uneconomic, or perhaps aesthetically unnecessary, on a larger scale, such as dead-heading, cutting back perennials mid-season to reduce height, regenerating plants through pruning, etc. (Thompson 1997).

3.9
***Rheum palmatum* dominates a planting, inspired by the *Lebensbereich* style on a moist fertile soil at Cowley Manor, Gloucestershire. Other species include *Persicaria bistorta* 'Superbum', *Euphorbia palustris*, with later flowering species including many geranium taxa and *Filipendula ulmaria* (June)**

3.10
The grass *Calamagrostis x acutiflora* 'Karl Foerster' stands above *Rudbeckia fulgida* and *Carex comans*. The planting also includes various geranium, monarda and aster taxa. Like all the plantings at Cowley Manor, a long flowering season is an important aspect of the design (September)

3.11
A native species, *Lythrum salicaria*, is included as a theme plant in one of the plantings at Cowley, its magenta being complemented by monarda taxa and the grey leaves of *Macleaya cordata* (August)

Informal naturalistic planting

Native flora as an artistic medium

It is possible to use locally native flora in a way that is entirely conventional in its design aesthetic, and with no intention of creating any kind of plant community. At first, this seems paradoxical. Yet it does have a rationale. Even used as monocultures, native plants will participate in the local ecology by acting as a source of food for specialist fauna. The use of locally native species is also a way of linking the immediate environment of the planting to the wider environment of the region, which can be a particularly valuable way of making this reference in a highly urban setting. The use of natives as an artistic medium, rather than an ecological one, is also a way of communicating their value, and that of the region, *vis-à-vis* the forces of centralisation and globalised blandness in a way that is acceptable to a large number of people. The classic example perhaps is of Roberto Burle Marx, who, when he became Director of Parks and Gardens in the northeastern Brazilian city of Recife in 1934, planted locally native plants in a public square. This scandalised all those who saw such flora only as worthless scrub, and the colonial mentality that appreciated the classical geometry of the metropolitan Portuguese garden as the only civilised way to grow plants. He went on to build a career that showcased Brazilian native plants but in ways that were totally design, rather than ecology, driven (Eliovson 1991).

Steve Martino's work in Phoenix, Arizona, USA, has had a similar impact, which he describes as 'bringing the desert back into the city after the city tried to push the desert away' (Martino 2001). As well as creating native-based plant communities, his practice also develops small plantings for urban settings that make use of the architectural qualities of desert flora, such as opuntia and ocotillo cacti. The highly defined textures and shapes of such plants stand out in a light that can be exceptionally harsh. These can be particularly effective when their shadows are thrown against flat-coloured walls of the kind favoured by Mexican architect Luis Barragan, who has been a major influence on Martino. An example of such a planting, which won an American Society of Landscape Architects award in 1992, is an arboretum designed for the Arid Zone Trees Company, who supply much of the material for Martino's practice. He has included sculptural elements, such as giant fin-like barbs, which echo the shapes of agaves (Thompson 1998).

A number of designers have used the structurally less-dramatic cool, temperate North American flora in an 'un-ecological' way, usually to make a particular educational or aesthetic point. For example, Burrell and Hagstrom, working with a community group in St Paul, Minnesota, made a prairie garden at the front and then used the same species in a much more stylised way at the back, 'like modern art' to encourage people to compare the different way the plants were used. Another project in the same city used bold patterns of native plants in a wetland, with different habitat zones forming concentric rings (Burrell 2001). Morrison has also used wildflowers in plantings at the National Wildflower Research Center in Austin, Texas, to emphasise to visitors their aesthetic possibilities (Leccesse 1995; Morrison 2001).

The 'xeriscape™' movement, which is aimed at encouraging US gardeners to conserve water, has also resulted in a considerable usage of native plants, especially in the drier southwestern and southern states. For the most part, they are used in design terms as 'normal' garden plants, replacing less drought-tolerant non-native species, rather than in self-consciously ecological designs (Ellefson *et al.* 1992). In some cases, this has been supported by the water authorities themselves, as in Florida, where the South Florida Water Management District was the first to implement xeriscape legislation in 1991, and built a demonstration water-saving garden in

West Palm Beach, where most of the plantings are native, combined with a few colourful exotics. The magnificent *Quercus virginiana*, a key southern landscape tree, are also now much more often planted (Tasker 1995).

Evoking nature

Two practices exemplify and highlight the problems we have in defining ecological planting design. Piet Oudolf in the Netherlands and Oehme/van Sweden in the USA have achieved high public-profiles for their innovative work. Both practices are noted for their extensive research of plant material and its use. They have both developed a distinctive aesthetic that is closely bound up with the visual qualities of the plants they use, which, in many cases, are species that have not been widely used in garden or landscape design previously, particularly ornamental grasses. Whether seeking such attention or not, their work has been seized upon by commentators anxious to promote a 'natural' approach to landscape design.

Oudolf's work has been very favourably written up in Britain by writers for consumer magazines and garden books, who confuse him with other, chiefly German, practioners, and hail him as a leading light of a naturalistic style (Brooks 1998; Buchan 2000). Practicing in the Netherlands, the UK and more recently in the US, his work dramatically counterposes a highly individualistic interpretation of the formal treatment of woody plant material with a floristically rich assemblage of ornamental forbs and grasses. An architectural and very contemporary use of clipped evergreens recalls the mentor of his youth, Mien Ruys, but it was his discovery of the dramatic power of perennials and grasses that led him to develop the style that established his reputation. 'My biggest inspiration is nature, not to copy it but to get the emotion,' he says, 'what I try to do is to create an image of nature' (Oudolf 1998). Much of the innovatory appearance of Oudolf's perennial plantings has been due to his use of grass species and of forbs that have traditionally been eschewed by horticulture, in particular the Apiaceae and genera such as *Sanguisorba*. A great many of the taxa used are genetically identical to wild stock, and of those that are not, many are cultivar selections of this wild stock, and of the hybrids used, nearly all maintain the proportions and, therefore, the aesthetic qualities of wild plants.

In addition to using plants to evoke wild places, Oudolf seeks to evoke nature by confronting his public with an aesthetic philosophy that celebrates the beauty of plants at all stages of their lifecycles. Setting himself firmly against the conventional horticultural practice of cutting back herbaceous vegetation in the autumn, Oudolf leaves his standing until the spring, waxing lyrical about the shades and shapes of dying leaves. He once said, only half-jokingly, 'a plant is only worth growing if it looks good when it is dead' (Oudolf 1994).

However, Oudolf's work pays little attention to ecological criteria in selecting plants, which instead are put together using a subtle and innovative set of aesthetic criteria, which stresses plant structure and visual texture. Unlike the German *Lebensbereich* practioners, Oudolf does not group plants by habitat, or use ecological criteria in selecting plants any more than the vast majority of garden design practitioners (Oudolf and Kingsbury 1999: 73). The design of his private garden features the placing of individuals of particular taxa in such a way as to evoke the intermingling of wild plants, although they are no more dynamic than that of many other garden designers who work with an informal approach – allowing a limited amount of self-seeding. His public work (e.g. Drömpark at Enköping, Sweden, and the Pensthorpe Waterfowl Trust at Fakenham, Norfolk) uses irregular-shaped blocks of herbaceous planting, each one characteristically using multiple individuals of a single taxon. The effect is thus profoundly different to that of natural vegetation.

In the US, the work of Wolfgang Oehme and James van Sweden has served to radically transform perceptions of the relationship between plants and landscape, particularly in public spaces. At first glance their work might seem to be profoundly 'un-ecological', featuring, as much of it does, large swathes of monocultural blocks of a limited number of taxa, especially in public landscapes (Kühn 1999). Their planting style has to work within some severe practical constraints (e.g. deer predation and a poorly developed horticultural tradition), and the cultural and ideological constraints of a society where anything other than mown grass is still seen by many as 'weedy'. Van Sweden himself once said, when looking at a planting of the author's in England, that 'the American public aren't ready for this yet' (Van Sweden 1998a). Like Oudolf, Van Sweden aims to evoke the emotion of wild landscapes, particularly the prairie plants he knew in his youth (Van Sweden 1998b). Massed grasses and tall perennials waving in the breeze are indeed very evocative, and have been taken to heart by the partnership's increasing band of admirers. However, those of a more ecological bent have criticised them for using non-natives, such as potentially invasive miscanthus grasses, and for producing work of a formulaic nature (Darke quoted by Burrell (2000)). Another prominent promoter of native plants (name withheld) told the author that if he proposed to include their work in this study he should 'go to Walt Disney World'.

Such criticisms, however, ignore the continuing evolution of their style. Sheila Brady, a partner in the practice, describes how they are 'moving much more towards interplanting whereas before we had masses of one species' (Brady 2001). Eric Groft, another partner in the practice, is emphatic in describing their work as 'natural', in that it aims to 'let plants be plants … clipped hedges for example, are not part of our vocabulary'. What is more, he sees their work as 'ecological', as 'plants have to be well-chosen for their environment' (Groft 2001). In some of the larger private plantings that the practice has worked on over the last 10 years, native plant community meadows have been used in situations where 'anything like our normal planting becomes cost-prohibitive' (Groft 2001).

The 'classic' work of Van Sweden and Oudolf is clearly not ecological in our understanding of the term, as they are not in any sense self-sustaining plant communities, plant selection is only loosely tied to ecological criteria and plant groupings are built around monocultural blocks of varying sizes. However, they successfully evoke 'nature' to many observers, and have played major roles in promoting the broad concept of naturalistic design. What is more, their undeniable creative skill, originality, professional boldness and success are an inspiration to all in the profession.

The larger-scale Oehme Van Sweden work is one that clearly has its roots in a 1950s German parks style, with its sculptural, almost Burle Marxian, flowing mass of perennials. Arguably, we have now come full circle, with German designer Petra Pelz working with perennials in public spaces in a bold style that is inspired by the two Americans, with little obvious reference to an ecological style (Kühn 2001). Pelz, like many designers, is acutely aware of the problems of maintaining plantings in public spaces, and finds from her experience or working in Magdeburg, that simple, very structural plantings are easier to maintain than more finely-structured ones. In seeking to develop planting combinations that form weed-suppressing carpets, her work is also arguably a simplified version of the *Lebensbereich* style (Pelz 2001).

Conclusions

It is clear from this survey that 'ecological design' covers a very wide range of practices. There is a need for practitioners to appreciate that this range and the flexibility offers a wide range of solutions for many different situations. Public and, indeed, large privately owned areas of green space often involve a patchwork of different situations, each with their own potential and problems. These can often be most easily appreciated as existing on one of several gradients:

- formal/architectural to wild/natural
- urban character to rural character
- the importance of aesthetic and cultural values being greater than ecological value to ecology and biodiversity being more important
- intensively used to not intensively used.

These complex and often geographically, aesthetically and functionally juxtaposed situations need practitioners who have a clear idea of what is appropriate for each area and who can handle the transitions between them subtly and skilfully. Understanding the full potential of the range of ecologically-based design options, and the relationships between them is crucial for the effective development and management of green space.

The desire to use locally native plants is an important part of the ecological planting movement. Yet, as this chapter indicates, there is a wide range of possibilities that involve the use of non-natives too. The normative and ideological aspects of the debate over the use of natives is arguably impeding the development of more adventurous strategies by creating divisions between people and professions who should be working together. More useful would be constructive debate over the role of natives and non-natives in different situations. Designing an aesthetic into native-only or native-dominated plantings is clearly an important issue, and one that needs more attention if these plant communities are to achieve recognition from the public and from decision makers. The native planting movement tends to be dominated by ecologists, yet a greater involvement of those with more of a design background could arguably do much to produce more aesthetically pleasing work.

Walser and several other practitioners, including Cassian Schmidt, the current curator at Hermanshof, stress how maintenance is the key issue for the long-term success of *Lebensbereich* plantings in public spaces. There seems to be a widespread feeling that there are not enough skilled personnel to maintain large plantings in public spaces, and that the relevant local government institutions do not provide the necessary resources or organisational support. A few cities that train their own staff, usually with one senior person who has a personal commitment to high standards and a genuine interest in the style, are able to keep plantings going. These include Stuttgart and Ingolstadt. It is not that a great deal of maintenance is needed, but it needs to be skilled and the timing of operations is crucial (Schmidt 2001). Walser also points out that 'overmaintenance' can be a problem, for example winter stems and seed heads cut down that could be a structural element (Walser 1998).

Ecological planting design faces a similar fundamental problem in both the private and the public sectors: a shortage of personnel skilled in the maintenance techniques necessary for successful and biodiverse development, and a frequent lack of understanding on the part of owners and managers of the importance of appropriate long-term management. Public landscapes, in particular, suffer from a combined and interrelated series of problems, lucidly described by Kühn: cuts in local government spending, a loss of the autonomy of open-space managers, and a consequent loss of pride and motivation. The increasing tendency for private companies to maintain open space is also a problem, tendering is all too often based on price and there is little continuity as contracts often have to be regularly renegotiated. Private sponsorship can sometimes help, but it is rarely of any use as a source of funding for long-term maintenance (Kühn 2001).

In the final analysis, only social and political changes can ensure a more certain future for well-managed green space. However, there is much that can be done under present circumstances to produce environments that are functional, aesthetically rewarding, sustainable and biodiverse, but understanding the full range of practices and the possibilities that they offer is vital for developing flexible strategies that can adapt to changing financial and political circumstances.

Green space needs designs and management techniques that minimise maintenance costs, for example a greater use of extensive management. With confidence in successful maintenance, decision makers and communities would be in a much stronger position to implement forward-looking and adventurous designs. Research geared towards extensive management and other ways of reducing maintenance costs could therefore do much to strengthen the hands of those who wish to see ecological plantings used more often.

References

- Baines, C. (1984). *How to make a wildlife garden*. Dent, London.
- Bartels, (1992). Restoring the North Eastern Meadow. *Landscape Architecture*, **12**, 74.
- Bowen, R. (2001). Telephone interview with author, 24 July.
- Brady, S. (2001). Telephone interview with author, 16 May.
- Brooks, J. (1998). *The New Garden*. Dorling Kindersley, London.
- Buchan, U. (2000). Country & Garden: 'I dream of Eden'. *The Independent*, 25 Nov.
- Burrell, C. (2000). Ornamental Grasses. *Landscape Architecture*, **3**, 26.
- Burrell, C. (2001). Interview with author, 10 April.
- Chatto, B. (1978). *The Dry Garden*. Dent, London.
- Chatto, B. (1982). *The Damp Garden*. Dent, London.
- Darke, R. (2001). Telephone interview with author, 30 April.
- Diboll (1998)
- Diboll, N. (2001). Telephone interview with author, 14 June.
- Diedrich, L. (2002). Promenade Architecture in the Riem Landscape Park. *TOPOS,* **37**, 58–63.
- Druse, K. (2001). E-mail correspondence with author, March.
- Dunnett, N. (1995). Coppice gardening. *The Garden*, March, 144.
- Dunnett, N. (1999). Annuals on the loose. *The Garden*, March.
- Dunnett, N. (2000). Tending God's Acre. *The Garden*, Dec., 886–889.
- Dutton (1997). *Some branch against the sky.* Timber Press, Portland, Oregon.
- Eckhardt, A., Obermüller, C. and Tauscher, A. (1999)
- Eliovson, S. (1991). *The Gardens of Roberto Burle Marx*. Sagapress/Timber Press, Portland, Oregon.
- Ellefson, C. *et al*. (1992). *Xeriscape Gardening*. Macmillan, New York.
- Flora Locale (2001) www.floralocale.org
- Franklin, C. (2001a). Telephone interview with author, 2 April.
- Franklin, C. (2001b). Letter to author, 26 Sept.
- Franklin, C. (2002). Telephone interview with author, 7 Feb.
- Gillette, J. B. (1994). 162 Birches. *Landscape Architecture*, Oct., 132.
- Gräfen, U. (2001). Telephone interview with author, 21 March.

- Groft, E. (2001). Telephone interview with author, 7 March.
- Gröning, G. (1997). Ideological Aspects of Nature Garden Concepts in Late Twentieth Century Germany. In Wolschke-Bulmahn, J. (ed.) *Nature and Ideology*. Dumbarton Oaks, Washington, DC.
- Gustavsson, R. (1994). *Det Nya Landskapet*. Skogstjrelsen, Jönköping.
- Gustavsson, R. (2000). Interview with author, 23 Oct.
- Gustavsson, R. (2002a). Telephone interview with author, 9 Feb.
- Gustavsson, R. (2002b). *Afforestation in and near Urban Areas. Dynamic Design Principles and Long-Term Management Aspects. Landscape Laboratories as Reference and Demonstration Areas for Urban and Urban-Rural Afforestation*. E12. Reykjavik, Iceland. 2000-09-17, Park-og Landskabsserien. Forskningscentret for Sov & Landskab, Miljöministeriet, Denmark.
- Hammer, M. (2000). Interview with author, 20 Oct.
- Hansen, R. (1993). pp. 39–46.
- Hansen, R. and Stahl, F. (1993). *Perennials and their Garden Habitats*. Cambridge University Press, Cambridge.
- Hickson, M. (1994). Conversation with author, summer.
- Heintz, M., Hofmeister, A. and Schulz, A. (1999). Spontane Vegetation in Städten und auf Industriebrachen; and Eckhardt, A., Obermüller, C. and Tauscher, A. (1999). Umsetzungsmöglichkeiten planerischer Vorstellungen. In *Planerischer Umgang mit Spontanvegetation*. Students' project at the Technische Universitaet Berlin. Unpublished.
- Hitchmough, J. (1994). Natural Neighbours. *Landscape Design,* May.
- Hitchmough, J. (1995a). Perennial pleasures in the urban sward. *The Horticulturalist*, **4**, No, 2, April.
- Hitchmough, J. (1995b). Planting Possibilities. *Landscape Design*, July/Aug.
- Kendle, A. D. (2001). Telephone interview with author, July 2001.
- Kendle, A. D. and Rose, J. E. (2000). The aliens have landed! What are the justifications for 'native only' policies in landscape plantings. *Landscape and urban planning*, **47**, 19–31.
- Kendle, T. and Forbes, S. (1997). *Urban Nature Conservation*. Spon, London.
- King, M. *Nieuwe Bloemen, Nieuwe Tuinen*. Terra, Amsterdam. (1997).
- Kingsbury, N. (1994). In a Cornish Garden (Chyverton, Cornwall, UK). *The Garden*, March, 104.
- Kingsbury, N. (1998a). The New Border. *Landscape Design*, Dec./Jan.
- Kingsbury, N. (1998b). Prachtstauden in der Wiese. *Garten und Landschaft*, 9.
- Kingsbury, N. (2000). Broad Vision (Fairhaven Garden Trust, Suffolk, UK). *House and Garden*, June.
- Kingsbury, N. and Von Schoenaich, B. (1995). Learning from Nature. *The Garden*, June, 366–369.
- Knoll, H., Kowarik, I. and Langer, A. (1997). Natur-Park Südegelände. *Garten + Landschaft*, **7**.
- Köhlein, F. (1992). 'Ökologisch-botanischer Garten Bayreuth. *Gartenpraxis*, **3**.
- Koningen, H. (1995). The Heemparks of Amstelveen. *Proceedings of the Perennials for Urban Habitats conference*, Freising Germany, 19 July.
- Koningen, H. (1997). The Process of managing naturalistic parks and wildflower. *Public green paper for New Trends in Planting Design II conference*, Kew, 24, June.
- Koningen, H. (2001) Interview with author, 23 Oct.
- Kühn, N. (1999). Ökologie und Staudenverwendung. *Stadt und Grün*, **12**, 819–823.
- Kühn, N. (2000). Spontane Pflanzen für urbane Freiflächen. *G.u.L*, **4**, 11–13.
- Kühn, N. (2001). Ein Blick zurück. *Landschaftsarchitektur*, **7**, 12–14.
- Latz, P. (1987). Die Hafeninsel Saarbrüken. *Garten + Landschaft*, **11**, 42.
- Leccesse, M. (1995). Texas tour de force. *Landscape Architecture*, **9**, 68.
- Loidl-Reisch, C. (1986). *Der Hang zur Verwilderung*. Picus, Wien.
- Loidl-Reisch, C. (1989). Let things take their course. *Anthos*, **3,** 18.
- Lovejoy, A. (1998). *Naturalistic Gardening*. Sasquatch, Seattle.
- Luken, J. (1997). Valuing plants in natural areas. *Natural Areas Journal*, **14**, 295–299.
- Luz, H. (1996). Points of focus in the city landscape. In Leopold, R. (ed.) *Perennial Preview*. Perennial Perspectives Foundation, Amsterdam, p. 61.
- Luz, H. (2002). The principle of dominant species. *TOPOS*, **37**, 16–21.
- Maguire (1998). Sustainable Simplicity. *The Garden Design Journal,* summer.
- Martino, S. (2001). Telephone interview with author, 15 June.
- McKormick, C. (1991). We don't 'do' wetlands. *Landscape Architecture*, **10**, 88.

- -- Morrison, D. (2001). Interview with author, 23 April.
- -- Oudolf, P. (1994). Interview with author, July.
- -- Oudolf, P. (1998). Interview with author, Dec.
- -- Oudolf, P. and Kingsbury, N. (1999). *Designing with Plants*. Conran Octopus, London.
- -- Plenk, S (1998) *Staudenpflanzungen für öffentliche Freiräume.* Unpublished doctoral thesis, Universitität für Bodenkultur, Vienna.
- -- Pelz, P. (2001). Großflächige Staudenverwendung – ein Weg aus der Pflegekrise? *Landschaftsarchitektur*, **7**, 17–19.
- -- Plenk, S. (1999). Stauden in der Stadtlandschaft. *Zolltexte*, No. 32, June.
- -- Reinhard, W. (1994). *Wild Pflanzen für jeden Garten*. BLV München.
- -- Robinson, W. (1870). *The Wild Garden*. John Murray, London.
- -- Rupp, C. (1991). Natternkopf und Rosen. *Die Gartenkunst*, 102–110.
- -- Schmidt, C. (2000). *Silbersommer – ein Projeckt des Arbeitskreises Pflanzenverwendung*. Arbeitskreis Pflanzenverwendung, Bernberg.
- -- Schmidt, C. (2001). Telephone interview with author, 24 May.
- -- Schönfeld, P. (2000). Gemischte Staudenpflanungen im Test. *Garten under Landschaft*, **4**.
- -- Schönfeld, P. (2001). E-mail correspondence with author, 6 July.
- -- Schönfeld, P. (2001a). E-mail correspondence with author, 6 July.
- -- Schönfeld, P. (2001b). Staudenmischpflanzung 'Silbersommer'. *Veitshöchheimer Berichte* 56, Bayerische Landesanstalt für Weinbau and Gartenbau.
- -- Schönfeld, P. (2002). E-mail correspondence with author, 11 April.
- -- Simon, H. (1990). Herbaceous Plants in Germany. *Anthos*, **1**, 10.
- -- Stein, S. (1993). *Restoring the ecology of our own backyards*. Houghton Mifflin, Boston.
- -- Tasker, G. (1995). Planting the Future. *Landscape Architecture*, **7**, 55.
- -- Thompson, J. W. (1998). Desert Redux. *Landscape Architecture*, **6**, 60.
- -- Thompson, J. W. (2000). Vacant Lot Eden. *Landscape Architecture,* **1**, 44.
- -- Thompson, P. (1997). *The Self-Sustaining Garden*. Batsford, London.
- -- Toll, J. (2001). Telephone interview with author, 24 Nov.
- -- Tregay, R. and Gustavsson, R. (1983). *Oakwoods New Landscape.* SLU Alnarp.
- -- Van Sweden, J. (1998a). Conversation with author, Oct.
- -- Van Sweden, J. (1998b). Interview with author, Oct.
- -- Walser, U. (1994). Interview with author, June.
- -- Walser, U. (1998). Cited in Plenk (1998) *Staudenpflanzungen für öffentliche Freiräume.* Unpublished doctoral thesis, Üniversitität für Bodenkultur, Vienna.
- -- Weisse, R. (1994). Nature and Art. *Proceedings of the New Trends in Planting Design conference*, Kew.
- -- Wiley, K. (2000). Natural Selection. *The Garden*, July, 526.
- -- Wiley, K. (2001). Interview with author, February.
- -- Woodward, J.W. (1997). *Signature Based Landscape Design*. John Wiley, New York, p. 222.

Chapter 4

The dynamic nature of plant communities – pattern and process in designed plant communities

Nigel Dunnett

All planting design, if it is to be successful, must to some extent be a compromise between what is desirable (artistic or creative vision) and what is possible (scientific reality). Of course, technology can be employed to push the boundaries of what is possible on any given site, but this is often at a considerable environmental cost. The great advantage of an ecologically-informed basis to planting is that it has the potential to achieve full creative vision with relatively little site modification. Having said that, even the terms 'ecological' or 'naturalistic' planting encompass a broad spectrum of approaches, ranging from pure restoration ecology (which aims to reproduce as closely as possible a target or reference of semi-natural plant community) through to ornamental plantings that may be highly naturalistic but bear no resemblance to any naturally occurring plant communities. But most points on this nature ↔ art continuum (described fully in Chapter 3) can be characterised by having some degree of creativity associated with them: achieving a 'natural' quality is of great importance and they are therefore driven at least partly by visual principles. Even habitat creation approaches involve some form of species selection and arrangement to distil the essence of a plant community.

The scientific underpinning of the different approaches to planting that are described as ecological can also vary widely. At the most basic level, for most ecologically-informed schemes, scientific thinking will come in at the plant-selection level: making plant choices based upon the 'right plant, right place' philosophy. This concept is fundamental: plants are the great interpreters of site conditions and accurately reflect and mirror what might be minute changes in soil type, topography, climate and management. Choosing plants according to *fitness to site* reduces the need for drastic and resource-intensive site manipulation. Plants from habitats that share similar environmental constraints tend to share common traits or characteristics, and this is a tendency that can be fully exploited in planting design (Dunnett 1995). At one extreme, this may involve putting together cosmopolitan mixes of plants that are adapted to certain site conditions, but with no regard to their geographical origin. At the other extreme, plant selection may have a strong geographical element to it and may aim to reproduce the character of a plant community (rather than trying to copy it completely) that is suited to particular site conditions. This 'biogeographic' approach may use very attractive reference communities from widely separated countries (for example, the contemporary 'prairie' and 'steppe' perennial planting styles in Western Europe), or be much more tied into local or regional reference plant communities.

But the value of scientific understanding goes much further than simply helping to put an appropriate plant list together. Applying scientific principles can actually guide the way that plants are arranged to achieve a fully naturalistic effect, but one that also actually works as a functioning plant community into the indefinite future. Plant communities tend to show identifiable *patterns* in the way that different species are arranged, both horizontally and vertically – these are related not only to environmental variation but also to the characteristics of the plants themselves and how they interact. As well as patterns in space, 'natural' plant communities show patterns in time: they are dynamic and change over a range of timescales, as a result of ecological *processes*. These changes in space and over time are directly related to each other, and manifest themselves in the way that naturalistic vegetation appears and functions. In this light, it is no coincidence that one of the first ecological publications that opened people's eyes to the dynamic nature of plant communities (and one of the most influential ecological publications of the twentieth century) was titled *Pattern and Process in the Plant Community* (Watt 1947). The aim of this chapter is to identify principles that enable us to understand *patterns and processes in designed plant communities*. The aim is not to repeat standard ecological texts but instead to provide insights into how a designed ecological landscape might function over time and space. Where ecological concepts are introduced they are clearly linked to their implications in terms of how vegetation is designed, established and managed. It should also be stressed that it is assumed that readers will be familiar with basic scientific concepts relating to the requirements for successful plant growth and these will therefore not be considered here.

The dynamic nature of plant communities

Any acceptance of an ecologically-informed approach to planting must fully embrace the concept of change. The common perception that plant communities in the wild are relatively static, with little alteration in their composition or appearance from year to year, is of course a misconception: change is fundamental to the processes that operate within semi-natural plant communities. Indeed, it could be said that every ecological principle that a designer or manager needs to be aware of is related in some way to this dynamic nature of plant communities. Change is apparent and important in all timescales, and for our purposes can be broken down into three main categories:

- changes in the way a unit of vegetation develops over a single growing season or year (processes related to the different rates of development and performance of component species, and generally referred to as *phenological* change)
- changes in the abundance, performance or visual presence of component species, or the overall biomass of the plant community between different years (generally referred to as *fluctuations* or *cycles*)
- longer-term changes in the character, composition or type of vegetation (generally referred to as *successional* change).

Change also operates at all spatial scales, whether this be at the level of two plants side by side competing with each other for space or resources, or the interaction between two plant community or vegetation types (again linked to competition), or at the largest landscape scale where the manner in which different vegetation units are linked together can affect the way that plants and animals (including humans) can move around any given area. Processes operating at all these scales manifest themselves in the vertical and horizontal structure of vegetation, and in the very survival and long-term integrity and persistence of any given vegetation type.

Vegetation change is partly driven by the obvious changes within the lifecycles of individual plants and populations of plants – establishment, growth, maturity, reproduction and regeneration, senescence and death – but is equally tied up with physical environmental factors and constraints, competition and plant-plant interactions, and, crucially, with the nature of the landscape context and the surrounding vegetation types.

Ecologically-informed or 'sustainable' planting has been defined as designed vegetation that maintains its integrity over successive generations with minimal resource inputs (Dunnett 1995). In order to disentangle this statement, we will first consider factors that maintain the integrity of vegetation. That is, how do more than one species co-exist in any given unit of space, and continue to co-exist? The question of how biodiversity is promoted and maintained, and its importance to the functioning of ecosystems, has been one of the fundamental questions in plant ecology and is the subject of much current debate. It also has great relevance to the aesthetics and functioning of designed vegetation. We shall then consider patterns of vegetation change over different scales of time and space.

Competition and co-existence – how plants interact

The successful combination of different plant species is one of the main functions of planting design and landscape management. In traditional, horticultural-based planting design, aesthetic and functional considerations predominate: how do the different component species work together visually and how do they perform the tasks (such as dividing or filling spaces) for which they have been designed? Biological questions relating to how plants interact with each other and their surrounding environment as a community or unit of vegetation receive little or no consideration. This is mainly because the planting environment is generally modified to suit the requirements of standard landscape plants, whether this be through modification and importation of soils, fertilisation or irrigation, or through pruning and other maintenance operations, all of which entail an energy, labour and financial cost.

An ecological approach to landscape vegetation can be radically different. Aesthetic and functional considerations can be equally applicable, but questions of ecological compatibility and long-term dynamics are also a central concern. Rather than specifically arranging plants in their final desired positions, and subsequently ensuring that that is where they remain, ecologically-informed planting can be more akin to starting and managing a successional process. However, compared to the vast bulk of ecological literature on the functioning of semi-natural plant communities in the wild, there has been surprisingly little application of ecological ideas in terms of the way plant communities function in landscape or ornamental planting: indeed, the vast majority of mainstream ecologists would probably not recognise this as a valid subject of study. Because, as discussed in Chapter 2, many so-called ecological approaches to landscape planting tend to emphasise the visual connection with naturalistic vegetation rather than the underlying processes going on in that vegetation, there is a real need to develop ecological models that address questions relevant to the way that vegetation may develop as part of human designed landscapes. At the most immediate level, these questions relate to factors that enable plants to co-exist under the wide range of potential environmental and site conditions, and to the characteristics of plants that enable them to be compatible with other plants growing in their immediate vicinity. In other words, factors that promote greater diversity and species richness in vegetation.

Why is biodiversity and species richness important?

The intrinsic value of biodiversity is a fundamental tenet of nature conservation. At a basic level, because a range of co-existing species can exploit more resources than can a single species on its own, diverse mixtures tend to out-perform any single species in terms of total biomass production. However, the greatest claim for the value of biodiversity is that diverse plant communities are considered to be more stable and resistant to change than simple systems. There are two main theoretical arguments to back this assertion (McCann 2000). One explanation is based on the assumption that as long as species do not react in identical ways to environmental variation, the greater the number of different species present, the greater the number of different responses, and that, as a consequence, variation will be smoothed out at the total community level. The second general explanation is based upon the idea that at greater diversity there is a greater chance of having species present that are capable of functionally replacing important species that may be adversely affected by external pressures, and that can therefore maintain ecosystem functioning.

Having said this, there is remarkably little scientific research evidence to fully back these claims: theory is definitely ahead of experience. It is clear that monocultures and very simple systems of low diversity are vulnerable to environmental fluctuations. But it is also apparent that chasing high biological diversity for its own sake is also open to question – certainly the notion that the greater the number of species the better (i.e. the greater the biodiversity) is not necessarily tenable on ecological grounds. The main indicators of ecosystem health and functioning, such as productivity, carbon sequestration, water relations, nutrient cycling and storage, and resistance and resilience to environmental change, are primarily dictated by the performance of vegetation dominants (i.e. those species that contribute the greatest amount to the total biomass of the community) and these are likely to be relatively few in number (Grime 1998), perhaps only 20–25% of the total numbers in a plant community (Schwartz *et al.* 2000). So do the remaining species have any ecological value, or are they merely exploiting available niches without contributing significantly to the functioning of ecosystems? Whilst many argue that the loss of any species can have profound and unforeseen consequences, more evidence is required to answer this question fully on purely ecological grounds

(Purvis and Hector 2000).

Some of these arguments may seem rather obscure and irrelevant to designers and managers of landscape vegetation, especially when maintenance techniques can be used to remove the dynamic element from designed plantings. However, an understanding of the value of biodiversity in landscape vegetation, and the mechanisms that maintain it, become crucial if visually and ecologically-rich vegetation is to be created with reduced maintenance input. Given that promoting biodiversity is one of the often-quoted advantages of an ecological approach to landscape planting, what are the real benefits in the context of designed vegetation? These fall into a number of areas, as follows.

- *Aesthetics and visual pleasure.* The aesthetics of naturalistic vegetation is a complex topic and is explored in full in Chapter 11 by Anna Jorgensen. Whilst simple low-diversity plantings work well in more formal settings where there may be a requirement for neatness, order and predictability, there is little doubt that diverse naturalistic vegetation has its own beauty in other less-controlled contexts. This may partly be a result of a rich assemblage of textures, forms and colours, or that in more diverse mixtures there is a greater chance at any one time of components of the vegetation being at the height of their visual display. Diversity and richness are also one component of *complexity*: one of four key factors identified by Kaplan and Kaplan (1989) that are said to result in attractive natural landscape. Certainly, many scientists who may question the absolute ecological value of biodiversity also say that they value it purely on aesthetic grounds.
- *Stability: removing vulnerability from simple systems*. This argument has the closest affinity to pure ecological theory. Introducing greater diversity into landscape plantings could be seen as an insurance policy against the failure of one or more component species caused by environmental disturbances such as climatic extremes or disease.
- *Setting up succession.* One of the most distinctive features (and one that is often the most difficult to accept) of naturalistic or ecologically-informed plantings is their unpredictability. As illustrated later in this chapter, different species or components rise and fall in their abundance over time. This may be a result of environmental disturbance, but is also likely to be a result of differences in the length of lifecycles of different species, and a result of the outcome of competition between component species. Including a diversity of *functional groups* of plants within an initial mix, both facilitates succession and again insures continuity of the integrity of the vegetation. A functional group in ecological terms refers to organisms (that may not necessarily be related) which behave in the same way in response to environmental change, or perform the same ecological function. For example, in planting new naturalistic woodland, both pioneer and longer-term forest trees may be included in the same mix to enable long-term species replacement to occur.
- *Supporting other types of organisms.* In general, the greater the diversity of plant species in a unit of vegetation, the greater the diversity of other types of organism (e.g. birds and insects) that it supports, through the provision of a wider range of food sources or habitat opportunities (Knops *et al.* 1999). As discussed in Chapter 1, there is not necessarily any relationship between whether vegetation is composed of purely native species or a mix of natives and exotics in terms of the number of organisms it supports. What is of more importance is the vertical or horizontal structure

of the vegetation in terms of the number of layers it is composed of, or of interactions between vegetation types across boundaries or ecotones.

- *Filling up available niches.* It is a cliché that 'nature abhors a vacuum'. Bare ground rarely remains in that state for long. Most weed control in landscape plantings involves the removal of undesired plants from gaps between desired plants. These undesirable plants, or weeds, are simply filling space that is not being exploited by the intended species. This may partly be because the planted species have not expanded to fill the space, or it may be that the other species are filling ecological niches that the components of the designed system are leaving empty. For example, bare ground beneath shrubs quickly colonises with aggressive species tolerant of light shade. By filling niches at the outset through the inclusion of additional species, for example by ensuring full ground cover throughout the year, and promoting a multi-layered vegetation structure, the need for weed control in this situation is reduced.
- *Maximising the length of display: phenological change.* Filling a wide range of available ecological niches also enables the length of visual display to be increased through the exploitation of species with different phenologies (specific patterns of growth and flowering) within the same unit area of vegetation. An obvious example is that of spring flowering bulbs and herbaceous plants within a deciduous woodland that exploit the light conditions at ground level before the leaves on the dominant trees cast dense shade below. Similar principles operate in many plant communities. The idea of exploiting phenological change is discussed later in this chapter.

Competition between plants and promoting diversity in landscape vegetation

Promoting diversity in vegetation is primarily about reducing the vigour of potential dominant species – it is simply not enough to include a larger number of species in a mix – that greater diversity of species has to be resistant to competition and elimination from aggressive species. Dominant species are those that, in the absence of constraining factors, tend to eliminate other species through *competition*, resulting in low diversity or mono-specific stands of vegetation. It is easy to think of plants as being essentially passive organisms, unlike animals that actively hunt and compete with each other for food resources. However, where resources are abundant, plants can be equally competitive, fighting for the same unit of water, nutrient or light, and often in an aggressive manner, moving both roots, shoots and foliage to capture those resources. In this situation, in the absence of constraining factors, the best competitor for those resources will tend also to be the winner in terms of space, eventually excluding less competitive species. This pattern holds for fertile, productive 'high energy' environments, but tends to fall apart when certain constraining factors are introduced to a habitat or ecosystem. It is therefore of great importance to understand what the constraining factors are that can increase the diversity of plant communities (through reducing the vigour of aggressive species), and equally to understand how to put together plant mixes with complementary competitive abilities so that no one species tends to eliminate all others. The most appropriate basis for our purposes to help understand how plants interact with themselves and with their environment in this context is Grime's Plant Strategy Theory (CSR theory). The CSR model has proved to be a remarkably powerful tool for predicting how plants and other organisms react to changes within their environment (Dickinson and Murphy 1998). Whilst the model has been used in nature conservation management, there has been only very limited application to the functioning of non semi-natural vegetation (although, for example, see Hitchmough (1994)).

The basic starting point for CSR theory is that there are two fundamental sets of environmental threats that limit the growth and survival of aggressive, potentially dominant species: those that hinder the functioning of the plant, and thereby its growth rate and production of biomass, or those that physically damage or destroy plant tissues or biomass already present. The first set of threats is termed *stress* factors, involving constraints that affect the physiological processes of the plant. Such factors include extreme low or high temperatures, heavy shade, drought or low nutrient availability. The second set of threats is termed *disturbance* factors and include grazing, cultivation and trampling. Every habitat on the earth's surface can be defined by the relative combinations of stress and disturbance factors that operate on it. Over the course of evolutionary time, natural selection has resulted in plants that grow in environments subject to such pressures developing adaptations that aid their survival and regeneration in those environments. What is remarkable is that unrelated species growing in geographically separated parts of the world show very similar responses to the same sorts of environmental pressures or constraints. Grime (1979) has identified three basic responses or 'strategies' for survival in environments that are subject to the various combinations of high and low stress or disturbance (Table 4.1)

The combination of low environmental stress and disturbance is characteristic of typical 'productive' conditions (i.e. where nutrients and water are not in limited supply and regular physical damage is rare) that encourage vigorous plant growth and the dominance of aggressive species that has been previously discussed. Such conditions may be found, for example, on abandoned fertile agricultural fields, old unworked allotments or gardens, or unmanaged productive grasslands: species that are well adapted to these environments tend to be tall herbaceous perennials, have spreading clonal growth and rapid summer growth rates. They are extremely effective *competitors* and tend to dominate vegetation, crowding out less vigorous species and resulting in low-diversity stands. Common competitors, or C-strategists, of northern Europe include rosebay willowherb, *Chamerion angustifolium*, and stinging nettle, *Urtica dioica*. In effect, the competitive strategy is to maximise the capture of resources (light, water and nutrients) and to invest these in further growth to capture still more resources.

Environmental stress and disturbance tend to limit the ability of competitive species to dominate. Restricted availability of resources (stress) prevents

Table 4.1. Combinations of environmental stress and disturbance resulting in the three basic plant response strategies

		Intensity of stress *Low*	*High*
Intensity of disturbance	*Low*	Competitors (C-strategists)	Stress-tolerators (S-strategists)
	High	Disturbance-tolerators (R-strategists)	Uninhabitable

rapid growth (both in height and spread), thereby allowing species better adapted to growth under harsh conditions. Where resources are in very limited supply (i.e. in stressed environments), plants have evolved very different strategies. Rather than exhibiting rapid rates of growth, *stress-tolerant* species tend to be slow growing and evergreen, with specialised physiologies and often with modified protective tissues. Vegetation tends to be unproductive, relatively sparse and with low biomass. In such 'low energy systems' (Dickinson and Murphy 1998), plants tend to reproduce primarily through vegetative growth rather than by seed. In effect, the stress-tolerant strategy is one of thrift: to make the most of captured resources by sitting tight rather than investing in rapid growth to capture more resources. The nature of competition between plants in such environments has been the main area of controversy in the development of CSR theory. Examples of relatively stressed habitats include low-fertility acid or calcareous grasslands and the understory habitat of woodlands.

Environments where the disturbance or destruction of vegetation is a regular occurrence have given rise to plant strategies that either avoid or enable rapid recovery from that disturbance. Although naturally disturbed environments include screes and landslides, shingle beaches and sand dunes, the majority of disturbed environments are human-influenced (e.g. cultivated fields and agricultural grasslands). Plants adapted to such environments tend to show rapid growth rates and a reliance on reproduction through seed as well as vegetative expansion. For example, annuals are adapted to regular severe disturbance: their rapid growth rate enables them to take quick advantage of bare ground following a disturbance event, and copious seed production ensures their survival into future generations before another disturbance. Biennials and short-lived perennials are similarly adapted to disturbances on a longer time-cycle. In effect, the *disturbance tolerant* strategy or *ruderal* stategy (named after the roadside habitats from which the disturbance-tolerant life-history was first described) is an insurance policy: investing resources in mechanisms that ensure a rapid response to predictable patterns of disturbance (Figure 4.1).

The three main strategies listed above are extremes. In reality, most species exhibit combinations of traits from the different strategies depending upon the exact environmental conditions to which they are adapted. The crucial point is that, in terms of the maintenance of diversity in vegetation, low stress combined with low disturbance is not good, favouring the aggressive competitor species. Equally, combinations involving high intensities of stress and/or disturbance produce hostile conditions for plant growth, restricting vegetation to a limited number of highly adapted species. In general, greatest species diversity is promoted at moderate intensities of environmental stress and/or disturbance. This is easily illustrated with reference to various grassland types. The more species-rich semi-natural grassland types tend to occur on relatively low fertility, free-draining acid or calcareous soils (moderately stressed) or, in the case of traditional hay meadows, on relatively fertile sites subject to moderate disturbance (hay cutting and after-grazing). The addition of fertilisers (reducing stress) or the removal of maintenance (reducing disturbance) will result in these grasslands becoming dominated by aggressive competitive grasses, with an associated loss of diversity.

The CSR model can be readily adapted to aid understanding of how designed vegetation functions. In the majority of landscape contexts, 'stress' generally equates to a lack of availability of resources (water, light and nutrients) and, in particular, nutrient status. Disturbance can be equated to the frequency and intensity of mechanical maintenance operations. Figure 4.1 illustrates the relationship of a range of herbaceous

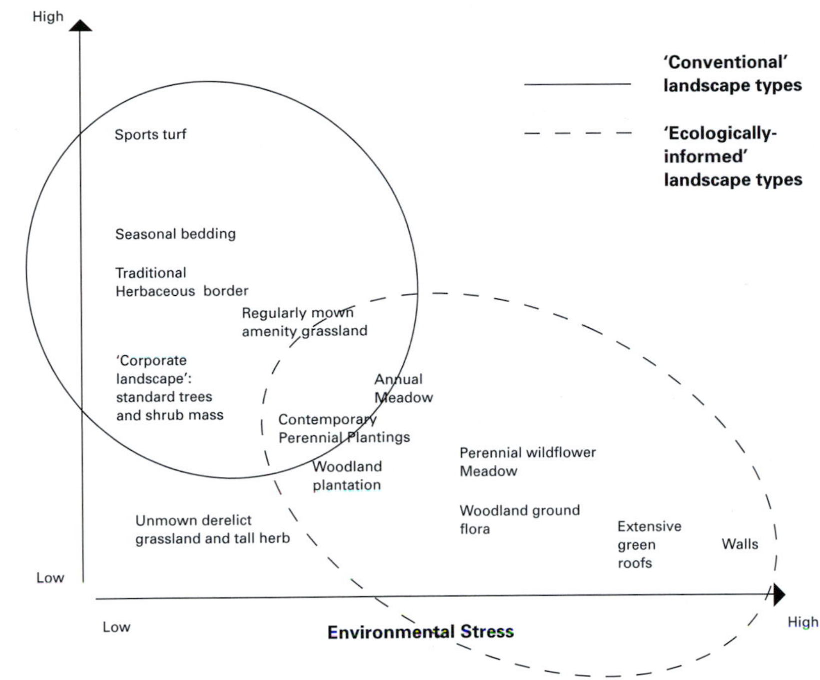

4.1
The relationship of urban landscape types to the intensity of environmental disturbance (maintenance operations) and/or environmental stress (site fertility)

landscape vegetations to the intensity of environmental stress and disturbance.

In general, the 'conventional' landscape types tend to cluster at the low-stress, high-maintenance corner of the diagram. Such landscape types prosper on sites with relatively moderate to high fertility, even though many of the component species growing in their native habitats are associated with low-moderate fertility. The desire of designers and horticulturists to achieve rapid plant growth has institutionalised the notion that highly cultivated plants 'need' fertile soils. Many stress-tolerant cultivated species will, however, grow well at very low-fertility levels. Conversely, the more ecologically-informed vegetation types tend to be suited to sites with moderate to low fertility and where maintenance input is also relatively moderate to low.

The value of CSR theory for ecologically-informed planting design lies in two areas:

1. *Plant selection*. Matching species with the same ecological strategies is one aspect of ensuring ecological compatibility with site conditions. For example, creating meadow-like herbaceous communities on fertile productive sites using stress-tolerant species from plant communities typical of low-nutrient free-draining calcareous soils (as is often recommended in the UK) will be unsuccessful without high management intervention. However, more vigorous species with a higher competitive element may be a far better option. As well as matching species to site, the CSR system also enables species matching within a planting mix so that competitive elimination with planted material is diminished and co-existence enhanced. A range of British native herbaceous species have been classified according to the CSR system (Grime *et al*. 1988). However, apart from some preliminary suggestions by Hitchmough (1994), there has been no attempt to date at classifying non-native species for landscape planting purposes.
2. *Vegetation management*. The CSR model provides an elegant framework for predicting the effect of different management regimes on the performance and diversity of vegetation. Again, there has to date been little application of the model away from semi-natural rural vegetation, although O. Gilbert (1989) has classified a range of urban vegetation types according to their predominant vegetation strategies. We return to this matter at the end of this chapter.

Patterns

We have seen how diversity can be maintained, through the promotion of the co-existence of species within a given area of space, but how does this actually work out on the ground? What is the visual and physical manifestation of diversity? Whilst the distribution of plants within more diverse

4.2
Examples of plants that exhibit different 'strategies':
(a) rosebay willowherb, *Chamerion angustifolium*, an aggressive, vigorous 'competitor';
(b) Juniper, *Juniperus communiis*, a slow growing, evergreen 'stress tolerator', growing in thin, free-draining soil and exposed conditions on a limestone pavement in North Yorkshire;
(c) vegetation adapted to hot arid conditions on Tenerife – a very different climate but the vegetation is also evergreen and slow growing; and
(d) Poppies, a typical 'ruderal' species, flowering on an abandoned cultivated field

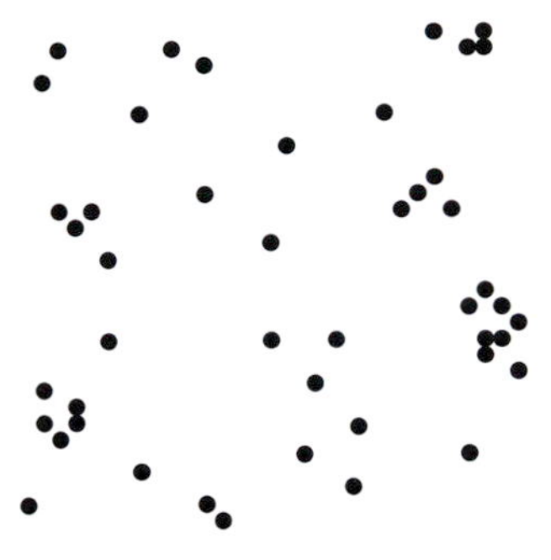

4.3
Aggregated plant distribution: hypothetical distribution of a species across an area of space showing patches of higher density imposed on a general distribution of lower density (modified from Greig-Smith (1964))

communities may, at first glance, appear to be random, ecological studies indicate that this is rarely the case. The distribution of a particular species may respond to (often small-scale) spatial changes in environmental factors such as soil moisture, concentration of particular nutrients, pH and so on, and the growth form of the plant (whether it spreads vegetatively or clonally by stolons or rhizomes, or how its seed is distributed), but it is also dependent upon competitive interactions with its neighbours. For example, a walk through a semi-natural woodland or forest reveals that many species occur in clumps or groups rather than as scattered individuals. This can be a result of many factors: some species form suckering clumps, others may have established at the same time as a result of some disturbance, such as a mature tree falling down to open up a glade. The main point here is that the plants are usually distributed in *patterns* and these patterns can be used as a basis for the design of diverse naturalistic plantings.

The detection of patterns of plant distribution has been an area of scientific study as well as for design inspiration. At the most basic level, distribution patterns within mixtures of plants can be described according to how *aggregated* and *segregated* the component species are (Pielou 1961). The degree of aggregation of a species is an indication of the amount of association of individuals or groups of individuals of that species. In effect, it is a measure of the non-randomness of the distribution of the species. In general, most species show some form of aggregation or clumping (see Figure 4.3). This may vary from a very loose association to a dense massing.

There has been a tendency to invest these naturalistic patterns with an almost mystical quality, presenting them as a set of rules that, if plants are

Table 4.2. Possible causes of plant distribution patterns

Distribution pattern	Possible cause
Singly or small clusters	Exacting requirements for regeneration from seed rarely met in the habitat. Spread by rhizomes is strictly limited. May indicate sensitivity to intense herbivory. Surrounding species may suppress expansion. Possible allelopathic effects
Larger cluster and groups	Species exhibit limited rhizomatous growth from initial colonisation or establishment centres. Indication of competitive balance within a habitat. Possible artefact of early successional stages, reflecting distribution patterns when habitat was originally more open to invasion
Patches	Potential reflection of patchiness of the environment, for example fluctuations in soil characteristics, or previous disturbance patterns. Possible early successional stage, indicating phase of expansion of competitors
Extensive stands	Species generally have rhizomatous growth habit, stoloniferous spread, competitively excluding other species. Possible artefact of low disturbance and environmental stress. Very common in competitors and stress-tolerant competitors

from another in terms of visual display. But other changes take place over periods of more than one growing season. These are of direct relevance to the design and management of naturalistic vegetation, partly because they affect the way that the vegetation may be managed, and partly because they highlight again the point that ecologically-informed design and management of vegetation is about setting up a system that is inherently dynamic and to some extent unpredictable into the long term. We can recognise two types of longer-term dynamic change: *fluctuations* or cycles, whereby species composition may change but the overall character of the vegetation remains relatively constant, and *successional* change, whereby the actual character and type of vegetation may change over time.

Cycles and fluctuations

There have been surprisingly few long-term studies that have monitored changes in the composition of plant communities over more than three to five years. As can be seen from Figure 4.7, the performance of a species over such a period really gives very little information about what it is actually doing over periods of decades. Those longer studies that have been carried out tend to confirm what most gardeners know by experience: plants tend to have good years and bad years, determined primarily by weather conditions, and perennial plants (both woody and herbaceous) tend to become over-mature and require rejuvenation in due course.

Figure 4.7 is taken from the Bibury dataset, one of the longest continuous studies of herbaceous vegetation in the wild, which is taken from productive grassland vegetation on a roadside verge in the south of England. The figure shows the yearly performance of a large stand of rosebay willowherb (*Chamerion angustifolium*), a vigorous tall perennial 'competitor' that forms large spreading clumps that tend to exclude other species, and which makes a dramatic display of tall pink flower spikes in mid to late summer.

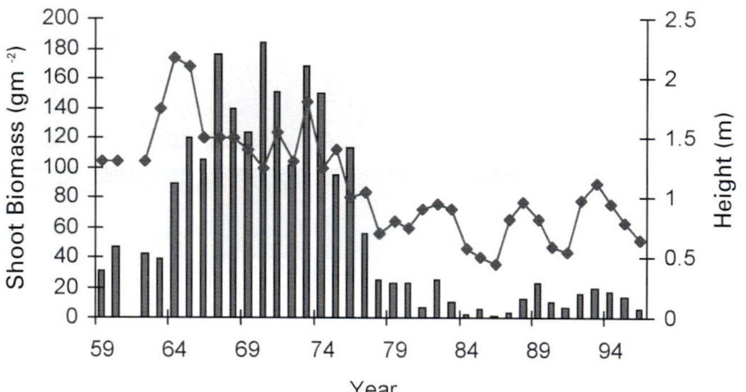

4.7
Comparison of maximum shoot height (♦) and shoot biomass of rosebay willowherb over the period 1959–1996 in the Bibury road verges. No measurements were made in 1961 (from Dunnett and Willis (2000))

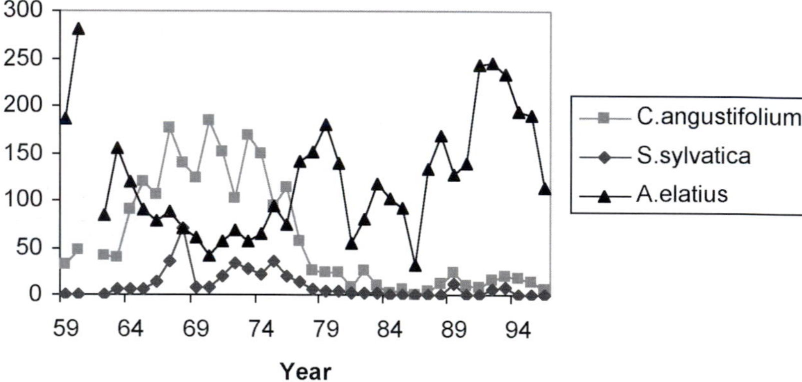

4.8
Comparison of the performance of *C.angustifolium, Arrhenatherum elatius* and *Stachys sylvatica* over the period 1959–1996 in the Bibury road verges. No measurements were made in 1961 (from Dunnett and Willis (2000))

Figure 4.7 indicates that there is considerable variation in both the height and bulk (biomass) of this species from year to year. The main factor determining these changes (in the absence of changes in management) is yearly differences in weather patterns. But there is also dramatic longer-term change, with a period of peak performance over the 12 years from 1964 to 1976. This rise and fall (which may be cyclical) is typical of the behaviour of many herbaceous perennials. Such processes in vegetation are again generally the result of the influence of dominant species going through four distinct phases (Watt 1947): pioneer (establishment of a species), building (growth to peak biomass),

4.9
Succession on railway sidings abandoned in Sheffield – grassland is being invaded by scrub and birch woodland

mature and degeneracy (breakdown of dominance and invasion by other competing species).

Whilst the increase in biomass and the lateral extent of the stand can be readily explained in terms of rapid clonal extension and elimination of subordinate species – *C.angustifolium* has a high potential for dominance (Grime 1973) – the sudden decline and break-up of the stand are less easy to interpret. One explanation for the change in performance of perennials in this way may be a progressive decline in vigour of the stand as resources are accumulated in living and dead components of the biomass, resulting in reduced nutrient supply (Watt 1947). Other explanations may include responses to extreme weather (such as drought), herbivory, allelopathy or disease.

The influence of such fluctuations is not limited to the individual species, but is played out through interactions with other species in the same community. Figure 4.8 illustrates the interplay of *C.angustifolium* with other components of the system at Bibury. *Arrhenatherum elatius* (False Oat Grass) is another 'competitor' and clearly benefits from the collapse in vigour of *C.angustifolium*, but the performance of *Stachys sylvatica* (Hedge Woundwort), which grows on the shady edges of the stand of *C.angustifolium* mirrors the performance of the willowherb.

There are very few such studies that demonstrate interactions between species over extended periods, but they generally indicate the major influence of dominant species on the behaviour of subordinates, and the overriding effect of climatic factors in causing yearly fluctuations in the abundance of different species (Watt 1971).

Succession

Succession is one of the fundamental concepts in ecology that is highly relevant to landscape design and management; indeed, it could be argued that a large proportion of landscape management operations are about preventing, promoting or diverting succession (although they are not often described in such terms). Succession differs from the cyclical changes and fluctuations described above in that it involves *directional* change in vegetation. Whilst cycles and fluctuations imply some sort of change within a defined vegetation type (i.e. although the precise species composition may change within a grassland, the vegetation remains as grassland), successional change implies a change not only in species composition, but also in vegetation character (i.e. grassland changes to woodland) (Figure 4.9).

In landscape terms, succession can be regarded as a force, constantly driving vegetation to alter its state, both in character but also species composition from the initial starting point. But just what is the end point? Classic succession theory suggests that in any given site, the progress of successional change can be predicted to a more or less predetermined outcome or 'climax' vegetation that is suited to a particular climate zone, with increasing species diversity, and structural complexity of vegetation as succession proceeds. However, this concept has been largely discredited and most ecologists recognise that 'mature' vegetation is far more dynamic, with many different mature species assemblages occurring in any climatic region, and that the mature vegetation is in a constant state of flux, subject to cycles and fluctuations caused by external disturbances (Burrows 1990). For our purposes, a far better model for succession is to consider that vegetation reaches an equilibrium over time with the balance of environmental stress and disturbance factors that are operating on that site. The further away from that equilibrium that the vegetation is, the greater is the energy input required to keep it in that state. For example, maintaining short amenity grassland in lowland England requires far greater inputs of energy than maintaining deciduous woodland. This model has important implications because it suggests that the outcome of succession can be manipulated by altering the intensity of stress and disturbance operating on the system. It also suggests that succession itself can be used to guide vegetation to a state that is 'sustainable' (i.e. on any given site it can be maintained with minimal resource inputs).

Although succession has been researched and discussed in depth for many decades, the application of this knowledge has been limited in natural conservation management (Luken 1990), and has certainly been rarely discussed in urban amenity landscape management. However, for ecologically-informed landscape vegetation, a succession-based approach provides a rational basis for creative and informed management. Luken (1990), summarising succession-based management models developed in the context of restoration ecology, proposed three main components of succession management: *designed disturbance, controlled colonisation* and *controlled species performance*. These terms are equally applicable to the management of naturalistic landscape plantings.

Designed disturbance refers to those factors that initiate new successions and vegetation

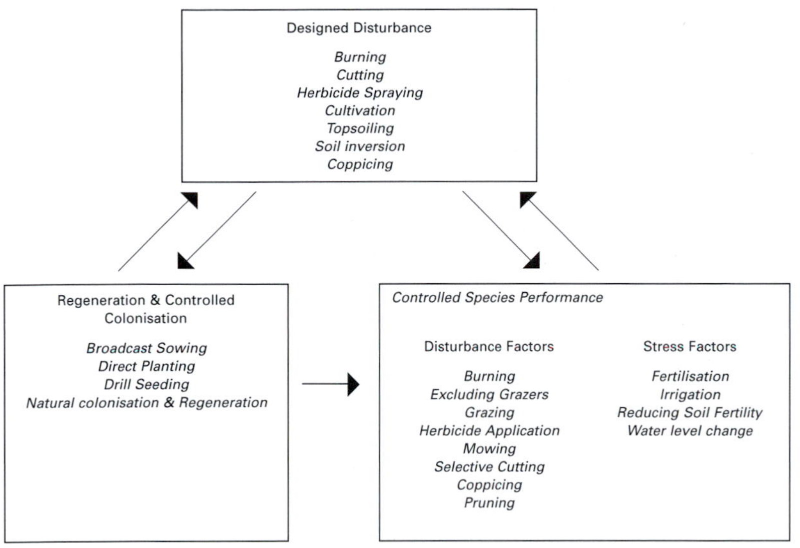

4.10
A succession-based model for the management of designed urban vegetation (arrows indicate sequential operations). Adapted from Luken, 1990

development, set back or slow down succession, or maintain cyclical change, i.e. periodic rejuvenation. In essence, designed disturbance is an artificial or human-induced operation that promotes suitable conditions for the establishment of new species or individuals on to a site. In most instances this will involve the removal of competition from existing vegetation and probably the creation of patches or areas of bare ground for seeding or planting. Some operations that can be used to create designed disturbance are listed in Figure 4.10. In effect, designed disturbances create or eliminate sites where succession can be initiated.

Controlled colonisation involves the manipulation of plant species' availability and establishment. Figure 4.10 lists operations that either directly introduce propagules of desired species, or selectively encourage certain species to establish or regenerate from species and propagule pools already present. It is clear that where non-native or ornamental species are to be included in a planting scheme, then artificial introduction is necessary. But even where vegetation is to be based on common native species, natural colonisation on its own is rarely satisfactory, partly because of the timescales involved and also because the resultant vegetation is likely to be composed predominantly of weedy ruderal species, at least in the short to medium term. Controlled colonisation and establishment increases or decreases the availability of plant species, according to whether they are desirable or not.

Controlled species performance includes techniques that increase or decrease the growth and reproduction of plant species to shape both the composition and form of the vegetation over time. We can relate the operations listed in Figure 4.10 that differentially control species performance to Plant Strategy Theory, discussed earlier in this chapter. Some of these factors, such as increasing or reducing soil fertility, or controlling water availability, differentially affect the rate of growth of species and can be termed *stress* factors, whilst others, such as grazing, mowing and pruning, selectively remove or damage plant biomass and, therefore, can be termed *disturbance* factors.

Figure 4.10 illustrates these three components as an integrated model for the management of landscape and garden plantings. Examples of applications of this model are given in James Hitchmough's chapter on herbaceous plantings (Chapter 6) and also more specifically in Hein Koningen's chapter on the creative management of ecological plantings (Chapter 10). The arrows in Figure 4.10 indicate direct sequential steps. Each component may also be repeated through time (for example, regular coppicing of woody plants or annual hay cutting of perennial meadows).

References

-- Burrows, C. J. (1990). *Processes of Vegetation Change*. Unwin Hyman, London.
-- Dickinson, G. and Murphy, K. (1998). *Ecosystems.* Routledge, London.
-- Dunnett, N. (1995). Harnessing Anarchy. *Landscape Design,* Nov., 25–29.
-- Dunnett, N. and Willis, A. (2000). The dynamics of *Chamanerion angustifolium* over a 38-year period in road verges at Bibury, Gloucestershire. *Plant Ecology,* **148**, 43–50.
-- Greig-Smith, P. (1964). *Quantitative Plant Ecology.* Butterworths, London.
-- Grime, J. P. (1987). Dominant and subordinate components of plant communities: implications for succession, stability and diversity. In Gray, A. J., Crawley, M. J. and Edwards, P. J. (eds) *Colonisation, Succession and Stability*. Blackwell Scientific Publications, Oxford, pp. 413–428.
-- Hansen, R. and Stahl, F. (1993). *Perennials and their garden habitats.* Cambridge University Press, Cambridge.
-- Hitchmough, J. D. (1994). Natural Neighbours. *Landscape Design*, **229**, 16–24.
-- Kaplan, R. and Kaplan, S. (1989). *The Experience of Nature.* Cambridge University Press, Cambridge.
-- Knops, J. M. H. *et al.* (1999). Effects of plant species richness on invasion dynamics, disease outbreaks, insect abundance and diversity. *Ecological Letters,* **2**, 286–294.
-- Luken, J. (1990). *Directing Ecological Succession.* Chapman & Hall, London.
-- McCann, K. S. (2000). The diversity and stability of ecosystems. *Nature*, **405**, 228–233.
-- Pielou, E. C. (1961). Segregation and symmetry in two-species populations as studied by nearest neighbour relationships. *Journal of Ecology*, **49**, 255–269.
-- Purvis, A. and Hector, A. (2000). Getting the measure of biodiversity. *Nature*, **405**, 212–219.
-- Schwartz, M. W. *et al.* (2000). Linking biodiversity to ecosystem functioning: implications for conservation ecology. *Oecologia*, **122**, 297–305.
-- Tilman, D., Knops, J., Wedin, D., Reich, P., Ritchie, M. and Siemann, E. (1997). The influence of functional diversity and composition on ecosystem processes. *Science*, **277**, 1300–1302.
-- Watt, A. S. (1947). Pattern and process in the plant community. *Journal of Ecology,* **35**, 1–22.
-- Watt, A. S. (1971). Factors controlling the floristic composition of some plant communities in Breckland. In *The scientific management of animal and plant communities for conservation.* Blackwell Scientific Publications, Oxford.

Chapter 5

A methodology for ecological landscape and planting design – site planning and spatial design

Darrel Morrison

The native landscape of the United States is richly diverse, both botanically and aesthetically. Tall-grass prairies with billowing waves of grasses and colourful wildflowers once covered millions of acres of the Midwest. Longleaf pine savannas with an incredibly rich ground layer of grasses, ferns and flowers blanketed some 92 million acres of the southeastern coastal plain. Majestic mixed forests of hardwoods and conifers covered much of the northeast; diverse desert vegetation grew in the arid southwest. Today, just tiny remnants of the pre-settlement landscape that have been protected by public agencies and private non-profit organisations, such as The Nature Conservancy, remain. These remnants remind us of our rich botanical heritage.

There has been, early in the twentieth century, and again for the last 25 years, an undercurrent within landscape design in the US which draws on these diverse natural plant communities for both inspiration and information. In the early twentieth century there was a movement to develop a landscape approach based on the native plant communities of the region. Jens Jensen was perhaps the most widely recognised practitioner of this approach. Born in Denmark in 1861, he emigrated to the US in his twenties, and practiced extensively in the Midwest from 1890 until his death in 1951. In the Chicago park system, and in a wide range of other public and private commissions, he became well known both for his masterful spatial designs and for his increasing reliance on the Midwestern prairies, savannas and forests as models for design.

He was careful to clarify that his work was not copied from nature, but was inspired by it.

In 1929, Dr Edith Roberts and Elsa Rehmann co-authored a book entitled, *American Plants for American Gardens*. Dr Roberts, a plant ecologist, and Ms Rehmann, a landscape architect, taught at Vassar College, and in their book discussed how a variety of eastern US plant communities could be used as a basis for designing gardens and landscapes that would be distinctively 'of the place' and also ecologically sound.

Other landscape architects pursued similar approaches during the first three decades of the twentieth century. Then the economic depression of the 1930s, followed closely by the Second World War, contributed to a decline in this approach.

It was only after the first Earth Day celebration in 1970 that the concept of using native plant communities as a basis for design re-emerged as a sizeable undercurrent in American landscape architecture. That undercurrent has been strengthened, at least in parts of the country, as a response to environmental concerns, such as water shortages and the excessive use of chemicals and energy in maintaining mowed and manicured landscapes. It is also reinforced by a desire to depart from predictable, generic landscapes that have destroyed regional uniqueness, and which are often aesthically dull.

Clearly, because of the presence – or dominance – of humans and human activities in the designed and managed landscape, it is unrealistic to believe that we can recreate a pre-settlement landscape over extensive areas. What we can do is to reconnect our designed landscapes with the natural heritage of the region and thereby begin to reinforce or restore regional landscape character. Further, the cumulative effect of many designed landscapes being based on the naturally evolved landscapes of the region can be a more 'sustainable' environment, less consumptive of water and energy resources than traditional ones; with the additional benefit of reintroducing many native species which have been eliminated from traditionally designed landscapes. Further, if a number of individual sites which are designed in this way are interconnected, they can begin to provide a network of 'corridors' through which wildlife can move.

In this chapter, we will discuss, first, traditional approaches to American landscape design as a basis for comparison with this alternative approach. Then, we will look at different degrees of departure from those current practices, in an effort to design more ecologically sound landscapes; and then we will look at a process that might be followed. Finally, a case study design project in the southeastern US Piedmont region will be presented. It should be noted that the emphasis in this chapter is on the use of native plant communities in landscape design, building upon the incredibly rich and underexploited resources that the US possesses in terms of its regionally distinct vegetation. This approach can be readily adapted for use elsewhere in the world, again drawing inspiration from appropriate native plant communities.

The use of native plant communities as a basis for a locally appropriate and distinctive landscape design provides a very strong underlying philosophy for plant selection. However, as discussed in Chapter 1, and in other chapters, naturalistic vegetation may, in certain contexts, include non-native species as well as native. This is perhaps most relevant in those regions where the native flora is limited (e.g. the UK, which has a much reduced native flora compared to continental Europe), or where cultural modification of the landscape has a far longer history than in the US. In these instances there may simply not be an appropriate native plant community type to provide for, say, a colourful flowering display in late summer in a prominent position in an urban park. The use of non-native species in ecological settings has been contentious (Chapter 1 discusses the issue in some depth), but in urban contexts the use of non-invasive exotic species in naturalistic vegetation can go some way to promoting a less resource-intensive public landscape whilst at the same time satisfying public demand for attractive plantings. The site-planning process described later in this chapter can be applied equally to native-only or to mixed plantings.

Current practices

Planting design, or composition with plants, has two basic components: plant selection and plant placement. A discussion of these two activities, as they are most often practiced in traditional landscape design, together with a summary analysis of the visual effects that result from them, is given below.

Plant selection

The primary criteria affecting the selection of plant species in traditional landscape practice are the following.

- Aesthetic characteristics, such as the form, texture, and seasonal colour characteristics, for example the colour of flowers, fruits or bark.
- Functional capabilities, such as the plant's usefulness at providing shade, windbreaking, visual screening or framing, and erosion and sedimentation control.
- Environmental tolerance, including hardiness, sun, shade and wind tolerance, and, increasingly, the ability to withstand the effects of soil, water and air pollution. Water requirements have typically been given only secondary consideration, until recently, because of the relative ease and low cost of providing supplemental water to plants needing more water than might naturally occur as precipitation in a particular region.
- Commercial availability is a prerequisite for any particular plant species being incorporated into a designed landscape. Because of its efficiency, the common practice has been for large nurseries to mass-produce hundreds of plants of a limited number of species that are well known (or well-marketed) and 'reliable', often because of wide environmental amplitude ('it'll grow anywhere'). These abundantly produced plants include a mix of native and exotic species, as well as hybrids and cultivars. It is unusual for growers to differentiate between these plants on the basis of origin, or to provide such information to buyers in catalogues or in nursery sales areas.

As a result of these influences on plant selection, there is little tendency in traditional landscape design to select a native species over a non-native, or exotic species, so long as it meets the criteria established for size, form, colour and function.

Following traditional plant selection practices, ornamental trees and shrubs that have conspicuous flowers, fruits and/or autumn colour, or that are evergreen, are the most likely selections. Furthermore, the same showy species are planted across broad geographic areas. In terms of general landscape treatment in the US, the most ubiquitous species are the ground-cover species. For example, the most often selected ground-covers in the US are a limited number of evergreens; for example English ivy (*Hedera helix* and its many varieties), periwinkle (*Vinca minor*) and Japanese spurge (*Pachysandra terminalis*), all of which were introduced to North America from Europe or Asia over a century ago and which are now being found to be invasive. The most widespread ground-cover plants in the traditionally designed landscape are the lawn grasses, estimated to occupy over 30 million acres in the US. With a few exceptions, these are exotic and/or hybridised species, typically requiring supplementary water (and fertiliser and pesticides) to provide the uniform dark green carpet that has been promoted as the 'ideal' cared-for landscape in this country.

Since neither the evergreen ground-covers nor

the turf grasses typically provide conspicuous flowers, the element of 'seasonal colour' is characteristically supplied through the introduction of spring-flowering bulbs and summer annuals. In commercial and corporate landscapes particularly, these 'seasonal colour' plantings are typically dug up and replaced several times a year.

Plant placement

Just as plant species diversity is vastly simpler in the traditionally designed environment than in the naturally evolved landscape, so are distribution patterns. Plantings may be geometric, reflecting either the geometry of building and urban settings within which they occur or a designer's wish to form architectonic spaces with plants. Or plantings may be consciously randomised. The latter approach, whilst often considered 'naturalistic', is rarely 'natural'. For example, it may take the form of a single-species tree planting set in either a lawn or an extensive evergreen ground-cover bed, without the structural components of middlestory or edge vegetation.

Where feasible, existing trees, fortunately, are often preserved and incorporated into designed landscapes, sometimes at great expenditure of money and effort. But even in these cases, simplification is typical, with the naturally occurring understory and ground layer plants removed from beneath the trees to be replaced with the 'cleaner' look of lawns, mulch beds or single-species ground-cover plantings.

Landscape maintenance/management

Once a landscape planting is installed, the subsequent management has traditionally had the effect of 'freezing' the composition, minimising change over time. Whilst the natural growth of trees is permitted, shrubs are often trimmed to give them a more compact architectural form. And, of course, lawns are kept at a perpetual height of approximately two inches (5cm) through frequent mowing. The species composition of traditionally designed landscapes is rarely permitted to change, with any invading plants considered 'weeds'. Woody invaders are often mechanically removed by pulling or cutting; broad-leaved herbaceous invaders in lawns or mulched areas are typically killed with herbicides.

The combined effect of prevailing plant selection, placement and management practices in the designed landscape is an ordered park-like appearance with smooth, deep-green lawn interspersed with predominately dense, dark-green shrubs planted as hedges, blocks or masses; and symmetrically shaped specimen trees planted either as individuals or in rows or in 'informal' groupings, often of a single species and size. The only noticeable changes in this landscape are the changing flower and foliage colours and, in some cases, the changing display of bulbs and annuals.

Alternatives to current practice

A variety of approaches to the use of ecologically-informed vegetation and plant communities may be taken when designing landscapes. Along a continuum, which goes from the most conservative (i.e. the most like currently-practiced traditional approaches) to the most complete departure from them, the following steps can be identified:

- substitution of native species for traditionally used exotics
- diversification of ground layer plantings
- stylisation/abstraction of native plant communities.

Substitution

This term implies a traditional approach to plant placement, i.e. forming spaces with plants and meeting functional criteria such as shading, windbreaking or the screening of views. But instead of selecting individual plant species almost solely on the basis of size, form, colour, and texture, one selects from an appropriate native community of plants those which can be expected to meet the aesthetic and/or functional criteria that have been established.

For most situations, there are native species that meet such criteria. Further, because plants of a particular plant community grow in association with each other in nature, they tend to appear harmonious when they are placed together in a designed landscape. Perhaps most importantly, they provide a link with the natural history of a site, and perpetuate or even intensify the local or regional identity, thereby counteracting the 'place-less' syndrome that has afflicted so many designed landscapes in US cities and suburbs.

The application of a 'substitution' approach on an upland site in the southeastern US Piedmont could draw on the upland Piedmont slope forest community for plants in a variety of sizes and forms. For example, the evergreen, low-growing herb, green-and-gold (*Chrysogonum virginianum*) could be used as a ground cover in a semi-shady area, instead of the commonly used, exotic, periwinkle. Shadblow (*Amelanchier arborea*), redbud (*Cercis canadensis*), flowering dogwood (*Cornus florida*), and sourwood (*Oxydendrum arboreum*) could make up the sub-canopy layer. Shrubs such as sparkleberry (*Vaccinium arboreum*), sweetshrub (*Calycanthus floridus*) and maple-leaved viburnum (*Viburnum acerifolium*), could make up much of the shrub layer under a canopy of white oak (*Quercus alba*), black gum (*Nyssa sylvatica*), mockernut hickory (*Carya tomentosa*) and American beech (*Fagus grandifolia*). As suggested above, the arrangement or placement of plants using the 'substitution' approach is not necessarily different from that in traditional design and, hence, may range from formal geometric arrangements to more informal, organic ones.

Diversification of ground layer plantings

A next logical step along the continuum of using native plants or native plant communities in the designed landscape is to depart from single-species ground-cover plantings by planting a diversity of species in mixes which are matched with the soil/light/moisture characteristics in different zones. Using the upland Piedmont landscape example again, a semi-shaded area might be planted with a mix of bracken fern (*Pteridium aquifolium*), fire pink (*Silene virginica*), bluestar (*Amsonia tabernaemontana*) and blue-eyed grass (*Sisyrinchium atlanticum*). In deeper shade, a ground layer mix might combine Christmas fern (*Polystichum acrostichoides*) with woods phlox (*Phlox divaricata*), wild geranium (*Geranium maculatum*) and hepatica (*Hepatica nobilis*). With mixed plantings such as these, the likelihood of a climatic extreme or disease or insect pest eliminating all the plants in the ground-cover bed is greatly reduced. Additionally, a wider array of plant species simply provides greater potential for aesthetic richness with a range of textures, colours, and flowering times, than does a single-species planting.

The practice of ground-layer diversification can range from combining two or three species in a few square feet to meadow-like plantings of 20 or more species replacing large lawn-areas. As in any planting design, the two components of this process are: the selection of species and designating their placement at the time of planting.

Species selection has both an ecological and an aesthetic basis. Ecologically, of course, it is essential that each species be placed in the appropriate soil/light/moisture environment. Aesthetically, colour and texture relationships, in particular, can be planned to create specific visual effects. Selecting from ground-layer species that occur together naturally in a native community, one may select analogous, or closely related, colours, as in the woods phlox-wild geranium-hepatica example mentioned earlier, with its pale blue-violet-pink flower colour combination. Or one could select complementary, contrasting colours, as with the yellow-flowered green-and-gold in combination with the blue-flowering crested iris (*Iris cristata*). In selecting plant textures, fine, fern and grass-like textures provide refinement and a soft appearance, creating a good backdrop for more dramatically textured species. An example of this might be the fine New York fern (*Thelypteris noveboracensis*) in a mass, with the bold, broad foliage of Mayapple (*Podophyllum peltatum*) as a contrasting texture.

In determining ground-layer plant placement patterns, the method of planting comes into consideration, i.e. whether seedlings will be individually placed or seed will be sown. The planting of propagated plants lends itself to shaded woodland plantings or to sunny borders. Seeding is best adapted to larger expanses, such as meadow-like plantings. The advantages of planting seedlings include the control one has over the placement of individual plants, and the competitive advantage such plants may have over weed species whose seed is in the soil. The disadvantages of using seedlings include higher costs and, in some cases, the limited availability of plants in the quantities required. Seeding has the advantage of being relatively inexpensive and often leads to a more natural distribution of plants, but has the disadvantage of being slow to establish and is therefore more vulnerable to weed invasion.

When starting with propagated plants, a useful model is the mingled 'drift' pattern which occurs so abundantly in naturally evolving landscapes. Using the 'drift' approach, an individual species is planted in a higher density in the centre of any particular group, but with more widely spaced individuals trailing away from the group. As one species diminishes in density, a second or third species increases. Thus, dynamic interactions between species are created. Because of the potential for the reproduction of the various species, open spaces may be left within mixed ground-layer plantings, just as there are open spaces on the natural forest floor. Up to a third or half of areas designated for woodland ground layer may be permitted to remain open initially, thereby providing an opportunity for the originally installed plants to spread into those spaces.

The alternative of planting by seeding, as noted above, lends itself particularly well to the planting of sunlit meadow-like communities. Using this technique, pattern is achieved through varying the composition of seed mixes in adjacent zones, leading to contrasts in colour and texture at a broad scale.

In such plantings, as in the natural prairies after which they are modelled, grasses play an important role, functionally and visually. They are effective at erosion control, with a network of deep roots beneath the soil and persistent leaves above the ground that intercept rainfall. Visually, they provide a linear filter of the broad-leafed and showy forbs or wildflowers with which they are planted. Further, their foliage tends to remain standing through the winter, providing structure in the winter landscape, often with the added benefit of rich, warm colour, as in the copper colour of various Andropogon species, and the gold and tan of switchgrass (*Panicum virgatum*) and Indiangrass (*Sorghastrum nutans*). Grasses might well constitute 80% of the seed mix in a meadow planting, with the remaining 20% comprised of a variety of forbs or broad-leafed wildflowers matched with the micro-environment.

In determining seed distribution patterns, zones that tend to 'flow' most closely emulate the patterns in natural landscapes, and relate well to undulating topography. In adjacent zones, there will be some variation of species, both grasses and forbs, but there should usually be some continuity of species between zones in order to present a soft 'continuum' effect as opposed to clearly defined lines between zones.

There are no hard-and-fast rules determining how many different species should be incorporated in a particular area of meadow/grassland planting, but some guidance can be drawn from earlier grassland studies. Most of the research on this community type has been done in the US Midwest, where a typical species density of 40–70 species per acre has been observed. By far the greatest proportion of the vegetation is made up of a small number of grass species, with the rest comprised of a large number of forb species in relatively small quantities. Translated into seed-mix terms for a zone within a meadow/grassland planting, this could suggest three or four grass species making up 80% of the mix, and 10 to 15 forb species constituting 20% of the mix. An adjacent zone might have a similar ratio of grasses to forbs, with, say, two of the same grass species carrying over into it and five to eight of the same forb species, whilst there may be a greatly reduced grass component in zones where a high-intensity floristic display is required. There would logically be less continuity between zones if there were sharp environmental differences between the zones, for example a low, poorly drained area bordered by an upland slope.

In implementing mixed grass-and-forb plantings, the seed of all grasses and forbs for a particular zone may be mixed and planted, either through broadcasting or drilling. Or the grasses may be drilled mechanically, and the forbs broadcast in 'drifts' within the zone. The second option provides a greater opportunity for controlling the distribution of forbs, and perhaps more closely emulating natural distribution patterns

Stylisation/abstraction of native plant communities

The next step along the continuum of design activity using native plant species is to incorporate stylised or abstracted versions of native communities as design elements. Whilst the design of such groupings is based on the botanical and aesthetic composition of naturally evolving communities, they will usually be abstractions of them, simpler in species composition and smaller in area than the natural models. Yet they will contain the most important species of those communities, ecologically and aesthetically, and distribution patterns which express or even heighten the unique character of those natural communities.

In many cases, this approach presents the potential of featuring more different plant community types on a designated site than would have occurred naturally on the same site prior to its 'development'. This results from two factors. First, new microclimates may have been created through the disturbances occurring with construction. For example, a previously wooded site may become a partially wooded site as a result of the cutting of some canopy plants, thus creating sunlit openings where the original woodland community species will not survive. Also, the presence of buildings and paved areas creates new micro-environments: a shaded zone on the north face of a building, or hot, dry zones where heat and light are reflected by paving and/or the south and west faces of buildings. Permanent or periodically wet areas may purposely be incorporated to collect stormwater and to let it slowly infiltrate. Furthermore, the human needs and activities introduced to a site may dictate or suggest the inclusion of a greater variety of plant community types than would have occurred there naturally. There may be a goal, for example, of keeping an open view unobstructed. So, instead of re-establishing a multi-layered forest throughout the entire site, a low meadow-like community might be designed for the viewing zone. Or, where eye-level screening is a goal, a forest edge community, consisting of Chickasaw plum (*Prunus angustifolia*), sumac (*Rhus* spp.) and Eastern red cedar (*Juniperus virginiana*) might be incorporated.

The abstraction of a native community in a designed landscape may include stylisation in the sense of giving more legible form to the distribution of plants than usually occurs naturally, or incorporating a higher concentration of plants than might normally occur. For example, in a visually prominent entrance area to a building set within a Piedmont forest planting, ground layer plants might be planted at both a higher diversity and higher density than that at which they typically occur in the native forest community. Additionally, the plants may be distributed in a way that heightens their effect, for example in directionally flowing drifts that relate to topographic form or to circulation routes, and/or in combinations that feature particular flower colour combinations. To be true to the community, though, they should be combinations which could logically occur together in the model natural community in the same region.

In some European countries, a further move away from the pure ecological plant community to a more horticultural abstraction has taken place, mainly as a result of a much reduced or depauperate native flora, as discussed in the introduction to this chapter. Whilst vegetation may be based largely upon native vegetation types (such as species-rich hay meadow or coppiced woodland edge), in appropriate settings, additional (non-native) species from similar habitats may be added, for example, to extend the season of flowering. It should be stressed that such an approach is limited to settings that are clearly cultural, for example urban parks and gardens.

A process for abstracting native communities in design

The use of somewhat simplified abstractions of natural communities of plants in designed situations combines some of the methods of traditional landscape design with others that depart from those methods. In the following section, a process is outlined, with the goal of facilitating the development of landscapes that feature elements of regionally appropriate communities of plants. It should not be viewed as purely a rigid, linear process, but one in which there is some flexibility and the potential for some back and forth movement among or between steps.

Study the natural model(s)

One could spend a lifetime studying a particular plant-community type and never learn all there is to know about it, in all its intricacies and complexities. That being the case, it is necessary to compress this learning process into a much shorter time-frame, trying to learn the most essential characteristics of community types – environmental factors; dominant, prevalent, and 'visual essence' species composition; community structure; and likely successional processes – in order to use such information in design. A logical starting point is to utilise others' quantitative and qualitative observations in the literature on the community or communities under investigation.

In order to relate such summary information to a specific site, it is extremely useful to supplement a literature review with first-hand field observations of one or more local stands of the community or communities under consideration. The unfortunate reality is that there may be no extant stands of a particular natural community remaining in the region. If there are, however, it can be extremely useful to observe them closely as a basis for design, looking for such elements as frequently occurring species combinations, striking aesthetic characteristics, the density and distribution habits of key species, and particular microhabitat preferences of certain species. The mapping and sketching of selected small areas can provide valuable insights for design in the abstraction or stylisation of the community type in a design context.

Inventory and analyse the site to be designed

A critical step early in the process is to do a thorough inventory/analysis of the site to be designed, just as it is in any landscape design or planning process. This will include all the 'standard' information-gathering relative to soil type, steepness of slopes, solar orientation, views (both on-site and off, desirable and undesirable), and existing vegetation (both as an indicator of site conditions and as a basis for determining what to retain and what to remove). Additionally, in adopting a native plant-community approach to designing the site, micro-environmental observations may be of special importance: zones with different shade-density and duration under trees and adjacent to structures; depressions, swales or poorly drained areas that will tend towards wetness during parts of the year; or exceptionally hot, dry zones, as in places where heat may be reflected by south- and west-facing walls or paved surfaces. Off-site features, such as buildings or trees, which may influence the microclimate, should also be identified and noted.

Identify users' needs and functional requirements

As in any landscape design or planning process, it is necessary to overlay an understanding of the existing physical characteristics of the site with an understanding of the spatial and experiential needs of the future users of it: vehicular and pedestrian circulation, parking and any other specific uses of the outdoor space, as well as climate modification (e.g., shading and windbreaking), screening and enclosure needs. If the future users of the site include wildlife, these species' needs for food, cover and water need to be included as part of this analysis.

Develop a mass/space plan

The site analysis will have identified the 'given' masses (e.g. buildings and existing vegetation masses), as well as open spaces (e.g. paved surfaces, rock outcroppings, open water and zones of low vegetation). The use analysis will have identified currently open areas where vegetation masses are needed for enclosure, screening or spatial formation. It will also suggest the need for open spaces to accommodate specific activities.

From these two sources, a mass/space plan can be developed. The importance of this plan, as the framework within which more detailed design will occur, cannot be overemphasised. Without such an overall structure, the designer can easily be diverted into selecting and placing individual plants and other elements in the landscape, rather than creating a cohesive, flowing design. Ultimately, the masses in the proposed mass/space plan will be translated into forest and shrub groupings, as well as enclosing structural elements (e.g. walls, fences and arbours) on occasion. The spaces will be translated into plant groupings based on naturally evolving old fields and meadows, wetlands and rock outcrops, or, in some situations, into lawns, open-water areas, decked and paved areas.

One of the major challenges in utilising native plant community groupings as design elements is to maintain coherence whilst accommodating the proposed human uses within a site which has many disparate and fragmented elements. Doing a series of quick mass/space diagrams can be of great help in meeting this challenge. Whilst there can be no formula for determining the form of masses and spaces, a useful analogy and inspiration in many situations is *the river*. The path taken by a meandering river characteristically creates a changing sequence of spaces and views, as well as a sense of mystery, always enticing the observer to see what is around the next bend. Furthermore, as a river carves out its channel, it tends to cut away at the outside of curves, and to deposit sand and/or gravel on the inside of curves. The result of this process is to form a flowing space in the landscape, wider in some places than in others, with an ever-changing view as one moves through it. Translated into a designed landscape, the river-like space may be interpreted as a pathway or zone of low-growing or periodically mown vegetation. Adjacent to the 'river' may be 'banks' of taller vegetation, for example grasses, sedges and wildflowers that grow to a height of two to six feet. This zone may vary in width, becoming broader at the inside of curves in the river-like space it encloses. It may grade into a zone of shrub drifts, which themselves may grade into a forest community, depending on the size of the area.

The width of river-like spaces obviously will vary from site to site, and with the need for enclosure or mass relative to openness or space. In some situations, it may emulate a broad, expansive river; in others, where space is more limited, it may more closely resemble a stream.

Match plant communities to the mass-space plan

Once the zones of mass and space have been identified, a list of potential plant community types that match the desired characteristics of those various zones can be generated. The designation of potential community-like groupings of plants to fulfil the design criteria for different zones must, of course, also be aligned with the environmental characteristics of each zone, for example soil, moisture, slope steepness and orientation. As noted earlier, the changes associated with site development may actually create new micro-environments, potentially increasing the number or range of community-like plantings that may be incorporated in the design.

In the southeastern US, the most likely plant community type to designate for 'mass' areas within a mass/space plan is a forest type (or types) appropriate to the soil-moisture-topography complex on the site. Such plantings may grade through transitional shrub zones into the spaces in the plan. Spaces will tend to be predominantly herbaceous plant zones, for example meadow plantings of various compositions, aquatic plantings, or, in some cases, lawns, pathways or paved areas. Those areas targeted for forest-like plantings can be planted to trees immediately, or can be permitted to evolve through stages of secondary succession, with the primary management activity being the removal or suppression of invasive exotic species. Those areas designated as herb-dominated meadows will require more management to suppress not only unwanted exotic species, but also woody species that will 'want' to occupy the space.

Select plant species and locate individual plants within community-like groupings

Once the spatial framework for a designed landscape is clearly identified in the mass/space plan, the very specific task of selecting appropriate plant species for each zone within the site may proceed, i.e. a planting plan may be developed for implementation.

Particularly in the case of forest-like plantings being installed on an open site, the initial species composition may be different from the long-term target composition. For example, a dense planting of early successional loblolly pines may be proposed, fulfilling the need for mass initially, after which successional processes will change the composition. Or an initial tree-planting plan may be supplemented with one or more additional layers of planting: later-successional tree saplings, seedlings or seeds to be added, or shade-tolerant shrubs and herbaceous ground layer species to be added as the initially-planted tree canopy develops.

For sunlit meadow plantings, the initial planting may well include the whole array of species which is desired in the area. And, as discussed earlier in this chapter, in the section on diversification of ground-layer planting, a meadow planting may appropriately be installed as seed rather than seedlings.

Examples of abstracted native plant communities for use in northwest Europe are given in Roland Gustavsson's (woodlands), Wolfram Kircher's (wetlands) and Hein Koningen's (ground layer) chapters in this book (Chapters 7, 8 and 10, respectively). For the remainder of this Chapter a case study will be used to show how the use of abstracted native plant communities can be applied in a designed setting.

5.1
Broomsedge (*Andropogon virginicus*) and other grasses in a 'roadside' community. Planted in spring 1994 and photographed in December 1994 at the Atlanta History Center

5.2
Showy evening primrose (*Oenothera speciosa*) in 'roadside' community, Atlanta History Center (spring 1996)

5.3
Roadside/woodland edge, Atlanta History Center, including red maple (*Acer rubrum*), flowering dogwood (*Cornus florida*) and American beech (*Fagus grandifolia*), as it looked in November 1997

Case study design: Atlanta History Museum

The landscape surrounding the Museum of History at the Atlanta History Center in Atlanta, Georgia, was designed by the author as an illustration of the use of regional plant communities as a basis for design, in collaboration with landscape architect Gary Gullatte. The majority of trees and shrubs were planted in the autumn of 1993; the herbaceous layer was planted in the spring of 1994.

In the inventory process, several distinctly different environments were identified, each suggesting a different Georgia piedmont plant community or successional stage as a model. In summary, these were categorised as follows.

1 Roadsides and 'edge of the woods' zones along the east entrance driveway leading to the museum.
2 An exposed, well-drained slope along the east façade of the building, both to the right and the left of a granite-paved entrance courtyard, with existing high canopied pines and oaks remaining in part of the area.
3 A partially canopied drainage swale in a depression between the front entrance drive and the adjacent street.
4 A circular, curbed area in the sunny granite-paved courtyard in front of the entrance foyer.

After the development of a mass/space plan, these different areas were translated into various plant community groupings.

Roadside/woodland edge

In these sunny zones along the entrance drive, relatively short sun-loving grasses and forbs (e.g. purple lovegrass, silkgrass, evening primrose and verbena) blend into taller herbaceous species (e.g. broomsedge, splitbeard bluestem and lanceleaf coreopsis) and then colonies of sassafras, sumac, Chickasaw plum and red cedar (Figures 5.1 to 5.3).

Herbaceous plants in this zone were installed as

seedlings, planted at approximately one foot spacing; woody species were planted as variably sized saplings. The natural reproduction of the planted species is permitted to continue, within limits, both by vegetative spreading and self-seeding. The invasion of the woody species into the zone nearest the roadway is purposely inhibited, however, by an annual mowing to 'hold' it as a sunny, flowering roadside.

Early successional forest

On the open slope along the east façade of the museum building, an early successional Piedmont forest is dominated by closely-spaced loblolly pines of various sizes. On the front, the pines grade into a woodland edge of sassafras, sumac and plum. As native hardwood species invade this zone, they will be permitted to develop as they do in a naturally evolving successional forest. Consequently, the scene will change: the pines will become more lofty, with sourwood, dogwood, redbud and other deciduous tree species forming a sub-canopy beneath them (Figures 5.4 and 5.5).

Hardwood forest

In the areas to the north of the Museum building, where there was a partial canopy of tall pine and oak trees, a Piedmont hardwood forest is being re-established, including white oak, hickory, red maple, blackgum and 'drifts' of American beech. Smaller trees, such as serviceberry, flowering dogwood and redbud provide colour and spatial variation at the midstory level, as do the shrubs, such as sparkleberry, sweetshrub and maple-leaf viburnum.

The herbaceous layer was designed in stylised, curving swaths of different species mixes, matched with different light levels that result from building shadows and from both the pre-existing and newly planted canopy trees. In semi-shaded areas, for example, a mix of bracken fern, columbine, firepink, bluestar and blue-eyed grass is planted (Figure 5.6).

5.4
Upland forest planting, Atlanta History Center, as it looked in November 1997

5.5
Upland forest planting, Atlanta History Center, as it looked in November 1997

5.6
Upland ground-layer planting for semi-shaded zone, including bracken fern (*Pteridium aquilinum*), columbine (*Aquilegia canadensis*) and bluestar (*Amsonia tabernaemontana*), Atlanta History Center (spring 1996)

In deeper shade, the evergreen Christmas fern is interplanted with woods phlox and wild geranium. Other mixes occupy other swaths; oakleaf-mulched zones occur between the planted zones with the expectation that certain of the planted herbaceous species will migrate into these areas.

In summary, in the hardwood forest planting, a framework of woody plants was established, and it is reflected in the layout of a stylised ground layer pattern. It is expected that there will be change in this landscape, brought about both by the growth and spread of initially planted vegetation, and by other species that may colonise. Management in this zone mainly consists of suppressing invasive exotic plant species that appear.

5.7 (far left, above)
Drifts of ragwort (*Senecio aureus*) and river oats (*Chasmanthium latifolium*) in drainage swale, Atlanta History Center (March 1995)

5.8 (far left, below)
Drifts of ragwort (*Senecio aureus*) and river oats (*Chasmanthium latifolium*) in drainage swale, Atlanta History Center (September 1994)

5.9 (left)
River oats (*Chasmanthium latifolium*) and sensitive fern (*Onoclea sensibilis*) at the edge of a drainage swale, Atlanta History Center (spring 1995)

'Streamside' forest and meadow

The low, periodically wet zone in front of the museum was planted with tree and shrub species that normally occur in streamside sites: red maple, musclewood, swamp azaleas, elderberry and strawberry bush. The 'river of space' in the middle of this zone was planted with river oats; it is bordered by a sequence of moisture-loving perennials, for example ragwort (*Senecia aureus*), cardinal flower (*Lobelia cardinalis*) and large, exuberant autumn-blooming Joe Pyeweed (*Eupatorium maculatum*), ironweed (*Veronica* spp.), sunflower (*Helianthus* spp.) and goldenrod (*Solidago* spp.) (Figures 5.7 to 5.9).

'Granite outcrop' circular garden

In the hot, exposed circle in the centre of the granite-paved entrance courtyard is the symbolic centrepiece of the native community plantings: a stylised version of a granite outcrop, utilising locally quarried granite and plant species from that environment (Figures 5.10 and 5.11). The design incorporates an ephemeral pool in a spiral form, a Georgia oak (*Quercus georgiana*) as the single, sculptural tree, and a variety of lichens, mosses and both annual and perennial herbaceous plants grow in crevices and openings between the flat granite stones that cover much of the circular area. The concrete-bottomed pool, lined with a layer of granite sand, varies in depth, grading from very shallow on the inside edge of the spiral to approximately 18 inches at the outer edge. The smooth line of the pool edge is interrupted once, with a lichen-covered boulder that slightly overhangs the outer edge of the pool. Rainfall provides water for the pool; its level fluctuates with rainfall patterns, and it is even permitted to dry out during dry periods.

5.10
Museum of History, Atlanta History Center, Georgia, with granite outcrop garden (autumn 1993)

5.11
Detail of a portion of granite outcrop garden, Atlanta History Center (winter 1994)

Because the plants of this community have adapted to extreme heat and drought, no supplementary water is supplied to them. Growth, re-seeding and vegetative spreading of characteristic granite outcrop vegetation will be permitted to occur, with the only management being the removal of non-indigenous species, and an early spring clipping of the previous year's herbaceous foliage.

In summary, the design of the approximately two acre landscape surrounding the Atlanta Museum of History was based on different Piedmont plant communities or successional stages, but with some level of stylisation, both in plant selection (drawing on 'visual essence' species) and in placement (forming perceptible masses and swaths of distinctive native species). The granite outcrop garden, particularly, is a symbolic representation: a sculptural composition designed to fit into a circular form, but one which expresses the essence of a unique and regionally significant natural community. Throughout the different community representations, the goal of sustainability is approached, with management inputs mainly limited to the removal and/or suppression of exotic species, once the initial plantings are established.

Conclusion

Whilst the use of native vegetation and natural dynamics in designed gardens and landscapes in American landscape architecture during the last quarter-century is increasing, it remains an undercurrent, rather than a mainstream activity. There is sometimes a misperception that designing with native plant communities and natural processes in not sufficiently artful. In reality, it can be considered to be a new art form appropriate to the twenty-first century: 'ecological art', which is simultaneously aesthetically rich, ecologically sound, evocative of place and dynamic.

Chapter 6

Naturalistic herbaceous vegetation for urban landscapes

James Hitchmough

Introduction

Naturalistic herbaceous vegetation differs from conventional herbaceous vegetation in that it mimics the spatial and structural form of semi-natural vegetation. Individual species are generally not planted in clearly defined groups or blocks, and where they are aggregated, 'outliers' of the same species will generally occur elsewhere in the planting. Aggregations of individual species will be largest and most prevalent with clone-forming forbs or grasses of moist fertile soils. As these species spread, they often eliminate their neighbours. On less fertile, drier sites, species will generally repeat across the planting, often many times over, creating distinctive rhythmical patterns, especially when plants are in flower. There will sometimes be several distinct canopy layers; shade tolerant vernal species near the ground, above these the main canopy species, punctuated, often at wide spacings, by tall emergent species. These spatial arrangements allow a larger number of species to be located within an area of planting. This facilitates a lengthy display season, with many dramatic changes of character, with fewer negative visual effects.

In conventional herbaceous planting, the use of spring flowering species is problematic, as post flowering these often look untidy or may even disappear completely in summer, leaving unattractive gaps. In naturalistic herbaceous vegetation, the decline of early species is effectively masked by the growth of adjacent later flowering species. The tall emergent species that form the uppermost canopy of the vegetation are normally late summer or autumn flowering. An additional virtue of naturalistic herbaceous vegetation is its capacity to act as a unifying element with disparate surroundings. With conventional planting the eye reads individual groups or blocks of plants, and unless these are repeated many times the vegetation has a clear grain or direction, often looking more comfortable from one side than another. This is problematic when the surroundings are complex and cluttered, as is the case in many urban settings. By comparison, naturalistic herbaceous vegetation reads as a continuous sheet, from which different species emerge to flower as the sheet grows taller, but without obvious directional grain.

The spatial arrangement, and multi-layered character of naturalistic herbaceous vegetation, also confer functional benefits to people and other organisms. Conventional herbaceous planting is based on either ground cover-like blocks, or widely spaced clumps surrounded by unplanted space to accommodate summer growth, with minimal competition with neighbouring clumps. The ground-cover model is highly functional, providing robust long-lived species are chosen, although if a taxon fails a large gap is inevitable. In naturalistic plantings the system can accommodate the failure of species without obvious gaps, as all plants are surrounded by 3–4 neighbours of a different species which expand into the space vacated. The loss of one species is an opportunity for other desirable species, as much as it is for invading weeds. In the widely spaced clump model, plants are heavily fertilised to maximise their size and luxuriance, however the diameter of the gaps are such that closure is not achieved until midsummer. In naturalistic herbaceous plantings, plants are present at much higher densities than in either the ground cover or clump and gap model, typically at least 10 plants/m^2 and in sown vegetation over 100 plants/m^2. At these densities, closure of spaces between plants has generally been achieved by May. The intense competition for water and light significantly reduces the vigour of many previously established weed species, and inhibits weed invasion from outside the planting. Weed-control requirements, the main impediment to the use of conventional herbaceous vegetation in urban landscapes, are reduced. As the individual plant is not the focus of attention in naturalistic planting, the traditional costs associated with 'titivating' are also avoided, as are division and replacement costs; the goal being for regeneration to occur from within the planting. Where management is required, it is generally compressed into critical phases of the lifecycle, often spring, and is undertaken as much as possible using crude unselective management techniques borrowed from nature conservation, for example burning or cutting.

Through typically being taxonomically and structurally diverse, naturalistic herbaceous vegetation is potentially of high habitat value. The degree of openness of naturalistic herbaceous vegetation will depend upon soil moisture and fertility, and also the species chosen. The drier and less fertile the site, the more open vegetation will become, and vice versa. The vegetation selected must change with the site, there is no standard version to be achieved. This illustrates one of the central tenets of naturalistic planting design, plants must be chosen to fit the site, and to be compatible with the other plants chosen if communities are to be created that are robust and sustainable. This requires the application of an ecological understanding to plant selection and management. Naturalistic herbaceous vegetation does not need to be confined to species native to a particular geographical region, although it is of course understandable that practitioners should make this connection. Providing attention is given to assessing the environmental and social context of the site, and the ecological needs and attributes of the species in question, naturalistic plantings may consist entirely of non-native species, native and non-native species mixed together, or native species alone.

Whilst naturalistic herbaceous vegetation aims to be more resource sustainable than conventional plantings, its key role is to create meaning and pleasure for human beings, and in urban contexts non-native species have a very important role to play in this process.

Although naturalistic herbaceous vegetation is not a new idea (see Chapter 2), in terms of scientific research it is still relatively poorly understood. Its creation and management fits less comfortably within the client-landscape architect-landscape contractor model than does traditional herbaceous planting. In addition, it represents something of a paradigm shift in visual terms; it often has no clear directional grain or apparent order, 'focal points' are absent and the individual plants are neither distinct nor cherished. This is a very different aesthetic for the public and landscape professionals to embrace and understand. To traditionalists in the horticultural world it represents poor cultivation practice, to the nature conservation movement it represents an unholy mix of species that should not be pretending to be naturalistic. Anna Jorgensen addresses some of these perceptions in Chapter 11. Some landscape professionals inspired by naturalistic form have rather naïvely perceived this style to be a 'magic bullet' that somehow arrests the normal ecological processes of colonisation and change in designed plant communities. This has led to disillusionment in the past, as it becomes apparent that this is not so. The author makes no such claims; ecologically-informed naturalistic herbaceous vegetation is less intensive to manage but is not management free. It is imperative that practitioners recognise that, whether native or exotic, these types of vegetation rely on informed management for the persistence of desired species. Where management is not informed, the vegetation will simply change into a less desired plant community.

Overall design considerations

Site planning

Naturalistic herbaceous vegetation is most dramatic when used on a relatively large scale, i.e. in blocks larger than 100 m^2. This is most likely to be economically possible when created by sowing, or a combination of sowing and planting (see the section 'Establishment by sowing in combination with planting'). When naturalistic vegetation is added as an afterthought, as small beds in paving or in mown grass areas, it can appear rather self-conscious, and even untidy. When designed as an integral part of a small space, for example in a garden or courtyard, it is much more successful. It is highly effective when combined with contemporary architecture and ground forms, providing a provocative contrast between the designed and the apparently spontaneous. In such situations, however, it is important to select a plant community that is attractive for as long a period as possible. Overall, however, the greatest range of opportunities for its use are probably associated with the refurbishment of twentieth-century public parks, which are often dominated by large expanses of mown grass that do not have a well-defined aesthetic or functional role (Figure 6.1).

Application to these types of landscape requires careful design and public consultation to ensure that areas selected do not have existing uses unappreciated by the designers. In many cases, plantings will 'hang' off the edge of woodland or parkland trees, providing a transition between shade and full sun. This also anchors the vegetation to the ground, although when used on a large scale, meadow or prairie-like vegetation will become the landscape and the visual problem of being unattached disappears. Location should also consider long-term management issues, for

6.1
Extensively managed prairie vegetation prior to flowering, acting as a bridge between a woodland edge and areas of mown grass – private garden, Wisconsin

example is it possible to get machinery to the site for cutting, is the site surround by mown grass that could act as a firebreak and so on. Planning for gathering and movement is important, people have an instinctive desire to experience the planting from within, and mown or hardened pathways can help to facilitate this whilst reducing the severity of trafficking damage.

The type of plant community chosen should reflect the likely needs and expectations of users, the overall design context and the environmental conditions. The timeless principle of intensively designed and managed landscapes close to buildings, or where people gather, becoming ever less intensive into the middle and distant landscape, remains a useful model to follow.

What type of naturalistic plant community is appropriate?

'Nativeness'

Plant communities can involve native species only, exotic species only or both. Making this decision is most straightforward in rural situations where native species predominate and are the overwhelming determinant of landscape character. Conservation of native biodiversity is a cornerstone in the management of these landscapes, and outside of gardens it is generally less appropriate to use exotic species. In such situations there is increasing pressure to use local genotypes rather than just native species *per se*, although the scientific and philosophical justification for this view are sometimes debatable

(Wilkinson 2001; Sackville-Hamilton 2001).

The native-only presumption becomes weaker as sites become increasingly urban, although where sites border onto areas of high conservation significance, native plant material may continue to be most appropriate. In urban situations where exotic species are often widely cultivated in gardens and public landscapes, and context is far more eclectic, it becomes very much a question of free choice, shaped more by the aspiration of local people and designers. Exotic species that spread aggressively by seed or vegetative means should, however, be avoided, especially in situations adjacent to semi-natural corridors, such as waterways, woodland, etc.

The fear of exotic species escaping and impacting negatively on native species has become much stronger as the biodiversity movement has developed. Whilst this is a rational concern, with naturalised species posing a significant local threat in some regions, it is simply scientifically incorrect to stigmatise all exotic species as invasive and all natives as non-invasive. It is understandable that some conservation biologists should support such dogma, but this view is untenable for designers and managers working in the cultural landscape of urban places. An excellent review of the native-exotic plant debate can be found in Kendle and Rose (2000). The idea of producing mixed communities of native and exotic species in urban landscapes is anathema to many conservation perspectives because it is seen as devaluing the spirit of nativeness. This is clearly no more than a philosophical-political notion rooted in romanticism and needs to be seen as such.

Habitat value

The general presumption is that habitat value of vegetation will be maximised by the use of communities that are based around native species. Again, this issue needs to be seen as a series of greys rather than black and white. If an overriding goal of a project is to provide habitat for a specific native organism whose habitat requirements are well understood, or replace a now lost semi-natural community that once occurred on a site, then native vegetation is most appropriate. However, it is also important to recognise that exotic vegetation also offers a habitat and is not a biological vacuum. Any vegetation that is structurally more complex than mown grass represents a significant habitat gain in urban landscapes, irrespective of where the species come from. This is clearly demonstrated by the research of Owen (1991) on invertebrate diversity in gardens of exotic species. In urban areas, in particular, it is generally necessary to balance habitat value with other values, for example, attractiveness and structure in relation to human preferences.

Ecological fitness and community stability

It is pointless to attempt to create plant communities that are poorly fitted to physical and biotic aspects of the site. Environment fit is, however, best considered at the level of individual species rather than the community, as some species in a stereotype plant community will be adequately fitted whilst others will not, and will disappear. The designed community only fails when sufficient numbers of the component species are poorly fitted. Where only a few species are poorly fitted, the better fitted species used will often expand into the space vacated by the ill-fitted species.

Key factors influencing gross ecological fit are site productivity in relation to the growth potential of individual species, local climate, soil moisture regimes, herbivore density and management regime. Site analyses need to identify likely levels of these factors across the site, so as to inform decisions on ground pattern, location of various plant communities and constituent species within a community. The placement of, for example, 'dry looking' plant communities should reflect where dry conditions occur on-site rather than were a designer might like such a community to be.

These factors are often only weakly related to

whether species are native or exotic, but again operate at the level of individual species. Small, slow-growing, stress-tolerating forbs sown as part of native wildflower mixes often fail to persist on highly productive urban sites. They are competitively displaced by larger and more vigorous native species. On such sites, sown or planted species with the latter growth characteristics are more likely to survive competition for light and soil resources, irrespective of whether they are native or exotic. Management in the guise of more frequent cutting, etc., may allow stress-tolerating species to be maintained on productive sites. It is more rational, however, to select highly productive species in the first place, for example tall north American prairie species as opposed to native chalk grassland species.

Aesthetic requirements

PHENOLOGY

Perhaps as a result of experiences within their own garden, there appears to be a widespread presumption among urban people in the temperate regions that vegetation should be 'attractive' throughout the summer months. This is particularly so for vegetation immediately adjacent to where people live or work. As herbaceous vegetation is highly seasonal in appearance, this is an important factor determining the type of plant community to be designed. Herbaceous vegetation that only flowers in spring, as in some woodland field layers, or needs to be cut in summer as hay meadow, is potentially problematic if used in situations that are subject to much public scrutiny in summer. These problems can be addressed by using zones of vegetation radiating out from buildings or gathering points, with long flowering or summer flowering material at the hub gradating to spring or other highly seasonal flowering vegetation further away. Phenology also needs to be addressed in terms of the duration of flowering of individual species within a community to ensure as dramatic and long a flowering period as possible.

HEIGHT AND TIDINESS

These two factors appear to be related. In a study using computer-generated photographic surrogates, Dai (2000) found that short, rather than tall meadow-like herbaceous vegetation was more preferred by the public, possibly because it was perceived as tidier, or perhaps even safer. Again, these preferences are probably influenced by location in relation to human activities, as previously discussed. Nassauer (1995) refers to the need for designers of naturalistic vegetation to provide the public with cues that affirm a vegetation is intentional and is cared for. Familiarity is also an important factor in public preference, Mynott (2000) found that local people came to tolerate the 'untidy' appearance of naturalistic herbaceous vegetation in winter because they knew how attractive it was in summer. Non-locals were strongly intolerant of the winter appearance because they did not know what it looked like in summer. Crisp edges between naturalistic vegetation and paths or mown surfaces are probably important contributors to gaining acceptance. The preference for naturalistic vegetation can clearly be learnt, either through travel and the familiarity this may develop, or through the media as an ecological or fashion icon.

COLOUR

This is an extremely important factor in designing plant communities in urban landscapes. Although tall green, grassy vegetation is not regarded very positively, Dai (2000) found that when colour is added to the scene the negative effect of height was cancelled out. Maximising the flowering impact of naturalistic herbaceous vegetation is a key means of maintaining public support. This requires these plant communities to be visually more dramatic than the semi-natural stereotypes upon which they are often based. This involves a departure from the tenets of restoration ecology, where the goal is to achieve a community that represents what species should be there. This is often most readily achieved in designed naturalistic vegetation by leaving out, or greatly reducing, the grass component, or managing the site post-sowing to eliminate or reduce grass abundance. It is also often desirable to abandon learnt ascetic theories on the use of colour in designed plantings in the public realm. There are two reasons for this. Firstly, there is little evidence that the general public do not like the brash colour combinations that lie outside those cherished by gardening writers, such as Jekyll (1908), Hobhouse (1985), and Pope and Pope (1998). These are clearly the learnt values of an elite, and do not represent any fundamental aesthetic truths. Secondly, even the most brutal colour combinations are visually much less shocking (even to people of 'good' taste) in naturalistic vegetation than in traditional block-like planting.

AVAILABILITY OF ADEQUATELY FUNDED, SKILLED, LONG-TERM MANAGEMENT

Naturalistic herbaceous vegetation varies in its infallibility and cost, although all are more fallible than vegetation such as mown turf or woody shrub mass. Within communities, individual species also vary in the same way, some are very reliable and inexpensive to establish, others are much more uncertain and potentially expensive.

As a generalisation, the least fallible naturalistic vegetation for a site of moderate productivity in Britain are those based around the stereotype mesotrophic native meadow. Sown at 4 g/m^2 the result is a grass-dominated community with a sprinkling of common forbs, such as *Centaurea nigra, Ranunculus acris* and *Leucanthemum vulgare*, plus 5–10 other species. Whilst slug predation on seedling forbs will reduce the number established, typically sufficient numbers survive. Even if some of the key forbs fail or decline over time, often due to inadequate management, the grasses and extra robust species, such as *Centaurea nigra*, will persist. The hay-cut in summer maintains the semblance of a meadow and, in most cases, some additional native species will gradually establish in the meadow. Equally robust is the same meadow with the addition of either exotic bulbous species (e.g. *Crocus, Narcissus, Camassia*) or well-fitted native and exotic forbs, such as *Euphorbia palustris*, *Geranium x magnificum*, *Geranium sylvaticum*, *Lychnis chalcedonica* and *Persicaria bistorta*. The combination of the annual hay-cut and the biomass of the plants themselves excludes most problem species.

At the other end of the spectrum are steppe and prairie communities that are not adapted to be dominated by native meadow grasses. Whilst not difficult to create in absolute terms, prairie-like vegetation is more demanding of understanding. Some of the species are highly palatable to slugs at germination and in subsequent years as they emerge from the soil in spring. They are also intolerant of competition in spring from colonising native grasses. Seed is more expensive per square metre than commercial native meadow-mixes, and if, for some reason, it all goes horribly wrong, you may be left with few visible signs of success. If, however, establishment is successful, the result is a visually dramatic vegetation, well suited to otherwise difficult highly productive sites. Practical aspects of these issues are discussed in greater detail in the section 'Creation of naturalistic herbaceous plant communities in practice'.

Types of herbaceous plant communities: habitat stereotypes

When creating naturalistic herbaceous plant communities, it is extremely helpful to base the design around a habitat stereotype. The rationale for doing so is that species that occur naturally together in a given plant community probably tolerate broadly similar conditions, and have similar management requirements. They are also likely to be broadly compatible with one another, although the

6.2
Wet meadow of British species in Richmond, North Yorkshire. Note the dense competitive foliage canopy on this relatively fertile site with *Persicaria bistorta* dominant. Smaller species dominate where soil fertility is reduced or the site is grazed

competitive capacity of individual species will often differ considerably. Even when using entirely non-native species, this provides a logical basis to include/exclude species, to assess how well the designed vegetation will fit the environmental and social conditions prevailing on the site, and to assess whether the proposed vegetation can be appropriately managed. As has previously been made clear in the introduction, even when using species native to the region around the site, the purpose of this text is not habitat restoration *per se*. The habitat stereotype is to be used as a guide only. In many cases it may be useful to include other species that do not naturally co-occur with the core species, but which experience has shown are broadly compatible. Tables 6.1 to 6.6 demonstrate how species from different parts of the world, but occupying broadly similar habitats, can be interchanged to produce a customised vegetation.

Meadows

This word is rather generic and, in terms of semi-natural vegetation, tends to be used to describe almost any community of forbs and grasses that do not grow beneath trees and shrubs. In planting design it has come to be used to describe herbaceous plantings in which the constituent plants mingle in a complex, random fashion. In many countries, 'meadow' is used more specifically to describe semi-natural communities that are the result of agricultural management, most commonly grazing by domestic animals and cutting for hay. This is, for example, the origin of most meadows in Britain and Europe. Many of these culturally amended sites would originally have been occupied by woodland and, in the absence of grazing or cutting meadows, are invaded by scrub and trees and return to woodland.

Meadow is also used to describe the more 'natural' grasslands that occur at high altitude (above the tree line) in many parts of the world. Most of these meadows are grazed, either by wild herbivores, such as deer, as in the sub-alpine meadows of the Rocky Mountains, or by a combination of domesticated animals and wild herbivores, as in the case of the European Alps and the Himalayan chain. Grazing is an important factor in determining the abundance of different species and the appearance of the meadow. Highly palatable plants, such as many grasses, are held in check, thereby promoting less palatable species.

Whilst a number of factors (soil moisture, soil fertility, soil pH and management regime) contribute to shaping species composition of meadows within a given geographical region, soil moisture is probably the single most important factor (Figure 6.2).

Dry meadows

Dry meadows (Table 6.1) occur in response to either low rainfall during the spring to summer period or dry, infertile soil types, often, but not always, derived from limestone. As a result, these meadows are dominated by predominantly small, slow growing, stress-tolerating species. The peak flowering season is generally early spring to midsummer, but earlier in southern European sites. When used as a vegetation in designed landscapes in higher rainfall climates, many of the constituent species are prone to displacement by larger growing species, especially on fertile soil. Many dry meadow species are highly intolerant of shade cast by taller plants. The use of highly infertile materials, such as crushed building rubble and sand, as soils for these communities will, however, improve persistence and ease of management. When established on these types of soils, cutting in summer as an aid to persistence is generally not required, as the competitive capacity of invading species is reduced by soil infertility and moisture stress. Because of the slow growth of many species, communities established by planting may take one to two years before they look attractive. This timescale will generally be longer for sown communities.

Moist meadows

These are found in many parts of the world, in the lowlands in the oceanic climates in western Europe through to high altitudes in more continental climates (Table 6.2). Generally, these plant communities are more dominated by various cool season grasses from the genera, *Agrostis, Alopecurous, Cynosurous, Festuca* and *Poa*, than are drier meadows, and the forbs are typically capable of tolerating this competition. These communities are typically associated with soils of moderate fertility, and consequently species grow faster and form larger, more widespreading or taller individual plants than species of drier habitats. As a result, they are generally better able to compete with invasive weedy vegetation on fertile urban soils. As a result they are more likely to persist under these conditions than are species of drier meadows. These plant communities are generally most attractive between late spring and midsummer. Moist meadows are generally heavily dependent on cutting or grazing for persistence.

Wet meadows

These may occur either locally along drainage lines or more extensively where rainfall is very high and/or drainage is impeded. Even the most moisture

Table 6.1. Commonly cultivated forbs and grasses characteristic of dry meadows in various parts of the world (derived from Polunin and Stainton 1984; Ellenberg 1988; Jelitto and Schacht 1990; Phillips and Rix 1991a, 1991b; Rodwell *et al.* 1992; Hansen and Stahl 1993; Fitter *et al.* 1995; plus the observations of the author)

Britain	Central Europe*	Southern Europe	Himalayan/East Asian
Campanula glomerata	*Aster amellus*	*Asphodeline lutea*	*Anaphalis triplinervis*
Centaurea scabiosa	*Aster linosyris*	*Convolvulus althaeoides*	*Festuca* spp.
Daucus carota	Buphthalmum *salicifolium*	*Dictamnus albus*	*Geranium himalayense*
Festuca ovina	*Dianthus carthusianorum*	*Echinops ritro*	*Nepeta clarkei*
Geranium sanguineum	*Eryngium alpinum*	*Euphorbia rigida*	*Nepeta nervosa*
Origanum vulgare	*Eryngium bourgatii*	*Euphorbia seguieriana*	*Perovskia abrotanoides*
Primula veris	*Melica ciliata*	*Festuca valesiaca*	*Phlomis bracteosa*
Pulsatilla vulgaris	*Salvia pratensis*	*Linum narbonense*	*Poa* spp.
Ranunculus bulbosa	*Stipa* spp.	*Phlomis lychnitis*	*Potentilla atrosanguinea*
Scabiosa columbaria	*Teucrium chamaedrys*	*Stipa gigantea*	*Salvia hians*

* Note that species listed under Britain also occur in Central Europe, but not vice versa.

demanding of these species, for example, *Primula* will generally grow acceptably well without irrigation on retentive soils in parts of Britain that experience greater than 1,000 mm rainfall per annum. They will survive with less in northern regions with particularly cool summers. Other species, for example, *Iris sibirica* and *Cirsium rivulare*, will tolerate drier conditions. Given the absence of moisture stress, many of the species associated with these habitats are relatively tall, competitive species. Some spread aggressively by underground stems forming monocultural 'clonal patches', for example *Filipendula ulmaria* and *Euphorbia griffithii*, and once established will compete effectively with many invading species. Most of these species typically grow among cool season grasses, although, on fertile sites, the shade cast by tall forb species may result in low densities of these. Some wet meadows are subject to cutting and grazing cycles, whilst others are a more semi-natural vegetation associated with sites that are too wet to support trees. Species from these habitats are typically less tolerant of the defoliation associated with cutting as hay.

Grasses are an important part of wet meadow vegetation. Where these grasses are either tussock forming, as in *Deschampsia cespitosa* or *Molinia caerulea*, or are tall clone-forming species, such as *Calamagrostis epigejos*, these species have a sufficent structural and textural quality to be used as grass only communities. On sufficiently moist soils, these communities provide an attractive transition between mown grass and woody vegetation types, and also provide strong design lines to contrast with architectural structures. Hitchmough (in press) has investigated the establishment of tussock grasses by field sowing.

More specialised wet habitats, in which tall vigorous plants may be restricted by infertility, low soil oxygen or grazing pressure, are often associated with small growing stress-tolerating forbs. Under these conditions, grasses are typically replaced by sedges (*Carex*) and rushes (*Juncus*). Many of the forbs in these habitats form discrete rosettes of

Table 6.2. Commonly cultivated forbs and grasses characteristic of moist meadows in various parts of the world (derived from Polunin and Stainton 1984; Ellenberg 1988; Jelitto and Schacht 1990; Phillips and Rix 1991a, 1991b; Chatto 1992; Rodwell *et al.* 1992; Hansen and Stahl 1993; Fitter *et al.* 1995; plus the observations of the author)

Britain	Central Europe*	Himalayan/East Asian	Caucasus
Cynosurus cristatus	*Achnatherum calamagrostis*	*Euphorbia longifolia*	*Brunnera macrophylla*
Festuca rubra	*Aconitum napellus*	*Euphorbia wallichii*	*Campanula lactiflora*
Galium verum	*Astrantia major*	*Meconopsis grandis*	*Centaurea macrocephala*
Geranium pratense	*Campanula latifolia*	*Persicaria affinis*	*Cephalaria gigantea*
Knautia arvensis	*Centaurea montana*	*Potentilla nepaulensis*	*Geranium platypetalum*
Leucanthemum vulgare	*Cirsium oleraceum*	*Primula alpicola*	*Geranium psilostemon*
Ranunculus acris	*Cirsium tuberosum*	*Primula denticulata*	*Papaver bracteatum*
Sanguisorba officinalis	*Ranunculus aconitifolius*	*Primula sinopurpurea*	*Scabiosa caucasica*
Stachys officinalis	*Veratrum album*	*Sanguisorba obtusa*	*Telekia speciosa*

* Note that species listed under Britain also occur in Central Europe, but not vice versa.

foliage, for example, asiatic *Primula* spp., *Succisa pratensis, Lychnis flos-cuculi* and *Geum*. Whilst often shade-tolerant, many of these species are not compatible with taller, more wide-spreading species. These species often reproduce by seed in plantings, whereas the tall clonal forbs of highly productive sites do not. Management to control larger invading species is required if these stress-tolerating species are to be successfully employed in designed vegetation. Almost all of the species in Table 6.3 are highly unattractive to slugs and snails as adult plants, and flower between spring and midsummer.

Steppe

Steppe is the term used to describe a diverse range of dry grasslands that occur from Central Europe through Eastern Europe, to Siberia and China (Figure 6.3). A number of types are recognised, for example, forest-steppe, tuft grass steppe, sagebrush steppe, mountain steppe, meadow steppe and semi-desert steppe (Archibold 1995). In Europe, the distinction between dry meadows and steppe is rather indistinct, with steppe representing

6.3
Steppe grassland in Eastern Austria, dominated by *Stipa* spp.

Table 6.3. Commonly cultivated forbs and grasses characteristic of wet meadows in various parts of the world (derived from Polunin and Stainton 1984; Ellenberg 1988; Jelitto and Schacht 1990; Phillips and Rix 1991a, 1991b; Chatto 1992; Rodwell *et al.* 1992; Hansen and Stahl 1993; Fitter *et al.* 1995; plus the observations of the author)

Britain	Central Europe*	Himalayan/East Asian
Caltha palustris	*Cirsium rivulare*	*Euphorbia griffithii*
Deschampsia cespitosa	*Delphinium elatum*	*Ligularia* spp.
Filipendula ulmaria	*Euphorbia palustris*	*Miscanthus* spp.
Geum rivale	*Hemerocallis flava*	*Persicaria amplexicaulis*
Lychnis flos-cuculi	*Iris sibirica*	*Primula bulleyana*
Lythrum salicaria	*Molinia caerulea* subsp. *arundinacea*	*Primula prolifera*
Persicaria bistorta	*Polemonium caeruleum*	*Primula pulverulenta*
Succisa pratensis	*Thalictrum aquilegifolium*	*Primula sikkimensis*
Trollius europaeus	*Veronica longifolia*	*Rodgersia* spp.

* Note that species listed under Britain also occur in Central Europe, but not vice versa.

communities exposed to particularly severe soil-moisture stress. As a result, in Europe some species are common to both dry meadow and steppe communities (Ellenberg 1988). Steppe becomes a more distinctive plant community as continental effects increase as one moves east. Steppe is typically associated with sites that experience extremely cold winters, moist springs and hot dry summers. The dominant plants are grasses with *Stipa*, the feather grasses, a characteristic genus. Many steppe grasses form distinctive discrete tussocks, in contrast to the more amorphous form of many meadow grasses.

The evolution of steppe grasslands is often ascribed to drying out of the climate during the Pleistocene, favouring the development of grassy vegetation. This straightforward explanation is increasingly challenged; most of the woody species occurring within the current steppe region are equally or more drought-tolerant than the grasses and forbs. In most arid parts of the world, it is woody, not herbaceous plants, that dominate. It seems possible that the combination of wild and domesticated herbivores and deliberate, regular burning by human hunter-gatherers have played a major part in the development of this vegetation type.

Because of the cold winters and hot dry summers, most steppe species grow and flower between mid-spring and early summer, then enter a dormant state and 'brown off'. Bulbous plants, such as *Tulipa*, are important spring components in Asia. In Central Europe, steppe is associated with very dry infertile, low-productivity sites. However, in Eastern Europe and Asia it is often associated with more productive ecosystems. In southern Russia, for example, steppe supports large growing species, such as *Phlomis tuberosa* (Table 6.4).

When steppe occurs on low-productivity sites, a very open, low-growing vegetation with a large percentage of bare ground (covered by mosses in autumn to spring) results. In a design sense this is the dominant visual stereotype for steppe vegetation. In the less continental climates of western Europe, 'designed' steppe communities that mimic this community are often difficult to manage, even on dry infertile soils. Due to mild winters and reliably year round rain, ongoing weed colonisation of the gaps between plants presents a challenge to managers. Closer spacing reduces weed invasion but many small growing steppe species are intolerant of shading and the planting design or sowing mix used must avoid too high a percentage of tall or widespreading species. An ideal site to undertake steppe-like plantings or sowings of this type are green roof systems involving a minimum of 90 mm of substrate of leca and composted organic material, as discussed by Dunnett (2002). Initially, these substrates are normally free of weed seeds and the severe summer moisture stress experienced assists in favouring the development of steppe species over vigorous weed species.

Table 6.4. Commonly cultivated forbs and grasses characteristic of steppe in various parts of the world (derived from BdB 1987; Ellenberg 1988; Jelitto and Schacht 1990; Phillips and Rix 1991a, 1991b; Hansen and Stahl 1993; Archibold 1995; plus the observations of the author)

Central Europe	Eastern Europe/ Western Asia
Adonis vernalis	*Chrysopogon gryllus*
Allium sphaerocephalon	*Clematis integrifolia*
Buphthalmum salicifolium	*Crambe cordifolia*
Euphorbia seguieriana	*Echium russicum*
Globularia punctata	*Eremurus stenophyllus*
Melica ciliata	*Gypsophila paniculata*
Pulsatilla pratensis	*Lathyrus rotundifolius*
Sempervivum spp.	*Paeonia tenuifolia*
Stipa pennata	*Phlomis tuberosa*
Teucrium chamaedrys	*Salvia nemorosa*
Veronica prostrata	*Stipa pulcherrima*

6.4
Tall grass prairie dominated by *Echinacea pallida*, Morton Arboretum, Chicago (early July). Note the C4 grasses that later in the year will dominate this prairie

Prairie

Prairie vegetation is naturally restricted to North America, where it stretches from the east of the Rocky mountains to the Appalachians (Figure 6.4). Its most northerly occurance is in Saskatchewan, Canada (45°N), and its most southerly, Texas. Prairie is a recent semi-natural vegetation, having developed within the past 10,000 years. Humans have played a major role in its evolution through the annual aboriginal burning of woodlands and savannah in combination with the grazing of wild ungulates. Without regular burning it is invaded by scrub, trees, weedy forbs and grasses, and slowly declines.

Whilst prairie is very rich in perennial forbs, it is typically dominated by warm season grasses. These are also referred to as C4 grasses, and are more drought-tolerant than the C3 or cool season grasses that dominate European and many montane grasslands in warmer parts of the world. As the name suggests, warm season grasses grow during the summer months and are fully dormant during the winter. The forbs in prairies are largely species that grow vigorously at lower temperatures. As a result of these two different growth strategies, there is, in essence, a window of low grass competition in spring that is exploited by the forbs. When cool season grasses invade prairie vegetation, whether semi-natural or created in urban landscapes, this has a detrimental effect on the vigour and survival of many forbs.

As can be seen from Table 6.5, soil moisture is again a key factor in determining the species composition of prairie, although some species occur across the full range of moisture conditions, for example *Aster laevis* and *Monarda fistulosa*. It is, however, unlikely that the genotypes of either of these species in a wet prairie are the same as those in a dry prairie. Species also have specific distributions within the prairie region, in east-west and north-south directions, for example *Aster turbinellus* is largely restricted to the region from central Illinois to Kansas (Gleason 1963). Most prairie species flower from July onwards. As a result of this and the presence of late developing warm season grasses, unlike most meadow vegetation, prairie is most attractive and 'tidy' in late summer and autumn. Prairie grasses remain structurally intact and attractive until the first frosts of autumn, when the foliage of many species turn yellow, orange or red.

As with all grassland vegetation, the height and openness of the community is determined by the combination of soil fertility and moisture availability. Dry prairie is more open than moist, and wet. Species of dry prairie are also typically shorter, for example *Asclepias tuberosa, Euphorbia corollata, Liatris aspera, Petalosporum purpureum* and *Schizachyrium scoparium*. They are also more intolerant of shading (particularly when grown in cooler climates) and, when used in designed landscapes on fertile moist soils, are likely to be eliminated by the growth of

Table 6.5. Commonly cultivated forbs and grasses characteristic of prairie vegetation in the northern US – grasses are in bold (derived from Curtis 1959; Gleason 1963; Ladd 1995; plus the observations of the author)

Dry prairie	Moist prairie	Wet prairie
Amorpha canescens	***Andropogon gerardii***	*Aster laevis*
Anemone cylindrica	*Aster ericoides*	*Aster novae-angliae*
Asclepias tuberosa	*Aster laevis*	*Cacalia atriplicifolia*
Aster ericoides	*Aster oolentangiensis*	*Dodecatheon meadia*
Aster laevis	*Aster turbinellus*	*Eupatorium maculatum*
Aster oolentangiensis	*Baptisia australis*	*Geranium maculatum*
Aster turbinellus	*Dodecatheon meadia*	*Helenium autumnale*
Coreopsis palmata	*Echinacea pallida*	*Helianthus grosseserratus*
Euphorbia corollata	*Echinacea purpurea*	*Liatris pycnostachya*
Helianthus laetiflorus	*Monarda fistulosa*	*Monarda fistulosa*
Liatris aspera	*Ratibida pinnata*	*Ratibida pinnata*
Monarda fistulosa	*Silphium integrifolium*	*Rudbeckia subtomentosa*
Petalosporum purpureum	*Silphium laciniatum*	*Silphium terebinthinaceum*
Schizachyrium scoparium	*Solidago rigida*	*Solidago ohioensis*
Solidago rigida	*Solidago speciosa*	***Spartina pectinata***
Sporobolus heterolepis	***Sorghastrum nutans***	*Vernonia fascicularis*
Verbena stricta	***Sporobolus heterolepis***	*Veronicastrum virginicum*

weedy species or taller growing prairie plant neighbours. As with meadows, dry prairie communities are most manageable when established on dry, infertile soils. They have the potential for use on low-volume roof gardens, as discussed by Dunnett (2002), however, they are generally less tolerant of extreme infertility and drought than European dry meadow species (Hitchmough *et al.* 2003).

Some prairie species are highly palatable to slugs and snails when cultivated in Britain, and this is a key factor in determining species choice. This is discussed in greater detail in the section 'Creation of naturalistic herbaceous plant communities in practice'. Many of the most robust of the prairie species that are traditionally cultivated in Britain (for example *Filipendula rubra* and *Veronicastrum virginicum*) are naturally associated with wet prairies.

Whilst prairie vegetation is generally thought of as a mixture of grasses and forbs, in some situations grass-only prairie communities can be developed. Prairie grasses require warm soil conditions for germination and establishment, but are not subject to mollusc damage and have highly attractive textures, subtle leaf colour and potentially stunning autumn leaf colour. Prairie grass establishment from seed is discussed further in the section 'Creation of naturalistic herbaceous plant communities in practice'. When planting is employed to create prairie-like communities, other C4 grasses, such as *Miscanthus*, can also be used.

Annual plant communities

Communities of annual plants are generally a response to either regular cycles of disturbance, as in agricultural situations, or highly seasonal rainfall patterns. In regions with temperate climates and reliable rainfall, annuals are mostly associated with agriculture (Figure 6.5). In Britain, cornfields with poppies, corn marigolds and other species are the best known and most charismatic annual plant community. Such communities are now rare due to improved seed cleaning and germination-inhibiting herbicides, and are best developed where low-intensity farming has been practiced. Before agriculture, annuals were far less significant plants in these regions, probably restricted to animal migration routes and other heavily disturbed sites. Most of the major annual plant communities of the world are, however, associated with winter rainfall, Mediterranean climates, for example, California, Arizona, southern Europe, northern Chile and Peru, southern Africa, western and central Australia, plus summer rainfall climates, such as eastern Mexico and Texas. Here severe seasonal drought restricts competition from perennial herbaceous plants other than bulbs, allowing the development of rich annual plant communities.

6.5
Annuals in fallowed field in Austria, *Papaver rhoeas* and *Consolida ambigua* dominate

Most of the winter rainfall species in Table 6.6 are referred to in the horticultural literature as 'hardy annuals', for example, Mansfield (1949) and Lloyd and Rice (1997), in that they can be established by sowing outside where they are to grow. As a designed vegetation, annuals are valuable because they often have very attractive flowers that are produced within three to four months of sowing.

6.6
Spontaneously occurring synanthropic vegetation, with lupins intermixed with native species, such as cow parsley, outside a garden in Hampshire

Table 6.6. Commonly cultivated annual forbs found in plant communities in various parts of the world (derived from Phillips and Rix 1999; plus the observations of the author)

European/Western Asian cornfields	Seasonally arid North America	Southern Europe
Agrostemma githago	*Argemone squarrosa**	*Chrysanthemum coronarium*
Agrostemma gracilis	*Clarkia pulchella*	*Iberis umbellata*
Anthemis arvensis	*Cleome serrulata**	*Lavatera trimestris*
Anthemis tinctoria	*Coreopsis tinctoria**	*Linum grandiflorum*
Centaurea cyanus	*Eschscholzia californica*	*Lupinus micranthus*
Chrysanthemum segetum	*Limnanthes douglasii*	*Nigella papillosa*
Consolida ambigua	*Lupinus texensis**	*Papaver somniferum*
Nigella damascena	*Mentzelia lindleyi*	*Salvia viridis*
Papaver commutatum	*Phacelia tanacetifolia*	*Scabiosa atropurpurea*
Papaver rhoeas	*Phlox drummondii**	*Silene coeli-rosa*

* Species found in climates experiencing summer rainfall. All other species are primarily from winter rainfall climates. Most species associated with European cornfields are essentially winter rainfall species, whose flowering is often delayed into summer by low winter and spring temperatures.

With such a short timescale, providing the soil is moist, if a sowing fails, it can be repeated and still get flowers in the same season. Many species demonstrate high-establishment rates, and are fast growing and initially able to compete with weedy species on-site. A significant disadvantage of annuals is that they are transient and, even with management to encourage regeneration from self-sown seed, often require over-sowing on a yearly basis. The key design challenges in developing annual plant communities is to select a range of species that will extend flowering from summer through to autumn, rather than the four weeks typically associated with standard cornfield annual mixes. In Britain, this sometimes involves the addition of annuals from summer rainfall climates, for example *Coreopsis tinctoria* and *Rudbeckia hirta*, which have higher temperature requirements for growth and, consequently, flower in Britain from late summer into autumn (Dunnett 1999) (Table 6.6).

Annuals also have a role to play in providing seasonal colour in the first year of sowings of perennial species, providing species are chosen that do not compete too aggressively with seedlings of the latter.

Human sponsored 'synanthropic' urban vegetation

Many of the plant communities described so far are associated with agricultural practice, and thus are intimately associated with human beings. More often, however, human-sponsored vegetation is seen as associated with the following.

Spontaneous occurring

These types of vegetation have been identified in many cities around the world, often on derelict land in transition from one use to another. They generally involve a mix of opportunistic native and exotic species. The resulting vegetation often reflects local variations in land use, cultural practices and climate. As a result, these spontaneous plant communities often differ substantially even between different cities within a relatively small geographical area

(Gilbert 1992) and are of considerable ecological interest (Table 6.7).

Spontaneous urban vegetation is generally associated with the subsoils, crushed building rubbles, and shallow layers of transported topsoils used as a surface covering. As many of the plants involved often have strong ruderal tendencies, there is often dramatic change in the vegetation during the first five years after the colonisation event. Community composition is often strongly related to soil productivity, with nitrogen-fixing legumes, such as clovers, medics and naturalised garden escapes such as *Galega officinalis*, dominating initially on the most infertile materials. These often decline in importance as they contribute to increasing soil nitrogen, and are replaced by taller non-nitrogen fixing forbs and grasses. In Sheffield, for example, there is a gradual increase in the standing biomass of perennial long-lived species such as *Chamaenerion angustifolium, Solidago gigantea, Saponaria officinalis* and *Centaurea nigra*. Many of these species will have been established as part of the initial wave of colonists, but are initially held in check by low soil nitrogen levels. High rates of seed production and dispersal are common characteristics of synanthropic species.

Table 6.7. Typical forbs of synanthropic plant communities in maritime versus continental climates in Europe (adapted from Gilbert 1992; Kühn 2000; plus the observations of the author)

Sheffield, UK	Berlin, Germany
Artemisia absinthium	*Aster lanceolatus*
Aster novi-belgii and Hybrids	*Aster tradescantii*
Chamaenerion angustifolium	*Centaurea stoebe*
Galega officinalis	*Diplotaxis tenuifolia*
Hypericum perforatum	*Doronicum pardalianches*
Leucanthemum maximum	*Geranium pyrenaicium*
Linaria purpurea	*Helianthus tuberosus*
Lupinus polyphyllus	*Impatiens glandulifera*
Oenothera biennis	*Oenothera biennis*
Saponaria officinalis	*Oenothera parviflora* agg.
Senecio squalidus	*Senecio inaequidens*
Solidago canadensis	*Senecio vernalis*
Tanacetum vulgare	*Solidago canadensis*
Taraxacum officinale agg.	*Solidago gigantea*

Although the public may consider these plant communities to be weedy, they are often unique assemblages closely associated with human environments. Some of these communities are extremely attractive, and, given that they are clearly well-fitted to urban conditions, in some cases they provide an attractive basis for developing truly sustainable naturalistic vegetation. In Berlin, Kühn (2000) is working on creating new urban plant communities based on the combination of spontaneous local species supplemented with non-naturalised species to add additional colour and interest. A potential disadvantage of these types of communities is that they may be viewed negatively by the public because of the visual associations of some species with derelict land and the notion of urban decay.

Designed urban herbaceous vegetation

There are many examples of these in gardens and parks, however very few are naturalistic (as defined in this text) in conception and their existence is dependent on traditional intensive maintenance. As such, they are essentially outside the scope of this text. A herbaceous vegetation that is relatively common and able to persist in perpetuity with only minimal maintenance input is bulbs planted in seasonally mown grass (Table 6.8). Over the past 20 years this has become a popular vegetation in urban parks, albeit in rather depauperate form, often involving *Narcissus* cultivars only. Far richer versions of this vegetation type can be found in botanical gardens and private gardens. Probably the best example in Britain of this style occurs in the garden at Great Dixter in East Sussex (Lloyd 1976a, 1976b).

6.7 (right)
Dutch crocus cultivars planted in grass at Kew. This produces a dramatic but short season display that can be extended by planting bulbs in meadows rather than mown grass

6.8 (above)
***Camassia leitchlinii* planted into a mixed native-exotic wet meadow by the author on experimental plots at RHS Harlow Carr, Harrogate**

Here a wide diversity of bulbs have been planted in relatively unproductive meadow grassland over the past 100 years. Flowering commences in autumn with *Colchicum* and *Crocus*, then continues with a succession of species through to early summer with *Gladiolus communis* subsp. *byzantinus* and *Iris latifolia*. The bulbs are complemented by native and non-native meadow forbs and grasses to create an Elysian landscape. The grass is cut as hay in early August and in some areas is given a second cut in September to allow the autumn crocus to display their flowers without too much competition from the meadow grasses. The management of this system is described by Garrett and Dusoir (2001). Bulbs are generally easier to establish in meadow grasslands than many forbs, as they often avoid strong competition with grasses by growing early in the year, when grass growth is restricted by low temperatures (Figure 6.7).

Bulbs are part of many semi-natural herbaceous plant communities and can be used to provide spring interest. Their successful establishment generally depends on integrating their leaf phenology into the management system necessary to maintain the core plant community. In many cases they restrict, for example, spring mowing in meadow situations (Figure 6.8), and interfere with spring burning and other forms of weed management in prairie-like vegetation.

Creation of naturalistic herbaceous plant communities in practice

Naturalistic herbaceous communities can be created by either sowing seed *in situ* where the plants are to grow, planting nursery grown transplants, or through a combination of planting and sowing. Which is most appropriate depends on the

Table 6.8. Bulbous species that successfully establish and persist in seasonally mown turf/meadow grassland in Britain (adapted from Lloyd 1976a, 1976b; Phillips and Rix 1981; Garrett and Dusoir 2001; plus the observations of the author)

Winter/early spring	Spring	Late spring/ early summer	Autumn
Crocus tomasinianus	*Anemone blanda*	*Camassia* spp.	*Colchicum autumnale* and cvs
Eranthus hyemalis	*Anemone nemorosa*	*Gladiolus communis* subsp. *byzantinus*	*Colchicum byzantinum*
Galanthus nivalis and cv	*Crocus chrysanthus* cvs	*Hyacinthoides hispanica*	*Colchicum speciosum* and cvs
Narcissus pseudonarcissus	*Crocus vernus* cvs	*Hyacinthoides non-scripta*	*Crocus nudiflorus*
	Fritillaria meleagris	*Iris latifolia*	*Crocus speciosus*
	Leucojum vernum	*Leucojum aestivum*	
	Muscari armeniacum	*Lilium martagon*	
	Narcissus (large flowered)	*Lilium pyrenaicium*	
	Narcissus bulbocodium	*Moraea spathacea*	
	Narcissus cyclamineus cvs	*Narcissus poeticus* and cvs	
	Narcissus triandrus	*Ornithogalum narbonense*	
	Ranunculus ficaria	*Tulipa sprengeri*	
	Scilla sibirica		
	Tulipa sylvestris		

6.9
Seeding produces a very naturalistic look, with high densities of species in this prairie sown in Sheffield

characteristics of the site, the plant community and the needs of the client. Table 6.9 summarises the characteristics of these three options.

Establishment by sowing in situ

Choice of communities and species

As has been discussed in the section 'Types of herbaceous plant communities: habitat stereotypes', basing choice of communities and species upon habitat stereotypes, as presented in Tables 6.1 to 6.6, helps to arrive at plants that are broadly compatible with a landscape site and one another (Figure 6.9). With native species it is possible to buy seed as individual species or pre-formulated as mixes for various soil conditions. Most practitioners lack the knowledge and experience to make up their own mixes, and buy pre-formulated mixes. Whilst these are satisfactory for general use they suffer from the following disadvantages.

Many provide a mix of grasses and forbs in the ratio 4:1 (by seed weight). This is fine if you want a very grassy vegetation to provide quick cover, but is less satisfactory where a meadow dominated by colourful forbs is desired. In our experience, most forbs flower earlier in life and more abundantly when sown in the absence of grasses. Some suppliers will provide forb and grass mixes separately.

You are limited to what is offered in terms of species and the relative proportions of these. This is very limiting in terms of producing specific effects, for example dramatic colour combinations or a high density of a specific species.

You can also buy 'off the peg' mixes for non-native species, for example various types of North

Table 6.9. Advantages and disadvantages associated with the main methods of establishing naturalistic herbaceous vegetation

	Key advantages	Key disadvantages
Sowing *in situ*	Inexpensive, cost of seed <£1.50 m^2	Requires specialised skills to weigh out small quantities of seed, pre-treat seed where required, calibrate sowing equipment
	Cost of implementation low	Access to accurate electronic scales is necessary
	Produces very fluid, naturalistic effects	Most contractors have little experience of establishing vegetation by sowing *in situ*
	High densities of plants readily achievable	Timing of sowing has a major impact upon success. This is not always possible in commercial landscape projects
	Complicated planting plans are not required	Successful establishment often requires good control of the germination environment. This is not always possible
	Can be used on mechanically hostile soils that are difficult to plant	Minimal initial impact
	Lower susceptibility of vandalism and, in particular, plant theft	Often requires control of slugs for high seedling establishment
	More sustainable, as energy intensive nursery facilities are not required	Weed control is more complex than with planting
	Essential for annuals and biennials	
Planting	High-initial impact	Expensive to very expensive for plant materials
	Can use particular cultivars	May require drafting of complex, difficult to follow planting plans
	Contractors are more familiar with planting as an establishment technique	Slow and expensive to implement, due to the high density of planting
	Can use mulching to reduce weed invasion	Tends to import nursery weeds into the site
	Allows for the use of plants that are highly palatable to slugs as seedlings but not as adults	
	Can be undertaken at any time of the year given irrigation, etc.	
Planting and sowing *in situ*	Allows for reasonably high initial-impact at relatively low plant material and implementation costs	Makes initial management more complicated, i.e. planted material inhibits mowing over to control seedling weeds
	Can use particular cultivars	Tend to import nursery weeds into the site
	Allows for the use of plants that are highly palatable to slugs as seedlings but not as adults	Shares some of the disadvantages of sowing *in situ* listed above

American Prairie plant communities, but they suffer from the same problems as the above. The advantage of 'off the peg' mixes is that you do not need to know as much about what you are doing, you instruct a contractor to sow at 4 g/m^2 and hope for the best. If you want to use sowing more creatively to produce designed naturalistic vegetation, it is necessary to formulate your own mixes.

To do this you need to think through your visual and functional requirements, then formulate a mix to satisfy these. A portable scientific balance (approximate cost £120.00) is essential to weigh out grams of seed. Examples of a successful seed mixes that the author developed for the prairie exhibit at the Eden Project are given in Table 6.10. This site had to look colourful from July to Autumn, and tolerate the dry, infertile, sandy soil but also the high rainfall climate.

Seed dormancy

Seed of herbaceous plants may be either dormant or non-dormant. Dormancy is the condition when the seed is capable of germination but fails to do so when provided with the appropriate conditions. If this phenomenon is not considered when selecting species for seed mixes, low levels of establishment are likely. A detailed discussion of seed dormancy is beyond the scope of this text but can be found in Baskin and Baskin (2001). A categorisation of dormancy is given in terms of landscape practice in Table 6.11.

Non-dormant species germinate in moist soil as soon as they experience high enough soil

Table 6.10. A prairie seed mix formulated by the author for the Eden Project, Cornwall

	Number of seed per g	Typical percentage of field establishment*	Desired plants per m^2	**g/seed/m^2 in order to achieve this**	Total amount of seed required (g/m^2 x total area of 1,250 m^2)
Aster azureus	2,877	15	15	**0.03**	43.4
Aster laevis	1,684	8	10	**0.07**	92.8
Echinacea pallida	175	40	10	**0.14**	178.1
Echinacea purpurea	232	30	15	**0.22**	269.9
Euphorbia corollata	351	20	10	**0.14**	178.1
Helianthus mollis	270	40	5	**0.05**	57.8
Helianthus occidentalis	456	20	10	**0.11**	137.1
Liatris aspera	474	20	10	**0.11**	132.0
Liatris pycnostachya	421	15	10	**0.16**	197.9
Petalosporum purpureum	714	15	10	**0.09**	116.7
Ratibida pinnata	947	30	10	**0.04**	44.0
Rudbeckia subtomentosa	1,614	5	10	**0.12**	154.9
Silphium integrifolium	140	40	2	**0.04**	44.5
Solidago rigida	1,614	40	10	**0.02**	19.4
Solidago speciosa	3,684	20	10	**0.01**	17.0
Total:			147.00	**1.35**	1,683.63

* Based on previous performance in field experiments.

Table 6.11. Seed dormancy in commonly cultivated herbaceous plants (data derived from Atwater 1980; Rock 1981; Baskin and Baskin 2001; Jelitto 2002; Prairie Nursery 2002; plus the experiments of the author)

Highly dormant	**Slightly dormant**	**Dormant, physical**
Aconitum	*Echinacea pallida*	*Amorpha canescens*
Astrantia	*Helianthus*	*Baptisia*
Deschampsia cespitosa	*Primula japonica*	*Lupinus*
Molinia caerulea	*Primula pulverulenta*	*Petalosporum purpureum*
*Paeonia**	*Rudbeckia fulgida*	*Stipa*
Persicaria bistorta	*Silphium*	*Thermopsis*
Primula veris	*Solidago speciosa*	
Pulsatilla vulgaris	*Veronicastrum virginicum*	
Rhinanthus minor		
Stachys officinalis		
Trollius		
Non-dormant	**Non-dormant, erratic**	
Aster (most)	*Aster laevis*	
Buphthalmum	*Euphorbia*	
Campanula (most)	*Geranium*	
Centaurea scabiosa	*Inula ensifolia*	
Echinacea purpurea	*Linum narbonense*	
Grasses (most meadow)	*Malva moschata*	
Grasses (most prairie)	*Ranunculus acris*	
Leucanthemum vulgare		
Lychnis chalcedonica		
Origanum vulgare		
Papaver orientale		
Primula (sikkimensis group)		
Primula denticulata		
Sanguisorba officinalis		
Solidago rigida		
Thalictrum aquilegifolium		

* Double dormant, requires warm then cold then warm cycles to germinate.

temperatures and are generally straightforward to establish by field sowing. Most annuals are non-dormant as dried seed; some species demonstrate dormancy immediately post-harvest but this disappears in dry storage. The most unreliable species for field sowing are generally either those with deeply dormant seed (see Table 6.11), or non-dormant with erratic germination. In both of these cases (even after treatment for dormancy), the percentage of seedling emergence tends to be low and extended over a period of time. On infertile sites with low numbers of weed seedlings, late-germinating seedlings may survive. On most fertile, weedy sites, these are eliminated as a result of competition for light with larger adjacent seedlings. Exceptions to this are species such as *Primula veris* and *Stachys officinalis* seedlings, both of which are highly shade-tolerant and unpalatable to slugs, and continue to appear up to two years post-sowing.

Treatment to overcome seed dormancy

Where treatments are necessary to break seed dormancy or to improve germination in non-dormant species, simplicity and efficacy are the key to choosing a technique. Commonly used techniques are as follows.

Winter chilling in situ

This is the most straightforward and, in many cases, most effective technique for deeply or lightly dormant seed. Seed is sown in autumn through to early winter and allowed to chill in the soil. Rain increases leaching of germination-inhibiting compounds from the seed coat. Deeply dormant species, such as *Astrantia*, need to be sown in the autumn to ensure sufficient chilling is experienced. The disadvantage of this technique is that small seeds, in particular, may be lost by being buried too deeply by worm casts, removed by seed predators or washed into deep fissures in the soils by heavy rain.

Chilling in a fridge

This is generally most effective with slightly, as opposed to deeply, dormant species. The seed is mixed with damp sand (not wet) in a sealed polythene bag and is placed in a fridge at approximately 4°C for between 4 and 12 weeks, depending on the species. It is also useful for reducing erratic emergence in non-dormant species. For recommendations on prairie species, see the guidelines produced by Prairie Nursery (2002a). Fridge chilling is not as effective as chilling *in situ* for more deeply dormant species due to the constant temperature and lack of leaching. Dropping the fridge temperature to 1°C improves germination for some of the latter species. Overall, however, where possible chilling *in situ* is to be preferred as it is less complicated and avoids risks of the seed being exposed to anaerobic conditions in excessively wet sand or germinating prematurely in the fridge. Fridge chilled seed is more sensitive to soil moisture stress during germination.

Mechanical abrasion

This is used for seed with impermeable seed coats, as in the pea family. Samples of the seeds are placed between sheets of fine-medium sand paper and are rubbed together until there is evidence of seed coat abrasion. This is effective, however it is rather difficult to be sure when sufficient abrasion has occurred. An alternative is to place the seed into hot or boiling water for various time-periods. This is easier to standardise but finding specific recommendations for a given species is often difficult, however see Hartmann *et al.* (2001).

Treatment with dormancy breaking plant hormones

Deeply dormant species, such as *Trollius*, can be made to germinate reliably by soaking in gibberelic acid, or in combination with other treatments, for example leaching (Hitchmough *et al.* 2000). Whilst this is essentially kitchen-level science, it is probably

Table 6.12. Typical percentage field establishment of prairie, wet meadow and dry meadow species given adequate pre-treatment (where necessary) to break dormancy and sown under ideal soil moisture conditions. Data derived from author's experiments

Low to very low field establishment (<10%)	Medium field establishment (10–30%)	High to very high field establishment (30–50%)
Prairie species	**Prairie species**	**Prairie species**
Aster laevis	*Aster oolentangiensis*	*Aster novae-angliae*
Solidago ohioensis	*Baptisia australis*	*Echinacea pallida*
Sporobolus heterolepis	*Coreopsis lanceolata*	*Echinacea purpurea*
Veronicastrum virginicum	*Helianthus mollis*	*Monarda fistulosa*
	Liatris aspera	*Ratibida pinnata*
Damp/wet meadow species	*Liatris pycnostachya*	*Solidago rigida*
Aconitum napellus	*Rudbeckia subtomentosa*	
Campanula lactiflora	*Schizachyrium scoparium*	**Damp/wet meadow species**
Primula denticulata	*Silphium*	*Lychnis chalcedonica*
Primula florindae	*Solidago speciosa*	*Polemonium caeruleum*
Stachys officinalis	*Sorghastrum nutans*	*Primula vulgaris*
Succisa pratensis		*Ranunculus acris**
	Damp/wet meadow species	*Rumex acetosa*
	Astrantia major	*Sanguisorba officinalis*
	Thalictrum aquilegifolium	
	Trollius europaeus	**Dry meadow species**
		Buphthalmum salicifolium
	Dry meadow species	*Daucus carota*
	Centaurea scabiosa	*Dianthus carthusianorum*
	Hieracium aurantiacum	*Lychnis coronaria*
	Malva moschata	*Primula veris*
	Origanum vulgare	*Salvia nemorosa*
	Papaver orientale	

* When sown in winter.

too complex for use in practice. Jelitto Seeds offers chemically treated seed (Jelitto GoldNugget Seed®) of a wide range of deeply dormant or erratic non-dormant species. This is more expensive than dry seed but gives very predictable results.

Germination requirements of a wide range of herbaceous plants are given in the Jelitto Seed Catalogue (Jelitto 2002), although, in some cases, germination is more erratic in field sowing than indicated, as recommendations are based on germination under controlled nursery conditions.

Cost of seed in relation to number of plants established

The cost of seed varies considerably between different species. Seed of agricultural strains of native grasses is the cheapest, followed by field-grown native wildflowers and the seed of wild collected native grasses and forbs. By purchasing the seed of species that are not native to Britain, for example North American Prairie forbs and grasses, from native seed producers in those countries, costs are often very comparable to that of British native wildflowers. For exotic species in general, there are a number of wholesale seed companies whose main market is the nursery industry. The company with the most extensive range of perennial forbs and grasses is Jelitto Seeds.

Comparing species only in terms of the catalogue price of seed is potentially rather misleading. A species with expensive seed may demonstrate very high percentage establishment when sown in the field, whereas species with inexpensive seed might show low percentage establishment. Individual seed weight is also important, the bigger the seed the fewer supplied per gram. Some seed price and seed weight differentials even out when percentage field establishment (the number of plants you expect to establish for every 100 seeds sown) is taken into account. For any given species, actual values for percentage field establishment vary between seed batches and from situation to situation according to soil moisture, temperature and sowing practice. Despite this, the research of the author suggests it is possible to categorise seed into broad categories, as shown in Table 6.12. Most annuals fall into the high to very high field establishment category.

Species that show low field establishment are often (but by no means always) those with very small seed, which are more sensitive to soil-moisture stress during germination and emergence.

How much seed is required per square metre?

When making up seed mixes it is desirable to set a target number of plants per m^2, both as a total for all species present and for individual species, and, from this, work out the amount of seed required. The total number of plants required will vary depending upon the size of the plants at maturity, the visual characteristics required and the weediness of the site. A typical total plant target would be between 100 and 200 plants/m^2. On weedy sites, higher seedling densities are desirable, as if one starts with a low density of sown species it is very difficult to dominate weedy species in the longer term. Sites that will be viewed from close quarters, plus the edges of sowings, also require higher than average densities. High-target densities are, however, potentially problematic, not only in terms of greater seed cost but also because this may lead to the elimination of the slower growing sown species by more vigorous species. In prairie sowings on fertile soil, for example, *Baptisia australis* and *Echinacea pallida* show relatively high establishment, but seedlings grow slowly and few seedlings survive the first year. Despite this, it is often better to go for higher densities, as at low densities on weedy sites, slow growing species may, in any case, be eliminated by weedy species. Low target densities are only sensible on sites where weed competition can be effectively managed, or with species that, in the longer term, will reliably fill in gaps through their own self-seeding.

Within the overall total target density (for example 100 plants/m^2), it is necessary to decide on target densities for individual species. This involves decision making analagous to that undertaken in conventional planting design. If, for example, you want more or less even numbers of plants of each species in the vegetation, you might go for a target density of 10 plants per species/m^2. In many cases, however, this would be unsatisfactory. It is more likely that you would want to establish one or less plants per m^2 of really tall emergent species, for example *Silphium terebinthinaceum*. Any more and you will lose the rhythmic emergent qualities and will end up with a dense stand. You might want to increase the numbers of key species, for example, those that have a particularly long flowering season, for example *Echinacea purpurea*, or flower at a specific time when it is desirable to maximise impact. Target numbers allows practitioners to 'design' sown vegetation, rather than be passive bystanders. This is contingent, however, on having access to percentage field establishment data, as shown in Table 6.12.

Following the example of a seed mix given in Table 6.10, pasting the following formula into an Excel spreadsheet will automatically calculate the weight of seed per m^2, where seed numbers per g, typical percentage field establishment, and target number of plants per species is known. For example:

> =SUM(1/(cell reference that contains seed number/g* cell reference that contains typical field % establishment/100)*cell reference that contains desired number of plants/m^2)

The total weight of seed sown per g are typically between 0.5 and 2.0 g/m^2, depending on the target numbers and the weight of the seed of individual species. Providing that species with extremely expensive seed are excluded, the cost of seed mixes of this type will generally be between £0.50 and £1.50/m^2.

Ecological/phenological compatability of species in mixes

The need for species in ecologically based vegetation to be broadly compatible with one another has been discussed previously. When creating novel plant communities that may lie outside the community stereotypes in Tables 6.1 to 6.6, it is particularly important to undertake a more detailed assessment of likely compatibility in terms of the growth characteristics of each proposed species. Key factors in determining this are as follows.

Growth rate

Mixing species with widely varying growth rates, i.e. very fast and very slow, often leads to the former eliminating the latter by shading. For slow or very small growing species to persist in mixture with vigorous species, they must be highly shade-tolerant or dormant during the summer months.

Growth habit

Wide-spreading species with dense foliage at grown level, for example *Coreopsis lanceolata* or *Rudbeckia hirta*, tend to eliminate slower growing shade-intolerant species. Tall, erect species, even when vigorous, have a less detrimental impact on seedlings of other species, due to reduced light-interception.

Phenology

This is often important in the second and subsequent growing season for either ecological or management reasons. Species that have evergreen winter foliage will, when mixed with species that are winter dormant, restrict the use of herbicides or burning to kill or defoliate colonising weeds. In some cases, of course, this winter foliage may preclude the need to burn or herbicide, by excluding weed species. It may also, however, provide habitat for molluscs that may increase damage to spring emerging species, or simply provide too much competition for light at a critical time. In meadows, winter evergreen species, such as *Papaver orientale*, may decline if closely mown, restricting the timing of cutting. One of the main challenges in developing ecological plant communities is to juggle with phenology to make the planting more sustainable but still manageable. North American prairie species are problematic in northern Britain because the climate is too cool to reliably establish prairie grasses. As a result, there is no cover of dead grass on the soil surface in winter to restrict weed invasion during mild wet British winters. A shade-tolerant, winter dormant, cool season tussock grass, such as *Molinia caerulea*, might be an effective replacement. Alternatively, a shade-tolerant, easy to establish, non-competitive, winter evergreen, such as *Festuca ovina* or *Primula vulgaris*, might be equally successful. The author has not yet tested such plant communities. They may not work for the reasons already given, but it demonstrates the necessary thought process.

Ecological strategy

This has been discussed in terms of the plant strategy models of Grime in Chapter 4.

These models, in essence, integrate some of the factors already discussed, with regard to growth rate, etc., and are very useful aids to plant selection. A rather demanding example of this can be found in Hodgson (1989). Strategy data on individual native species are provided in Grime *et al.* (1988). Hitchmough (1994) has speculated on the strategies of a number of exotic species.

6.10
The effect of slug control during the first four weeks post-germination on the survival of sown North American prairie forbs: (a) the plot was pelleted with metaldehyde; and (b) the plot was not pelleted

Table 6.13. Relative palatability of seedlings to slugs and snails (from Hanley *et al.* 1995; Scheidel and Brueheide 1999; and as yet unpublished research of the author)

Highly palatable	Low palatability
Arnica montana	*Aster oolentangiensis*
Asclepias tuberosa	*Aster laevis*
Baptisia australis	*Aster novae-angliae*
Cacalia atriplicifolia	*Geranium sylvaticum* and many other spp.
Centaurea orientalis	*Knautia arvensis*
Echinacea purpurea	*Lychnis chalcedonica*
Helianthus mollis	*Persicaria bistorta*
Liatris aspera	*Primula veris*
Ratibida pinnata	*Ranunculus acris*
Salvia nemorosa	*Rudbeckia subtomentosa*
Silphium terebinthinaceum	*Rumex acetosa*
Trollius europaeus	*Schizachyrium scoparium*
	Silphium integrifolium
	Sorghastrum nutans
	Sporobolus heterolepis
	Stachys officinalis
	Succisa pratensis
	Veronicastrum virginicum

Palatability to slugs and snails

Relatively little is known about the palatability of seedlings of different species to slugs and snails. As a general rule, as seedlings age they become increasingly less palatable, due to increases in the concentrations of various chemical substances and, in some cases, morphological features, such as surface hairs (Table 6.13). *Trollius europaeus*, for example, is rarely grazed by slugs as an adult, but is highly palatable as young seedlings (Hitchmough 2003). The same also appears to be true for many *Primula* species. Some forbs are attractive to molluscs even as adults and are correspondingly ephemeral in landscape projects. In sites with high densities of slugs and snails, control of these

Table 6.14. Examples of particularly robust but non-invasive forb species

Dry meadow	Damp-wet meadow	Prairie	Annuals
Buphthalmum salicifolium	*Centaurea nigra*	*Aster laevis*	*Agrostemma githago*
Dianthus carthusianorum	*Euphorbia palustris*	*Eupatorium maculatum*	*Centaurea cyaneus*
Galium verum	*Geranium sylvaticum*	*Helianthus mollis*	*Chrysanthemum segetum*
Malva moschata	*Geranium x magnificum*	*Rudbeckia fulgida* var. *deamii*	*Papaver rhoeas*
Origanum vulgare	*Persicaria bistorta*	*Rudbeckia subtomentosa*	*Papaver somniferum*
Papaver orientale	*Sanguisorba obtusa*	*Silphium integrifolium*	*Phacelia tanacetifolia*
Primula veris	*Sanguisorba officinalis*	*Veronicastrum virginicum*	*Rudbeckia hirta*

herbivores during the emergence period will normally greatly increase the diversity and density of sown and weed species (Figure 6.10).

'Robustness' as established plants

This characteristic derives from the combination of high tolerance of competition, longevity and low palatability to slugs as established plants. When dealing with very weedy sites or sites where management is likely to be restricted, at least a core of the species selected should possess these characteristics. These species may, however, be those most likely to naturalise beyond the site, and so caution needs to be exercised (Table 6.14).

Establishment practice

TIME OF SOWING

The key factor that determines successful germination and establishment of all herbaceous plants is soil moisture (Fuller 1987; Wilson and Gerry 1995; Hitchmough *et al.* 2003). Consequently, the optimal time for sowing generally coincides with the months of lowest soil-moisture stress that are warm enough for germination to occur. Within this generalisation there are some specific times that research or practice have shown to be optimal for specific communities and species, as shown in Table 6.15.

Site preparation

WEED CONTROL

This is a fundamental requirement for successful establishment and longer-term community development. Most urban sites support large populations of aggressive weed species. If these are not controlled prior to sowing, they will eliminate many of the sown forbs that germinate. In the longer term, some weed species will be controlled in grassy, meadow-like plant communities by the mowing-grazing regime. By this time, however, many of the desired species are likely to have disappeared. The practice of eliminating one vegetation to achieve an ecologically-based successor may seem to be a contradiction. Regeneration by seed in many semi-natural ecosystems is, however, an occasional event, with most seedlings eliminated by competition from the surrounding established vegetation (Grubb 1977; Morgan 1995). The potentially beneficial effects of established plants reducing soil-moisture stress by providing shade are outweighed by the harmful effects of shade on photosynthesis and root competition for water and nutrients. In most cases, competition is uniformly detrimental to the establishment and survival of sown species (Aguilera and Lauenroth 1995; Hutchings and Booth 1996). It is, however, important to assess the existing botanical significance of sites prior to finalising

Table 6.15. Optimal sowing times for herbaceous vegetation

Vegetation type	Sowing dates	
North American prairie grasses	March–July	Seed have high-temperature requirements for germination (C4 species), but are also intolerant of soil-moisture stress. As with prairie forbs, sowings beyond July are often unsuccessful. Frost heave and surface erosion results in low seedling survival
North American prairie forbs	March–June or October–February	A diverse group of species that germinate at lower temperatures than prairie grasses. Most species show most reliable germination from October–February sowings as the chilling requirements of species are automatically met. March–June is, however, satisfactory for many species when fridge pre-chilling in moist sand is employed, and is essential if prairie grasses are to be included
Eurasian meadow grasses and forbs	March–June, August–September or October–March	Again, a very diverse group, although many species establish from spring or early autumn sowings. Overwintering losses are often less than for prairie-type species. Species that require lengthy winter chilling for germination, for example *Primula veris, Astrantia* and *Rhinanthus*, must be sown between October and December
Annual forbs	April–June	Providing the soil is moist, time of sowing will often be determined by when a flowering display is required. Species from warm, summer rainfall climates, for example *Cosmos*, *Cleome* and *Helianthus annua*, establish poorly when sown into cold soils under short day conditions

decisions on replacement vegetation.

Established weedy vegetation is most effectively eliminated through application of the translocated herbicide glyphosate, which is available as a range of proprietory products, for example 'Roundup Biactive'. This herbicide has extremely low mammalian toxicity. It can be used throughout the year, when weed foliage is present, but has no effect on dormant, leafless weeds or weed seeds in the soil. Most effective control is achieved when applied to actively growing weeds between March and October. One application will kill highly sensitive weeds, however, a second or even third application at three to six week intervals may be required to control stoloniferous or rhizomatous perennial weeds, such as couch grass, *Elymus repens*. Weeds must be controlled prior to moving or cultivating soil, as this inevitably complicates getting the herbicide into weeds via their foliage.

Where there are philosophical or legislative objections to the use of glyphosate, other weed-control techniques can be used, for example repeated cultivation, steam sterilisation and mulching with opaque sheet mulches. Some of these techniques can be reasonably successful but generally require a longer timescale and cost substantially more than herbicidal weed-control.

The most problematic weed source when sowing herbaceous plants *in situ* is the weed seed bank. Herbicides such as glyphosate make control of established weeds straightforward, however the process of seed bed production and raking to incorporate sown seed generates a weed germination 'pulse'. With plant communities where there is typically a lengthy lag between sowing and germination (for example as in autumn sowings of prairie forbs that will not germinate until spring), it is possible to overspray sowings with a herbicide such as glyphosate prior to emergence. There is always a fear of harming the sown seeds, however, in an unpublished study undertaken by the author on 10 species of prairie forbs there were no apparent adverse effects on the germination of the latter. This practice substantially reduces winter weed colonisation but does not give 100% control.

On long cultivated topsoils, the weed seed bank is numerically huge. Given sufficient time, the practice of shallow surface cultivation to promote weed germination followed by secondary cultivation some weeks later to kill these seedlings can reduce the weed seed bank. This is often referred to as the 'stale seedbed technique'. Where it is possible to do so, having a year to prepare a site is extremely helpful, but is only rarely possible. The density of the weed seed bank declines with soil depth, and is sparse or absent on many soils below 200 mm. Consequently, the use of the lower topsoil or subsoil as a sowing medium is an effective strategy, providing these soils are sufficiently well-structured to support plant growth. It is not, however, always possible to strip off areas of topsoil, but where a site has already had the topsoil removed, then a subsoil is often a better choice for direct seeding than a topsoil. Because most subsoils are composed of fine soil-particles that hold large amounts of water and readily maintain continuity of moisture films with germinating seeds, they sponsor high establishment of sown species.

Weed seed banks in topsoil can also be suppressed by blanketing with shallow layers of weed-free materials, such as subsoil or mineral aggregates. In our research in Sheffield we have found that a 40–50 mm layer of coarse sand gives very effective control of weed seed banks. These mulch layers are spread then seed is sown into them and lightly raked in. Percentage emergence is generally lower when the sand sowing technique is used due to the increased moisture-stress experienced. This can result in excellent weed-control but very poor establishment when dry conditions are experienced concurrent with germination. Except where irrigation is available, sand mulching is most appropriate for winter sowing. For sowings made during the spring to summer period, sowing into a subsoil mulch is likely to be a better alternative. These mulch layer techniques add significantly to the cost of sowing and are most appropriate for plant communities where the aim of management is to try to permanently exclude winter-growing grasses, as in the case of prairie-type vegetation or dry meadow-steppe vegetation dominated by forbs. For moist-wet meadow species tolerant of competition from cool season grasses, they are not justified.

Soil types

As can be gathered from the section 'Types of herbaceous plant communities: habitat stereotypes', there is potentially an attractive naturalistic herbaceous vegetation for every site, no matter how wet or dry, fertile or infertile, providing the community is thoughtfully matched to site soils. In general, the most difficult soils to deal with are those traditionally prized by landscape architects and horticulturists – the moist fertile loam. On these soils, competitive exclusion as a result of the rapid growth of weeds and the most vigorous sown species is often a problem, and the use of uniformly vigorous sown species is the most sensible strategy. These soils are, however, very suitable for many annual forbs that are able to compete by growing vigorously. In some cases, such soils may be better planted with conventional herbaceous or woody plants and managed by mulching to suppress the weed seed bank. Extreme soil conditions, for example, dry infertile soils and, to a lesser degree, wet soils offer designers an opportunity to produce highly interesting vegetation that really does respond to the site context. Plant growth is, however, often slow on marginal soils and it is important to prepare clients for this, so they do not misinterpret this as failure. Designers need to establish the range and nature of the soils present on a site prior to earthworking and before overall master-planning commences so that various substrates present can positively inform the design concept.

In semi-natural habitats, soil pH is often an important factor in determining which species are present plus typical species diversity. Typically, more diverse plant communities are often associated with limestone-derived soils. Some of the species associated with such soils (calcicoles) perform better under alkaline conditions, others grow satisfactorily on neutral and acid soils. In many cases, high plant diversity is often related to the fact that limestone-derived soils are not very fertile and, as a result, highly vigorous dominant species are absent or checked, allowing more species to co-exist. In our research on slightly acid soils in Sheffield, we have found many species that are often associated with limestone-derived soils, for example *Origanum vulgare*, to establish and persist satisfactorily. Overall, potential soil productivity appears to be more important for many species than soil pH *per se*.

Soil cultivation

In some cases, deep soil cultivation is essential, for example on crushed rubble soils to incorporate, for example, composted green waste, to improve root penetration and moisture retention. The cultivation of heavily compacted clay soils is also needed to improve root penetration and soil oxygenation. On less extreme soils, where established weeds have been controlled by herbicides, deep cultivation is often unnecessary and sometimes seriously detrimental. After standard rotavation to 200 mm, many soils can take more than six months to return to their pre-sowing density. This is often exacerbated by the destruction of soil structure due to too many passes with the rotavator. As a result, they tend to crack very deeply during dry periods and the surface layer containing the germinating seeds dry out more quickly, leading to lower seedling emergence and higher mortality. On most soils, cultivation for sowings of perennial species should be restricted to approximately a 25 mm deep surface layer to create a fine tilth for sowing.

Sowing practice

The goal of sowing is to obtain an adequate density of seedlings, relatively evenly distributed across the sown area with few bare patches.

Seed distribution

Depending on the area to be sown, broadcast sowing can be undertaken by hand by a chest-mounted spinning disk, a wheel-mounted spinning disk spreader or tractor-mounted equivalent. For really large-scale application, a tractor-mounted agricultural precision drill can be used. These are capable of giving very good results, however these are rarely available to urban projects. Their use in relation to seeding into existing meadow grassland and creating prairie vegetation on cultivated soils are discussed by Wells *et al*. (1987) and Morgan (1997), and see www.prairienursery.com.

To obtain even distribution when broadcasting, it is necessary to calibrate your application technique. The principles involved in doing this are the same for all types of equipment. If hand broadcasting, a bulky carrier, such as sawdust, chick feeder crumbs or sand, is used to make sowing easier. Sand is the most readily available but the heaviest material to work with:

- from your seed mix calculations, establish the weight of seed that you wish to sow per m^2
- calculate the total weight required for the area to be sown, i.e. if the area is 200 m^2 and your mix is to be sown at 1.5g/m^2, you need 300 g of seed mix
- for every m^2 of the area to be sown add one handful of your seed-sowing carrier (e.g. sand) to a clean wheelbarrow. If your area is 200 m^2, add 200 handfuls. This is made much quicker by marking a plastic bucket to show the volume equivalent to 50 handfuls of sand
- add the seed for this area (300 g) to the sand in the wheelbarrow, mix thoroughly
- mark off the area to be sown with string lines into a series of 1 m wide corridors
- transfer some of the sand-seed mix to a bucket and walk along the corridor distributing a handful of sand-seed mix over each metre of travel. Work across the site to be sown in this manner.

The above technique gives accurate sowing and the string lines corridor approach provides feedback to inexperienced sowers that reduces the risk of running out of seed halfway across the area to be sown. Precision in seed sowing is most important for sowings close to buildings and with species and communities that will not readily fill-in large gaps by self-seeding. Less precision is required with native meadows sown with a grass component. With spinning disk seed-applicators, the seed is sown without a carrier. Calibration is still necessary and involves walking over a large sheet of black polythene at a standardised walking rate, with the disk spinning at a standardised speed for a set distance, for example 5 m. The time taken to travel the 5 m is also recorded. The width of the seed distribution swathe can be observed (for example, 2 m), and since the distance travelled is also known (5 m), so is the area sown, i.e. 10 m^2. The seed on the polythene sheet is then carefully collected up and weighed on a balance. If the aim was to sow at 1.5g/m^2, there should be 15 g of seed on the sheet. If there is 7.5 g, the sower needs to half their speed of travel; if there is 30 g, then the speed of travel needs to double, and so on.

Depth of sowing-seed incorporation

Incorporating seed into the soil post-sowing by raking or harrowing on a large scale increases seed contact with moist soil and improves germination and establishment. The germination of small seed is sometimes (but not always) inhibited by darkness, and this may negate some of the benefits of incorporation post-broadcasting. Since most seed mixes will contain large, medium and small seed, there are several options:

- sow and rake into the top 5–10 mm of the soil
- mix the seed as two batches based on approximate seed size – medium-large and small. The former is sown first and is raked in. The small seed is then oversown onto the

6.11
The effect of controlling aggressive grass weeds on density and diversity of sown forbs: (a) a plot in an experiment with no grass control in year one; and (b) the same experiment but with grass control in year one

surface. Given that incorporation by raking or harrowing is a very crude process, with some seed always remaining on the surface, in our experience splitting the seed into two batches is rarely justified.

Where possible, sown sites should be rolled with a heavy roller post-sowing, especially if small seed has been surface sown. Rolling improves seed-soil contact and is most important on dry sites or with species that are particularly sensitive to moisture stress at germination.

Slug-snail control

Although not normally undertaken for sowings of native wildflower meadow species, some common native species are highly palatable to slugs (Hanley *et al.* 1995; Scheidel and Brueheide 1999), and on sites with dense mollusc populations, their establishment may be greatly reduced. The author's research on non-native species suggests that slugs have a major impact on the establishment of palatable species, and that a single application of metaldehyde-containing pellets will at least double the number of seedlings that establish. In this particular experiment, additional applications did not further improve seedling survival. Decisions on controlling slugs at germination need to balance possible adverse non-target effects with the likely failure of palatable species.

Weed management

This is more complicated than in planted vegetation due to confusion as to which seedlings are weeds and which are sown. There is also the physical problem of uprooting sown species as weed species are removed, and crushing sown species when moving through sown areas. Because of these difficulties, it is often necessary to adopt unconventional approaches to weed management in the first year. The basis of this is to try to minimise weed germination by a combination of the previously discussed techniques, stale seedbed techniques, use of soils with low-weed seed banks and the use of mulches, etc., as previously discussed. Weeds compete

6.12
The same experiment in year three, showing how plots with no grass control are essentially devoid of sown forbs

for light, water and nutrients, however, in the first year of a sowing, the most critical of these factors is often light. Dense shade cast by weeds causes the elimination of light-demanding sown species.

Weeds also have an adverse effect in that, when present in high densities, they provide habitat for slugs and this exacerbates the loss of palatable species. The impact of weeds on sown species varies considerably depending upon combinations of these factors in relation to the site.

The most effective weed-management technique we have investigated is a 50 mm deep-coarse sand mulch spread over the soil surface. Sand mulching has an additional long-term benefit in that it appears to reduce slug predation in spring as plants emerge from the soil. The problems of sand mulching reducing seedling establishment have been discussed under the section 'Weed control'.

Where it is not possible or desirable to use sand mulching, and sowings are made onto a weed seed rich topsoil, weed management will often rely on the mowing of sown vegetation to a height of approximately 50–100 mm (depending on the growth habit of the sown species). As most weeds grow faster than the sown species, weeds are more defoliated, improving the establishment chances of the former. Mowing needs to commence before the weeds get too tall, i.e. at 100–150 mm, typically in May or June. If left too late, the large volumes of cut trash left may shade-out sown seedlings. Typically, mowing can continue at fortnightly to monthly intervals. The effectiveness of mowing depends on the weeds present. It is most successful with annual dicots. Even with these, however, mowing changes the form of many erect weeds; they branch close to the ground casting denser shade than they might otherwise do.

Mowing is least effective on vigorous perennial grasses, as it encourages these to tiller and smother adjacent seedlings. Grasses can, however, be removed from sowings of forbs, by overspraying with selective grass herbicides. In Britain, sethoxydim (Checkmate®) had off-label approval for use on ornamental herbaceous plants (Whitehead 2002). We have used it on seedlings of a wide variety of species in our experiments with no obvious damage to forbs. It does not damage narrow-leafed fescues. The effect of this type of control on both the density and diversity of sown forbs on productive, weedy sites is very great (Figures 6.11 and 6.12).

Nurse crops are sometimes recommended to improve the establishment of sown species, often using annual or short-lived species, such as *Lolium multiflorum*. The benefits of such nurse crops are extremely dubious. Pywell *et al.* (2002) recorded a decrease in the number of grass weeds following the use of a *L. multiflorum* nurse crop, but no corresponding benefit in the establishment of sown meadow forbs. This is because vigorous nurse crops pose similar competitive pressures to non-sown weed species. Slower growing, less-aggressive nurse crops, for example annuals such as *Linum grandiflorum*, may confer some benefits to sown species, however it is difficult to see how they can effectively compete with weed species but not with sown species. The most valuable role of nurse crops of colourful annuals is probably to provide interest in year one, although this may be at the expense of the long-term success. In one of the author's prairie vegetation experiments, the inclusion of the fast-growing biennial *Coreopsis lanceolata* seemed successful in the first year when this species dominated the sowing. By year two, many had died out but, by then, they had also eliminated adjacent perennial prairie species. These gaps gradually colonised with weed species, leading to the collapse of the prairie community.

Where trained and diligent labour is available, it is possible to physically remove weeds in the first year of sowings. Owing to identification problems and the risk of uprooting small sown seedlings, this is often combined with mowing early in the season. By midsummer it is much easier to distinguish between weeds and sown species. Weeds can often be controlled with minimal surface disturbance by either dabbing them with a 50% solution of glyphosate through a mini wick wiper, or by using a very sharp, thin-bladed knife (we use serrated fish-filleting knives) to cut the weeds below ground by rotating the knife in the soil. The latter is also effective for controlling seedling docks (*Rumex* spp.), providing the tap root is cut more than 5 cm below soil level. String lines are placed across the sowings to provide a 1–2 m wide corridor to work through. Inevitably, some sown species are crushed but this has to be seen in a cost-benefit framework. Annual weeds need to be removed before they flower and set seed.

Weed control in the first year is crucial, especially in forb-only vegetation. By maximising establishment and growth, sown species are given the opportunity to dominate in the second year. If one enters the second growing season in the absence of intensive maintenance with low densities of sown species, and high densities of weeds, the prognosis is not good. The number of plants of sown species to provide a dense cover varies according to the size of individual plants, their growth habit and site productivity. Our research suggests that typically between 50 and 100 plants/m^2 are a minimum value.

Establishment by planting

Choice of communities and species

The key advantages of planting are that it allows you to establish species that perform poorly when sown as seed *in situ* and it fast tracks the whole process of creating a vegetation. Most critically, it allows a client to see that something positive has happened. It is, however, important to understand that, in the longer term, interactions between the nature of the site, management and the characteristics of the planted species will determine what species survive. Many species that are initially successful may decline and disappear by year five. Some of the factors that promote this change in species composition are largely independent of choice of planted species, however plant selection remains the key design input in determining long-term outcomes. Information given under the section 'Establishment by sowing in combination with planting' on ecological traits of herbaceous plants, plus the effect of soil productivity, soil moisture regime etc., is equally relevant to establishment by planting.

One factor that does differ when establishing naturalistic vegetation by planting is palatability to slugs and snails. Planted herbaceous plants are usually morphologically and physiologically adult, and are generally less palatable to molluscs. This allows the establishment of species that are very palatable as young seedlings, for example *Trollius europaeus* (Hitchmough 2003), in slug rich sites. Information on the typical palatability of adult herbaceous plants to molluscs in spring is given in Table 6.16. Palatability does, however, vary

Table 6.16. Relative palatability of adult herbaceous perennials to molluscs when emerging in spring (derived from the observations of the author)

Highly unpalatable	Intermediate	Highly palatable
Aconitum	*Aster laevis*	*Asclepias tuberosa*
Alchemilla mollis	*Aster novae-angliae*	*Cacalia*
Aster divaricartus	*Aster turbinellus*	*Delphinium*
Caltha	*Astrantia major*	*Echinacea purpurea*
Campanula lactiflora	*Astrantia maxima*	*Hosta*
Dianthus carthusianorum	*Baptisia australis*	*Liatris aspera*
Euphorbia	*Brunnera macrophylla*	*Ratibida pinnata*
Filipendula	*Cephalaria alpina*	*Salvia pratensis*
Geranium spp.	*Coreopsis tripteris*	
Grasses (most species)	*Echinacea pallida*	
Helianthus cvs	*Eupatorium maculatum*	
Helianthus mollis	*Hemerocallis*	
Liatris pycnostachya	*Iris sibirica*	
Lychnis chalcedonica	*Monarda fistulosa*	
Miscanthus	*Rubeckia*	
Papaver orientale	*Salvia nemorosa*	
Pulmonaria	*Solidago*	
Rodgersia		
Rudbeckia fulgida var. *deamii*		
Sanguisorba		
Silphium integrifolium		
Thalictrum		
Trachystemon orientale		
Trollius europaeus		
Veronica longifolia		
Veronicastrum		

depending upon circumstances. Species that typically escape damage in a traditional planted-border may be severely damaged when surrounded by dense planting or grasses. This is, for example, the case with typically robust species, such as *Astrantia major, Brunnera macrophylla* and *Cephalaria alpina*. Plantings which are shaded for part of the day also suffer more damage. The extent of damage also seems to be inversely proportional to the density of palatable species, and damage to palatable species increases as the proportion of unpalatable species increases in a planting.

Planting design

Factors influencing the location, composition and overall design of herbaceous plantings in relation to spatial and other site-characteristics have previously been referred to in the section 'Overall design considerations'. Often, there will be gradients across a site generated by factors such as light-shade, soil moisture and user patterns. Planting design generally needs to respond to these gradients, as

6.13 (above)
Similar principles applied in designed herbaceous vegetation in a German park

6.14 (left)
Distribution patterns in semi-natural vegetation. *Hebe* sub-alpine scrub and grassland in New Zealand

well as to more abstract design notions if it is to be sustainable, i.e. shade-tolerant communities need to be placed in shade, wet-tolerant communities in wet areas, and so on. Within each of the community types that this process generates, decisions have to be made on the spatial arrangement and the density of the various species, and their percentage contribution to the planting mix.

Planting patterns and spatial arrangement

In naturally occurring plant communities, spatial arrangement often varies according to the site productivity and the levels of environmental stress. On highly productive, low-stress sites, for example moist fertile soils adjacent to a lake or river, tall vigorous herbaceous plants, which often spread by rhizomes or stolons to form large monocultural patches, eliminate other species in the process. Cultivated species typical of these situations include *Filipendula*, *Lysimachia*, *Helianthus laetiflorus* and *Solidago gigantea*. On low-productivity, high-stress sites, for example a south facing slope on dry limestone soils, short, slow-growing clump-forming herbaceous plants are favoured. In contrast to highly productive sites, low-productivity conditions tend to support a high diversity of different plants because no plant has the means to dominate its neighbours. Species occur as individuals or small groups, repeating across the site and intermixed with individuals of other species.

Sites that are intermediate between these two extremes will host a mix of individuals, small groups and occasional monospecific patches. These natural patterns should inform design. If one tries to implement a dry infertile planting concept on a fertile productive site, the most vigorous weeds and planted species (and especially those with spreading rhizomes, etc.) will always be trying to colonise and eliminate their less vigorous neighbours. Consequently, larger blocks of species are more sensible on productive sites, and are also satisfactory on unproductive sites, although visually they may not fit the anticipated visual stereotype for such sites. Typically, the pattern of repeating individuals is likely to be visually preferred on unproductive sites (Figures 6.13 and 6.14).

Species composition within each community

Typically, the design process commences by drawing up a short list of species based on an understanding of different habitat stereotypes (see Tables 6.1–6.6). It is helpful to enter these names into a spreadsheet and reorganise them in terms of flowering season, i.e. spring, early summer, mid-late summer and autumn. This provides an indication of where the non-flowering times are likely to be in relation to likely public expectations of, and use, of the site. It also assists in the planning of colour combinations and the likely structure of the planting. If you find that half your short-listed species flower in spring to early summer, then you can compensate by adding additional later-flowering species.

At the end of this initial design phase, it is

necessary to approximate the percentage of planting sites within the community to be created that are to be occupied by species a, b, c and so on. This allows you to refine the appearance and function of the planting mix. It is, of course, axiomatic that you can only do this if you have, or are prepared to develop, an in-depth understanding of the plant materials. You may, for example, have identified the 3 m tall yellow daisy, *Coreopsis tripteris*, as a late autumn component. If you decide to use this species as an occasional dramatic emergent, rather than a block that will obscure views through and across the planting, then you probably only need occupy 5% of the planting spaces with this species.

In a dry meadow planting you may have decided that the peak flowering display is to occur in late June and July, however you want to have some spring colour. As a result, you limit your spring flowering species, to blue *Ajuga genevensis*, yellow *Primula veris*, and acid yellow *Euphorbia polychroma*, and to no more than 10% of total planting spaces for each species. To create the required drama in midsummer you occupy 30% of your planting spaces with *Salvia nemorosa,* with a further 20% to *Centaurea orientalis* and 10% to *Euphorbia seguieriana* subsp. *niciciana*, and so on until all the planting spaces are allocated.

On a more subtle level, this approach allows you to plan the ecological structure of planting. For example, you may wish to have a distinctive spring flowering ground layer composed of species such as *Ajuga* and *Primula*, through which later flowering layers of plantings emerge. If this is to work, the shortest layers have to be extremely shade-tolerant (as in the examples given) or they will be eliminated by the later flowering, generally taller, species. If this is what you desire (it may assist in preventing an invasion of undesirable natives as well as providing some winter greenery), then the percentage of *Ajuga* and *Primula* will have to be increased from the previously identified 10%. Where shade-tolerant ground layer species spread rapidly by self-sowing, stolons or runners, lower percentages may be satisfactory.

In relatively open-plant communities, such as dry meadow and steppe, the lower layers in plantings may avoid being shaded because even the tallest species are relatively short and are widely spaced. Consequently, in these types of plantings, low-growing summer flowering species, such as *Thymus* and *Sedum*, may be used as a ground layer.

You can work out the approximate number of planting spaces in an area by deciding on a notional planting grid of 200–500 mm, giving between approximately 4 and 16 plants/m^2. The grid spacing used will depend on the size and spread of plants, both at purchase and in the longer term, how closed a canopy is required, and how quickly. Closer spacings will generally produce a more weed-resistant vegetation. For an average site of moderate productivity, 9–10 plants/m^2 is a typical planting density. It is, however, important to re-state that where you design plantings that include plants of very different growth habits and rates, i.e. fast and slow, many of the slow-growing, shade-intolerant species will eventually be eliminated at these densities. Plant selection needs to ensure that most plants in a community are of similar growth rate and size. Despite adopting a rather confusing plant

6.15
On highly productive herbaceous plants, deep mulches of organic debris can be spread over the top of plantings to suppress weed colonisation without having an adverse effect on the desired species

6.16
With stress-tolerating species, crushed rock or gravel mulches are less effective but more visually and functionally appropriate

sociology based approach, Hansen and Stahl (1993) is a useful source of information on plant compatibility in planting.

Planting and initial weed control

Given the large number of plants that need to be planted in naturalistic planting schemes, one litre pots represent a workable compromise between excavating large planting holes and plants being large enough to reliably survive the planting process. Small plants in plugs or 9 cm pots often fare badly from typical commercial planting, and even when planted acceptably well are often lost due to burial beneath too great a depth of mulch. Where available, bare-root stock are often better value than container stock in terms of plant size in relation to cost, but they limit planting to the dormant season. They may also be planted upside down by adequately supervised, under-skilled staff.

Site preparation for planting needs to be undertaken as previously discussed in the section 'Establishment by sowing *in situ*'. Soils cultivated to 200 mm and left as uncompacted as possible are much quicker and easier to plant into. Concerns about weed seed banks are much less significant, as in most cases a mulch will be applied post-planting to suppress weed development from this source (Figure 6.15). Mulch choice will generally reflect planting character and, for tall herbaceous plant communities of moist, productive sites, will generally be a 50 mm layer of coarse, composted organic debris. With dry looking plantings, a 50 mm layer of gravel or grit sand is generally used. This is far less effective than organic debris in restricting weed seed development, but is still helpful in the first year (Figure 6.16).

Establishment by sowing in combination with planting

As suggested in Table 6.9, this approach combines the advantages of both establishment techniques. It also complicates first-season management by creating a mix of large and small plants. Despite this, it is sometimes a useful approach, particularly where initial impact is important and where more control over appearance than is possible with seeding is necessary. Sowing is essentially used as a low-cost technique to establish seedlings in the gaps between the planted material, although inevitably these seedlings far outnumber the planted material and are likely to eventually create the long-term character of the community.

Planting into a sown vegetation dominated by meadow grasses

The author has experimented with sowing a native grass and wildflower meadow in year one, into which cultivars of native and exotic meadow plants are planted in year two (Hitchmough 2000). The resulting meadows were cut as hay in August, defoliating both planted and sown species, to maintain a diverse native meadow. The problem with this approach is that the planted material has to establish in the face of severe competition, especially from the sown native-grasses. Because of this competition, and the defoliation of the hay cut in this particular study, only a few species established satisfactorily when planted into a 200 mm diameter meadow-free area or 'gaps'. Growth of planted forbs is very slow under such conditions; even successful species tend to remain much the same size as when originally planted. Subsequent research into the next generation of these experimental hay meadows has found that by providing 450 mm gaps, the number of species that are capable of establishing, even when mown off in August, is potentially increased.

Species that establish best when planted into established, grass-dominated communities are generally those that are unpalatable to molluscs, are shade tolerant or possess leafy upright shoots (Davies *et al.* 2000). The provision of a gap at planting around each plant only aids long-term

Table 6.17. Establishment success of species planted into purpose-sown native meadows subject to an August haycut in Ayr, Scotland, and Harrogate, North Yorkshire (from Hitchmough 2000, and unpublished data)

Successful species	Intermediate*	Unsuccessful species
Euporbia palustris	*Aconitum napellus*	*Astrantia major*
Geranium psilostemon	*Aruncus dioicus*	*Astrantia maxima*
Geranium sylvaticum	*Cephalaria alpina*	*Brunnera macrophylla*
Geranium x magnificum	*Hemerocallis* cvs	*Campanula glomerata* 'Superba'
Geranium x oxonianum	*Iris sibirica*	*Campanula lactiflora*
Persicaria bistorta 'Superba'	*Lychnis chalcedonica*	*Campanula latifolia* var. *macrantha*
Sanguisorba obtusa	*Lythrum salicaria*	*Geranium* 'Johnsons Blue'
Thalictrum aquilegifolium	*Trollius europaeus*	*Polemonium caeruleum*
		Primula pulverulenta
		Rheum 'Ace of Spades'
		Stachys grandiflora
		Trollius chinensis cvs

* Some individuals establish satisfactorily, whilst others decline.

establishment in species that are fundamentally well fitted to competition with grasses. Species that are not well-fitted decline as the competition-free gap around them is colonised by sown species. This is the final arbiter of what survives in a sown-planted meadow. Where gaps are maintained by weeding or herbicides beyond the first year, the plants grow much faster, however many species then decline in size as soon as this weeding ceases, resulting a year later in plants that are much the same size as they were when initially planted! Another characteristic of species planted in meadows managed by an August hay cut is that most species are dwarfed by the recurrent defoliation and subsequent crash in photosynthesis. Species that reach 1.5 m in a garden border are often no taller than 500 mm, making it very difficult to 'design in' emergent species. One species that seems to lie outside these biological rules is *Euphorbia palustris*, which continues to get bigger, even with a hay cut, after planting gaps close up.

The responses of species that have been planted into sown wildflower meadows on damp to wet soils, cut for hay in August, are given in Table 6.17. When the grassy vegetation is not mown until October, a wider range of species are able to establish, as documented by Hitchmough and Woudstra (1999). Overall species diversity may however decline under a late-cutting regime. In a three-year trial (Dunnett unpublished data), winter cutting of vigorous perennials, such as *Geranium sylvaticum, G. psilostemon* and *Persicaria bistorta*, planted into existing amenity grassland resulted in significantly enhanced performance compared with late-summer cutting. This management regime also promoted the abundance of 'evergreen' native herbaceous species, such as *Taraxacum officinale* and *Ranunculus repens*.

Maintaining competition-free gaps around planted material in sown meadows is troublesome in practice, and in some situations a more satisfactory approach is to plant first and then sow over the top of these species, as previously described. The disadvantage of this approach is that if planted stock is planted close together it makes raking in of seed

a

6.17
(a) Creating mixed native-exotic meadow through sowing native meadow-species followed by gap clearance and planting cultivated species – an experiment by the author at RHS Harlow Carr; and (b) the same experiment five years later showing how a complex finely detailed meadow vegetation has developed

b

slow and difficult. It also restricts the use of weed-control techniques for sown vegetation, such as 'high' mowing (Figure 6.17).

Planting into a sown vegetation dominated by forbs

The author's experience suggests that, as a result of diminished competition, herbaceous plants are more readily established by planting in these types of vegetation, for example, forb-only prairie. As with establishment from planting only, the positions of key visual dominants are detailed on a planting plan, whilst other species are simply planted

6.18
Creating prairie vegetation at the Eden Project by, first, planting then immediately afterwards sowing a prairie mix over the top: (a) the site immediately after the completion of planting and sowing in March; and (b) the same site two growing seasons later in August

6.19
The same principle applied to a garden. May to June flowering herbaceous plants, such as *Iris sibirica* and *Thalictrum aquilegifolium* flower above a sown sward of late summer flowering prairie plants. By July, the former will have finished flowering and will be hidden by the 1 m plus prairie plants

randomly at the specified intervals. The timing of establishment is typically determined by the needs of the sowing, as with container-grown stock, the planting date is much more flexible. Over-sowing previously planted stock is well suited to situations where relatively weed-free subsoil, sand mulching or abundant skilled labour is available. The author has used this technique to successfully establish prairie vegetation on a number of sites, including the Eden Project in Cornwall (Figures 6.18 and 6.19).

Management

The goal of the management of naturalistic herbaceous vegetation is to achieve a satisfactory balance between maintenance costs and the appearance and persistence of the sown or planted species. As a result, the management of such plant communities requires a greater understanding than traditionally planted herbaceous vegetation but generally substantially fewer maintenance hours. The reason for this dichotomy is that in traditional herbaceous planting the objective of management is very clear; any colonising plants that are not part of the original planting scheme are weeds to be removed. The practice of maintenance is in effect to maintain a plant community in a state of suspended animation. Plants that fail are replaced and gardened until they succeed. This may be highly demanding of labour but the objective is clear even to the most unskilled gardener or manager.

With naturalistic vegetation, managers need to recognise that suspended animation is not a realistic concept, some plants will succeed, some will fail, and some of the former will colonise territory (by seeding or vegetative means) vacated by the latter. Species that were not included in the establishment mix will establish; some of these will be welcome (or at least acceptable), others will be unacceptable. The role of the manager therefore involves walking a tightrope between what is perceived by them and members of the community to be acceptable or unacceptable. Unless there are abundant resources for management, there is, however, no longer a simple stereotype to manage towards. There may be many different points on the gradient from acceptable to unacceptable. Management becomes the art of defining the limits to acceptable change.

Judgements on this will depend not just on the values of the manager but also on their perception of how site users feel about the vegetation, which, in turn, will be dependent upon the site's context and role. The final arbiter in this decision-making soup will be biological and, in particular, the impact, for example of invading plants or animals, on the capacity of the desired species to persist and do what they were selected for. Managers can only make this latter judgement satisfactorily if they have experience of what is likely to happen, backed up by a scientifically based ecological and horticultural understanding of the impact of factors such as weed density and slug grazing on the persistence of a given species.

From an intellectual perspective, this is much more professionally challenging than the management of conventional decorative herbaceous vegetation. Do vegetation managers see it this way? People who are capable of integrating these intellectual and practical aspects appear to be very uncommon in public landscape management where the world is dominated by generalists with very limited depth in vegetation management *per se*. The richest vein of managers with these skills exist as head gardeners in large private and institutional gardens, and as managers of semi-natural vegetation of high-conservation significance. Few of these people are likely to choose to ply their trade in the world of public green-space management and landscape contracting, where extraneous factors often severely restrict what can be achieved. These problems are not restricted to Britain, as Hein Koningen describes in Chapter 10.

The successful management of herbaceous vegetation obviously starts at conception; if inappropriate species or communities are chosen, then management is almost doomed to fail from the outset.

Management to aid the persistence of desired species

Assuming that species are broadly well-fitted to the site, there are three factors that primarily determine persistence: typical longevity-capacity to establish offspring, competitive displacement by other plant species, and predation by herbivores such as slugs and snails.

Longevity and capacity for regeneration

Species vary considerably in the longevity of individual plants, and this is very much affected by site factors such as the degree of moisture and nutrient stress. Under traditional garden cultivation, many herbaceous plants are far shorter lived due to the low-stress environments provided. Species such as *Scabiosa columbaria* may only live for three as opposed to 10 to 15 years as is typical on dry, infertile soils in semi-natural habitats. Being short lived is not necessarily a problem for persistence, providing that the species produces adequate seed that is capable of germination and establishment under the site conditions and management regime. This is discussed further in the section 'Management to aid regeneration'. Some species are, however, almost immortal, essentially forming clonal communities as the rhizomes expand outwards. In most cases, plants with the latter growth-forms are more robust and are more likely to persist in the longer term.

Competitive displacement

This is an ever-present source of plant loss in naturalistic plant communities. It results from one species being better able to capture light, water and nutrients in order to produce leaves and stems that will further diminish the capacity of neighbouring species to compete for these resources. Species doing the displacing can be either native or exotic species, sown-planted or spontaneously occurring. In some cases they are weedy native species recruited from the soil seed bank.

Competitive displacement is most problematic on highly productive sites when relatively slow growing, small statue plants (stress tolerators) are sown or planted. Under low-intensity maintenance, these sites are soon colonised by highly productive competitor and ruderal weeds, which, if not managed, will competitively displace the desired species. On highly unproductive sites, these plants still invade but because of the lack of resources for growth are less able to dominate and eliminate the sown species.

Although most obvious in the management phase, this problem needs to be addressed first at the design stage by matching plant ecology, size and growth habit to the productivity of the site soil. Rather than use small stress-tolerators on productive sites, go for wide-spreading, dense, tall and vigorous species that will have similar growth rates to weedy colonists.

Selective weed management techniques

These require maintenance staff to be able to distinguish between desirable and undesirable species, and kill the latter. This is only possible when staff are reliably able to make these distinctions. Many of the high costs associated with naturalistic herbaceous vegetation in Germany and Holland are generated by the practice of selective weeding, often at the seedling stage. Despite this, given skilled staff, selective weeding in spring can be highly cost-effective with plant communities that develop a dense foliage canopy later in the growing season. For weeds that cannot sensibly be controlled by physical removal, for example bindweed (*Calystegia sepium*), the spot application of glyphosate via a narrow paint brush or mini-wick wiper can be very effective.

Non-selective techniques applied to the community as a whole

These are largely borrowed from nature conservation practice, and during the past 10 years have been applied by the author and Nigel Dunnett to the management of naturalistic herbaceous plant communities. Although alien to traditional garden plant maintenance, they are often relatively inexpensive to undertake and, more importantly, because they are applied to the vegetation as a whole, it is not necessary for practitioners to be able to distinguish between desirable and undesirable species.

6.20
Cutting, raking up and removal of meadow vegetation in August

Defoliation at critical times to check the vigour of potential competitive dominants

CUTTING

This is commonly associated with meadow management. These are mostly mown in spring and are cut as hay with a strimmer in summer or early autumn. The principle behind this is that by mowing in spring, as grasses (and other species) are beginning to grow vigorously, they will be temporarily checked, thereby favouring slower-growing species. Complete defoliation associated with the summer hay cut imposes a further check on grasses and forbs. Hay cutting is, however, a very blunt instrument, and the author's work on establishing native and exotic forbs in sown meadows shows that the vigour of many forbs is also severely reduced by this practice and is leading to the elimination of some species. This is particularly marked with early cutting, i.e. in July. In a 10-year study of the effect of management on vegetation change in upland native hay meadows, Smith *et al.* (2002) found no significant difference in the numbers of different species present in plots cut in June, July and September. The cutting date did, however, have a significant effect on the percentage cover of some species.

Forbs that most obviously benefit from early cutting are low-growing rosette formers, such as *Plantago*, and species that either rapidly replace lost foliage or are winter green, and are able to make use of the additional sunlight at ground level post-cutting. For some forbs it seems very likely that the benefits of cutting in summer, which are derived from temporarily reduced grass competition, are outweighed by the disadvantages of the loss of photosynthetic productivity. In an urban context, the simple mantra of cutting in summer, based on traditional agricultural, native hay meadows warrants reassessment. Research is needed to identify grass-based plant communities and species that, on balance, are best cut in summer and those that are best cut in autumn or winter. To do this, one needs to target key species that one may wish to promote, rather than just looking to see what maximises overall species diversity. As of yet, information of this type is not available.

Cutting can also be used in non-meadow vegetation. In North America, mowing in spring is considered to be a reasonable substitute for burning in the management of restored prairie vegetation (Prairie Nursery, 2002b). In applying this to Britain, the author has only looked at the mowing of prairie vegetation in early spring. By itself this is not very effective, as few tall invasive native species are defoliatated at this time and grasses rapidly regrow before most of the prairie species emerge. Cutting in early May when weeds and prairie plants are more advanced would probably be more effective, but we have not yet attempted this (Figure 6.20).

BURNING

The notion of using fire to 'care for' a vegetation is counter intuitive in the urban psyche, but fire is a very useful device when it can be adequately controlled. In Britain, many dry agricultural meadows were traditionally managed by fire (Wells and Barling 1971) but this practice has now passed out of the public consciousness. In Central and Eastern Europe however, it is still common to see dry meadows managed by spring burning. Green (1996) provides an excellent review of burning rural grasslands to promote conservation values, and laments the negative attitude to this. Clearly, fire is potentially dangerous and can generate nuisance, but these problems are resolvable. In North America, the burning of restored prairies in urban areas is becoming commonplace, and there are many information sources on how to do this safely (Pauly 1997). Burning has additional benefits to cutting in that it darkens the soil's surface and clears away leaf litter and other debris, and it facilitates the germination of many species (including weeds). It also kills some invertebrates and, in particular, molluscs, some seed on the soil surface, young seedlings and annual weeds. Most of the nitrogen in organic debris is volatised at 200°C (Wright and Bailey 1982), so in the absence of legumes, regular burning will tend to decrease soil nitrogen levels, generally to the detriment of weed species. Burning is normally undertaken in spring to combust dead overwintering foliage and to defoliate winter-growing weeds. In the author's prairie research, we generally use propane gas-fired triple burners from the tool-hire industry that are designed to soften tarmac in road-repair works. These devices have a work rate of approximately 3 min/m^2 where used to 'ash' all foliage present. Burning is very effective against annual weeds, but defoliates rather than kills many perennial herbaceous plants. It is very effective against some short lived but problem perennial weeds, for example the *Epilobium* species of nursery container plant production. It will also check, but not eliminate, creeping buttercup *Ranunculus repens*. Burning greatly reduces the scale of weed-management problems and allows managers to focus better on the selective management of the weeds that remain.

Most of the author's use of fire as a management tool has been in conjunction with prairie plant communities, for which burning is the standard management treatment in North America (Figure 6.21). We normally burn between mid-March and mid-April. The later the burn the greater the amount of foliage of weeds and desired species destroyed. This takes great courage but we have not observed any obvious lasting damage to the prairie species. All of the species listed in Table 6.5 other than the vernal *Dodecatheon*, tolerate spring burning, including the semi-evergreen, surface rooting *Rudbeckia fulgida* var. *deamii*. The advantage of burning later in spring is that you are likely to kill or check a wider range of weeds than will be encountered earlier. When burning, no attempt is made to avoid sown or planted species unless these are known to be sensitive. With North American prairie grasses and forbs, the blackened soil warms up more quickly, allowing these species to grow away more rapidly, shading the ground and

6.21
Use of burning to manage North American prairie grasses. The dead overwintering foliage is burnt in early April to defoliate invading weeds on an experiment involving small discrete blocks. For safety, we normally cut down the dead foliage and remove, prior to burning with a propane-fuelled burner

eliminating later germinating weed cohorts.

Burning can also be used on steppe-like and dry meadow communities, although there is little or no research as to the response of individual species. In Europe and Eurasia, many of these communities have traditionally been managed in this way as a means of encouraging fresh grass growth for domestic stock. Many species should therefore tolerate this practice. *Linum narbonense* and *Origanum vulgare*, and presumably many other evergreen perennials, recover rapidly even when burnt in late March in full leaf.

HERBICIDES

These are somewhat different to cutting and burning in that many kill or severely damage, as opposed to defoliate, adult herbaceous plants. This is potentially advantageous but increases the risk of damage to desired species. Herbicides are most useful for addressing weed-management problems that cannot be satisfactorily addressed by other means. In most cases, this means occasional, as opposed to routine, use. Clearly the use of herbicides in managing decorative vegetation is a contentious issue. As with burning, but more so, herbicides are typically seen as counter-intuitive to 'caring for' vegetation and especially 'ecologically' based vegetation. Herbicides are also commonly regarded to lie outside of sustainable practice, even though it is clear that low-toxicity herbicides, such as glyphosate, are the most sustainable means of controlling large areas of unwanted vegetation and are used by England's governmental nature conservation agency ('English Nature') for precisely this reason. It is entirely rational to shun herbicides that are highly toxic to humans and other animals, indeed all herbicide use in public areas is problematic and alternative techniques are preferable where this is possible. To the author, however, it seems rather confused in a highly technological society to reject extremely low-toxicity herbicides simply on the grounds they are synthetic organic chemicals.

The most toxic herbicide by far is paraquat/diquat, sold to and widely used by amateur gardeners as 'Weedol'. Owing to its extremely limited capacity to translocate through plants, the author has used this in experiments as a chemical defoliant in comparison to cutting and burning in managing American prairie plant communities. We are currently in the process of evaluating a low-toxicity alternative (Glufosinate-Ammonium, 'Challenge') that would be much more acceptable in practice. When applying these contact herbicides, no attempt is made to avoid the foliage of desired species. Despite this, the only prairie species that we have observed damage from overspraying with paraquat/diquat in spring has been *Rudbeckia fulgida* var. *deamii*, although clearly it will potentially cause serious damage to evergreen species. It will eliminate all annual weeds, and will give effective control of creeping buttercup and creeping bentgrass (*Agrostis stolonifera*).

Herbaceous plant communities and species that are completely winter dormant, i.e. have no overwintering green buds or leaf rosettes, can be oversprayed with the non-selective herbicide glyphosate in winter. This has proved, for example, to be extremely effective in eliminating *Agrostis stolonifera* from sown swards of North American prairie grasses. Dunnett and Hitchmough are currently evaluating the effect of winter overspraying with glyphosate on a wide variety of winter-dormant herbaceous plant species.

Many of the most problematic colonists of forb-rich meadow or prairie-like vegetations are perennial grasses, such as creeping bent, couch grass, *Elymus repens* and Yorkshire Fog, *Holcus lanatus*. All of these species can be selectively controlled without damaging the forbs by overspraying with grass-specific herbicides, such as sethoxydim (Checkmate®) as previously discussed in the section 'Establishment by sowing *in situ*' (Table 6.18).

Table 6.18. Weed-management techniques for specific herbaceous plant communities

Moist meadows	Mow very closely and remove cuttings once between late autumn and spring (depending on the phenology of the species present). Cut as hay and remove cut material between June and October (depending on the target species present). A second mowing in either autumn or spring may be desirable on highly fertile soils. With problem species not controlled by this regime, for example docks, cut out below ground or paint with appropriate translocated herbicide
Dry meadows/steppe	Mow and remove cuttings in late winter to early spring. Timing depends on the species present. Winter colonisation by weedy annuals may be controlled by burning in early spring. Where colonisation by weedy grasses is a problem, the spot application of glyphosate or an overall application of a graminicide (avoiding *Stipa* and other desirable grasses) may be used between March and July. Cutting as hay in late summer may sometimes be useful on productive soils
Wet meadows	Where these contain tall late flowering-developing species, mow in spring, then cut as hay between autumn and early spring and remove from the site. Where species develop and flower earlier, they can be treated as for moist meadows
Prairie	Burn in March to April and each year if possible. The standing debris from the previous year can be either strimmed off and removed before this, or burnt *in situ*, although this is potentially hazardous where there is a lot of dry fuel and where propane-fuelled burners are to be used. More infrequent burning is satisfactory if weed invasion is limited. Where the invasion of stoloniferous grasses becomes a significant problem, spot apply glyphosate in early spring or employ overall application of graminicide prior to the prairie grasses emerging from the soil. Clump-forming problem species, such as docks, can be cut out below ground level
Annual meadows	Cultivate once between autumn and spring. The precise timing will depend on the species present in the soil seed bank from the previous year in relation to what is desired. In many cases, annual oversowing at reduced rates is essential. Where there is a substantial invasion of rhizomatous grasses, overspraying pre- or post-cultivation with glyphosate may be essential. Alternatively, a specific graminicide can be used, or the planting rotated to a new site

Predation by slugs and snails

These herbivores feed on the young emerging shoots of herbaceous plants in spring and have a potentially significant impact on species' persistence. As is discussed in the section ' Establishment by planting', species vary considerably in their palatability to molluscs as adult plants and there is much variation in the degree of damage experienced by individuals of the same species within a planting. It is not clear whether this is due to the feeding preferences of individual slug species, their spatial distribution or varying palatability of individuals of a species. The author's research into the long-term persistence of prairie plant communities in slug-rich environments suggests that there is a relationship between weed density in spring and the degree of damage to the prairie plant species. Prairie plants on weedy plots suffer more competition from colonising weeds, they also have to contend with more intense predation. In the moist, shady environment generated by dense weed-cover, molluscs are present in higher densities and feed for longer. Where this type of vegetation is subject to this intense competition/predation regime, the most palatable species decline and disappear over a number of years, resulting in low densities of the most robust/least palatable species. Although there has been very little research into these ecological relationships in other types of naturalistic vegetation, this is probably the most common reason for the disappearance of many native and non-native species from designed herbaceous vegetation.

Until an inexpensive, effective, yet low-toxicity molluscide is developed, the most satisfactory means of dealing with this phenomenon is to select less palatable species, and/or manage to reduce spring weed-cover. The biological control of slugs with nematodes can be effective, however it is currently too expensive to use on a large scale. The practice of sand mulching to aid weed management also appears to reduce mollusc damage.

Management to aid regeneration

Herbaceous plants regenerate by either vegetative means via stolons/rhizomes or from seed, and in some cases by both. Species that can do this successfully in naturalistic vegetation are useful (providing they are not too aggressive), in that they are more likely to be able to fill in gaps in planting and to compete with invading species irrespective of initial sowing or planting density. This process potentially makes such communities sustainable in the long term, by providing a buffer against the loss of key species to aging, competition or herbivory.

All herbaceous plants spread outwards as they add another 'layer' of growth points to the previous year's growth. In many species this process slows down with aging, restricting the area any one plant can cover. This area may then diminish as individual plants age and decline, as, for example, in *Achillea* species and *Echinacea purpurea*. Other herbaceous species are more permanent and they slowly grow larger, as in the case of many *Aster* and *Geranium* species. The next group of species are those that spread aggressively by vegetative means, for example *Filipendula ulmaria*, *Inula hookeri* and *Euphorbia griffithii*, forming what are known as 'clonal' patches as a result of competitively displacing sown, planted or spontaneously occurring neighbours. With these types of forbs, a monoculture is likely to result in the longer term, unless the forbs chosen all share the vigour and growth habit of the most aggressive species present. The spread and persistence of clone-forming species is often relatively independent of management. Species with these growth habits are, in any case, essentially immortal and, therefore, the need to employ management to aid persistence is greatly reduced.

Species that have the first growth habit rely on regeneration from seed for their long-term persistence and are much more dependent on management. This is clearly most marked in annuals and biennials. The successful establishment of seedlings in naturalistic herbaceous vegetation is often an occasional event for the following reasons:

- low seed production or heavy seed predation by weevils or birds
- insufficient germination microsites free of competing plants
- a layer of moss or organic debris restricting seedling access to mineral soil
- intense slug predation on seedlings
- the elimination of seedlings through shading by surrounding adult plants.

As the potential productivity of a landscape planting increases, the likelihood of species establishing successfully from seed in established vegetation decreases. Germination and establishment requirements often differ considerably even between species in a genus, for example in *Solidago*, see Goldberg and Werner (1983). In general, however, breaking up layers of organic surface debris to improve seed access to mineral soil, and increasing light availability at the soil surface, are important. In grass-dominated native meadows, seedlings of many species often germinate in late summer to autumn, as well as in spring. Cutting these meadows close to the ground in late summer to autumn, followed by heavy scarification of the surface, appears to be effective. In plant communities not subject to defoliation during the growing season, for example North American prairie vegetation, seedling germination and emergence rarely takes place before March or April. Seedling establishment can often be promoted by avoiding burning or similar forms of management in that year. This assumes, of course, that the community is relatively weed-free. Seedling survival will be further improved by high mowing to maintain higher light-levels for seedlings in early summer. Even with these inputs, the author's experience suggests that relatively low levels of seedling establishment should be anticipated.

Within communities of annual and biennial species, management to promote germination from the previous year's seed is essential if the community is to continue to exist. This often takes the form of shallow cultivation to disturb surface debris and weed colonisation, and to stimulate buried seed to germinate. On sites that have become heavily colonised by perennial grasses, the use of a non-residual herbicide, such as glyphosate, prior to the germination of the desirable annual species may be necessary, as few annual species can germinate and establish satisfactorily in the presence of adult plants.

Summary

Naturalistic herbaceous vegetation is a potentially valuable addition to the repertoire of planting styles for public and institutional landscapes. In aesthetic terms, it is likely to challenge the preconceptions of many lay observers, however there are reasons to believe that this will gradually change as this type of planting becomes more common. At present, this is hampered by a lack of understanding at both a scientific and practical level of these types of vegetation, however this is gradually changing. Successful creation and management does, however, require that designers, clients and managers are prepared to adopt a more ecological approach than is normal in conventional herbaceous vegetation. It remains to be seen whether this will materialise in practice.

References

- Aguilera, M. O. and Lauenroth, W. K. (1995). Influence of gap disturbances and type of microsites on seedling establishment in *Bouteloua gracilis*. *Journal of Ecology,* **83**, 87–97.
- Archibold, O. W. (1995). *Ecology of World Vegetation*. Chapman Hall, London.
- Atwater, B. R. (1980). Germination, dormancy and morphology of herbaceous ornamental plants. *Seed Science and Technology*, **8**, 523–573.
- Baskin, C. C. and Baskin, J. M. (2001). *Seeds, ecology, biogeography, and evolution of dormancy and germination*. Academic Press, San Diego.
- BdB (1987). *Handbuch Wildstauden für Wiesen und andere Feiflachen*. Grün ist Leben, Pinneberg, Germany.
- Chatto, B. (1992). *The Damp Garden*. Dent, London.
- Curtis, J. T. (1959). *The Vegetation of Wisconsin*. The University of Wisconsin Press, Madison, Wisconsin.
- Dai, L. (2000). Public perception of naturalistic herbaceous vegetation in urban landscapes and key elements that determine response.

MA thesis, University of Sheffield. Unpublished.
-- Davies, A., Dunnett, N. P. and Kendle, A. D. (2000). The importance of transplant size and gap width in the botanical enrichment of species-poor grasslands in Britain. *Restoration Ecology,* **7**, 271–280.
-- Dunnett, N. (1999). Annuals on the Loose. *The Garden,* **124**, 168–171.
-- Dunnett, N. (2002). Up on the Roof. *The Garden,* **127**, 380–383.
-- Ellenberg, H. (1988). *Vegetation Ecology of Central Europe*, 4th Edition. Cambridge University Press, Cambridge.
-- Fitter, R., Fitter, A. and Farrer, A. (1995). *Grasses, Sedges, Rushes and Ferns of Britain and Northern Europe*. Collins, London.
-- Fuller, R. M. (1987). Vegetation establishment on shingle beaches. *Journal of Ecology,* **75**, 1071–1089.
-- Garrett, F. and Dusoir, R. (2001). Bulbous plants for use in designed landscapes. *Plant User Specguide*, **7**, 5–14.
-- Gilbert, O. L. (1992). *The Flowering of the Cities. The natural flora of 'urban commons'*. English Nature, Peterborough.
-- Gleason, H. A. (1963). *The New Britton and Brown Illustrated Flora of the North Eastern United States and adjacent Canada*. Hafner Publishing Company, New York.
-- Goldberg, D. E. and Werner, P. A. (1983). The effects of size of opening in vegetation and litter cover on seedling establishment of goldenrods (*Solidago* spp.). *Oecologica,* **60**, 149–155.
-- Green, B. H. (1996). Countryside Management; Landscape ecology, planning and management. Spon, London.
-- Grime, J. P., Hodgson, J. G. and Hunt, R. (1988). *Comparitive Plant Ecology, A functional approach to common British species.* Unwin Hyman, London.
-- Grubb, P. J. (1977). The maintenance of species richness in plant communities: the importance of the regeneration niche. *Biological Reviews*, **52**, 107–145.
-- Hanley, M. E., Fenner, M. and Edwards, J. (1995). An experimental field study of the effects of mollusc grazing on seedling recruitment and survival in grassland. *Journal of Ecology*, **83**, 621–627.
-- Hansen, R., and Stahl, F. (1993). *Perennials and their Garden Habitats*. Cambridge University Press, Cambridge.
-- Hartmann, H. T., Kestler, D. E., Davies, F. T. and Geneve, R. (2001). *Hartmann and Kester's Plant Propagation: Principles and Practices*, 7th Edition. Prentice Hall.
-- Hitchmough, J. D. (1994). Natural Neighbours. *Landscape Design*, **229**, 16–24.
-- Hitchmough, J. D. (2000). Establishment of cultivated herbaceous perennials in purpose-sown native wildflower meadows in south-west Scotland. *Landscape and Urban Planning*, **51**, 37–51.
-- Hitchmough, J. D. (2003). Effect of sward height, gap size and slug grazing on emergence and establishment of *Trollius europaeus* (globeflower). *Restoration Ecology,* **11**, (1), 20–28.
-- Hitchmough, J. D. and Woudstra, J. (1999). The ecology of exotic herbaceous perennials grown in managed, native grass vegetation in urban landscapes. *Landscape and Urban Planning*, **45**, 107–121.
-- Hitchmough, J. D., Gough, J. and Corr, B. (2000). Germination and dormancy in a wild collected genotype of *Trollius europaeus*. *Seed Science and Technology*, **28**, 549–558.
-- Hitchmough, J. D., Kendle, A. and Parakevopoulou, A. (2003). Seedling emergence, survival and initial growth in low productivity urban 'waste' soils; a comparison of North American prairie forbs with meadow forbs and grasses native to Britain. *Journal of Horticultural Science and Biotechnology,* **78**, (1), 89–99.
-- Hobhouse, P. (1985). *Colour in your Garden.* Collins, London.
-- Hodgson, J. G. (1989). Selecting and managing plant materials in habitat construction. In Buckley, G. P. (ed.) *Biological Habitat Reconstruction.* Belhaven Press, London, pp. 68–78.
-- Hutchings, M. J. and Booth, K. (1996). Studies of the feasibility of re-creating chalk grassland vegetation on ex-arable land. II. Germination and early survivorship of seedlings under different management regimes. *Journal of Applied Ecology,* **33**, 1182–1190.
-- Jekyll, G. (1908). *Colour Schemes for the Flower Garden.* Country Life, London.
-- Jelitto, L. (2002). *Perennial Seed Catalogue*. Schwarmstedt, Germany.
-- Jelitto, L. and Schacht, W. (1990). *Hardy Herbaceous Perennials, Volumes 1 and 2,* 3rd Edition. Batsford, London.
-- Kendle, A. D. and Rose, J. E. (2000). The aliens have landed! What are the justifications for 'native only' policies in landscape plantings? *Landscape and Urban Planning*, **47**, 19–31.
-- Kühn, N. (2000) Spontane Arten für urbane Freiflächen. Garten & Landschaft, **4**, 11–14.
-- Ladd, D. (1995). *Tallgrass Prairie Wildflowers*. Falcon Press, Helena, Montana.
-- Lloyd, C. (1976a). Meadow Gardening, Part 1. *The Garden*, **101**, 323–329.
-- Lloyd, C. (1976b). Meadow Gardening, Part 2. *The Garden*, **101**, 350–355.

- Lloyd, C. and Rice, G. (1997). *Garden Flowers from Seed.* Penguin, London.
- Mansfield, T. C. (1949). *Annuals in Colour and Cultivation*. Collins, London.
- Morgan, J. W. (1995). Ecological studies of the endangered *Rutidosis leptorrhynchoides*. II. Patterns of seedling emergence and survival in a native grassland. *Australian Journal of Botany,* **43**, 13–24.
- Morgan, J. W. (1997). Plowing and Seeding. In Packard, S. and Mutel, C. F. (eds) *The Tallgrass Restoration Handbook for Prairies, Savannas and Woodlands*. Island Press, Washington, DC, pp. 193–215.
- Mynott, L. (2001) User perception of naturalistic Meadow Vegetation in Parks, unpublished MA Thesis, Department of Landscape, University of Sheffield.
- Nassauer, J. (1995). Messy ecosystems, orderly frames. *Landscape Journal*, **14**, No. 2, 161–170.
- Owen, J. (1991). *The Ecology of a Garden, the first fifteen years*. Cambridge University Press, Cambridge.
- Pauly, W. (1997). Conducting Burns. In Packard, S. and Mutel, C. F. (eds) *The Tallgrass Restoration Handbook for Prairies, Savannas and Woodlands.* Island Press, Washington, DC, pp. 223–244.
- Phillips, R. and Rix, M. (1981). *The Bulb Book.* Pan, London.
- Phillips, R. and Rix, M. (1991a). *Perennials Volume 1, Early Perennials*. Pan, London.
- Phillips, R. and Rix, M. (1991b). *Perennials Volume 2, Late Perennials.* Pan, London.
- Phillips, R. and Rix, M. (1999). *Annuals and Biennials*. McMillan, London.
- Polunin, O. and Stainton, A. (1984). *Flowers of the Himalyas*. Oxford University Press, Oxford.
- Pope, N. and Pope, S. (1998). *Colour by Design; Planting the Contemporary Garden.* Conran Octopus, London.
- Prairie Nursery (2002a). *Guidelines on seed treatment for germination*. Westfield, Wisconsin.
- Prairie Nursery (2002b). *Guidelines on establishment and management of prairie*. Available at www.prairienursery.com.
- Pywell, R. F., Bullock, J. M., Hopkins, A., Walker, K. J., Sparks, T. H., Burke, M. J. W. and Peel, S. (2002). Restoration of species-rich grassland on arable land: assessing the limiting processes using a multi-site experiment. *Journal of Applied Ecology*, **39**, 294–309.
- Rock, H. W. (1981). *Prairie Propagation Handbook*, 6th Edition. Department of County Parks, Recreation and Culture, Milwaukee, Wisconsin.
- Rodwell, J. S., Piggott, C. D., Ratcliffe, D. A., Malloch, A. J. C., Birks, H. J. B., Proctor, M. C. F., Shimwell, D. W., Huntley, J. P., Radford, E., Wigginton, M. J. and Wilkins, P. (1992). *British Plant Communities. Volume 3. Grasslands and Montane Communities.* Cambridge University Press, Cambridge.
- Sackville Hamilton, N. R. (2001). Is local provenance important in habitat creation? A reply. *Journal of Applied Ecology*, **38**, 1374–1376.
- Scheidel, U. and Brueheide, H. (1999). Selective slug grazing on montane meadow plants. *Journal of Ecology*, **87**, 828–838.
- Smith, R. S., Shiel, R. S., Millward, D., Corkhill, P. and Sanderson, R. A. (2002). Soil seed banks and the effects of meadow management on vegetation change in a 10-year meadow field trial. *Journal of Applied Ecology*, **39**, 279–293.
- Wells, T. C. E. and Barling, D. M. (1971). *Pulsatilla vulgaris* Mill. (*Anemone vulgaris* L.). *Journal of Ecology*, **59**, 275–292.
- Wells, T. C. E., Cox, R. and Frost, A. (1989). Diversifying grasslands by introducing seed and transplants into existing vegetation. In Buckley, G. P. (ed.) *Biological Habitat Reconstruction.* Belhaven Press, London, pp. 283–298.
- Wilkinson, D. M. (2001). Is local provenance important in habitat creation? *Journal of Applied Ecology*, **38**, 1371–1373.
- Wilson, S. D. and Gerry, A. K. (1995). Strategies for mixed-grass prairie restoration: herbicide, tilling, and nitrogen manipulation. *Restoration Ecology*, **3**, No. 4, 290–298.
- Whitehead, R. (2002). *The UK Pesticide Guide 2002*. British Crop Protection Council/CABI Publishing, Wallingford, Oxford.
- Wright, H. A. and Bailey, A. W. (1982). *Fire Ecology.* Wiley, New York.

Chapter 7

Exploring woodland design: designing with complexity and dynamics – woodland types, their dynamic architecture and establishment

Roland Gustavsson

Introduction – discoveries and rediscoveries for an innovative design

We are rooted in an age that seeks instant landscape effects but, from an environmental viewpoint, instant effects are not really what are wanted. Instead, a far more sustainable approach is required that involves greater richness and complexity evolving over time, directed in a knowledgeable way. Healthy cities need effective green-space networks and woodlands; not just to promote healthy living for city dwellers, but also to sustain wider biodiversity, to promote water and air quality, and to regulate climatic extremes. All this is well known, but is rarely reflected in landscape design. Rather than trying to freeze parks or gardens and making them static entities, they would be greatly enhanced if their long-time dynamic and structural changes are treated from a deep and active understanding. Moreover, rather than claiming that landscape architecture needs simplicity to be successful, it would be of great interest for the future to promote design concepts in which complexity plays a role. Considering the importance of both the outdrawn time-perspective and complexity in design, it is surprising how few books and articles are written focusing on planting design and vegetation in a city or urban rural fringe context, bridging the gap between architecture and an ecological-technical understanding.

In temperate climates, woodland is the natural state for the long-term development of landscape

7.1
There are many possibilities for discovering the qualities of interior woodland rooms, whether they have a closed canopy or are open to the sky (upper diagrams) as opposed to the most commonly used 'open room' style (lower diagram) where woodland is seen purely as a structural element to define outdoor spaces

vegetation. However, the view of woodland discussed in this chapter is very different to the way it is generally conceived by designers and managers. Indeed, one of the main aims of this chapter is to rediscover the traditional meaning of woodland or forest as a rich diversity of land uses; some open, some half-open, others closed, but all within a wooded framework (Rackham 1986). A further aim is to place greater emphasis on the interior of woodlands as rich environments that appeal to all the senses, rather than viewing woodland plantations as simple structural elements in landscapes that define exterior spaces. The interior woodland should mean a choice between a whole series of interesting options, of types which all should be able to become very distinct and supplementary to each other, giving harmony or drama by contrast (Figure 7.1). Sadly, this has often been forgotten in day-to-day design. Furthermore, the chapter presents an alternative to conventional landscape design and planning, and is based on a view of woodland, forest, scrub and small-scale mosaics with open glades and meadows as a dynamic and ecologically functioning cultural concept, whether or not one is not restricted to the choice of native species.

The approach taken in this chapter is to identify a whole set of specific structural-dynamic components of woodland landscape types and to describe them in a way that makes them concrete as visions or ideal types. These types include high forest, low forest, woodland edge, half-open land, small-scale mosaics and shrub-dominated vegetation. Such types can be combined and integrated to result in a rich landscape that can cater for a wide range of uses and functions. But first we will consider in much more detail what woodland actually means, along with general design principles, before looking at the more technical aspects of the different structural types.

Rediscovering the wide and rich cultural meaning of the term 'woodland'

The role, value and perception of woodlands has altered throughout the many periods in the history of landscape architecture, from being an essential part and an extension of the more formal approaches, such as the baroque gardens, to being related to more informal periods, such as the picturesque and the English Landscape style, and, more recently, to the naturalistic style (Kendle and Forbes 1997). However, through much of the twentieth century when modernism (functionalism) dominated, woodland design, particularly in urban areas, was almost thrown out as something where a visionary approach was not possible. The modernist approach was to see woodlands as structural elements in landscape, giving form and shape to outdoor spaces or 'rooms'. In the visions of modernism, the interior room or environment of the woodland became almost non-existent. Rather, the 'room' was reduced to belonging just to the open grass or water landscape (Gustavsson 1981). Today, if we consider that period as an interruption which is past, there are now good reasons to talk about the need for discoveries of brand new concepts as well as a need for rediscoveries of old values as part of a fruitful search for an innovative, articulated and diverse woodland design for the future.

In contrast to the views that predominate about urban woodlands, a virtually opposite viewpoint

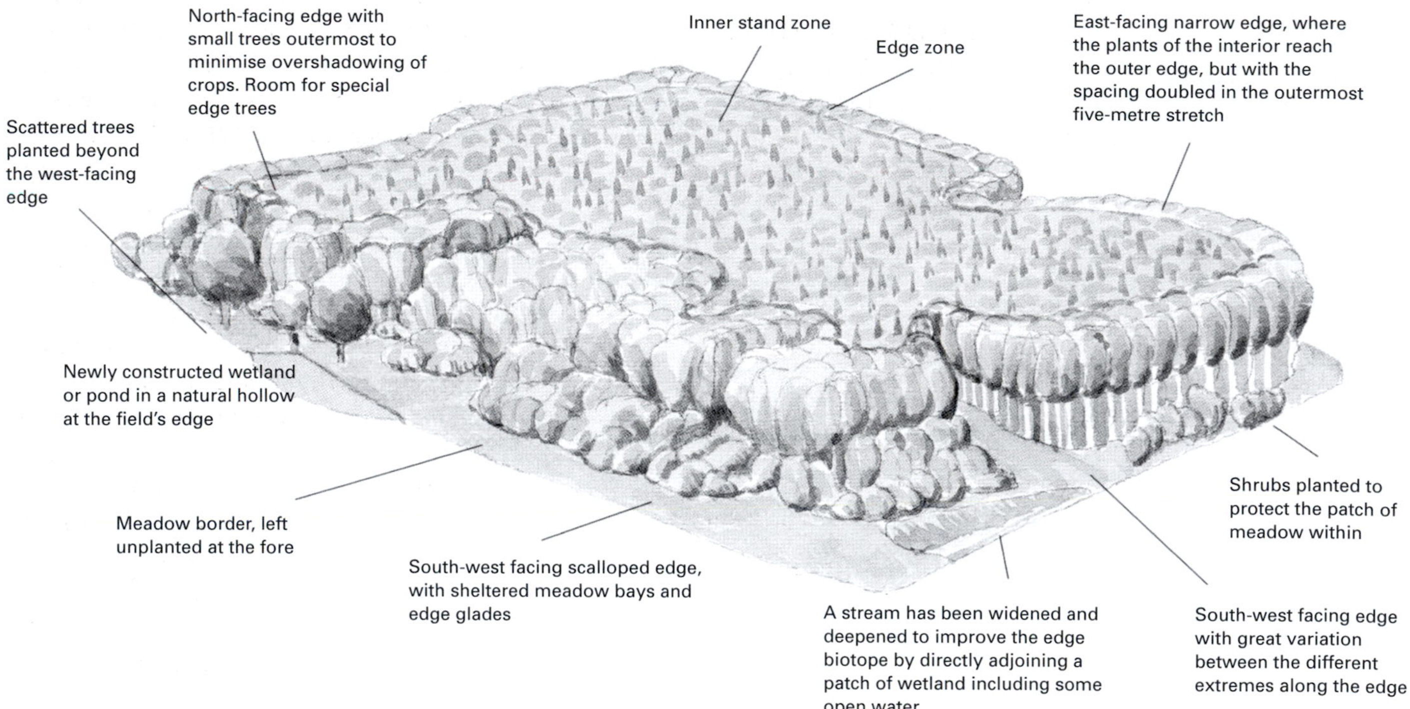

7.2
A woodland design that focuses on the edges of the wood as well as the quality of the interior.

determines the creation and management of woodlands in the countryside that have forestry, recreation or nature-conservation objectives. Here it seems that woodlands exist mostly of inner parts, whilst the outer parts are forgotten. These rural design traditions, with a few exceptions, have seldom had design issues at the top of the agenda, and have therefore rarely developed articulated woodland design concepts for aesthetics or multiple use. Consequently, there is great scope for innovative visions and concepts in relation to woodland design. Design in this instance can act as an important bridge between landscape architecture and other related knowledge fields, such as 'silviculture', forest and landscape ecology, landscape art, landscape history and knowledge areas related to mixed or mosaic land-uses.

Today, among practising experts as well as among many of the general public, the meaning of the terms 'woodland' and 'forest' is quite vague. It would be very fruitful to move away from the current narrow view of woodlands and forest landscapes as being composed of large-scale and monotonous dense masses of trees, and move towards the more original meanings of the terms as diverse, mosaic landscapes, integrating open spaces, open woodlands, half-open and closed woodlands, tree- and shrub-rich types and water bodies, all mentally forgotten as visions. Furthermore, what happens in-between the stands of trees might be of equal importance to what happens within the stands. Research into how people experience forests stresses the importance of not only considering the individual stands, and their quality, one by one as isolated elements, but also in what order the stands are placed on a 'local forest area level'.

Experiencing a woodland might, for a few, mean to use your arms to climb up a tree and see it from the top-down but, for others, the quality will very much be concentrated on the understorey of a stand and the qualities around their eyes, ears, nose and feet; thinking about the interior rooms, the views, the changes in light, the small birds, the butterflies, the perennial woodland herbs and grasses, the autumn-coloured leaf carpets, but also about the paths, the walks, etc., which will mean as much as the trees themselves. Consequently, greater notice should be taken of the woodland as a whole unit. In addition, much more importance has to be given to the fringes of the woodland, the woodland edges, the entrances, the open parts inside the woodland areas, the streams and the small waters. Figure 7.2 illustrates an alternative focus, in which the design efforts focus on the edges, which also includes glades and special woodland stand types that are in direct contact with the woodland edge, and takes into consideration the orientation and aspect, with a special emphasis on the southward and the westward directions.

Historical woodland types – rediscovering a rich language belonging to landscape

A woodland means much more than an area filled with trees for timber production, a collection of species belonging to an identified 'woodland type' or a set of habitats. It is a culturally rich term, which has been heightened with meaning over thousands of years. Traditional place names and old words reveal a host of old woodland terms, which together cover an extremely rich variety of characters and management regimes – landscape words like wood-pasture, coppice woodland, holt (a wood, perhaps a single-species wood), lund, lound, grove and launde (woodland glade, lawn) are all found in old landscape documents in Britain (Muir 1999), and corresponding terms can also be found in all the Scandinavian countries or in Germany. They just give a hint of how many types and aspects there have been in relation to a woodland through time – types and aspects that should be more interesting as an inspiration and as a base of knowledge for the future compared to what we see around us today and feel obliged to use in the design of a woodland. Such an historical retrospective should provide a rich base for design. We should, however, be careful in trying to 'copy' woodland concepts from not only forestry but also from nature conservation or forest ecology that concern the descriptions of countryside or historical types. The urban context means new situations and functions, and therefore possibilities to rethink historical types and also to include a whole series of new types or variants.

Finding the necessary reference landscapes

Many stakeholders, designers and managers of newly constructed landscapes have probably too few reference landscapes in their minds concerning woodland types, because too few and well-developed types exist in the landscape today – this is particularly true of urban contexts. For example, in Britain people probably think of an urban woodland as a thick green mass or a mixed forest stand with a lot of nettles and shrubs with no real visual attractiveness. Further, there is probably no articulation between individual trees or tree layers, no interesting field layer, and very little else that inspires you to walk right through. With such a woodland in mind you are better to keep to the clayish paths and accept the litter found along it. In order to come closer to a more positive and articulated meaning of a woodland and its possible attractive qualities through management, there is a need to re-find and re-use a different language, with a whole variety of words for describing different sizes, structural patterns, architectural individual

7.3
A montado landscape from Portugal, probably the most famous grazed tree-rich landscape in Europe, with its grass sward and its unending open canopy of oaks, which is sometimes grazed by cattle and sometimes by goats, sheep or the Iberian pig, and which is sometimes more open and sometimes more rich with trees. It is an interesting reference landscape type, with a remarkable closeness to an ideal of a savannah landscape or a designed area within the classic English Landscape park-style

life-forms and management regimes. We can do this partly by finding good reference landscapes that embody greater complexity and that stimulate active use and enjoyment. We can do this by looking at historical woodland types (because in many regions woodlands were taken away from the landscape by farmers many hundreds of years ago, and here it is sometimes difficult to imagine woodlands as parts of possible and desired future landscapes), but also by looking at traditional management systems that are used in different countries at present.

Open woodlands and 'silvi-pastoral' systems

One of the most interesting woodland design concepts is the 'wood pasture' of open woodlands, with a grassy layer beneath the trees that would traditionally be open to grazing animals. In Britain we have to go back to medieval times to find systems expressed in very old-landscape words, such as 'silva pastilis' (wood pasture) and 'denes' (swine pastures) (Muir 2000). In Southern European countries, such as Portugal, the chance is greater through their still-living 'silvi-pastoral' system of 'montado' (Figure 7.3). Also in Sweden, Norway and Finland, and in the Baltic countries, these kinds of grazed or hayed tree- and shrub-rich landscapes are still found quite easily, and an increasing amount are also being restored to be part of the urban landscape (Figures 7.4 and 7.5). Here, such design concepts should be considered as a rediscovery today, due to their influence in park and garden design in the so called 'Stockholm School' up until the 1950s (Bucht 1997, 2002). Even in the Netherlands, despite

7.4(a) and (b)
The wooded meadow Laxareänget on the island of Gotland in the Baltic sea. Many of the traditional wooded meadows were grazed during a short period in the autumn, but the basic management of the grass sward was hay cutting. The photographs show two different degrees of closeness, the characteristic shift in-between *storrum* ('large room') with a dominance of grasses and light-demanding herbs, open corridors as enclosed rooms with colourful carpets of flowers up until about midsummer, hundreds of pollards of lime-trees and ashes, and interior woodland entities with a few large trees in an interaction with coppiced multi-stemmed trees and shrubs

having virtually no living remnants of old woodlands, a somewhat similar half-open, grazed landscape has been regarded as belonging to an important part of the future landscape for recreation and nature conservation. The Dutch have, in several places since the 1980s and 1990s, succeeded in reconstructing and putting into practice a complex open or half-open landscape with, probably, a similar character to what existed before 'the farming culture' came to totally dominate the European countryside (Vera 2000).

7.5
A grazed, half-open landscape from Sweden that was the inspiration for one of the most well-known nature parks in Warrington New Town, which was designed in the 1980s. The existing cluster of elements, the richness of form, symbolised by the shift between one, two, five, ten, or even more than 30 stems in one single tree clump, provide a base for impressionistic gradients in openness and closeness in a long-term sustainable pattern. Later, the same area was chosen for a PhD study about landscape perceptions and the attractiveness of grazed countryside landscapes. Out of 60 different areas, this area was chosen as one of the most attractive areas in southern Sweden by city dwellers from a sample of 120 people (Hägerhäll 1999)

Wilderness woodland areas

Ancient woodlands are obvious reference landscapes when dealing with nature conservation as a fundamental base in order to understand long-term dynamics and the importance of unbroken continuity over time and in space. However, when dealing with an urban context and woodland design, such references can also help a great deal but partly for other reasons. There might be similarities with more virgin woodland systems, and it could be a long-term goal for plantations as well. Certainly for educational purposes, such goals can be of great importance. Wilderness areas might also be among the most appreciated because of the mythologies, the ethics and the aesthetics which are tied to them, and they can serve management, create interest and deepen the experience for the visitors. An internationally well-known example in which such natural woodlands have been used as explicit references for recreational forests is Amsterdam Bos, the forest park in Amsterdam, the Netherlands.

The adventurous woodland

As well as the need to rediscover traditional woodland concepts, there is a challenge to search for new concepts. One such concept is termed the 'adventurous woodland', with its concern for the user's direct interaction with woodlands and its particular focus on children. The importance of designing woodlands which support children, their development, their creativity and their play in groups as well as individually, has recently been stressed by many researchers. However, the question of how to design for children is not a simple one, and it should not be. It should rather be respected as an important design issue, in which you need to know the wishes from the point of view of the children and the adults involved, and what that means in terms of vegetation structure, plant choices, dynamics and management. Certainly, the design solution – 'the design concept' – is very much a question of several complementary ways rather than one, and also very much a combination of different woodland qualities and types.

Concerning the design of woodlands for children's enjoyment, researchers seldom or never point at particularly designed places as examples of 'good practice'. Rather, they focus on places which are not designed. The best examples seem to be found by accident rather than through a professional design, which of course is a remarkable fact. There are, however, exceptions, but they seem to be very few. One of the early successful cases was Balloon Wood in Nottingham, England, which was partly designed.

Children have, step by step, been allowed to interact more and more with plants in their play. In housing areas of the 1930s to the 1970s, plants were something that stopped children playing, keeping them on the 'right' side of an area rather than integrating them with plants or vegetation patterns. The designers used thorny plants because of the assumption that nothing else would survive. In the 1970s *Salix* species were suddenly introduced as a framework that could, to some extent, also be actively used by children to build huts, etc. But it was actually first in 'the naturalistic style' that children were actively allowed and stimulated to enter and experience plantations with trees and shrubs. A Swedish example that has been very successful and influential is the 'Rosengården play park' in Helsingborg. Unfortunately, the day-care activity was closed at the 'Rosengården play area', and today it functions as a local nature park area,

7.6.
Balloon Wood in Nottingham, England – this heavily used adventurous woodland in the 1970s was one of the most influential examples of woodland concepts for children's play in the 'early years'

7.7
(a)–(c) The experimental housing area in Delft showing the early development and development up until now. In the late 1990s, a restoration programme was undertaken and after that an English Landscape park-style took over. In some parts the high quality is still there and has increased with the growing maturity of the vegetation, in other parts the management has not really succeeded in articulating the vegetation architecture or in keeping all the 'micro-rooms' that the children created and used. Today, children still very much use the area, but the strong, active relationship between the adults, the children and the landscape has been reduced
(d) A beloved glade in an adventurous woodland in Warrington, England.

with just a few children coming to the place now and then. The adaptation to the new, more ordinary, park situation can today easily be seen by more conventional management, compared to the early park situation, which was strongly directed to the children and their use.

One of the most far-reaching experiments in Europe, with a particular emphasis on children, their uses and wishes, was the Gillis experiment in Buitenhof, Delft, in the Netherlands. In one of the nature-inspired yards, the children could take advantage of a large area which was to be the dominating part, and which was constructed by a combined planting and seeding, in which small tree and shrub plants were introduced as dense planting, with an immediate seeding of grasses. As a result, a fluent gradient between tree-rich and more open rooms occurred in a kind of emerging open woodland. This was later articulated by creative early management of thinning and pruning. The pedestrian ways were very much a result of an action-oriented design. The children were allowed to run, play and have fun, and the pattern of paths which where created in this way were followed up by the construction people. In the early years, a Dutch research team from Leiden found surprising results of how successful the design had become with regard to how much the children played and how varied their play was. It also inspired many of the adults to be outdoors.

It is important to stress robustness in order to enable the long-term survival of the woodland character and the key trees in areas that are attractive and are heavily used by children. In particular, this means a focus on low woodland types with standard trees or many layered high woodland structures, which enable a shift from one individual to another when one gets damaged or is removed by the children. The increased openness on less fertile soils can, to some extent, compensate for the need for fertility to give the necessary re-growth. In management there also has to be special

a

b

c

d

individual care of the climbing trees, with a special understanding of important positions and the need to integrate more than seems to be necessary for the long term. There is also a need to reach an area size that should extend at least 20 × 20 m, and even more if open areas, like glades, are to be integrated as well. The activities of the children lead to a certain pattern in the vegetation. The children create their places, and that can be very violent, but then they often stop. What the children seem to do can be excessive and hard for the vegetation and its long-time survival, but they stop at a certain point, rather than being simply negative: they want to actively form a place for adventure, and the damage to trees and shrubs normally does not extend any further. The result also points out the importance of long-term research if we want to find out what are good and bad design concepts; for a strikingly high number of areas have gone up and down in quality over time (Figures 7.6 and 7.7).

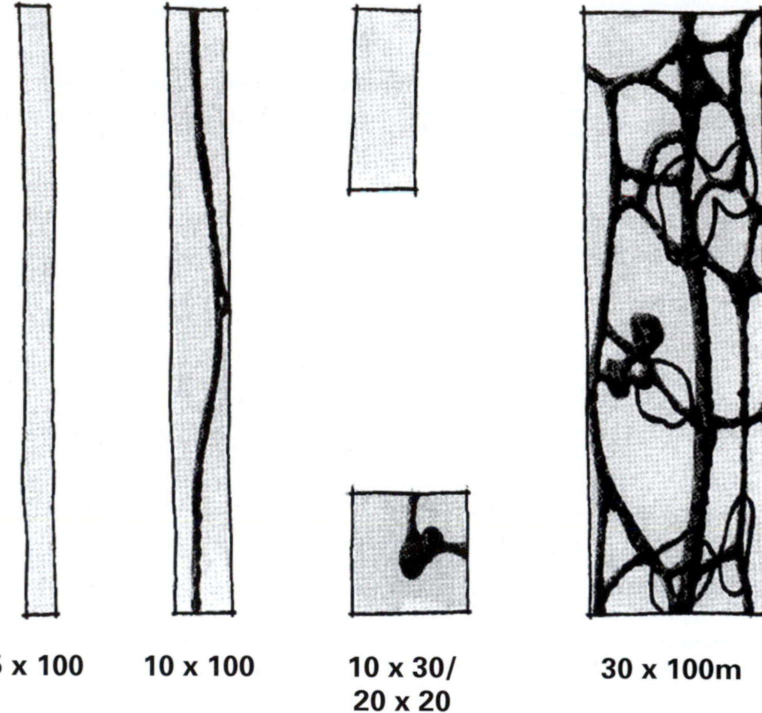

7.8
Possible paths in woodland belts of different dimensions give rise to different possibilities for path networks, nodes and glades. Dimensions in metres

Woodland belts and other shelter belts

In many urban locations and also in many other landscape situations as well, one is often required to work in a restricted space and to use this restricted space in a very effective way. It might be a green string in-between a housing area and a traffic road, it might be a green isolated pocket in a sub-urban environment, or it might be in-between two agricultural fields. Many questions are raised in dealing with such very small plantations. When do the interior rooms and the interior woodland habitats occur? When can you start to differentiate between outer and inner edge zones? When does it become a wood as opposed to a shelter belt? How can woodland perennials survive in the long term? At what size can we start to talk about long-term sustainable systems? Such, and similar, questions have not been discussed enough, but they are as important as it is for a football team to have a pitch of a certain size in order to be able to play football (Figures 7.8 and 7.9).

When do interior qualities develop in a piece of woodland? This is a question focusing on critical minimum sizes. The ability of plants to survive or to grow well is related to size. In small plantations the chance is reduced, especially in a hard climate or with hyperactive wildlife. Also, human use is dependent on scale. Figure 7.8 shows the possibilities for paths in woodland belts of different widths. When does the first informal path start to occur? When do you also get a chance to create a parallel path? When do the children create a whole system of paths and somewhat enlarged 'micro-rooms'? Empirical studies have shown that critical sizes are often found around widths of 10–12, 25–30 and 60–100 m. In practice, long, narrow

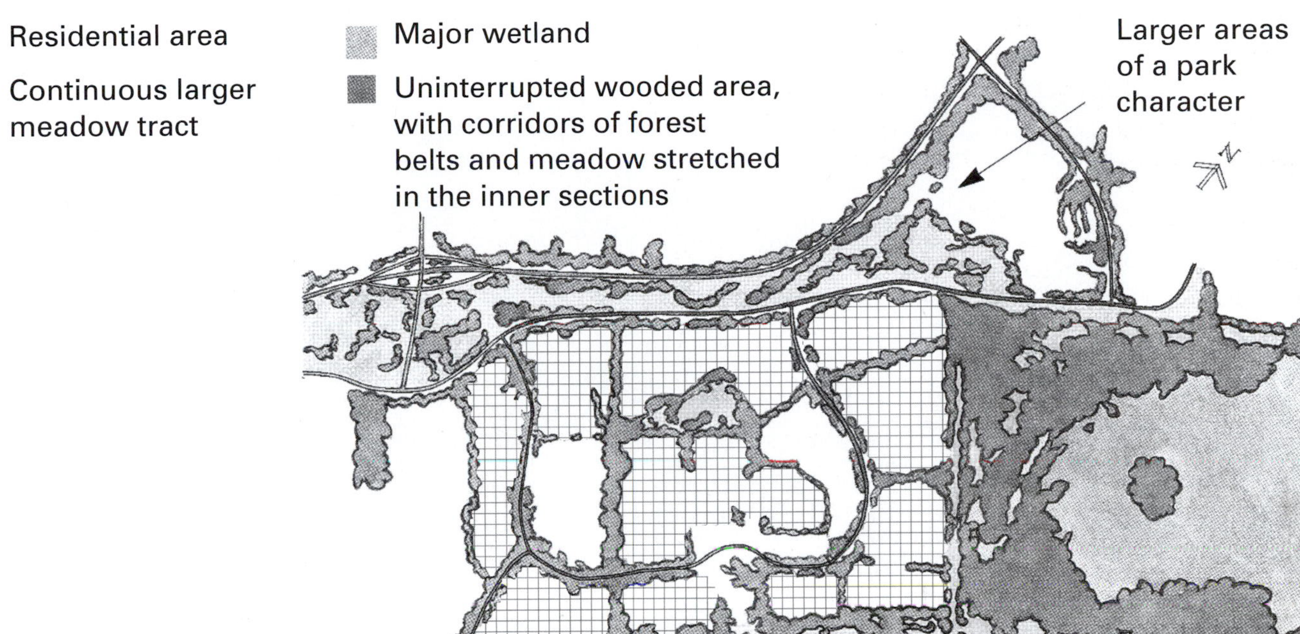

7.9 (a)
Oakwood, Warrington. The design concept for this British New Town was based on 'nature fingers' linking woodland blocks with residential areas

plantations are too often 2–4 m: too narrow to give the important 'interior qualities'.

The quality, size and width of woodland belts in practice on a green structure level, in Oakwood, Warrington, UK, provides a contextual discussion (Figure 7.9(a)). Here a design concept was used in which 'nature fingers' are meant to meet 'garden approaches'. Furthermore, the woodland belts were meant to play an important mental role in separating and cutting down the size of housing areas to a human scale, and underlining a landscape identity to enable an understanding that you are living in front of, or behind, the woodland belt in question. The woodland belts also function as part of an overall green network, creating the necessary 'good' contact with parks and natural areas in the outer zones. But the questions should be taken deeper: what does the choice of different widths mean in practice, for human appreciation, for children's play or for the plants and their growing conditions? (Tregay and Gustavsson 1983).

Figures 7.9(b) and (c) show photographs from a woodland belt in Oakwood over a period of 20 years. Ecologically, many of the woodland perennials have started to form viable carpets, and there is a high amount of flexibility when undertaking coppice-inspired management, keeping a good balance between light and shadow. The location of the walk road is problematic, by creating an experience of being outside and not really belonging to the interior world if the coppice is used with too short intervals or is too mechanically focused on the road-verge zones. The use of 'rough' plants, especially nettles, is also problematic, considerably reducing the feeling of a woodland character.

b

c

7.9 (b) and (c)
Woodland belt in Oakwood, Warrington (b) 1978, shortly after planting. (c) 20 years later

Plantations as buffer zones and air filters

Woodland belts will probably be used more frequently in the future as buffers or filters for air pollution and acidification, to reduce nutrient leakage, or as general protection. Tree planting alongside traffic routes and around dwellings is often recommended today for environmental benefit. The importance of such planting is illustrated by an investigation of the environment in western Scania in Sweden (SOU 1990: 93), which found that road traffic is responsible for 80% of nitric oxide emissions and 60% of hydrocarbons. Following this, it is estimated that, in Sweden alone, 20,000 people are constantly exposed to harmful levels of nitrogen dioxide and carbon dioxide. Considerably more people are exposed to air pollution that can give rise to cancer, allergies and asthma. About 300,000 people in Scania live in areas where noise levels are troublesome. A series of different measures is therefore required to improve the situation.

Example of a buffer planting

Figure 7.10 illustrates an example of the principles used when planting to counteract traffic emissions, stressing the importance in design of focusing on both structural and dynamic aspects. The main purpose is to screen off the traffic from the areas behind, to reduce the psychological impact of the traffic and to reduce large-particle pollution. The plantation also has a wind-reducing effect. Similar principles can be applied when industry or allotment gardening are the main concerns. As the planted trees and shrubs face a major road, a 50 m broad planted zone has been used. Along a less heavily trafficked road, 15–20 m would be sufficient. Groups of trees and shrubs planted in overlapping patterns act as a windbreak and reduce noise pollution more effectively than a homogeneous mass plantation. A particularly dense edge at the roadside is essential for noise reduction. In Figure 7.10, zone A comprises nurse trees of birch, alder or larch (later removed) and bushes. If wind reduction is important, an open front edge with just trees is added to 'catch' the wind.

Zone B in Figure 7.10 is made up of wooded belts using low woodland types with standards constructing an open canopy and a dense lower vegetation with trees that are valuable in the longer term, such as oak, lime and maple. There is a scant understorey of bushes, which functions as a filter but

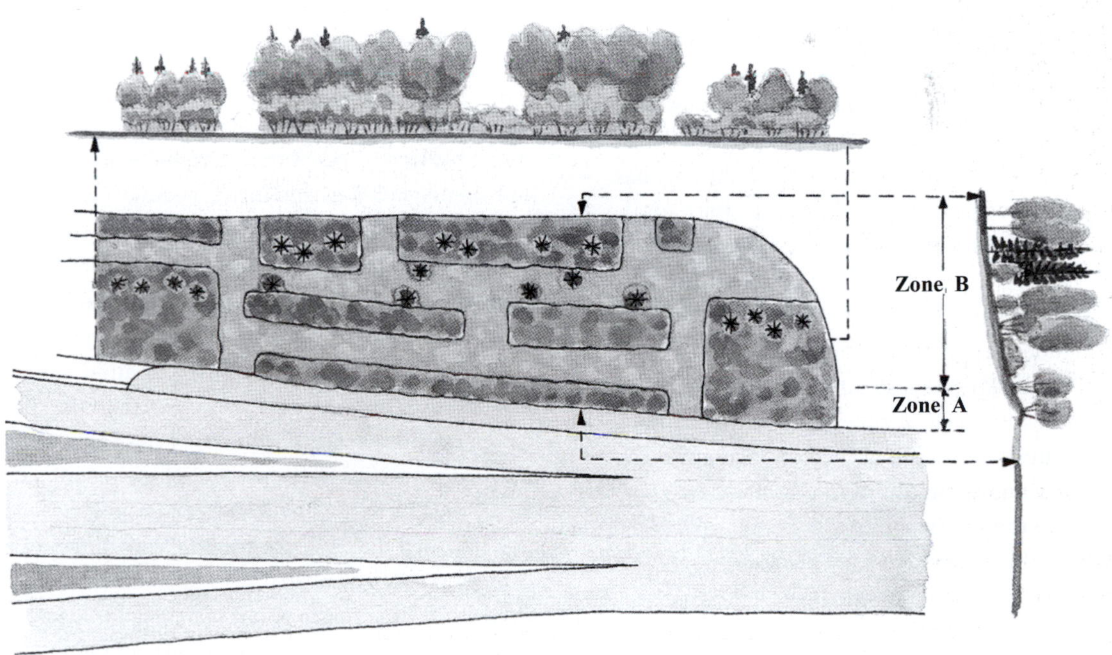

7.10
Planting to counteract traffic emissions

7.11
A private garden in Dalby, Sweden

does not prevent access to the interior of the plantation. To provide an efficient filter, this zone may be extended further to include spruce, which, during the summer has a filter capacity that is at least as good as that of deciduous trees. In the winter, the difference is pronounced; air only has to pass through a 10 m wide belt of spruce for the amount of particle-bound pollutants to be reduced to a few per cent. However, spruce is one of the tree species most sensitive to pollution. Having a deciduous screen in front protects the spruce sufficiently for it to also act as a filter.

The intermediate zones comprise meadows alternating with zones of shrub or 'energy' forest. These zones create contrast in distant views, but also improve the sustainability in zone B by giving more light to the understorey individuals.

Playing with the extremes when designing woodlands

Much vegetation establishment focuses on the need for ideal conditions of good fertile soil. Maybe it is time to reflect deeper with regard to the dominating soil-water conditions and their consequences for design in different cities or for reaching an attractive, multi-functional landscape, rich in contrast, variety and identity. Maybe we could gain a lot if, rather than trying to force the vegetation into a narrow 'good, medium soil-water situation', we instead try to use the whole spectrum, from the extremes of dry and nutrient-rich to wet and nutrient-poor. If we focus particularly on woodland types, then these are found along the whole gradient, and their use will result in very different characters when compared to each other. This stresses the importance of not searching for ideal types that just belong to the rich soils but rather

7.12
Aachen. Open woodland planting that is suggestive of the sparse vegetation patterns of extreme conditions

those that belong to the more acid soils, if we consider the 'normal' city situation. Many semi-natural vegetations with a strong and attractive character are actually found in extreme situations, which might make us consider what we can gain by a complementary approach, in which we utilise the normal 'good' conditions to create robust vegetation and to create very special places by utilising the extremes.

Figure 7.11 shows a private garden in Dalby, Sweden, with acid, open-grown woodland with birches, pruned spruces (a Swedish type of bonsai), blueberries, heather and mini-mires with mosses, created in a region in which very few would expect such a landscape, though it could be said to be more typical for other Scandinavian regions. The garden is supplemented with many plants belonging to the present biotope types but coming from other parts of the world. It is a garden area with many names: the secret garden, the moss garden, the blue berries garden and the Mattis garden.

The photograph in Figure 7.12 is from Aachen on the border between Germany and the Netherlands. Sides of concrete, a floor of gravel and an open planting with trees belonging to this extreme habitat creates a strong character. This can be compared with similar situations, for example in which a pedestrian walkway passes under a motorway, and concrete is used in a conventional way to form a functional tunnel.

Figures 7.13 to 7.15 show how wetland forests are used, or could be used, as inspiration in a design. Wetland forests are said to belong to the most species-rich habitats (Figure 7.13). As such, they can offer extremely rich experiences of landscape. Increasing interest in environmental solutions to urban drainage will give us more possibilities in the future to explore fields within designs that have so far been hardly touched.

Figure 7.15 presents a diagram of a very old wetland forest of *Salix*, showing how the *Salix*

7.13
An ancient wetland forest of alder

7.14
Designed wetland forest in the new housing area of Västra Hamnen in Malmö, Sweden – the national exhibition of experimental houses and green surroundings in 2001

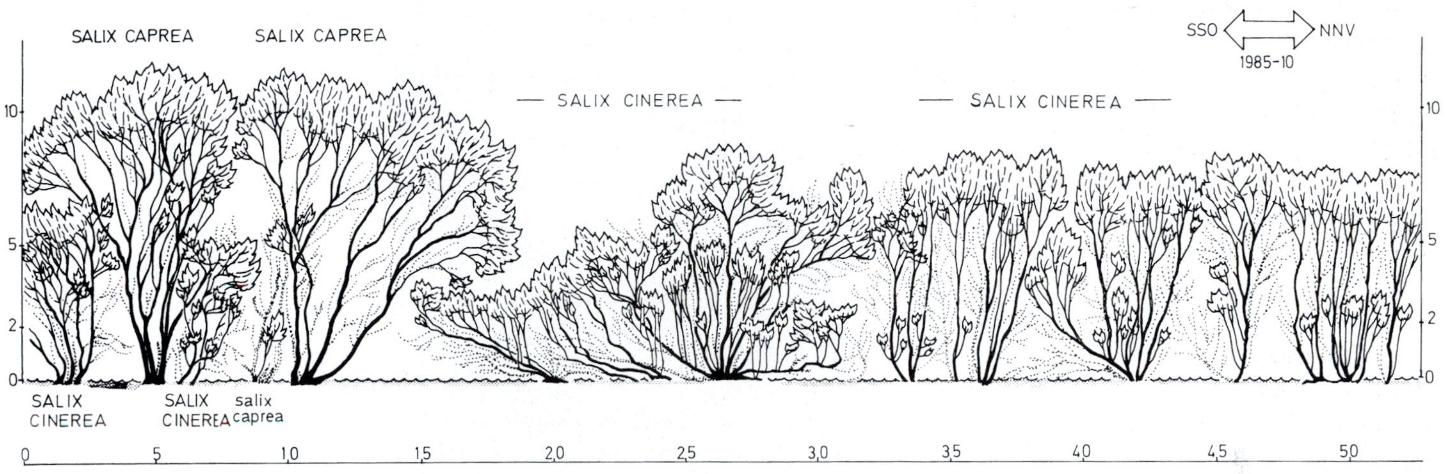

7.15
Very old wetland forest of *Salix* (from the PhD thesis by Gustavsson (1986)) showing how the willow species form self-regenerating woodland

species, through an 'intelligent strategy', are able to spread step by step, making it difficult for other species to evolve. When the outer branches get older they sink due to the weight, and some go under the water and come in contact with mud or other kinds of substrates, thereby giving a chance to new roots. A new individual is therefore formed and the old links become rotten within a few years.

Woodland aspects on an area level – overall design principles and approaches to a contextual design

So far a lot of general principles for use in a woodland design have been presented, with the main goals being to reach beyond mainstream solutions and stressing more long-term dynamic thinking. Here, landscape character, basic landscape types to widen the understanding and the meaning of 'urban woodland', and reference landscapes have been the key words. In thinking about a design situation, there is a complementary need to be strongly contextual, which stresses both an intuitive ability and also training in a more contextual design relating to questions such as the following.

- How can you recognise different parts of the woodland as a series of places, walks, entrances, landmarks, views, focus points and zones in-between? Are there reasons for a division of the woodland into different zones when thinking about the management level and strategies, stressing main strategies for: certain places for activities; places with a woodland park character; zones based on an aesthetic of care aimed at a character with a strong emphasis on scenic values; zones in which a mix of traditional forestry or agricultural methods and a production outlet would be appreciable in an aesthetic of care; and wilderness zones, including areas with no management at all involved in an aesthetic of wilderness? (Nassauer 1997).
- What natural processes are important for you to start, and what should actually be avoided to allow for later natural processes or cultural-social events?
- What is preferable in the choice of a formal or an informal design language? How can you create

strong and distinct atmospheres, spans in-between harmony and chaos, uniformity and complexity?

- How does the woodland area relate to other woodlands, other recreational areas as well as housing areas and traffic zones, and how should it relate? Does it create an illusion of a world in itself, with a lot of surprises hidden inside, or does it belong to the surroundings as an extension which gradually changes in character but stimulates contacts in-between through its openness along its fringes?
- How will the users reach the woodland? Will there be possibilities to provide better links, to give a whole series of alternative routes?
- Is it possible to distinguish between different routes in a hierarchical way by considering length as well as atmosphere and seasons: broad walks, narrow paths and rides, providing a place for more 'rational' people or for those who want to socialise or feel secure, but also places for those who want to be alone, to feel a closeness to nature, or who are searching for more informal contacts?

Figure 7.16 shows Bulltofta Park, Malmö, which is the largest park area designed within a 50-year period in Sweden. Its design was influenced by the Amsterdam bos in the Netherlands. Conceptually it was also influenced by German 'plant sociology' and 'potential natural vegetation'. Furthermore, it represents an example of the implementation of a basic structure of both open and woodland areas but also of a hierarchical network of walks. In a development perspective, ideas have now been raised as to whether parts will, in the coming years, be transformed to silvi-pastoral systems. Other questions concern the diversification of the woodland edges and how woodland interior zones can be improved for the experience of the visitors. The latter very much concerns how the network of paths should be changed.

7.16
Bulltofta Park, Malmö, Sweden

Figure 7.17 shows major design principles for a woodland area. Figure 7.17(a) is the wall concept, creating an illusion of a world of its own by dense outer zones. In parallel, it creates feelings of surprise when discovering a pillared hall or an open room in the middle. Figure 7.17(b) is the open outer zones, half open or a light-giving pillared hall character, grazed or not grazed, creating links to the surroundings. It has an increased density; the more you enter the woodland, the idea of 'the more we walked into the forest, the more it closed itself around us' is strengthened. Figure 7.17(c) illustrates a concept which suggests a basic skeleton of robust vegetation, with indigenous species, which comprise both outer zones and interior 'walls'. The robustness improves long-term sustainability for the woodland as a whole but, in particular, for the blocks in-between, in which a more sensitive vegetation can be sheltered; like spruce stands or stands with exotics if you want them to be long lasting.

7.17
Major design principles for a woodland are: (a) open outer zone concept; (b) wall concept; (c) robust vegetation

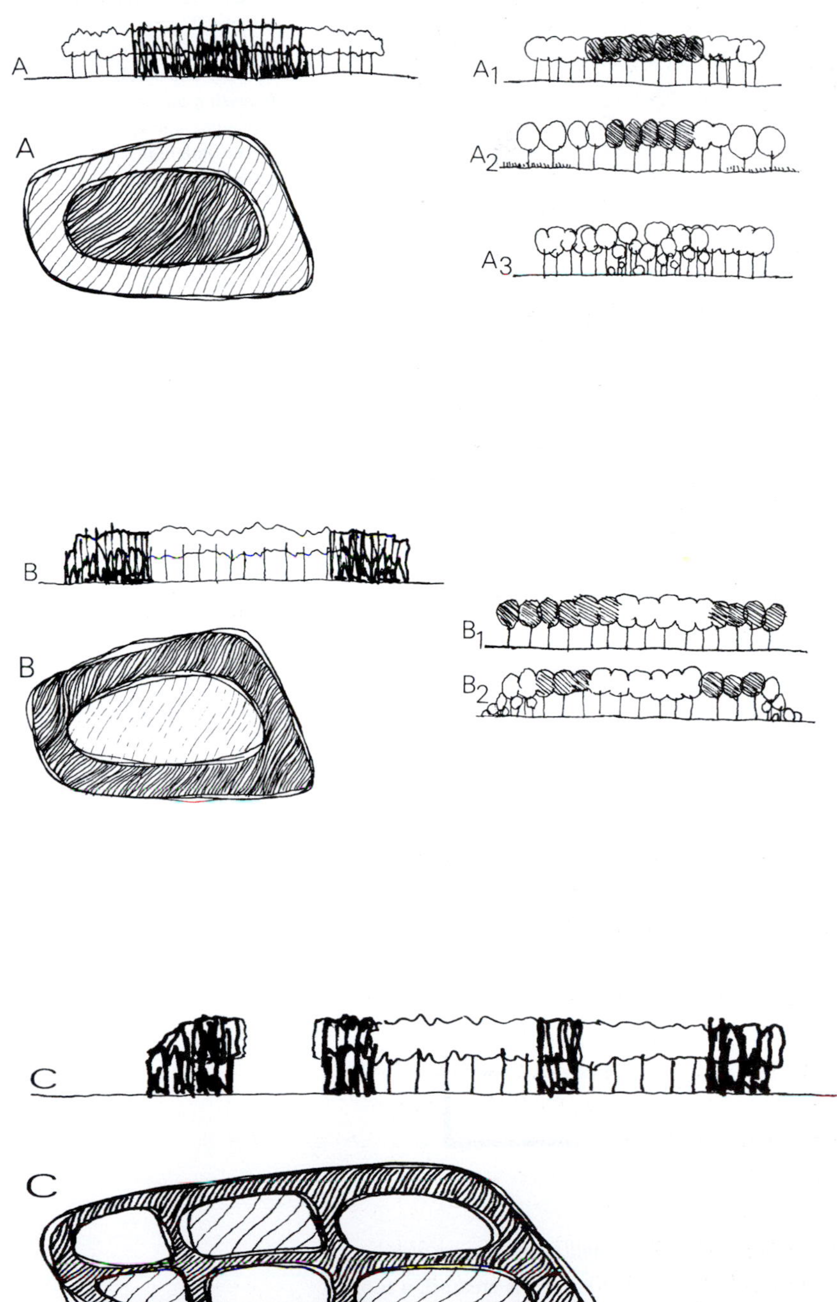

Woodland types: their dynamic architecture, establishment and management – the structural dynamic approach to woodland design

There are two main approaches to 'vegetation architecture' or planting design that can be characterised as follows.

- *Physiognomic* (textural) – this has been the dominant approach until now, focusing on individual plant qualities: forms, colours and shapes of flowers, bark and leaves, etc.
- *Structural*, focusing on vertical and horizontal patterns, stressing the direct links between vegetation architecture and ecology, and offering an improved knowledge base involving design, long-term development and management principles.

The structural approach allows us to increase our understanding of the relationships between forms and dynamics, and of how these dynamics can be actively used, thereby stressing the fact that natural processes are always part of the design in parks and gardens. Furthermore, it allows us to deepen and sharpen our image of links between cultural expressions and natural processes, rather than dividing the two into separate worlds. To combine trees and shrubs in different patterns means that a certain architecture will be created. If we are to speak truthfully about long-living, sustainable, environment-friendly solutions, there is a need to understand much more about how different species interact, and the resultant expressions in terms of vegetation architecture.

Conventional design traditions sometimes make people sceptical about identifying types because it is said to diminish the world of possibilities and narrow the scope of creativity. However, even if some frames, focus areas and ways of thinking are suggested, this should be seen as open-ended and as a way of stimulating the discovery of other

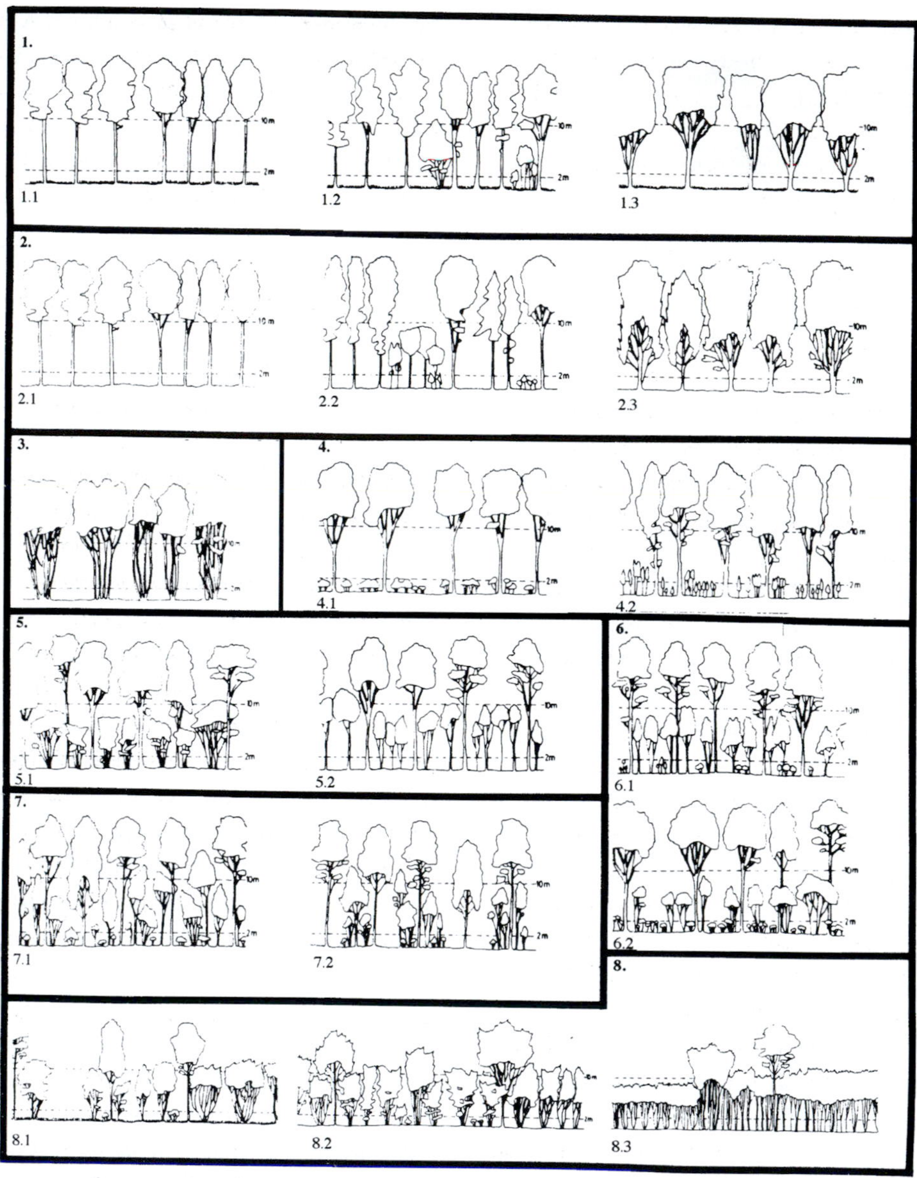

7.18
An overview of different structural types of vegetation dominated by trees and shrubs focussing on high and low woodland types. 1. The dark high woodland; 2. The light high woodland; 3. Multi-stemmed, one-storied high woodland; 4. Two-storied high woodland with shrubs; 5. Two-storied high woodland with well developed middle layer; 6. Three-storied high woodland; 7. Multi-layered high-woodland; 8. Low woodland types

possibilities other than those presented here. The invention of 'types' and 'sub-types' on a habitat or stand level, which is chosen here as the main scale area, does not need to end with the identified types. It structures thinking in a way that easily finds combinations and unidentified types as part of a design process. Thereby, a tool-box is created, a tool-box from which it is possible to pick and combine in an unending way in order to aid the design of local parks, gardens or other urban semi-natural areas.

Very few attempts have been made through the years to achieve an articulated view of how it may be possible to create the different major characters of vegetation as an essential part of a new woodland creation in the design of parks and gardens, or, broadly, of landscape architecture. The structural vegetation approach, with its spatial interest, developed initially with the 'Cambridge School' of botanists and their applications in tropical rain forests. In the 1950s, Dansereau (1951, 1958) and Dansereau and Arras (1959) tried to identify a universal system of structural types of vegetation. Some years later, more incomplete, attempts were also made by forest ecologists, such as Rackham (1975), Kira (1978), Peterken (1996) and Koop (1989), and by foresters like Mayer (1992). Despite these and some other exceptions, very few attempts have been made to identify structural types, and thereby to focus on the architecture and the character of vegetation. No one has so far seen the possibilities to directly link the research of vegetation structure to landscape architecture and city contexts.

These were the main reasons why research at the Department of Landscape Planning in Sweden in the 1970s and 1980s focused on the structure of vegetation as an approach for urban woodland design and long-term management. An overview of the main structural types of vegetation with trees and shrubs was developed, and was presented in a series of practical projects in Sweden as well as in Britain, including the well-known example of Oakwood in Warrington New Town (Tregay and Gustavsson 1983). As a result, a classification scheme was made based on North and Central European vegetation, published in the early 1980s as a series of research reports about naturalistic (nature-like) areas in parks and housing areas, focusing on different kinds of native and ornamental plantations (Gustavsson 1981, 1995; Gunnarsson and Gustavsson 1989). Later the identification of woodland types was taken some steps further, identifying more sub-types that should be regarded as important for practice. More recently, improvement has been made through a better integration of dynamic concepts (Rizell and Gustavsson 1998). In parallel, questions were raised about how frequently these vegetation types were found in the Swedish cities of today, within different time rings in a city development. The original scheme covered 29 identified structural types, including both open and more tree- and shrub-rich characters. Of these, only 10 were commonly used in the investigated Swedish cities, and several of what could be considered as the most interesting were totally missing. The reason for this 'character poorness' was mainly thought to be a lack of knowledge of what structural types could possibly be used.

Below, some of the main types have been selected in order to illustrate such aspects as key characteristics, use of nursery species during the first years, species, recommendations for the choice of planting scheme, and other aspects which might be practically relevant. It should be noted that the structural approach includes both indigenous and exotic species, and does not only cover naturalistic characters. Furthermore, there are also important links between the number of layers, dominating trees, light and shadow, and the field layer with its characteristic perennial herbs and grasses.

Indigenous species and their interactions in woodland systems

Indigenous species will often continue to be seen as the most secure basis for a long-term living system because we have scientific and practical experience of them, and they should, more than others, be hardy and trustful from a very long-term perspective – a point of major importance in 'stressed' urban situations. Systems with indigenous species have strong symbolic cultural values because of their familiarity to many people. Most of these experiential qualities are related to the older woodland stages, and they are therefore of crucial importance if it is possible to prolong the life of plantations into these older stages.

However, of equal importance is to increase the knowledge and the use of urban woodlands based on ornamental plants. These have, over centuries, fascinated city dwellers because of their exotic flowers, strong autumn colours, or because they are from foreign, distant countries, with all the curiosity that this can awake. And there is no sign that city people will be less fascinated about exotic plants in the future. There has been some experience in the northwestern part of Europe and Scandinavia of the hardiness and long-term survival ability of a range of exotic tree-species, but if we want to extend or deepen our knowledge and look at these species and their ability to grow in long-term systems, as well as their interactions with neighbouring individuals or their place in a succession, there is so far very limited knowledge.

Main structural types

The rest of this chapter contains a description of the main structural types of woodland. These types include: high woodlands (uniform, open woodlands with a high canopy and sparse shrub-layer); many layered woodland; low woodlands (more dense woodlands with a low canopy and a high proportion of shrubs and multi-stemmed trees); shrub-based systems; edges; and half-open land and small-scale mosaics. In each case, the character of the woodland is described, key species are listed, suggestions for planting densities are given, as well as details of field-layer establishment. Finally, some examples of the application of these types are given.

Dark high woodland: one storey high stand type

Basic characteristic

Homogeneity, co-dominance between the trees. One tree-species should be chosen to dominate the scene by itself, or a combination consisting of one nursery species and one key character species could be chosen. The crowns should be lifted high, the trunks should be without forks, to give the impression of a large space or hall with a roof supported by pillars: a 'pillared hall'.

Sub-characteristic

There is a need for a necessary area before sub-groups and sub-characteristics can even be discussed, otherwise homogeneity will be too disturbed. If the size is sufficient, solitary individuals or distinct groups in the undergrowth can increase effects, but just very, very few. Also, if done with care, very few individually grown trees could be included as an exceptional part of the canopy. If these solitary grown trees have canopies that do not cast dense shade, then an interesting effect of light pockets can be created, with light finding its way down the stand.

Key character species

Beech, maple, lime tree, horse chestnut, hornbeam, elm and spruce (Figure 7.19).

Nursery species

Not too many, and not too vigorous. Absolutely under 25%, maybe even under 10%, of the canopy. Sometimes it is wise to avoid nursery species totally because they are often forgotten in the later thinning programs and thereby often become part of the later phases, thereby introducing an unwanted heterogeneity.

Edges

Closed edges, especially towards the south and west, are recommended to increase the sense of an inner room and darkness, but also to reduce processes which cause heterogeneity.

Field layer, type and establishment methods

A very poorly developed field layer or a field layer dominated by low perennials and mosses that will develop in the long term is likely to occur spontaneously. In order to introduce a more diverse spring and early summer flowering field layer, direct seeding and planting should be used.

Planting schedule

Very short distance between the plants gives fewer forks at the stem and a higher inner roof, whereas a larger distance gives a lower inner roof, which will be a variant between the pillared hall character and another more open type.

7.19(a)
Dark high woodland: an old beech stand

7.19(b)
Dark high woodland: a horse chestnut stand in a park in Hanover, Germany, giving the typical 'pillared hall' effect

The light high woodland

Basic characteristics

Homogeneity, created by the use of one species or a combination of two supplementary tree species, i.e. birch and oak, or birch and wild cherry. Co-dominance, high uplifted crowns. Solitary shrubs and small trees in the undergrowth.

Key character species

Poplars, birch, ash, pine, oak and cherry (Figure 7.20).

Edges

Open edges could be favoured, stressing the importance of incoming light, the visual overview and homogeneity.

Field layer and establishment methods

A field layer dominated by grasses and high perennial herbs, and young tree plants, develops spontaneously. Establishment methods include direct seeding of shadow-tolerant grasses and herbs belonging to the inner edge zone.

Basic management principles

More regular but careful thinnings. No selection of main trees as a basic principle.

The many layered woodland type

Basic characteristics

Species-rich plantation – there can be as many species as individuals. The more layers and the more species, the more important is the careful design and management, based on the special strategies each species have and their characteristic groupings in a very diverse type of woodland system. These woodlands are characterised by a many layered, species-rich high woodland, but are often also found with open glades, meadow corridors, individually open grown trees, and thickets of shrubs as part of its structure. As a basic principle for long-term co-existence, there has to be a balance between light-

a

b

c

demanding species in the upper layers and more shadow-tolerant species the lower you come in the system. A full use of native species belonging to these kind of systems can create a fascinating landscape experience, with most of what is considered as a woodland at its best, and with many characteristic individual trees, dramatic interactions between neighbours living extremely close to each other, each finding their own niche, and, in turn, the pattern as a whole giving a strong harmonious experience with the stems, the layers and the colourful carpets of flowers in spring.

Sub-characteristics

If the area is large enough, species richness can be achieved by a horizontal change of species mixture over the area. Here sub-groups with or without distinct layers can be recommended as part of a larger pattern. Moreover, a large enough size also makes it possible to increase the complexity even more by including glades and denser thickets. When used in the park tradition, it has been important to keep the different layers apart in a strict manner, using shrub species for the shrub layer, whilst in the conservation and forestry traditions the different layers are often more difficult to separate from each other, and the shrub layer normally consists of young tree species which have future roles in the layers above. Very similar systems and design principles are used within the 'garden woodland' as a widely spread design concept. Here exotic species are widely used, and the shrub layer and the perennials in the field layer are given prominence. A rule 'of the wandering sunlight' is often referred to here: the upper canopy is designed to be open so that rays of sunlight illuminate the woodland floor throughout the day.

Key character species

Upper tree layer: ash, oak and aspen. Lower tree layer (middle layer): lime, rowan, whitebeam, hornbeam, beech, wild cherry, bird cherry, maple and hazel. Higher and lower shrub layers: hazel, hawthorn, bird cherry, young individuals of shadow-tolerant tree species, *Cornus*, *Viburnum* and *Ribes* species.

Edges

The edges can be very varied.

7.20(a)
Light high woodland: middle-aged birch stand from southern Finland – further south in Europe other species, such as *Betula ermani* or *B.jackmontii*, can replace the European species if the wish is to have white stems

7.20(b)
Light high woodland: old Populus stand in Sjöarp makes a strong effect in a local recreational landscape with its contrast of dark giving stands to the surroundings

7.20(c)
Light high woodland: open pine stand, with its strong response in its character to the climate limitations, with its low height, the leaning stems and the poor but light-demanding field layer (Madrid, Spain)

Establishment methods – trees and shrubs
An ambitious weeding in the first two to three years always creates a fast start, especially for the slow starters. However, strong competition from the herbaceous layer can support diversity and differentiation in the various layers.

Establishment methods – the field layer
Direct seeding in combination with strategic planting in groups. The soil conditions and the type of litter that is created is critical for the choice of species.

Basic management principles
This multi-layered high woodland type is only possible on soils with good water and nutrient conditions. To some extent you can, however, compensate for somewhat poorer conditions by a vague opening of the high canopy, and by artificial watering during drought periods. However, there are questions about long-term viability if these woodlands are unmanaged: in practice, a well developed, many layered structure like this is rather unusual – it normally does not exist by natural processes but is instead a combination of historical, multi-functional and complex management methods, as stages within 'lund' management, and management of wooded meadows or as the later stages of an overgrown coppice with standard systems. A knowledge-based management system which focuses on the selection of main trees, neighbour trees, the development of a multi-layered structure in-between, the combination of strict individual and group treatment, and a utilisation of spontaneous processes is therefore important.

Low woodland types (low stands)

Basic characteristics
Low woodland types with multi-stemmed trees and high shrubs, with a possibility to enter physically, even if in the younger stages this may be difficult due to its density. Many have suggested that traditional coppice systems should be used in city situations much more. In these systems the traditional management never enables anything resembling a high woodland type to develop. However, after a period of no management they stop their development as low woodlands, with or without standard trees emerging here and there. Coppicing, which uses the spontaneous re-growth of the species, is arranged on a rotation cycle, sometimes on short cycles of six to eight years or less, or on longer cycles up to 20–30 years. This gives a dense mass of multi-stemmed individuals that have many similarities with high shrubs – it is a collective, anonymous and dense mass, that is higher than a shrub. They become almost impossible to enter and have almost no visual openness, if planted densely. However, if we include the longer intervals and wider spacings or also include the 'overgrown' or 'left' stages, then, suddenly, physically and visually more open types are found. These latter, totally new types, but based on similar principles and also on some of the traditional principles, should all be considered as important for the future.

Sub-characteristics and sub-types
Low woodlands should still be very much related to the traditional coppice systems but should be regarded as something wider, and with other possible types and stages which fit into a city context. There are several distinct sub-types that should be identified:

- the more open grown, with close links to woodland meadow types
- the visually semi-open types
- the very dense type, with a closeness to shrub types
- a differentiation into different types based on the presence of standard trees and by the height ('high coppice systems' and 'low coppice systems').

Key character species
Hazel, lime, *Salix* species, hawthorn, hornbeam,

oak, beech, rowan, ash, maple, elm, alder, birch and bird cherry. Among the exotics, chestnut, *Amelanchier* species, *Cercidiphyllum*, *Hamamelis*, *Pterocarya fraxinifolia*, etc., should be considered as interesting, but more species should be tested (Dunnett 2003).

Planting scheme

A choice of key character species – many or one – in a mixture with nursery species. For some variants, nursery species should not be necessary, but, it could have disadvantages in the longer term. Consider how to place standard trees, as well as sensitive species that have to be controlled or helped.

Edges

Owing to its low height, the interior part can melt together easily with the edge zones. However, sometimes sensitive species or species with particular beauty should be placed in the edge zone so they will be noticed and can be taken care of in any difficult stages of low management periods.

Field layer and establishment methods

The field layer should be considered of particular importance, especially when considering the visually more open types. The establishment methods comprise a combination of seeding and planting.

Basic management principles

The basic characteristics of multi-stemmed trees and shrubs makes management differ from a normal woodland forestry practice. Management can become difficult because coppice is quite unknown in urban areas today, so we have to adopt new practices, based on a deep understanding of how coppice systems can work in a wider meaning of the term. Particularly, it should be stressed that we have to notice the completely new city functions: functions such as aesthetics, play areas for children, filters for cleaning the air, etc. Therefore, management strategies should be goal directed rather than just trying to copy traditional management ways (Figure 7.21).

7.21

(a) Small-scale mosaic with ongoing coppicing, dominated by hazel. Scania, Sweden (b) Low woodland type of hazel 15 years after planting in Warrington, England, successfully used by children; (c) *Pterocarya fraxinifolia*, an exotic species used in the Alnarp landscape laboratory, Sweden, as a characteristic low woodland type after 15 years

Shrub types

Basic characteristics

Shrub types are probably the most used structural type in parks and gardens. Because of this there is a lot of experience within the horticultural tradition of how to design with shrubs. However, it must be said that there are many problems with the standard treatment of shrubs: 'shrub mass' plantings, characterised by block plantings of ornamental shrubs, can be visually monotonous, offer little in the way of seasonal change or wildlife value, and are usually maintained in a very crude manner that prevents dynamic development (Dunnett 2003). Moving on to a more dynamic approach to designing with shrubs means, to some degree, a change of perspective and maybe even the development of new design concepts. Furthermore, most shrubs that are used are pioneer species, but how do these interact with each other and with shrubs and small trees which are not pioneer species? Also, a lot of new knowledge is waiting to be explored concerning how shrub types develop in the very long run, and concerning what patterns and species are characteristic of old age and renewal phases.

The shrubs should sometimes be designed so they remain as long as possible as vital shrub areas or zones, perhaps enabling the human-scale division of spaces. At other times they should be designed as pioneer phases that lead to both high and low woodland types, providing a lot of flowers, berries and shelter for birds, whilst we are waiting for the trees to develop, notably trees which can be quite anonymous for the first years. Compared to most other types, shrub species and shrubs are short lived, but, on the other hand, they also gain a mature character relatively early.

Sub-characteristics and sub-types

Many sub-types can be identified:

- a dense, varied scrub type, characterised by its diversity and richness in form
- high scrub with solitary trees or groups of trees as a mixture between a homogeneous base and elements that stick out
- high, even shrub type – a very homogeneous type
- combination of high and low shrubs
- low shrub with solitary trees
- low, even shrub.

Key character species

The key species consist mostly of shrub species. However, to some degree we also find some tree species among the important species, but very few herbs and grasses of importance. Indigenous shrub systems have a lot of qualities for local flora and fauna, their hardiness, flowering period and their colourful autumn season. However, outside of this we also find all the possibilities that the use of exotic species can bring.

Among the indigenous key character species we find light-demanding shrubs, such as blackthorn and roses, or more shadow-tolerant species, such as *Ribes alpinum*, *Sambucus* species, *Euonymus europaeas*, *Viburnum opulus*, etc. When suitable, a lot of interest should also be directed to the many exotics with high ornamental qualities.

Edges

More often shrubs are part of a more open grass countryside landscape, found as isolated shrub islands but maybe even more common as part of a hedge landscape or a woodland edge. Notice the spontaneous expansion that is typical for many of the species; it can be an opportunity as well as a potential problem.

Planting scheme

In order to extend the sustainability of shrubs, the shrub species can be planted in groups, separated from trees and taller scrub species. The selected trees should be light-giving rather than shadow-giving, and should have a small, narrow crown rather than a wide one. Moreover, the presence of tree species should be minimised in planting schemes to figures below 10%, and probably even much lower.

Field layer and establishment methods

Considering the field layer and its establishment, special focus should be directed to the outer edge zones. Establishment methods often comprise a direct seeding as a base, complemented with a plantation of smaller groups and individuals.

Basic management principles

An estimation of what will happen in the long run can be seen in shrubs growing in the countryside. Over a long period it seems that tree species experience difficulties in entering shrub-dominated communities but, in the long run, they do. Even if the trees do not invade the shrub area, it will break down. Especially for *Rosaceae* species like *Prunus spinosa*, this will happen within a maximum period of a 100 years. Coppicing is important as part of the management principles for shrubs. It might help to keep them young, but not to keep them 'forever young'. Other important principles explaining their possible diversity and long-term sustainability are grazing and mowing regimes.

Half-open land and small-scale mosaics

Basic characteristics

Plantations and open rooms should form interactive systems, creating informal or more formal patterns, in a logical relationship to land form, soil fertility and hydrology. The choice of principles for tree and shrub plantings should shift from larger and smaller group plantings to individual planting in the open rooms. There should also be a shift from very dense plantings, following the plants' natural sociability strategies, to plantings based on large distances in-between the individuals, giving each other support by their relative closeness but still standing far enough away from each other that they will be 'open grown' in character.

Sub-characteristics

- Small-scale mosaic with glades, open meadow or grass corridors and copses, and clumps of trees or high shrubs in a very diverse architecture.
- Evenly or unevenly spread trees over grassland, in a half-open character.
- Shrubs spread over a grassland or a meadow area in a distinct formal or informal pattern.

Key character species

Tree choice should be selected with a priority for light-giving, small and narrow-crowned species, which also, in many cases, are species creating an attractive flowering period. Common trees and shrubs for half-open landscapes are birches, wild cherry, bird cherry, rowans, hawthorns, hazel and roses. However, the principles should not be too simplistic. Large, open grown, and shadow-giving trees used for larger areas could create a majestic character. Trees such as oaks, beeches, hornbeams, lime trees and maples, and exotics like horse chestnut and sweet chestnut have been used a lot in old traditions for this kind of landscape.

Edges

The field layer and its species for a half-open landscape often have much in common with species for a woodland edge community. The architectural pattern of trees and shrubs should also be designed with specific notice of how they relate to the closed landscape in the surroundings.

Field layer and establishment methods

Perennial plants should be part of the aesthetic highlights, with a choice of species related to open meadow, grassland, woodland edge and woodland interior communities. Establishment methods comprise a combination of direct seeding and planting.

Basic management principles

The long-term management regime will be very important for keeping and developing qualities belonging to this type. The open areas can shift from short cut-grass to hayed meadows and free-growing grass areas for regeneration zones, with direct or spontaneous seeding. This is often a very dynamic landscape, although people believe it to be one of the most stable over time. This concept can be difficult for management staff to grasp and the qualities of the small-scale pattern can easily be destroyed and become overgrown.

Edge types

Basic characteristics

Even if you do not decide to plant a particular edge to a new woodland, an edge zone will develop. If so, why not make a special design for the edge zones if you have the chance? There are many advantages, such as aesthetic improvement, increased wind shelter for the woodland interior behind or increased wildlife value. The edge zone is also a preferable zone for children and their play. Here they can find shelter and construct huts, and here they should be able to find good climbing trees from which they can obtain an overview of the more open surroundings (Figure 7.22).

Sub-characteristics

Edge types can vary in-between the extremes, from a three-staged edge with an outdrawn profile to a one-staged edge. When enough space is available, the 'three-staged edge' can get a depth of 30–50 m, and several zones can be identified, from the inner edge zones to the middle edge zones and the outer edge zones. In the inner edge zone, a high woodland type with specific edge trees can be found. In the middle edge zone, a low woodland type can sometimes be found, but this is uncommon in practice. Finally, the shrubs dominate the outer edge zone, but not all of it. This may interact with a special attractive grass- and herb-rich zone, with species that are favoured by having the shrubs and the edge trees at the back: this is a dynamic equivalent to gardens with their shrub and perennial borders. However, considering woodland edge design, variation *along* the edge must also be considered. The same profile might be chosen to create uniformity and a greater sense of harmony, or the opposite, with all the extremes composed in one and the same edge, can be chosen. Furthermore, specific elements should be considered as a contribution on *'an area level'*. Such elements are glades placed in the inner edge zone, 'in-drawn' grass wedges like creeks or inlets, 'out-drawn' points or tips of shrubs or trees, solitary trees and clumps placed as a forefront, small water and wetlands which are placed to maximise its function as a wildlife habitat and to increase its beauty. Such an element is also the edge path. The sensibility of how this is drawn in a designed edge zone has characterised many well-known landscape designers.

Key character species and field layer

In the science of plant sociology, specific plant communities of the edge zones in different climates and soil types have been identified, and should be able to be used as a reference.

Basic management principles

In recent times, woodland edges are often left without management, with the obvious risk of missing a lot of interesting qualities, and with the risk that most of the edges will look the same. In the long term, particularly the 'out-drawn', shrub-rich types and the visually open, short edges will disappear.

Conclusions

To explore woodland design opens up new possibilities – possibilities which have stayed undiscovered for many reasons. To step back, reflect and rediscover a rich (both cultural and natural) woodland history is an important recommendation of this chapter. It is also suggested that visually attractive and structurally interesting reference landscapes and woodlands are identified that provide inspiration for future design. But that is far from all. There must be other, completely new concepts to discover as well as new theoretical fields to explore. The most interesting of the theoretical concepts should be taken into reality and thereby enable new reference landscapes to be created. This chapter has tried to present some of what have been considered as the most interesting or promising. The examples are from many corners of Europe today, and, as types, many of them are, so far, rare.

7.22(a)
Open edge with wild perennials from a garden at Dalby – the perennials often move around until they find their best situation

Woodland design includes a whole range of basically very different concepts, which it helps to develop an articulated, deep knowledge about. It stretches from physiognomic perspectives, so well-known in practice today, to structural perspectives, which are much less used, and it gives the chance to bridge in-between architectural and biological knowledge fields. A chapter like this can hopefully serve as an eye-opener, a starting point or as a stimulating mental processes. The many references to both research and practice provide a good opportunity to dig deeper.

It should also be stressed that woodland design is an activity aiming to be far-reaching in time and to succeed in bringing a gift to future generations. It is therefore an activity, which, more than many other design activities, plays with dynamics – to set a long journey which should be highly enjoyable right from the start and through the complete process. A set of key elements are introduced to interact with each other and also with other dynamic natural processes, which can disturb or enrich the system over time. Within the chapter we also included a breakdown of the main types and sub-types, which can be seen as a basis for further design inspiration and interpretation. For example, if we want to use similar thinking concepts for the exotic or ornamental plants, or if we want to investigate other parts of Europe, North America and elsewhere, as well as the primarily Western European models that have been used here.

7.22(b)
An extremely diverse edge zone in Oxhagen, Sweden. In many grazed landscapes the outer edge zone is sometimes very complex, with many pockets and shrub islands. To design something similar in housing areas can be done but there is often a problem with resources being available for longer-term management

References

- Bucht, E. (1997). *Public Parks in Sweden 1860–1960. The Planning and Design Discourse*. Thesis Agraria 56, Swedish University of Agricultural Sciences, Alnarp.
- Bucht, E. (2002). Traditions in Urban Park Planning and Management in Sweden and other European Countries. In Randrup, T. B. *et. al*.(eds) *Urban Forests and Trees; Proceedings No 1. COST Action E12*. Directorate-General for Research, EUR 19861, Brussels, pp.215–227.
- Dansereau, P. (1951). Description and recording of vegetation upon a structural basis. In *Ecology*, No. 2.
- Dansereau, P. (1958). A universal system for recording vegetation. *Contributions de l´Institut Botanique de l´Université de Montreal*, No. 72.
- Dansereau, P. and Arras, J. (1959). *Essais d´application de la dimension structurale en phytosociologie Vegetatio*. Acta Geobotanica, Haag, pp. 49–99.
- Dunnett, N. (2003). Natural models for shrub planting: shrub mosaics and woodland edge. In Hitchmough, J. and Fieldhouse, K. Blackwell Scientific Publications, London.
- Grahn, P. (1991). Om parkers betydelse (The Meaning and Significance of Urban Parks). *Stad and Land*, No. 93.
- Grahn, P. and Stigsdotter, U. (2002). Landscape architecture and stress: How a green city could affect people's stress-related depressions and burnout syndromes. *Urban Forestry and Urban Greening*, Vol. 1, supplement, 30.
- Gunnarsson, A. and Gustavsson, R. (1989). Etablering av lövträdsplantor. *Stad and Land*, rapport Nr 71. MOVIUM, SLU, Alnarp.
- Gustavsson, R. (1981). Naturlika grönytor i parker och bostadsområden – en beskrivning av forskningsprojektets bakgrund, dess experimentella del samt en kort genomgång av viktiga vegetationstyper, klassificerade utifrån deras uppbyggnad, struktur, form. *Landskap* 58, Alnarp.
- Gustavsson, R. (1995). A structural approach to woodland plantations. In Griffiths, G. H. (ed.) *Proceedings for the IALE (UK) Conference in Reading 1995,* IALE (UK), Garstang.
- Kendle, T. and Forbes, S. (1997). *Urban Nature Conservation. Landscape Management in the Urban Countryside*. E. & F. N. Spon. London.
- Kira, Y.T. (1978). Community architecture and organic matter dynamics in tropical lowland rain forests of south east Asia. In Tomlinson, P. B. and Zimmermann, M. H. (eds) *Tropical trees as living systems.,* pp. 561–601.
- Koop, H. (1989). *Forest Dynamics. Silvi-Star: A Comprehensive Monitoring System*. Springer-Verlag. Berlin.
- Mayer, H. (1992). *Waldbau auf soziologisch-ökologischer Grundlage. 4., neu bearbeite Auflage*. Gustav Fischer, Stuttgart.
- Muir, R. (1999). *Approaches to Landscapes*. MacMillan Press, London.
- Muir, R. (2000). *The New Reading the Landscape. Fieldwork in Landscape History*. University of Exeter Press, Exeter.
- Nassauer, J. (ed.) (1997). *Placing Nature. Culture and Landscape Ecology*. Island Press, Washington CD, California.
- Peterken, G. (1996). *Natural woodland*. Cambridge University Press, Cambridge.
- Rackham, O. (1986). The History of the English Countryside. Weidenfield & Nicolson, London.
- Richards, P. W. (1952). *The tropical rain forest*. Cambridge University Press, Cambridge.
- Rizell, M. and Gustavsson, R. (1998). Att anlägga skogsbryn. Modeller och referenser för anläggning och rekonstruktion. Forskningsrapport. *Stad and Land*, No. 160, MOVIUM, SLU, Alnarp.
- SOU (1990: 93). *Miljön i västra Skåne*. Statens Offentliga Utredningar, Stockholm.
- Tregay, R. and Gustavsson, O. (1983) Oakwood's new landscape: designing for nature in the residential environment. Stad OCL Land; rapport nr. 15, Sveriges Lantbruks-universitet, Alnarp, Sweden.
- Vera, F. W. M. (2000). *Grazing Ecology and Forest History*. CABI International Publishing. Wallingford.

Chapter 8

Wetlands and water bodies

Wolfram Kircher

Introduction

This chapter describes the design and establishment of naturalistic plantings for wetlands and water bodies. Although, in many ways, wetland vegetation is relatively straightforward to establish, it is also perhaps the least developed in terms of the range of options that are available to designers. There is a tendency to work with a very limited range of species and vegetation types. This chapter not only intends to widen the aesthetic and ecological scope of designed wetland plantings but also aims to promote a wider range of opportunities for such plantings. The main focus is on vegetation – information describing the technical construction of artificial water bodies can be found in the relevant literature, for example in Agate (1976), Archer-Wills (2002), Hagen (1995), Eppel (1996) and Niesel (2002), and technical landscape architecture terms comply with Evert (2001).

Wetland areas within public open space can be excellent examples of multi-functional landscape planting. Not only can such vegetation be very attractive but it also has high habitat potential. Moreover, with increasing interest in Sustainable Urban Drainage Systems (SUDS), there is new potential for urban green space to become part of co-ordinated flood prevention and water management schemes. Wetlands not only function as temporary water-storage bodies but also as biological filters, removing impurities from runoff (and possibly 'grey water' output from buildings) before joining water courses. Whilst the technology for constructed reed beds is now well known, the visual and habitat dimensions have not, as yet, been explored in urban contexts, and, in particular, the potential ornamental qualities and the potential for wetland planting of such constructed wetlands have not been exploited.

Factors determining the character of wetland vegetation

There are many factors that influence the development and character of vegetation, of which the nutrient loading and the pH of the water are the most important.

Nutrient loading

The amount of dissolved nutrients in the water body (particularly nitrogen, but also phosphorus and potassium) have a profound affect on both the productivity of wetland vegetation and its species composition. Water bodies with very low nutrient levels are called *oligotrophic*, those with medium levels, *mesotrophic*, and those with high levels, *eutrophic*. *Hypertrophic* means an extremely high nutrient content. Hypertrophic conditions are often found in newly filled ponds and result in the undesirable development of murky water due to a 'bloom' of floating algae and dense carpets of Duckweed (*Lemna minor)* on the surface. In water bodies without a permanent high nutrient inflow, this situation will rectify itself in time, as bacterial denitrification releases nitrogen back into the air, dissolved phosphorus will be precipitated into the sediment and nutrients become locked up in plant tissues. However, in many natural water bodies this inflow is strong enough to cause long-term eutrophic or even hypertrophic conditions. As well as promoting algal blooms, high nutrient levels result in the vigorous growth of aggressive competitive higher plant species (both submerged and emergent), leading to low biodiversity and a requirement for continuous management to maintain open water.

Water hardness

Water hardness is a function of the concentration of dissolved carbonates (HCO_3^- – known as temporary hardness) and other salts (permanent hardness): the greater the concentration of such salts, the greater the 'hardness' of the water. In more acidic waters, dissolved carbonates are converted to CO_2 and H_2O; acidic water therefore tends to be less hard than alkaline water. The concentration of CO_2 in hard water is generally very low, limiting the ability of submerged plants to absorb it for photosynthesis. Instead, plants typical of hard water tend to use HCO_3^- as a carbon supplier. This is especially true for many undesirable filamentous algae. Therefore, the problem with this kind of weed increases with water hardness. On the other hand, several submerged perennials are not able to assimilate bicarbonate, and so need a higher amount of dissolved carbon dioxide, which is only available at low water hardness or in 'soft water'. For this reason, species such as the highly demanding *Hottonia palustris* are not cultivatable in hard water. Figure 8.1 shows approximate values for trophic and hardness levels and their related chemical parameters.

8.1
Classification of water bodies according to trophic level and water hardness

Classification according to trophic level

tendency for floating algae and lemna spp. to increase

	oligotrophic	mesotrophic	eutrophic	hypertrophic
NO_3^-	1 mg/l	5 mg/l	10 mg/l	> 20 mg/l
NH_4	<0,5 mg/l	2 mg/l	5 mg/l	> 10 mg/l
PO_4^{--}	<0,1 mg/l	1 mg/l	2,5 mg/l	> 5 mg/l

Classification according to water hardness

tendency for flamenteous algae to increase

	low	medium	hard
temporary hardness	1°dH	10°dH	20°dH
HCO_3^-	10 mg/l	100 mg/l	200 mg/l
~pH	3 – 7	6 – 9	7 – 11

Running and standing water bodies

In nature we find standing water bodies as ponds or lakes. Ponds are shallow enough to be populated completely by green plants whilst lakes have a deeper zone. Running water types include springs, streams or rivers. In running water, plants are more mechanically strained than in ponds or lakes. So typical plants of this vegetation do form no wide leaves, but narrow, thread-shaped bodies. Sometimes the same species produces quite different phenotypes in standing and running water.

In running water, warm layers will be continuously substituted with cooler ones through the action of the current. So standing water will reach higher temperatures than running water.

Oxygen and carbon dioxide are better incorporated in running waters than in standing ones because turbulence on the surface gives rise to a larger interface with the air. For that reason, some plants typical of streams grow poorly in ponds. The vegetation found in running water is also better supplied with nutrients. In still water, a nutrient depletion zone may form around plants because of their uptake. In comparison, in rivers and streams fresh supplies of nutrients are carried to roots and submerged shoots continuously. Typical species of running water, such as *Veronica beccabunga*, therefore should be cultivated under conditions rich in nutrients.

Flow rate also has a considerable influence on the range of plants that can be grown. Vegetation within the water body of swiftly running streams and rivers is likely to be limited, whilst the vegetation along the banks of rivers subjected to regular flooding and disturbance is likely to be composed of ruderal species able to tolerate periodic disturbance.

Standing water bodies and wetlands in nature

In common with other chapters in this book, the starting point for the consideration of naturalistic wetland plantings is a consideration of naturally occurring 'model' or 'stereotype' communities that might provide the basis for modified designed vegetation types. Figure 8.6 shows possible vegetation sequences in five different types of lakes in Central Europe. In very simple terms, we can distinguish three broad vegetation groupings within water bodies themselves.

1 *Submerged zone*. Submerged species can live as 'hydrophytes', fixed by roots into the ground (e.g. *Potamogeton, Myriophyllum*), or as floating 'pleustophytes' (*Ceratophyllum, Utricularia*).

8.2
Organic-shaped natural ponds convey the impression of distance in space (LWG Veitshöchheim, Germany)

8.3
Small pond in the author's garden with water lilies and shallow-water zone. To get the best visual effect, it is important not to cover the water surface too densely with plants

8.4
Formal ponds allow the development of a multitude of several habitats on small space – here a raised bed for water lilies is surrounded by L-shaped swamp-beds at the Anhalt University for Applied Sciences, Bernburg, Germany

8.5
A formal concrete pond in the botanical garden at Würzburg, Germany: water lilies and helophytes are raised up in pre-cast concrete units. The rampantly growing *Typha* species are kept from spreading by being planted in enclosed receptacles

Potamogeton perfoliatus can grow in water up to 6 m deep. Under nutrient-poor conditions, carpet-forming *Characeae* are typical, whilst in eutrophic water stands of *Myriophyllum* or *Elodea* are found. Water pressure and light intensity determine a plant's ability to grow in deep water. In oligotrophic water, submerged plants can reach deeper zones than in more eutrophic waters because lower levels of floating algae mean clearer water and greater light-intensity at depth.

2 *Floating-leaf community*. Rooted hydrophytes, such as Water Lilies (*Nymphaea*) or *Nuphar*, and floating pleustophytes can be found here also. The roots of the latter hang into the water without being fixed into the bottom (as in *Hydrocharis*, or in the tropics, *Eichhornia*). In eutrophic and hypertrophic water, Duckweed (*Lemna minor*) forms dense carpets and shades out sunlight, reducing the abundance of submerged species.

3 *Emergent aquatic plant communities*. 'Helophytes' are those plants that are rooted underwater or in saturated soil but with stems and leaves that rise at least partly above the water surface. Whilst a species such as the Tall Rush, *Schoenoplectus lacustris,* can grow in 3 m depth of water, many *Carex* species or *Iris sibirica* will survive in only temporarily flooded wet meadows. The most common emergent aquatic plant is *Phragmites australis*, which is found throughout the world and forms extensive reed communities facilitated by rampantly spreading rhizomes. Under hard water oligotrophic conditions, Twig Rush (*Cladium mariscus*) is typical, whilst in eutrophic water *Butomus umbellatus*, *Iris pseudacorus* or *Typha angustifolia* are common and in very nutrient-rich water, *Glyceria maxima* or *Bolboschoenus maritimus* are common. In a zone of fluctuating water, often a belt of Tufted Sedge (*Carex elata*) occurs in front of the real emergent plant community. Under oligotrophic or mesotrophic conditions a very special shore vegetation can develop: rhizomes of *Eriophorum angustifolium*, running *Carex* species, *Potentilla palustris* and *Menyanthes trifoliata* grow out, floating upon the water surface. They can produce a dense blanket that may be settled by other plants, forming what is in effect a floating meadow.

Silting of lakes and bog development

Much of the annual production of water-plant biomass eventually accumulates on the lake floor together with organic material carried in from outside. In an anaerobic environment, this material only partially mineralises and forms organic mud, mixed with inorganic sunken particles. Together with peat, formed by plant debris resistant to

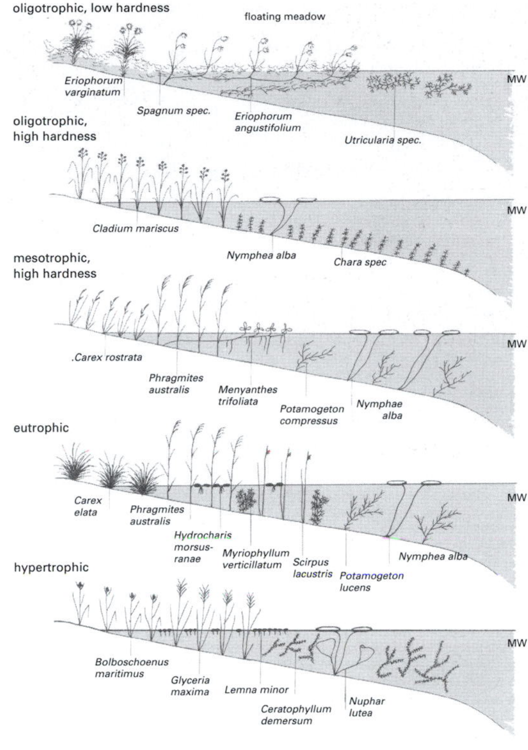

8.6
Vegetation sequence along the depth zones in five different types of standing waterbodies in Central Europe (MW = middle water-line)

decomposition, this mud leads to the silting up of water bodies from the edges inwards and the shore zones develop from reed vegetation into carrs or fens.

Carrs

The saturated, periodically flooded edges of lakes are naturally colonised by Reed (*Phragmites australis*) and tall sedges (for example, *Carex elata*). This stage of reed or tall sedge swamp is followed by moisture-loving woody plants, such as *Alnus glutinosa, Prunus padus* and several *Salix* species, forming a wet woodland or carr. Shade-tolerant helophytes, for example ferns, *Carex elongata* or *Calla palustris*, dominate the ground layer (Figure 8.7).

8.7
Acid-mesotrophic site with carr vegetation near Hagen, Germany – *Alnus glutinosa* shades a ground cover dominated by *Molinia caerulea, Carex elongata* and ferns

Fens and straw meadows

Only if the environment is very poor in nutrients will a wood-free fen or low bog form naturally. In Central Europe, such plant associations mostly result when carrs have been cleared. In the long term they can only be preserved if mown once a year. Mowing has been practised in the autumn since the Middle Ages to obtain straw for farm animal bedding. Typical plant communities of wet straw-meadows are low sedge swamps, formed by shallow growing *Carex* species, such as *Carex davalliana, C. flava, C. nigra* or others, along with attractive flowering perennials. The construction of drainage ditches results in dryer types of straw meadows, characterised by the Purple Moor Grass (*Molinia caerulea*), again including visually attractive forbs.

Raised bogs

The above mentioned fens are fed by nutrient-containing water from streams, springs and groundwater. When peat accumulation leads to a raising of the surface to a height where groundwater is no longer accessible to plants growing in the fen, the water supply is limited to that supplied by rainfall and, consequently, nutrient supply diminishes, resulting in acidification in the peat body. The number of plant species declines and only several specialists remain. The appearance of typical Peat Mosses (such as *Sphagnum magellanicum* and *S. rubellum*) indicates the start of a development to a raised bog. The prerequisite for this is sufficient equally distributed rainfall. Figure 8.8 shows an artificially created raised bog. *Sphagnum* mosses have special cells (Hyalocytes) that are able to exchange cations for hydrogen (H^+). This causes further acidification. *Sphagnum* mosses form a layer covering the whole bog-surface and grow constantly upward whilst their lower parts die and, at the very low rates of decomposition under such acid conditions, they thereby form bog peat. Figure 8.11 shows a section through an idealised type of a silted-up lake in the northern alpine foothills of Central Europe with carr, fen and straw meadow, such as a convex bent raised bog. The wet centre accommodates typical bog flora, such as Harestail Cotton Grass (*Eriophorum vaginatum*) or

8.8
Artificial raised-bog planting at Erich Maier, Altenberge, Germany. The water level is maintained by the use of storage containers, hidden in the peat substrate. Besides central European plants spectacular North American insectivorous *Sarracenia* species increase diversity

8.9 (below left)
***Dactylorhiza majalis* (orchids) between *Molinia caerulea* on a drained oligotrophic lime-fen**

8.10 (below right)
Mesotrophic wet meadow with *Fritillaria meleagris* and *Cardamine pratensis* in the Sinntal Valley, Germany

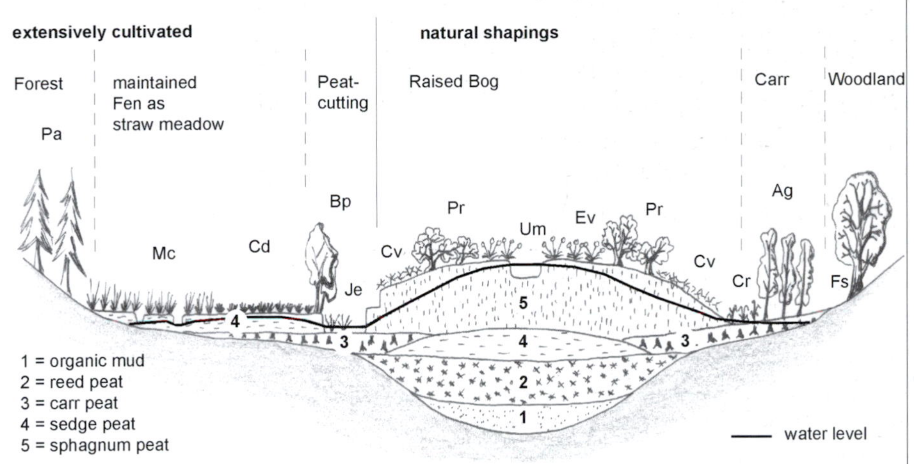

characteristic species:

Pa = *Picea abies* planted
Mc = *Molinia caerulea* on drained straw meadow
Cd = low sedge (*Carex davalliana*) on well drained straw meadow
Bp = *Betula pendula* at the ditch edge
Je = *Juncus effusus* as pioneer in the peat cut ditch
Cv = *Calluna vulgaris* on the bog slope
Pr = *Pinus rotundata* at the bog edge
Ev = *Eriophorum vaginatum* on the bog-plateau
Um = *Utricularia minor* in the bog-lake
Cr = *Carex rostrata* in the lagg
Ag = *Alnus glutinosa* in the carr
Fs = *Fagus sylvatica*

8.11
Possible fen and bog types above a silted-up lake in the northern alpine foothills – heights are considerably exaggerated for illustrative purposes

insectivorous *Drosera* species, growing between *Sphagnum* mosses. Of course there are several other possibilities of bog-development, for example described in Succow and Jeschke (1986) or Ellenberg (1996).

Wet meadows cut several times a year and wet pastures

When drained and fertilised, many former fens became so productive that they have to be mown regularly throughout the year or be used as pastures. However, meadows mown up to two or three times a year, even with some enrichment of nutrients, can support a good number of perennial species: *Polygonum bistorta, Trollius europaeus, Cardamine pratensis* or *Fritillaria meleagris* are some striking examples (Figures 8.9 and 8.10). The higher the level of nutrients and the greater the frequency of mowing cycles, the poorer the species diversity will be because nutrient-demanding species are more rampantly growing and are more competitive ('C-Strategists', see below) than species from nutrient-poor sites ('S-Strategists', or 'stress tolerators'). Ecological strategies are discussed in greater detail in Chapter 4.

Vegetation on exposed mud and disturbed or uncultivated wetland

The ground of drained ponds or the disturbed soil surface of ditches and ploughed wetland has a ruderal character. Such sites will be populated first by Short-lived Rush (*Juncus*) species, annual *Bidens* species or *Alopecurus aequalis*, followed by *Carex canescens, Ranunculus flammula, Epilobium* spec. and other tussock plants with a rich seed-bank. These fast-growing ruderals (R-strategists – Grime 1986) can become annoying weeds on the shore zone of artificial ponds. During the early years after completion, such a site is effectively disturbed and therefore prone to long-term invading weeds. These can be problematic in the gaps between planted individuals at high nutrient level. Without regular maintenance, the vegetation of fertile wet meadows will develop into a willow shrubland or a reed bed with *Phragmites australis* or to a tall forb community. The latter stage is populated mostly with *Filipendula ulmaria, Lysimachia vulgaris* and *Lythrum salicaria*. These species produce a spectacular flowering effect, but are only recommended where space is not limited. In North America, *Lythrum* has become a notorious invasive neophyte, so it is not recommended to use it there in planting design.

Exposed mud on the edge of water bodies is of particular value to invertebrates, whilst periodically flooded herbaceous vegetation around the edge of ponds and lakes is also beneficial to amphibians. It is therefore important, where space allows, that room is given for very shallow margins in places that enable fluctuations in water levels to produce periods of exposed mud and also flooded vegetation.

Design considerations for wetland planting

Location, size and shape

In nature, wetlands and water bodies are always found in depressions or at the bottom of slopes. Accordingly, man-made naturalistic ponds and wetland plantings and wet meadows should be placed at the lowest part of a park or garden site. If this is not possible, partial ground modelling or shrub plantings along the edge where the terrain is sloping down can conceal this unnatural impression. Partial shading by trees or tall shrubs is not problematic, as the accumulation of nutrients caused by leaves falling in autumn is largely overestimated (Figures 8.2 and 8.3). However, dense shade will reduce the possibilities for aquatic planting: traditional practices of pollarding or coppicing water-side trees periodically reduces intense shade. If the planted area of a pond or wetland planting is to be smaller than about 200 m^2 and a good diversity of species is intended, the range of hydrophytes and helophytes should be selected carefully. Many species are very competitive and suppress less vigorous ones.

Artificial ponds can either be shaped in a formal or a naturalistic style, depending on the visual environment. Very conspicuous hybrids or cultivars, such as large flowered water lilies or variegated cultivars, are only suitable in formal situations (Figures 8.4 and 8.5). On the other hand, wild plants and natural-looking cultivars can look pleasing in both formal and informal situations.

Plant grouping

Besides water depth and nutrient conditions, Plant Sociability has to be a consideration in the way that plants are arranged, drawing guidance from the way plants arrange themselves in nature. Vegetation planted in a naturalistic style achieves its visual appeal not from groups of single species in neighbourhood arrangements, as is practiced in ornamental borders, but mostly from combinations in different layers. For example, tall growing species should be used in much smaller numbers than lower growing ones. The largest percentage should be made up by shallow ground-covers. It must be admitted that in more productive sites and water bodies, and over larger areas where maintenance will be extensive, there is little purpose in devising detailed planting arrangements or drawing up an intricate planting plan: wetland plants tend to form spreading masses that soon obliterate any patterns imposed by the designer. However, in oligotrophic waters, in smaller-scale sites or where maintenance can be more intensive (in a garden situation, for example) then the following categories may be of use – the six categories can be characterised in accordance with Borchardt (1996), conforming to wetland habitats.

- *Monoculture forming plants* – invasive competitors, forming extensive populations and suppressing other species. Loose-growing species can be combined with shade-tolerant ground-cover plants. Vigorous grass-like species belong to this category, for example *Phragmites australis, Typha* spp. and *Zizania latifolia.* In wet meadows and marginal vegetation there are also competitors with dense growth, for example *Petasites hybridus, Matteuccia struthiopteris* and *Carex acutiformis*.
- *Dominant plants* – usually tall-growing clump-forming tussock plants. These have to be used at a distance from other solitary species to achieve the best visual effect. Planted densely, a meadow-like impression will be produced. In this case not too many different flower colours should compete at the same time. Examples include *Iris pseudacorus, Carex pendula* and

8.12
***Butomus umbellatus*, a companion plant for use in clusters and clumps**

8.13
***Aster nemoralis* is an important late flowering wetland species**

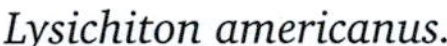

Lysichiton americanus.

- *Companion plants* – mostly semi-tall plants forming clusters and clumps. These should be planted in small groups or as neighbours for the structural solitary species. Examples include *Iris laevigata, Pontederia cordata* and *Carex diandra.*
- *Ground-cover plants* – these should be distributed more or less under all plants of the above categories. In plantings designed to achieve a clear structure with perceptible layers, ground-covers should be more than 50% of the total number of plants. If a more or less dense meadow-like character is intended, lower amounts are justified. Examples include *Veronica beccabunga, Lysimachia nummularia* and *Carex davalliana*. In bog plantings, *Sphagnum* mosses are used as ground-covers simply by pressing them flatly on to the wet substrate surface.
- *Scattered plants* – in this category we find several important forbs without a great need of space and with a limited display period. They should be loosely distributed between ground-covers and companions. In bog and fen plantings, many of these species, such as orchids, sundew or gladioli, are expensive, so initially only a few can be planted but they should propagate themselves by seeding. With suitable conditions, three *Dactylorhiza* plants can generate a hundred-strong group of flowering offspring from seed within about five years.
- *Sown species* – these particularly involve hemiparasites, which cannot be established by planting. Hemiparasitic species tap into the roots of host plants and obtain some of their nutrition from the host plant but are also able to photosynthesise for themselves. They are typical of less fertile sites and are relatively common in nutrient-poor wetland systems. The best date for sowing is in the autumn, as cool temperatures break the seed dormancy, and germination starts in early spring. Many such species have a long-term flowering display. The growth rate of the parasatised species will be reduced, but not disturbed too heavily by the semi-parasites. Hemiparasites are primarily members of the *Scrophulariaceae*-sub-family *Rhinanthoideae: Rhinanthus serotinus* (annual), *Pedicularis palustris* (biennial) and *Pedicularis sceptrum-carolinum* (perennial).

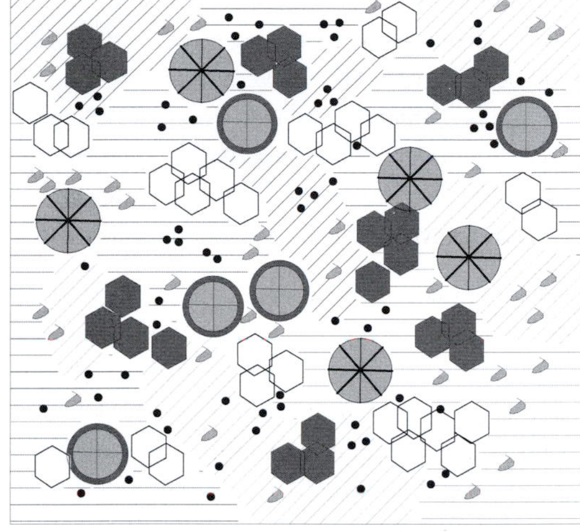

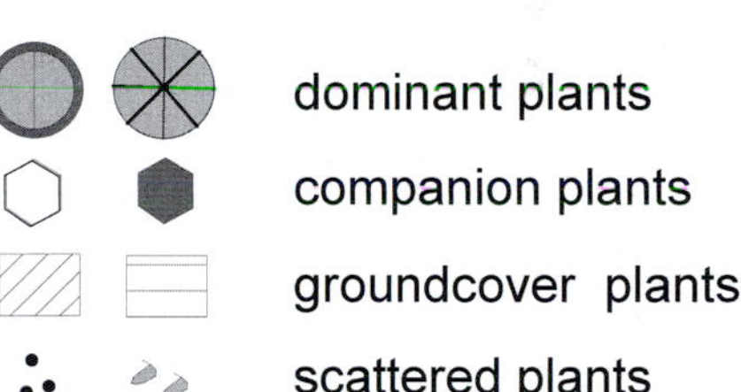

8.14
Distribution pattern of plants according to grouping categories

Besides hemiparasites there are also several short-lived perennials, biennials or annuals that may be introduced into planted vegetation by sowing. However, competitiveness has to be considered very carefully when choosing these species, for some spread extensively by seeding themselves. Short-lived species from fertile wet-meadows, such as *Bidens* spp., *Juncus articulatus* or *Aster tripolium,* can look very pleasing but are only suitable to sow in small amounts between competitive tall forbs (*Filipendula, Lythrum,*

Mimulus ringens). The establishment of herbaceous plants by sowing *in situ* is discussed in detail in Chapter 6. Several short-lived *Primula, Linum catharticum, Carex viridula* or even scattered plants, as mentioned above, can also be sown successfully into low growing plantings with the character of poor bogs or fens.

These grouping categories should be followed in both planted and sown vegetation. On flooded sites, vegetation is established mostly by planting, but wet meadows on terrestrial sites can be initiated by pure sowing too. The grouping categories can be applied to the proportions of seed numbers per species. Further information on the grouping of plants according to Plant Sociability is given in Chapter 9.

8.15
In a pond with a tiered profile it is possible to have a sharp transition from the swamp and shallow-water zone to the Water Lily zone

Seasons of development

A further basis with which to compose visually pleasing naturalistic vegetation is to use species with different cycles of growth, flowering and dormancy. Thus, there is a permanent change of seasonal aspects. In spring, wet sites need longer to warm up than dryer ones, so vegetation growth starts relatively late. It is important to use the very few early developing hydrophytes, such as *Caltha palustris, Lysichiton americanus* or *Primula elatior*. Spring bulbs for wet sites include *Leucojum vernum* or *Fritillaria meleagris*. In early and high summer, many species make an attractive display: this is the main growing period. Late summer and autumn need particular attention. *Lythrum salicaria, Pontederia cordata* or *Allium suaveolens* are examples of late flowering forbs, whilst *Euphorbia palustris* is very decorative with bright orange autumn-leaf colour.

Ecological strategy and competitiveness

To accomplish low-maintenance-plantings, it is necessary to combine species of similar competitiveness according to the fertility of the site. Fertile sites should be planted with 'C-Strategists' (competitiors) that produce a dense cover. In depth zones 3 and 4 (see section 'Vegetation zones'), this will mean reed-forming plants. In zone 2, vigorous tall forbs (*Filipendula ulmaria*) and rhizomatous species (*Carex acuta*) are able to form durable communities needing virtually no maintenance. During the first few years of development, short-lived ruderal plants, such as *Lychnis flos-cuculi,* and *Mimulus luteus,* form a dense cover until they are eventually overgrown by competitor species.

Artificially sealed water bodies with a poor substrate tend to become very low in nutrients. This is desirable for guaranteeing clear water conditions. In zones 3–5, plants from richer native sites are suitable, especially when some water movement exists. Even

Water Lilies or other floating leafed plants develop satisfactorily after a certain period of slow growth. In zone 2, however, plants from rich wet meadows mostly react with symptoms of deficiency. This area is ideal to establish bog or fen vegetation with stress-tolerators: small, slowly growing species that tend to occur naturally on sites poor in resources. Unfortunately, these plants are rarely to be found in the nursery ranges of swamp plants.

Geographical origin of the plant material

From at least the 1970s onwards, landscape architects in Germany have been required to use, wherever possible, native species in planting design. When wetland and water plants are to be used in the semi-natural landscape outside the urban area, as part, for example, of bioengineering works along riversides, it is important to use only appropriate native species. In an urban environment, aesthetic considerations need to be given a much higher priority. In public green spaces, as in private gardens, it should be seen as important to optimise the visual effect of artificially established vegetation even when foreign plants are to be included. For example, if there is a lack of flowers in late summer or early spring, and native plants with these characteristics are not available, consideration should be given to non-invasive exotics with these species. The city landscape is, by its very nature, a human-generated environment. This is, however, a highly contentious subject. Whilst isolated ponds in designed urban and garden contexts can support both native and non-native species, the use of non-native species should not occur alongside streams or other wetland types that may be intertconnected. Use of extremely invasive foreign species must be avoided. Examples are the East Asian *Impatiens glandulifera*, a wetland ruderal invading riversides in Western and Central Europe, or *Lythrum salicaria* from Europe, which causes major problems in nature protection in North America. Because of the reduced barriers to dispersal by seed or vegetative fragments, wetland species have a higher than average capacity to colonise native plant communities.

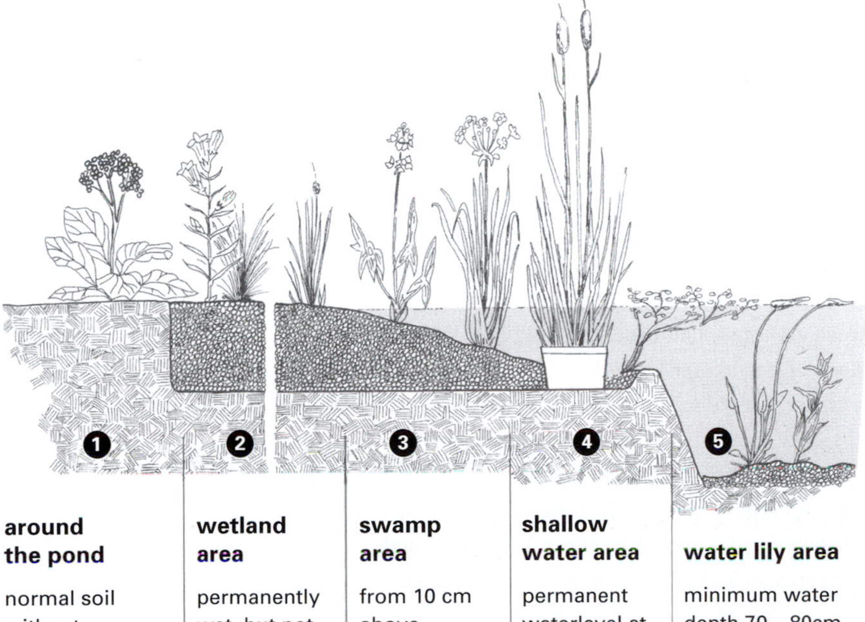

8.16
Depth zones of an artificially sealed pond, adapted from a plan of the Association of German Perennial Nurseries (BdS)

Vegetation zones

The character and composition of wetland communities is closely related to water depth. It is possible to distinguish five main zones of aquatic vegetation in artificially sealed ponds (Figure 8.13):

- *zone 1 – external edges*: normal soil without contact with the waterbody. Plants should be chosen that visually fit the wetland character but ecologically correspond with the conditions in the vicinity of the pond
- *zone 2 – wetland area*: permanently wet soil, but without being flooded. Here perennials of wet meadows, fens and bogs can be established
- *zone 3 – swamp area*: between about 10 cm above and 10 cm under water level – the place

for emergent aquatic plants of the reed zone
- *zone 4 – shallow water area*: a permanent water level of 10 to 40 cm is an ideal position for several emergent aquatic plants or small growing water lilies
- *zone 5 – water lily area*: more than 70 cm depth – most floating and submerged plants.

We will now consider each of these zones in greater detail. The species identified in the lists will not form vegetation displays that copy nature, but rather will resemble natural plant communities, improving their appearance by emphasising conspicuous flowering forbs and reducing or excluding aggressive grasses. The plant lists are arranged in Plant Sociability categories. The proposed amount of plants within each category can be distributed among the listed species more or less regularly or according to intended proportions of colours, textures, shapes and other aesthetical criteria. All plants mentioned in the lists below are hardy in Central Europe to at least minus 25°C. A few exceptions requiring protection are marked.

Zone 1 – external edges

The edges of artificially sealed ponds and wetlands often show an extremely sharp transition between a wet area within and a more or less dry area outside the lining material. It is recommended that plants are selected for zone 1 that look similar to wetland plants but are able to withstand periods of dryness. These can be lush looking grasses or forbs with wide leaves, for example species of the genera *Miscanthus, Hemerocallis, Helianthus* or drought-resistant Irises for sites rich in nutrients. On nutrient-poor sites, a possible bog or fen vegetation can be continued outside the sealing, for instance with small *Allium, Carex, Sesleria, Briza* or *Anthericum* species.

Zone 2 – the wetland area

The margins of water bodies, periodically flooded zones, wet flushes, bogs and fens represent an untapped resource for the designer. Whereas water-body margins are usually planted with a very limited range of species, there is great scope to adapt and modify a whole range of vegetation types, including wet and damp meadow-based vegetation and wet woodland and shrub-based communities.

The main types of vegetation to be considered in this zone include carrs (wet woodland), tall herb communities, wet meadows and pastures, fens and straw-meadows, and raised bogs.

Carr vegetation

On naturally wet sites and around large ponds and lakes, carr-like woodland can be established. Trees and large shrubs have a high transpiration rate and are able to drain soggy soil. They are, therefore, useful in wet depressions. However, along the edge of sealed water-bodies the loss of water is generally too great when tall woody plants are used. Designed carrs can develop a clear stratification into a tree layer, shrub layer and herb layer. The herbs can be sown, if the soil is largely free from weeds. Tall perennials can be established – this can be among short-lived ruderal weedy herbs. Competitive weeds, such as *Urtica dioica* or *Phalaris arundinacea*, should be removed before planting the desired perennials. Another possibility is to plant only trees and shrubs between existing spontaneous vegetation. If vines (for instance, *Humulus lupulus* or the North American *Vitis riparia*) are wanted to climb among the trees and tall shrubs, they should not be planted before the woody plants have reached a sufficient height.

In carr vegetation, woody plants will be responsible for the long-term effect. Perennials and short-lived species include shade-tolerant species and plants that are tolerant of open sites to guarantee a satisfying visual effect even before trees and shrubs shade the herb layer sufficiently.

Examples of woody plants include the following.

1 Alder carr: soggy soil, moderately flooded in spring, eutrophic, pH lightly acid to lightly alkaline, species native in Central Europe – proposed quantities for 100 m^2:

– trees:
  - 15 *Alnus glutinosa*
  - 5 *Prunus padus*

– shrubs:
  - 5 *Cornus sanguinea*
  - 5 *Euonymus europaeus*
  - 30 *Ribes nigrum*
  - 5 *Salix cinerea*
  - 5 *Viburnum opulus.*

2 Birch pine carr: wet soil, not flooded or only moderately flooded for a short time in spring, oligo-mesotrophic, pH acid to lightly acid (<6), species native in Central Europe – proposed quantities for 100 m^2:

– trees:
  - 10 *Betula pubescens*
  - 3 *Pinus sylvestris*

– shrubs:
  - 10 *Frangula alnus*
  - 50 *Vaccinium uliginosum*
  - 5 *Salix aurita*
  - 20 *Ledum palustre*

– dwarf shrubs:
  - 300 *Calluna vulgaris* (sowing is possible on weed-free sites).

3 Mixed decorative carr: soggy soil, moderately flooded in spring, meso-eutrophic, pH lightly acid to neutral, species native mostly to North America, added with other origins to produce a colourful effect – proposed quantities for 100 m^2:

– trees:
  - 3 *Taxodium distichum*
  - 2 *Liquidambar styraciflua*
  - 5 *Sorbus decora*

– shrubs:
  - 10 *Cephalanthus occidentalis*
  - 10 *Clethra alnifolia* – along the edges
  - 5 *Ilex verticillata*
  - 5 *Physocarpus opulifolius* or *Magnolia virginica* on acid soil in mild climate
  - 15 *Myrica pensylvanica* or *Rhododendron viscosum* on acid soil
  - 15 *Spiraea tomentosa*
  - 5 *Viburnum trilobum.*

Along the woodland edge, *Rubus idaeus* (Raspberry) can be established in groups. If not too wet, this can also be a cultivar producing fruits in autumn on shoots of the same year, such as 'Autumn Bliss'. This enables simple maintenance: the edge can be mown late each winter or spring and there will be a visually attractive development of flowers and fruit in the same year.

Trees and shrubs can either be planted together with perennials or integrated into an existing wet meadow with site conditions suitable to each other. These herbaceous communities should be maintained as meadows until the canopies of the woody plants develop a shade that leads to a decline in the growth of the perennials. Shade-tolerating perennials can be introduced, when this occurs.

When trees and shrubs are planted together at the same time with shade-tolerating perennials, these should be combined with several tall wet-meadow forbs (dominant species) as interim shade creators. With increasing shading these tall perennials will be weakened and will gradually become substituted by the more shade-tolerant perennials (Table 8.1).

Meso-eutrophic tall herb communities

If no trees and shrubs are required on an area with wet conditions, a yearly hay-cut in late autumn or spring is necessary. On sites rich in nutrients, tall herb communities develop. Established artificially, they produce an aesthetically pleasing display when enriched with sufficient amounts of flowering forbs between the grasses. Examples for mesotrophic and eutrophic sites are combined in one table because several species can be used in both conditions (Table

Table 8.1. Shade-tolerant perennials

	Origin*	Soil/water conditions	Height (cm)	Flowering Months	Flower Colour
Dominant species (5–10/10 m²)					
Aconitum napellus	Eur	Eutrophic	80–120	VI–VII	blue
Carex pendula	Eur	Meso–eutrophic	80–140	V-VII	brown
Chaerophyllum hirsutum	Eur	Eutrophic	60–110	V–VI	white-pink
Ligularia dentata	E-As	Eutrophic	100–150	VIII–IX	yellow
Matteuccia pensylvanica	N-Am	Eutrophic	150–200	fern–plant	
Molinia arundinacea	Eur	Oligo-mesotrophic	180–200	VIII–XI	brown
Osmunda cinnamomea	N-Am, O-As	Eutrophic	120–150	fern–plant	
Osmunda regalis	N-Am, Eur, As	Eutrophic	150–200	fern–plant	
Solanum dulcamara	Eur, As, N-Afr	Eutrophic	100–150	VII–VIII	purple
Telekia speciosa	E-Eur, W-As	Eutrophic	120–150	VII–VIII	yellow
Thalictrum aquilegifolium	Eur, E-As	Eutrophic	80–100	V–VI	pink, white
Companion species (10–30/10 m²)					
Carex elongata	Eur, W-As	Meso-eutrophic	30–60	V–VI	brown
Carex grayi	N-Am	Meso-eutrophic	70–80	VI–VII	green
Dryopteris cristata	Eu, As, Am	Mesotrophic	60–60	fern–plant	
Lysichiton americanus	N-Am	Eutrophic	80–100	IV–V	yellow
Lysichiton camtschatcensis	E-As	Eutrophic	80–100	IV–V	white
Lysimachia vulgaris	Eu, As, N-Am	Eutrophic	100–120	VI–VIII	yellow
Mimulus ringens	N-Am	Meso-eutrophic	70–90	VII–VIII	blue
Molinia caerulea	Eur, W-As	Oligotrophic	80–100	VIII–IX	brown
Peucedanum palustre	Eur, W-As	Mesotrophic	60–120	VII–VIII	white
Symplocarpus foetidus	N-Am, E-As	Eutrophic	40–60	II–IV	red – brown
Saururus cernuus	N-Am	Meso-eutrophic	70–80	VII–VIII	white-yellow
Ground-covers (20–50/10 m²)					
Calla palustris	Cosmopolitan	Eutrophic, acid	15–20	V–VI	white
Carex sylvatica	Eur, W-As	Mesotrophic	20–40	IV–VI	green
Geum rivale	W-As	Meso-eutrophic	20–30	V–VI	red
Hydrocotyle vulgaris	Eur	Oligo-mesotr., acid	10–20	inconspicuous flowers	
Lysimachia nummularia	Eur, W-As	Meso-eutrophic	3–5	VI–VII	yellow
Mimulus guttatus	N-Am	Meso-eutroph	30–50	VI–IX	yellow
Myosotis palustris	Eur, As	Mesotrophic	10–40	V–VIII	blue
Stellaria aquatica	Eur, As	Eutrophic	20–60	VI–IX	white
Stellaria palustris	Cosmopolitan	Oligotrophic	10–45	V–VII	white
Thelypteris palustris	Cosmopolitan	Mesotrophic	30–60	fern	
Sphagnum-mosses – cuttings pressed on wet soil surface of acid, oligotrophic sites: *S.palustre, S.squarrosum, S.angustifolium, S.magellanicum*					
Scattered plants (up to 50/10 m²)					
Leucojum vernum	C-Eur	Eutrophic	15–20	III–IV	white
Trientalis europaea	Eur, N-As	Oligotrophic, acid	10–15	VI–VII	white
Caltha palustris	Eur, As, N-Am	Meso-eutrophic	20–35	IV–VI	yellow
Primula florindae	C-As	Eutrophic	25–70	VII–VIII	yellow
Primula japonica	E-As	Eutrophic	20–50	V–VI	red
Ranunculus ficaria (bulbs)	Eur	Eutrophic	5–20	III–V	yellow
Sown species					
Bidens cernua	Cosmopolitan	Eutrophic	5–100	VIII–X	yellow
Impatiens noli-tangere	Eur, As, W-Am	Mesotrophic	30–100	VII–VIII	yellow
Monoculture species – not to combine with species mentioned above (10–30/10 m²)					
Petasites hybridus	Eur	Eutrophic	70–80	III–IV	red
Equisetum hyemale	Cosmopolitan	Meso-eutrophic	50–70	horsetail	
Matteuccia struthiopteris	Eur, As	Meso-eutrophic	70–80	fern	
Scirpus sylvaticus	Eur, As	Oligo-mesotrophic	70–100	VI–VII	green-brown
Onoclea sensibilis	N-Am, E-As	Meso-eutrophic	50–80	fern	

* Eur = Europe; As = Asia; Am = America; N = North; E = East; S = South; W = West; C = Central

Table 8.2. Meso-eutrophic and eutrophic tall herb communities

	Origin*	Soil/water conditions	Height (cm)	Flowering Months	Flower Colour
Dominant species (10–20/10 m²)					
Asclepias incarnata	N-Am	Eutrophic	90–120	VII–VIII	pink
Aster puniceus	N-Am	Eutrophic	90–200	VII–XI	purple
Carex muskingumensis	N-Am	Meso-eutrophic	70–90	VI–VIII	brown
Carex paniculata	Eur, W-As	Mesotrophic	60–90	V–VII	brown
Carex pseudocyperus	Eur, As, N-Am	Meso-eutrophic	60–90	V–VIII	green
Eupatorium cannabinum	Eur, As	Eutrophic	100-140	VII–IX	pink
Eupatorium perfoliatum	N-Am	Meso-eutrophic	120–150	VII–X	white
Euphorbia palustris	Eur, W-As	Eutrophic	70–100	IV–V	yellow
Filipendula purpurea	E-As	Eutrophic	80–110	VI–VII	white-pink
Filipendula ulmaria	Eur, As	Meso-eutrophic	80–110	VI–VII	white
Filipendula rubra	N-Am	Meso-eutrophic	120–160	VI–VII	pink-red
Iris pseudacorus	Eur, W-As	Eutrophic	80–120	V–VI	yellow
Leucanthemella serotina	E-Eur	Eutrophic	120-150	IX–X	white
Lythrum salicaria	Eur, As	Meso-eutrophic	70–120	VII–IX	pink
Mentha aquatica	Eur, As	Eutrophic	40–80	VII–IX	pink-lilac
Senecio paludosus	Eur, W-As	Meso-eutrophic	100–140	VII–VIII	yellow
Veronica longifolia	Eur, W-As	Eutrophic	80–120	VI–VIII	blue
Companion and ground-cover species (30–60/10 m²)					
Achillea ptarmica	Eur, As	Mesotrophic, acid	60–90	VII–VIII	white
Bistorta officinalis	Eur, As, N-Am	Mesotrophic, acid	40–90	V–VII	pink
Cardamine amara	Eur	Mesotrophic	10–60	IV–VI	white
Carex canescens	Cosmopolitan	Mesotrophic, acid	20–45	V–VI	gray-green
Carex diandra	Cosmopolitan	Mesotrophic, acid	30–50	V –VII	brown
Carex flacca	Eur, W-As	Mesotrophic, alkaline	15–20	V–VI	black
Carex ovalis	Eur, As	Mesotrophic, acid	30–40	V–VII	yellow-brown
Carex nigra	Eur	Mesotrophic, acid	20–30	V–VII	black
Carex panicea	Eur	Mesotrophic	20–50	VI	green-brown
Geum rivale	W-As	Meso-eutrophic	20–30	V–VI	brown-red
Hypericum tetrapterum	Eur	Mesotrophic, acid	50–70	VII–VIII	yellow
Juncus articulatus	Eur, As	Mesotrophic	20–50	VII–IX	brown
Lychnis flos-cucculi	Eur, W-As	Mesotrophic, acid	40–70	V–VII	pink
Mentha pulegium	Eur, W-As	Mesotrophic, acid	20–30	VII–IX	pink – purple
Mimulus guttatus	N-Am	Meso-eutrophic	30–50	VI–IX	yellow
Myosotis palustris	Eur, N-As	Meso-eutrophic	20–30	IV–VII	blue
Scutellaria galericulata	Cosmopolitan	Eutrophic	10–40	VI–IX	blue – purple
Ranunculus acris	Eur, As, N-Am	Mesotrophic	25/50	V–VI	yellow
Scattered plants (up to 50/10 m²)					
Caltha palustris	Eur, As, N-Am	Meso-eutrophic	20–35	IV–VI	yellow
Cardamine pratensis	Eur, As, N-Am	Mesotrophic	15/30	IV–V	white-purple
Potentilla erecta	Eur, W-As	Mesotrophic, acid	5–10	V–IX	yellow
Succisa pratensis	Eur, W-As	Oligo-mesotrophic	15–80	VII–IX	blue-lilac
Sown species					
Aster tripolium	Eur, As	Saline soil	40–80	VII–IX	purple-lilac
Anthoxanthum odoratum	Eur	Mesotrophic	30–40	V–VII	green
Rhinanthus serotinus	Eur, W-As	Mesotrophic	10–70	V–VIII	yellow
Monoculture species – only to combine with shallow ground-cover species mentioned above (10–50/10 m²)					
Carex acuta (=C. gracilis)	Eur, As	Mesotrophic	60–90	V–VI	brown
Carex acutiformis	Eur, W-As	Meso-eutrophic	70–100	V–VI	brown-green
Carex riparia	Eur, As, E-Am	Mesotrophic	70–110	V–VII	brown-green
Carex rostrata	Cosmopolitan	Oligo-mesotrophic, acid	30–70	VI–VII	green
Cladium mariscus	Cosmopolitan	Oligo-mesotr., alkaline	80/160	VIII–X	brown
Darmera peltata	N-Am	Eutrophic	100/50	IV–V	pink
Sparganium erectum	Eur, As	Eutrophic	60–80	VII–IX	green

* Eur = Europe; As = Asia; Am = America; N = North; E = East; S = South; W = West; C = Central

8.2). Tall herb communities are not only suitable for wet meadows but also along the shore of streams too, when only a short period of flooding in spring usually occurs. Table 8.2 includes only a few typical ruderals because with the establishment of such a vegetation the soil will be strongly disturbed and there will be enough short-lived forbs appearing spontaneously.

Oligotrophic bogs and fens

All the species mentioned in Table 8.3 are dependent on low-nutrient levels. In artificial ponds, sealed with a chemically inert material, such as plastic sheets or synthetic resin, this situation can often be found when nutrient poor substrates and rainwater or mains water is used (Figure 8.14). Only if such conditions are guaranteed is such a planting sustainable in the long term. Normally such plantings will only be established in small areas. Depending on the hardness, or rather the acidity of water, we can distinguish between lime-fen, acid-raised bog and transition-bog plantings.

Vegetation of raised bogs grows best under conditions with low water hardness and pure *Sphagnum* peat substrate, or around 5 cm of peat stacked on lime-free sand. On this wet acid-substrate, *Sphagnum* mosses can be established as ground-cover vegetation. Pure raised bog-species are able to grow within this living *Sphagnum* layer, as they are able to grow continuously through the permanently expanding mosses. Conditions between both the aforementioned possibilities can occur, for example, on a poor acid substrate and semi-hard water. Here it is possible to establish most of the plants recommended in Table 8.3. Even here scattered clumps of *Sphagnum* species can be established. The acidification caused enables adequate growth conditions for raised-bog plants placed just into the moss-clumps.

Although in several European countries, *Sphagnum* peat is viewed as a renewable resource and is acceptable as a horticultural product, in other countries (notably the UK), the use of peat is actively discouraged. This is because semi-natural raised bogs are a rare and declining habitat, and are threatened by peat extraction. In these instances, lime-free sand can be used as a lower layer and be covered with a thin peat layer (2–3 cm are enough) or living *Sphagnum* plants. In a correctly worked out planting, the *Sphagnum* plants will not die but will develop into a dense blanket. Coir or composted pine-bark can be used as a substitute, as can timber-fibre substrate ('Toresa').

Artificial-bog vegetation can produce an exciting effect with intricate combinations of cotton grasses, insectivorous plants, dwarf shrubs, orchids, semi-parasites, and several ornate species between dwarf grasses and mosses. The ground-covers are indispensable for both an optimal visual effect and the best growth of bog forbs. These are mostly rooted very weakly and need the strength of the surrounding vegetation to secure them in place (Figure 8.15).

For example, the author has observed the best germination of orchids between grasses and Irises. Semi-parasites of the genera *Rhinanthus, Pedicularis* and *Castilleja* should be sown near grasses in autumn, so that they can find and penetrate the roots of these potential hosts after germination in early spring. Their long-lasting flowering period results in a little weaker growth of the grasses. The poorly competitive *Mimulus primuloides, Pinguicula grandiflora* and *Primula frondosa* should be placed on bare soil. They will be overgrown by invading ground covers but can move to new gaps by self-seeding.

8.17
Oligotrophic lime-fern with Cotton Grass in Southern Germany

8.18
Wooden half-barrel used to store rainwater in a winter garden. This oligotrophic environment is suitable for establishing bog vegetation, carnivorous *Darlingtonia californica*, and *Drosera* species grow well

Table 8.3. Oligotrophic bogs and fens

	Origin*	Soil/water conditions	Height (cm)	Flowering Months	Flower Colour
Dominant species (5–20/10 m²)					
Andromeda polifolia	Eur, N-Am, As	Raised – transition bog	15–25	IV–V	white
Carex diandra	Cosmopolitan	Transition bog – lime-fen	20–60	V–VI	brown
Cypripedium reginae	N-Am	Transition bog – lime-fen	50–80	V–VI	white, pink
Darlingtonia californica⁺	N-Am	Raised bog	30–40	VI–VII	red
Eriophorum latifolium	Cosmopolitan	Transition bog – lime-fen	40–80	IV–V	white
Eriophorum vaginatum	Cosmopolitan	Raised bog	30–50	IV	white
Gentiana asclepiadea	Eur, W-As	Transition bog – lime-fen	30–40	VII–IX	blue
Iris sibirica	E-Eur, W-As	Transition bog – lime-fen	70–80	V–VI	blue
Kalmia polifolia	N-Am	Raised bog	30–50	V	red
Ledum groenlandicum	N-Am	Raised – transition bog	50–100	V–VI	white
Lythrum salicaria 'Robert'	cultivar	Transition bog – lime-fen	30–50	VII–VIII	pink
Molinia caerulea	Eur, N-As	Transition bog – lime-fen	40–80	VIII–IX	brown
Sarracenia flava⁺	N-Am	Raised bog	40–60	VI–VII	yellow
Schoenus nigricans	Eur, Am, W-As	Lime-fen	30–50	V–XI	black
Trollius europaeus	Eur, As, N-Am	Transition bog – lime-fen	40–50	V–VI	yellow
Zigadenus elegans	N-Am	Transition bog – lime-fen	50–90	VI–VIII	white
Companion species (20–60/10m²)					
Arnica montana	Eur, As	Raised-transition bog	30–40	V–VI	white-pink
Carex capillaris	Cosmopolitan	Lime-fen	15–25	V–VII	
Carex echinata	Cosmopolitan	Transition bog	20–40	V–VII	green
Carex flava ssp. flava	Eur, N-Am	Transition bog – lime-fen	30–40	VI–VIII	green
Epipactis palustris	Eur, W-As	Transition bog – lime-fen	40–50	VI–VIII	red-white
Erica tetralix	N-W-Eur	Raised-transition bog	20–30	VI–VIII	pink
Eriophorum russelianum	N-As, N-Am	Raised-transition bog	20–40	VI–VII	orange
Gentiana pneumonanthe	Eur, W-As	Transition bog	20–40	VII–IX	blue
Helonias bullata	N-Am	Raised-transition bog	20–40	V–VI	pink
Iris setosa ssp. *canadensis*	N-Am	Transition bog	20–30	V–VI	blue
Narthecium ossifragum	Eur	Raised bog	10–30	VII–VIII	yellow
Sarracenia purpurea	N-Am	Raised bog	15–30	VI–VII	red
Tofieldia calyculata	Eur	Transition bog – lime-fen	15–30	VI–VII	yellow
Trichophorum caespitosum	Cosmopolitan	Raised bog	5–20	V–VI	white
Vaccinium macrocarpon	N-Am	Raised bog	3–5	VI–VIII	red
Vaccinium oxycoccus	Eur, N-Am	Raised bog	3–5	VI–VIII	pink
Ground-cover plants (up to 120/10 m²)					
Carex davalliana	Eur	Transition bog – lime-fen	10–40	V–VII	brown
Carex viridula	Eur, N-Am, As	Transition bog – lime-fen	10–15	VI–VIII	green
Mimulus primuloides	N-Am	Transition bog – lime-fen	3–5	VII–IX	yellow
Schoenus ferrugineus	Eur	Lime-fen	15–30	V–XI	brown
Trichophorum alpinum	Cosmopolitan	Transition bog	10–20	V–VII	white
Sphagnum-mosses – cuttings pressed on wet soil surface of acid, oligotrophic sites: *S. palustre, S. squarrosum, S. angustifolium, S. magellanicum*					
Scattered plants (up to 50/10 m²)					
Allium angulosum	Eur, W-As	Transition bog – lime-fen	30–60	VII–VIII	red
Allium suaveolens	Eur	Transition bog – lime-fen	20–40	VIII–IX	pink
Aster nemoralis	N-Am	Raised – transition bog	15–25	IX–X	pink-violet
Dactylorhiza spec. & Hybrids	Eur	Transition bog – lime-fen	20–40	V–VI	pink
Dianthus superbus	Eur, N-, E-As	Transition bog – lime-fen	30–40	VII–IX	pink
Drosera anglica	Cosmopolitan	Raised – transition bog	5–20	VII	white
Fritillaria meleagris	Eur, As	Transition bog – lime-fen	25–30	IV–V	white/violet
Gladiolus palustris	E-Eur, C-Eur	Transition bog – lime-fen	40–50	VI–VII	pink-red
Pinguicula grandiflora	Eur	Transition bog – lime-fen	5–15	V–VI	blue
Parnassia palustris	Eur	Transition bog – lime-fen	10–20	VII–IX	white
Pogonia ophioglossoides	N-Am	Raised – transition bog	10–15	V–VI	pink
Rhynchospora alba	Eur, N-As	Raised – transition bog	25–30	VI–VIII	white
Primula frondosa	E-Eur	Transition bog	5–10	IV–V	pink
Spiranthes cermia	N-Am	Transition bog	30–40	IX–X	white
Swertia perennis	Eur	Transition bog – lime-fen	15–50	VI–VIII	violet
Viola palustris	Eur	Transition bog	5–12	V–VI	blue
Sown species (hemiparasites)					
Castilleja miniata	N-Am	Transition bog	20–50	V–VIII	orange
Pedicularis palustris	Eur, As	Transition bog – lime-fen	20–50	V–VI	red-pink
Pedicularis sceptrum-carolinum	Eur, As	Transition bog – lime-fen	50–100	VI–VII	yellow
Rhinanthus serotinus	Eur	Transition bog – lime-fen	30–50	VI–VIII	yellow

* Eur = Europe; As = Asia; Am = America; N = North; E = East; S = South; W = West; C = Central
⁺ Slight frost protection recommended in cold regions

8.19
Wastewater treatment system with plantings of *Carex acutiformis* and *Scirpus lacustris* in Friedrichsrode, Germany. In the middle there is a pebble bed planted with bactericide *Mentha aquatica*

Zones 3 and 4 – the shallow water and swamp area

Along the edge of standing water bodies with a fluctuating water level (zone 3), *Carex elata* can develop to be the dominant species of a tall sedge swamp. It can be linked with a tall forb community outwards (zone 2) and with a reed swamp inwards. The typical reed swamp vegetation is dominated by a few very competitive species sending a dense net of rhizomes and roots through the saturated soil and protecting it from erosion (Table 8.4). The most widespread reed species, *Phragmites australis*, prefers edges of standing water bodies and invades wetlands too. In wastewater treatment wetlands, it is the most effective purifying species because its thick, aerenchym-containing rhizomes optimise the site as a habitat for micro-organisms that aid the reduction of pollutants and nutrients (Wissing 1995) (Figure 8.16). Along streams and riversides *Phragmites* communities are substituted by *Phalaris arundinacea*. Its roots and rhizoms only penetrate a shallow soil-layer and are, therefore, not very effective at protecting river banks from erosion. Bioengineering objectives are best realised when *Phragmites australis* is used together with *Schoenoplectus lacustris* in transition zones to deep water. Rampantly spreading *Carex* species (such as *C. acutiformis*) are recommended for shallow water and wetland zones. Together with *Carex elata*, some other tussock species and low-growing or less-competitive rhizome perennials are suitable for a diverse planting design in several layers as explained above.

Menyanthes trifoliate and *Potentilla palustris* as ground–covers prefer meso- to oligotrophic water and mediate between zones 4, 3 and 2 as well because they develop floating mats toward zone 5. A wide range of inhabitable water depths is to be found by *Calltriche palustris*, *Crassula recurva*, *Hippuris vulgaris*, *Hottonia palustris* and *Sparganium* spp., being able to form very diverse bodies according to water-depth. The 'land type' develops a tough,

Table 8.4. Shallow water and swamp area

	Origin*	Soil/water conditions	Height (cm)	Flowering Months	Flower Colour
Dominant species (5–20/10 m²)					
Carex elata	Eur	Mesotrophic	30–100	IV–V	green
Iris pseudacorus	Eur, As, N-Afr	Meso-eutrophic	80–100	V–VI	yellow
Nuphar advena	N-Am, S-As	Eutrophic	50–80	VI–IX	yellow
Pontederia lanceolata⁺	N-Am	Eutrophic	80–120	VI–X	blue
Peltandra virginica	N-Am	Meso-eutrophic	80–100	V–VI	green
Companion species (10–30/10 m?)					
Butomus umbellatus	Eur, As	Eutrophic	50–100	VII	pink
Hippuris vulgaris	Eur, As, N-Am	Eutrophic	25–30	inconspicuous flowers	
Iris laevigata	W-As, S-Am	Meso-eutrophic	70–80	VI–VII	blue
Lysimachia thyrsiflora	Eur, As, N-Am	Oligo-mesotrophic	70–80	V –VI	yellow
Mentha aquatica	Eur, As	Eutrophic	40–80	VII–IX	pink-lilac
Mimulus ringens	O-, N-Am	Mesotrophic	60–100	VI–VII	blue purple
Pontederia cordata	N-Am	Eutrophic	60–70	VI–IX	blue
Ranunculus flammula	Eur, W-As	Mesotrophic, acid	20–50	VI–VIII	yellow
Ground-covers (20–40/10 m²)					
Juncus ensifolius	N-Am	Mesotrophic	15–20	VII–X	brown-black
Menyanthes trifoliata	Cosmopolitan	Oligo-mesotrophic	15/30	V–VI	white
Nasturtium officinale	Eur, As	Meso-eutrophic	20–80	V–X	white
Pilularia globulifera	Eur	Mesotrophic, acid	5–15	fern plant	
Potentilla palustris	Cospoplolitan	Oligo-mesotrophic	30–40	V–VI	brown-red
Sparganium minimum	Eur	Mesotrophic	5–20	VI–IX	green
Veronica beccabunga	Eur, W-As	Meso-eutrophic	25–30	V–VIII	blue
Scattered plants (up to 30/10 m²)					
Alisma lanceolatum	Eur, W-As	Eutrophic	50–60	VII–VIII	white
Alisma subcordatum	N-Am	Eutrophic	30–50	VII–VIII	white
Alisma plantago-aquatica	Eur, As	Eutrophic	40–100	VII- VIII	white
Baldellia ranunculoides	Eur	Oligo-mesotr. saltresist.	5–30	VII–X	white, pink
Juncus bulbosus	Eur	Oligo-mesotr., acid	5–15	VII–IX	brown
Orontium aquaticum	N-Am	Meso-eutrophic	5–10	V–VI	yellow
Sagittaria latifolia	N-Am	Eutrophic	50–60	VI–VII	white
Sagittaria sagittifolia	Eur, W-As	Eutrophic	40–60	VI–VII	white
Monoculture species – only to combine with shallow ground-cover species mentioned above (10–30/10m²)					
Acorus calamus	S-, E-As	Meso-eutrophic	60–100	V–VI	white
Bolboschoenus maritimus	Eur, As, E-Am	Meso-eutrophic	30–100	VI–VIII	brown
Cladium mariscus	Cosmopolitan	Oligot-mesot, hard	80–200	VII–XI	brown
Cyperus longus	C-Eur, As	Mesotrophic	100–130	VII–IX	brown
Dulichium arundinaceum	N-Am	Mesotrophic ?	40–80	VII–IX	brown
Phragmites australis	Cosmopolitan	Meso-eutrophic	100–400	IX–I	brown
Ranunculus lingua	Eur, W-As	Meso-eutrophic	70/100	VI–VII	yellow
Schoenoplectus lacustris	Eur, As	Eutrophic	200–250	VI–VIII	brown
Schoenopl. tabernaemontani	Eur, As, N-Am	Eutrophic, saltresistant	50–150	VI–VIII	brown
Sparganium erectum	Eur, As	Meso-eutrophic	50–120	VI–VII	green
Sparganium simplex	Eur, As, N-Am	Meso-eutrophic	50–100	VI–VII	green
Typha angustifolia	Eur, As, N-Am	Meso-eutrophic	150–200	VI–X	brown
Typha latifolia	Cosmopolitan	Meso-eutrophic	150–200	VI–VII	black
Typha laxmannii	Eur, As	Meso-eutrophic	120–160	VI–X	brown
Typha minima	Eur, As	Oligo-mesotr., hard	40–60	V–VII	brown
Typha shuttleworthii	Eur	Meso-eutrophic	90–120	VI–VII	grey-black
Zizania latifolia	As	Meso-eutrophic	100–150	flowering only in warm climate	

* Eur = Europe; As = Asia; Am = America; N = North; E = East; S = South; W = West; C = Central
⁺ Hardy if planted 50cm below water level

Table 8.5. The water lily area

	Origin*	Soil/water conditions	Water depth (cm)	Flowering Months	Flower Colour
Floating-leaved species (not fixed into the bottom with their roots)					
Hydrocharis morsus-ranae	Eur, As	Mesotrophic	> 10	VII–VIII	white
Riccia fluitans	Eur, As, Am	Mesotrophic?	> 10	moss plant	
Salvinia natans	Eur, As	Meso-eutrophic, hard	> 10	fern plant	
Stratiotes aloides	Eur, As	Mesotrophic, hard	> 70	V–VI	white
Clump-forming and moderately running rooted floating-leaved species					
Caltha natans	N-Am	Mesotrophic?	10–40	VI–IX	white
Nuphar japonica	E-As	Meso-eutrophic	70–120	VI–IX	yellow
Nuphar lutea	Eur, As	Meso-eutrophic	70–120	VI–X	yellow
Nuphar minima	Eur, As	Oligotrophic, acid	50–90	VI–IX	yellow
Nymphaea alba	Eur, W-As	Meso-eutrophic	80–120	VI–X	white
Nymphaea candida	Eur, W-As	Mesotrophic	70–100	VI–X	white
Nymphaea odorata	N-Am	Meso-eutrophic	70–100	VI–X	pink
Nymphaea tetragona+	N-As	Oligo-mesotrophic	20–40	VI–X	white
Nymphaea tuberosa	N-Am	Meso-eutrophic	70–100	VI–X	white
Nymp. 'Berthold'	Cultivar	Meso-eutrophic	40–60	VI–X	pink
Nymp. 'Candidissima'	Cultivar	Meso-eutrophic	60–90	VI–X	white
Nymp. 'Gladstoniana'	Cultivar	Meso-eutrophic	90–120	VI–X	white
Nymp. 'Marliacea Carnea'	Cultivar	Meso-eutrophic	60–90	VI–X	white-pink
Nymp. 'Moorei'	Cultivar	Meso-eutrophic	40–70	VI–X	yellow
Ranunculus aquatilis	Cosmopolitan	Mesotrophic	50–90	V–IX	white
Trapa natans	Eur, As	Eutrophic	50–120	VI–VIII	white
Monoculture rooted species – very competitive and not to combine with other species					
Nymphoides peltata	Eur, As	Meso-eutrophic	40–100	VI–VIII	yellow
Persicaria amphibia	Cosmopolitan	Meso-eutrophic	10–100	VI–VIII	pink
Potamogeton natans	Cosmopolitan	Meso-eutrophic	40–100	inconspicuous flowers	

* Eur = Europe; As = Asia; Am = America; N = North; E = East; S = South; W = West; C = Central

+ Requires slight proctection in very cold climates

Table 8.6. Submerged zone community

	Origin*	Soil/water conditions	Water depth (cm)	Flowering Months	Flower Colour
Rooted species					
Callitriche palustris	Cosmopolitan	Meso-eutrophic	> 10	inconspicuous flowers	
Chara fragilis	Eur, As, Am	Oligo-mesotrophic	> 20	alga – plant	
Eleocharis acicularis	E-As, Am	Meso-eutrophic	> 10	inconspicuous flowers	
Elodea canadensis	Am	Meso-eutrophic	> 20	inconspicuous flowers	
Fontinalis antipyretica	Eur, As, N-Am	Oligo-mesotrophic	> 30	moss – plant	
Hottonia palustris	Eur, As	Meso-eutrophic, acid	> 10	V–VI	pink
Littorella uniflora	Eur	Oligotrophic	> 20	inconspicuous flowers	
Myriophyllum spicatum	Cosmopolitan	Oligo-eutrophic, hard	> 30	inconspicuous flowers	
Myriophyllum verticillatum	Cosmopolitan	Meso-eutrophic	> 30	inconspicuous flowers	
Nitella flexilis	Eur, As, Am	Oligotrophic, acid	> 20	alga – plant	
Potamogeton crispus	Cosmopolitan	Mesotrophic	> 50	inconspicuous flowers	
Potamogeton lucens	Eur, As	Eutrophic, hard	> 50	inconspicuous flowers	
Floating species (without roots)					
Ceratophyllum demersum	Cosmopolian	Eutrophic	> 40	inconspicuous flowers	
Ceratophyllum submersum	Eur, As	Eutrophic	> 40	inconspicuous flowers	
Utricularia vulgaris	Cosmopolitan	Mesotrophic, acid	> 40	VII–VIII	yellow

* Eur = Europe; As = Asia; Am = America; N = North; E = East; S = South; W = West; C = Central

upright body, while the 'submerged-type' produces smooth, feathery leaves on soft branches, increasing the gas-exchanging plant surface. Floating branches develop to more or less dense growing blankets covering the water surface.

Zone 5 – The Water Lily area

WaterLilies (genus Nymphaea) are the most important representatives of this deep zone. There is a very wide range of cultivars with different flower-colours and different recommended water depths. Table 8.5 shows only a few examples. For further information Wachter (1998) is recommended. Though Water Lilies prefer meso- to eutrophic conditions, they thrive well in water poor in nutrients if they have enough space to develop a large root system. Whilst *Nymphaea* species and Hybrids prefer sunny conditions, *Nuphar* species withstand even shady sites. Most of the other deep-water plants tend to be very invasive by producing rampantly growing rhizomes either penetrating the mud (*Persicaria amphibia*) or floating along the water surface (*Nymphoides peltata*).

Rooted submerged hydrophytes can cover the pond's bottom with spectacular carpets. It is advised to avoid the extremely competitive *Elodea canadensis*: this can overgrow even Water Lilies. Instead, oxygenation can be guaranteed by rootless *Ceratophyllum* species: these are easily removed when too prolific. *Potamogeton* species can spread rampently too, but species of this genus are suitable even in deep water in large ponds.

Callitriche palustris, *Crassula recurva* and *Hottonia palustris* mediate between zones 5, 4 and 3, forming mats submerged in deep and emerged in shallow water or on soggy soils. *Hottonia*, however, is suitable only in water with low hardness. *Ranunculus aquatilis* is a short lived species that can cover the pond's surface in the first seasons and completely disappear in others. *Salvinia natans* will only survive in winter in continental climates when it can lodge between dense reeds.

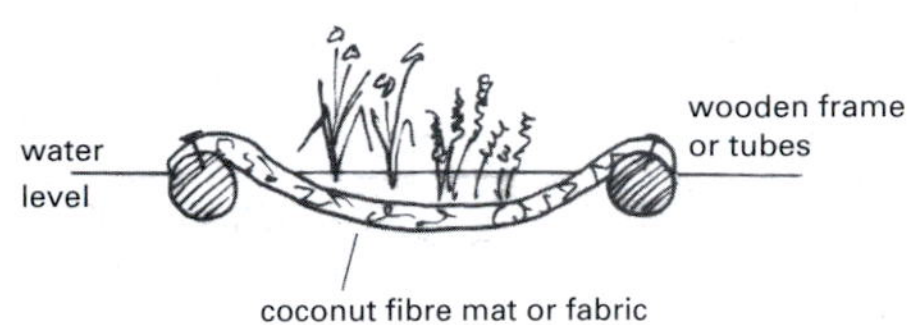

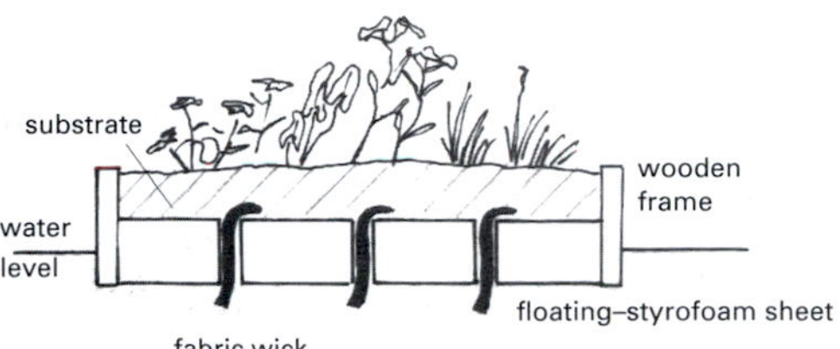

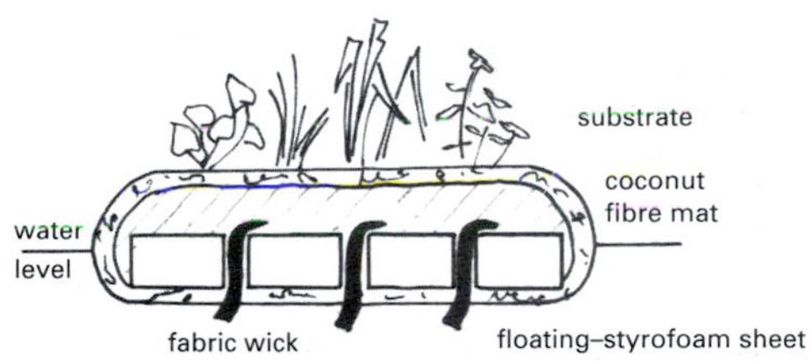

8.21
Possibilities for floating islands

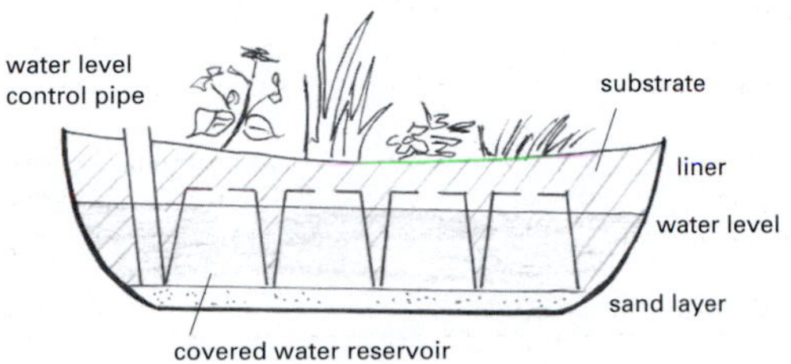

8.20
Swamp-bed-construction

Special applications of wetland planting

Artificial bogs and wetland

In nature, extensive bogs often occur without any connection to open-water surfaces. This principle can be transferred into urban landscape design. An artificially sealed swamp-landscape corresponds to a man-made pond containing only zone 1 and possibly zone 2 plant communities. It must be remembered that when the whole volume of the swamp bed is filled with substrate, the transpiration of plants and the evaporation of soil will dry out the swamp body very rapidly in summer. The volume of the substrate pores is too small to store enough water for a dry period. A certain amount of water should therefore be stored in covered hollow bodies (Maier 2000: 16–18), as shown in Figure 8.20. These bodies can be plastic-pots, buckets turned upside down or canisters. They are to be drilled at the top and bottom, so that water can flow in and out. More than half of the volume should be filled with these hollow bodies, saving substrate and optimising the water balance. The depth of swamp beds is recommended to be between 40–50 cm, if tall forb communities are to be established, or 30 cm for bog or fen vegetation.

Waterfalls, fountains, artificial springs and streams

The zone around constructions with intense water movement has to be fixed with stony substrate, such as a gravel or pebble covering, to protect it from erosion. Between these stones, ruderals susceptible to competition with other plants can be used. In oligotrophic conditions these can be *Pinguicula grandiflora* or *Primula frondosa*. Mesotrophic sites along streams allow the establishment of species with higher demands in nutrients because of the constantly moving water. Tall plants should be used sparingly and the vegetation should not cover the substrate completely, in order to accentuate the dynamic character of these water features. Recommended species along streams are *Trollius europaeus, Caltha palustris, Cardamine pratensis, Myosotis palustris, Veronica beccabunga* and tussock-forming *Carex* species.

Floating islands

If there is no possibility to establish plants in a pond's swamp-zone, floating structures can be built as vegetation carriers. Figure 8.21 illustrates several possibilities for how to construct such drifting islands.

8.22
Coconut-fibre mat planted with *Phragmites australis*. The matting, thoroughly rooted through, is ready for installation along erosion-endangered shores

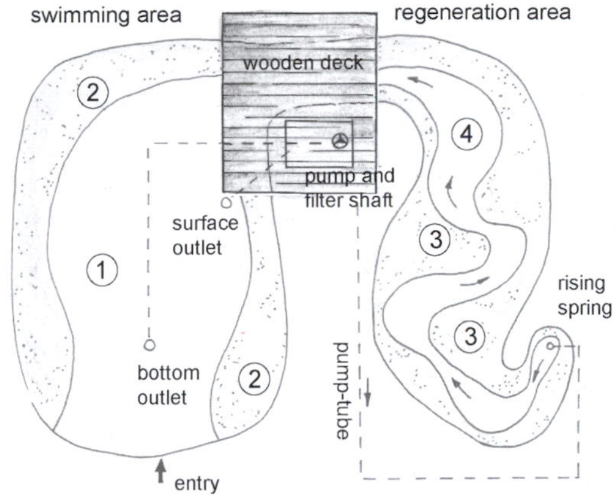

8.23
A roof garden on the Possmann cider factory (Frankfurt/Main, Germany). *Carex acutiformis* and other helophytes are irrigated with circulating water which helps to cool the building and significantly reduces its electricity consumption

8.24
A natural swimming pond system

If they are fixed at the shore they then have the advantage of balancing fluctuating water levels by moving upwards and downwards, thereby guaranteeing a steady waterlevel for the planting. Any number of square metre sized elements with frames of timber, or even steel tubes, are used to establish reed vegetation on water reservoirs with heavy water-level variations (see Schlüter 1996: 140–142). Figure 8.22 shows coconut fibre mats with reed-vegetation, ready to be established either to an erosion-threatened shore or between the frames of floating islands mentioned above. Large, extensive mats of floatable synthetic fabric ('Repotex') can cover purification ponds for contaminated water. Arnold and Mählmann (2002) recommend planting *Scirpus lacustris* and *Carex acuta* (syn. *C. gracilis*) on to the mats.

On a smaller scale, floating islands can skirt ponds that have been built without wet-meadow and shallow-water zones. Here, for example, floating–styrofoam sheets — a special hard structured kind that cannot suck water — with fabric wicks passed through several holes can be used as a substrate carrier. A 5–10 cm substrate layer, covered and fixed by a coconut fibre-mat is sufficient to feed low and semi-high perennials, such as plants of fens or bogs. A floating bog is a recommended feature to brighten up open rainwater reservoirs, particularly as the chemical quality of the water fits best to the vegetation of raised bogs.

Extensive roof plantings

Shallow substrate layers on flat or moderately sloped roofs are usually planted with drought-tolerant perennials, especially *Sedum* species. But it is also possible to establish wetland vegetation when the substrate surface is permanently supplied with water. Even synthetic fabric mats are sufficient to support wetland or swamp-vegetation. The main reason for installing such a vegetation system is the effect of cooling the building efficiently without too high an energy input (Ziepke 1992) (Figure 8.23). The permanently moving water allows the use of wetland plants from Table 8.2 (in particular, monoculture species), even if it has got a low nutrient content. Lightly contaminated water can be purified by running through such a large area of suitable substrate and water plants. On small roofs – mainly in private gardens – a covering with low growing oligotrophic fen or bog vegetation (see Table 8.2) is feasible to gain an exciting visual and botanic diversity, by saving roof-loading.

Swimming ponds

Natural swimming ponds are becoming popular in Austria and Germany as a natural alternative to pools treated with chemicals. These pools have many advantages. They combine the ornamental character of richly vegetated pond margins with the recreational feature of the swimming pool. They enable wetland vegetation to be established in a water body where space may otherwise be limited. They support a wide range of pond wildlife and they filter pool water in a natural, chemical-free manner.

To obtain clear water, nutrient input must be minimised; it is worth striving for oligotrophic quality. One of the most common systems works by pumping water from the surface and bottom of the bathing area, which is planted only along the edges, into the regeneration zone filled with dense, proliferating vegetation. From there it flows back again into the main body of the pond (see Figure 8.24). It is not the direct uptake of nutrients by the plants, but microbiological reactions at the surfaces of substrate particles and plants that cause the intended cleaning effects. The most effective purifiers are rampantly spreading helophytes and hydrophytes with aerenchyme-containing rhizomes, referred to as 'monoculture species' in Table 8.2, 'shallow water and swamp area' and *iris* species or *Asclepias incarnata. Iris pseudacorus* and *Mentha aquatica* improve hygiene by emitting bactericide substances, if the water depth is sufficient. Planted at a high density, tussock plants with intensive root systems are suitable, such as *Carex elata. Ceratophyllum, Stratiotes* and *Potamogeton* species are suitable submerged plants.

The regeneration zone is most effective when it is narrowly shaped or even takes the form of a stream because then the increased water movement brings about improved nutrient supply of demanding vegetation. On the other hand, the nearly motionless water of the wider swimming zone is responsible for the very low nutrient supply of the planting along its edges (Figures 8.25 and 8.26). Here plants from meso- or even nature sites are susceptible to nutrient-deficiency symptoms, so these are therefore optimal conditions for oligotrophic bog and fen vegetation. More or less narrow strips of this vegetation around the swimming area surprise the users with unusual effects: frogs and other animals can be watched easily from inside the pond between a low-growing vegetation of insectivorous plants, orchids, cotton grasses and other specialities. Occasional heavy waves have no negative effect to the planting when the substrate surface lies more than 10 cm above water level. There should be no plants under the water surface in the sphere of influence of the swimming zone, because their dying leaves would cause unpleasant mud-accumulation and whirling up of organic particles. Only Water Lilies can be accepted here. Their leaves can easily be cut and removed in autumn.

8.25 (left)
Transition-bog planting at the edge of a swimming pond in the author's garden – *Sarracenia flava* beside *Castilleja miniata,* a hemi-parasite that is presumed on the roots of *Carex flava* and *Lythrum salicaria* 'Robert'

8.26 (above)
Along the wetland zone, framing the swimming area of the author's pond, a fen has been developed with *Dactylorhiza* (orchids), *Eriophorum latifolium* and attractive flowering gems between *Carex davalliana* and ground-cover grasses. Behind the wooden deck the densely planted regeneration-zone

Practice of carrying out plantings

Planting substrates

In natural wetlands and water bodies, the existing soil is usually planted without drastic modifications.

Thus, the range of plants has to be co-ordinated sensitively with the existing trophic level, chemical reaction and soil textural class. To avoid germination of weeds, a 5 cm mulch-layer of bark chips or gravel can be beneficial. On the other hand, planting beds of artificially sealed ponds should be covered with a substrate, chosen according to the intended planting habitat.

In zones 4 and 5 in small water bodies, baskets are sometimes recommended as a way of economising on substrate. Enclosed containers offer the advantage of preventing rhizomes from escaping, but nutrients are quickly used up and demanding species show symptoms of deficiency, especially nitrogen. Therefore, containers should be fertilised with a slow release nitrogen source such as hoof and horn chips (2–3 g/l), and re-potted after dividing the root stock every two to four years. Containers with helophytes emerging high above the water level are easily knocked over by gusts of wind. In large, deep ponds, pre-cast concrete ring-units are preferable as planting beds for water lilies, lifting them up to a suitable depth.

Generally, it is preferable to plant into a substrate layer spread directly over the lining material of the water body. To avoid nutrient accumulation in the water body, nutrient-poor substrate material is recommended. For rooting of helophytes and hydrophytes in zones 3 to 5, it is sufficient to use a 10 cm layer of lime-free pebbles 2–16 mm in size. In the wetland zone (zone 2), more fine-grained material should be used the more the substrate surface is raised above the water level. The following recommendations are valid in ponds as well as in swamp beds and other applications.

Raised-bog plantings can be established in pure *Sphagnum* peat, thoroughly soaked with water before use. As a substitute, lime-free sand is suitable as a lower layer, covered with only 5 cm peat, coconut–fibre–wool or unfertilised timber–fibre (Toresa). *Sphagnum* mosses should be pressed on parts of the wet peat-surface to develop a living substrate. Substrate for transition bogs can be composed likewise when supplied with semi-hard water. A very poor and acid water quality can be compensated by a 5–10 cm layer of base-containing gravel (lava, pumice, expanded clay) underneath the peat, or a very thin layer of limestone or dolomitic gravel. For lime-fen vegetation, limestone gravel (2–8 mm) should be used as a substrate, the layer above the water level can be mixed with 50% *Sphagnum* peat.

The substrate depth for meso-eutrophic to eutrophic tall forb communities should be more than 25 cm. The submerged substrate should be sandy or granular in order to support the influx of water and nutrients, whereas clay or loamy subsoil can become mixed into the layer above the water level. The contained clay-minerals improve the chemical buffering. Topsoil is unsuitable because of its high nutrient content and because of its weed-seed loading. The substrate surface can be covered with gravel as a mulch. Substrate used for transition bogs, fen and meso- to eutrophic tall forb communities can be mixed with 30% shredded bark. Water and swamp plants from eutrophic sites can be supplied with nitrogen by starting fertilisation with horn chips (up to 50 g per plant respectively per m^2) mixed into the substrate.

Plant size and quality

Typically wetland and water plants are available in 9 cm pots. Vigorous reed plants are occasionally sold in 11 cm pots and water lilies in 13 cm pots. Plants must have a well-established root system. Bare-rooted plants and plants in trays with a root-ball size of about 3–4 cm are suitable for wet sites because there is very little danger of drought damage. However, there should be low weed competition for successful establishment, and planting should be carried out after the possibility of spring floods and before the end of June. Water lilies should be planted in shallow water, the shoot heads have to be located above the substrate's surface.

Plants for zones 3 to 5 should be reliably fixed to prevent them from being pulled out by currents or waves. In Germany, good results were achieved with Flor-Recult-Logatainer plants, which are cultivated in special trays (Ziepke 1990). Each plant develops a flat root ball of 100 cm², shaped like a cigarette box. Planting with a spade is rapid and, if the flat rootballs are lined up parallel to the current, they withstand erosion better along the riversides and streams. Vegetation mats on floating islands or roof gardens can be planted by laying Flor-Recult-Logatainer plants flat on to the surface (see, for example, Ziepke (1992)). New roots will anchor the perennials and their shoots will emerge within a few weeks.

Several companies offer ready planted mats and fascines with reed- or tall forb vegetation (see, for example, BGS (2002)) for establishing along shores that are strongly exposed to erosion. These elements consist mostly of coconut fibre and should be fixed with wooden stakes or stones (Bestmann 1993; DIN 2002).

Submerged and floating-leaved species without roots are traded in transparent plastic bags or boxes. Closed receptacles must not be stored in full sun because the heat would destroy the sensitive plants. They are best stored in an open water bucket in the shade. Rooted submerged plants should be fixed with their base in the substrate, whereas floating species should be just thrown into the water.

Planting densities

Plant distances are suggested as numbers of plants per area, as proposed for wetland and shallow-water plants in Table 8.4. These can be adapted in practice, depending upon factors such as the period of time until a dense ground cover is to be reached, whether the vegetation is established by sowing, planting or a mix of both methods, the available financial budget or the desired proportions between tall and low plants.

The habitat's 'reed-swamp' or 'tall forb community' tend towards a density of 5–7 plants/m². For rampant growers, 1–3 plants/m² is sufficient in monoculture planting: these can be optionally combined with 4–6 ground covers. Raised-bog and oligotrophic fen vegetation can be planted with up to 20 plants/m² because of their slow growth. Between a *Sphagnum* carpet, 5–10 perennials are sufficient. Not included in these calculations are 'scattered plants' and sown species.

Planting time

Wetland and water sites should be planted from May to mid-July. Before this period, temperatures are too low for satisfactory establishment. Later planting means that slow-growing plants, in particular, are not able to fix themselves sufficiently, and winter frost can lift them easily out of the substrate. Potted reed species can be planted until August, whilst bare-rooted water lilies can be put in at any time up to June.

Sowing practice

Nearly all perennials, apart from ferns, can be established by sowing, if seeds are available. Some seeds will need to be broadcasted as fresh as possible (*Symplocarpus, Rhinanthus* and *Pedicularis*). Many species need a period of cool temperatures, around 0°C–+4°C for at least four to six weeks, to break dormancy (Kircher 1994). The best option is to sow in late autumn, but this is only suitable on sites that will definitely not be flooded in winter or spring. Otherwise, seeds can be mixed with moist sand and stored at the temperatures mentioned above. When the site is no longer flooded, seeds can be broadcast. A thin cover with sand fixes the seed and prevents it from drying up. It should not be thicker than 1 cm because several wetland plants need light to trigger germination.

Maintenance (water management, weed control, cutting and protection in winter)

Water management and algae control

In a sealed pond, transpiration can cause a fall in the water level of more than 5 mm during a hot summer day. The more the mains-water has to be refilled, the greater nutrient levels become. Generally, water with low hardness and nutrient content should be preferred to prevent algal growth, just as in swamp beds with bog and fen vegetation. The refilling of water can work automatically, when the supply pipe is controlled by a floating switch.

In newly filled ponds, it is quite normal that after some weeks the water becomes murky because of floating algae. After a while, natural predators, especially water fleas, develop that eat the algae. In the long term, the nutrient-level should decrease, so that floating algae will not be so abundant. To prevent persistent problems with floating algae, the following recommendations are made for artificially sealed ponds:

- use of water with low hardness and low nutrients
- avoiding lime-containing and nutrient-rich substrate and fill material; hard limestone without porous structures can be used
- nutrient-enriched surface water from outside the pond should not overflow the edges in bigger amounts and get inside
- use sufficient helophytes along zones 2 to 4 and hydrophytes in zone 5 – floating leaved plants cover and shade the water surface, this weakens the vitality of algae.

If trees shade parts of a pond, the effect of cooling and reduced light intensity causes deterioration in conditions for algae. Leaves falling into the pond can cause moderate nutrient enrichment, but this is often overestimated. Pine trees are recommended pond shaders because their needles are very poor in nutrients and lead to an acid reaction when falling into the water.

Even in oligotrophic ponds, filamentous algae can cause unpleasant displays. There are species with a rough surface (*Cladophorales*) and others with a slimy surface (*Zygnemales*). Both are able to assimilate hydrogencarbonate, leading to an increase in pH in their surroundings. Acidifying the water can destroy the algae effectively, but it also has catastrophic influences on other living organisms in the pond. So the adding of acid into the water should be carried out carefully and only in cases of emergency. Filamentous algae need a fixed surface to anchor themselves with rhizoides, this works best above lime- containing structures. From there they grow through the water body. Besides the avoidance of lime, the following are possibilities for controlling filamentous algae:

- manually removing filamentous algae with a rake or a small net mounted on a long handle – together with the plant mass, nutrients, especially phosphorus (algae are prone to a considerable consumption of phosphorus), are withdrawn
- water movement or blown-in air can increase and optimise the level of dissolved CO_2, which seems to reduce the growth of filamentous algae
- barley straw is said to have an algae-repressing effect – though the reason for this effect is still disputed, practical experience strongly suggests that this is very effective (Newman 1997)
- several herbicides are available that prevent algae growth but damage to the water plants can occur (Hafner and Eppel 2002)
- dyes which produce a turquoise colouration of the water – if its artificiality is not a problem, this is a very effective way to control algae.

Mowing and weed control

Sites above the water level are much more endangered by invading weeds than the floating zones. Ruderals, such as *Ranunculus sceleratus, Alopecurus aequalis, Epilobium* spp., *Bidens* spp. and *Juncus* spp., are the most common weeds in the wetland zone of newly established plantings, and should be removed before fruiting. This is possible with weed control about four to six times a year during the first two years (establishment maintenance) until the planted species have reached a high percentage ground-cover. In oligotrophic wetland zones, the above mentioned weeds will develop slowly and only to a small size, so that weed control two or three times a year will be enough. More dangerous than short-lived weeds are competitors, especially *Calamagrostis* spp. and other invasive grasses. They have to be removed together with their rhizomes. If discovered too late, only a treatment with the herbicide Glyphosate will be successful. It must be painted directly on to the weed leaves but must not be allowed to come into contact with the desired plants.

This intensive weed-control maintenance is only practical on small plantings. On large urban plantings, development should be directed by mowing in early spring or late autumn, and removing the cuttings. Tall forb communities do not have to be mown each year, but a regular cycle creates tidy looking plantings. The cut material should be removed so that the sites become impoverished in nutrients. There should also be an occasional control of invasive competitor weeds. Bog and fen vegetation is best mown in autumn (October to November) to remove as many nutrients as possible.

Newly established carrs should be mown in spring each year or each second year until the tree canopies begin to shade the soil lightly. Later, only one or two cuts are enough to remove over-aggressive forbs and grasses. Trees can be coppiced every 15 to 25 years to prevent them from becoming senile and to protect them from wind damage. Weeds of zones 4 and 5 are algae, and, in smaller ponds, some invasive submerged plants, in particular *Elodea canadensis*. This rampantly growing plant should be substituted by *Ceratophyllum* species. Water-plant specialists recommend smothering *Elodea* populations by covering them up with large amounts of *Ceratophyllum* (Wachter 1996).

Fertilising

If a planting is designed according to the site's trophic level, fertilising is not necessary. However, in artificially sealed ponds, it is recommended to reduce nutrients as efficiently as possible to achieve clear water and reduce *Lemna minor* carpets and other weeds. On the other hand, in such an enclosed system, species with a high nutrient absorption can suffer from deficiencies, especially in nitrogen. Symptoms show up as small, yellowed leaves, shorter branches and a low and halting growth. *Butomus umbellatus* even reduces the production of inflorescences. Other nutrient-demanding plants are species of the genera *Pontederia, Iris, Hibiscus, Sagittaria, Alisma, Orontium, Trapa, Lysichiton* and *Calla*. To increase nutrient availability, nitrogen should be applied directly to the needy plants without fertilising the water: either hoof and horn chips can be injected into the substrate surrounding the root-system (20 – 50 g per plant) or urea-solution (1%) is sprayed upon the emerged surface of the plants. Floating plants can only be treated with the spray method because they are not fixed in the substrate with roots. Fertilising should be carried out only when symptoms of deficiency are to be seen. Hoof and horn chips should be used only in spring (May to June). According to the author's experience, even in bog- and fen-plantings nitrogen deficiencies can appear when they are fed with rain-water and there is no water movement through their substrate. In this case one to two urea treatments in spring are recommended as explained above.

Winter protection

Planted in the indicated water depth, nearly all

species mentioned in this chapter are hardy. Protection in very cold climates, such as in Central Europe, particularly when temperatures fall under –15°C for several days, is recommended for:

- *Darlingtonia californica* and *Sarracenia flava* (brushwood layer)
- *Pontederia lanceolatum* (hardy when planted deeper than 50 cm under the water level)
- *Nymphaea tetragona* (overwinter under frost-free conditions)
- *Salvinia natans* (but light is also required).

Ponds can be protected from blown or fallen foliage by stretched-out nets. If this is not suitable, thick layers of leaves accumulated above the bottom of the pond can be removed with a small net mounted on a long handle or with a pump.

Acknowledgements

- Special thanks to Noël Kingsbury and Nigel Dunnett for reading and improving the text, and to Anja Wendorf and Michaela Wetzel for helping with the diagrams and tables.

References

- Agate, E. (1976). *Waterways and wetlands*. British Trust Conservation Volunteers, Doncaster.
- Archer-Wills, A. (2002). *A complete Guide to Design, Constructing and Planting Water Features*. Todtri Productions Ltd.
- Arnold, R. and Mählmann, J. (2002). *Hygienization of contaminated surface waters using floatable textile islands with (repo-)plants (Scirpus lacustris, Carex gracilis) – first results*. Information paper of Sächsisches Textilforschungszentrum e.V., Chemnitz.
- Bestmann, L. (1983). *Uferzonen – lebende Baustoffe*. Sonderdruck aus: Wasser und Boden 3.
- BGS (Bestmann-Green-Systems) (2002). *Catalogue of BGS-Ingenieurbiologie- und -ökologie GmbH*. Tangstedt, Germany.
- Borchardt, W. (1996). Pflanzenverwendung im Garten- und Landschaftsbau. *Der Gärtner*, Vol. 6. Ulmer, Stuttgart.
- DIN (Deutsches Institut für Normung e.V.) (ed.) (2002). DIN 19657 – Sicherung von Gewässern, Deichen und Küstengewässern. In *DIN: Landschaftsbauarbeiten. DIN Taschenbuch,* **81**, 9th edition. Beuth, Berlin, Wien and Zürich.
- Ellenberg, H. (1996). *Vegetation Mitteleuropas mit den Alpen*. 5 Auflage. Ulmer, Stuttgart.
- Eppel, J. (1996). Natürliche und naturnahe Dichtungsmaterialien für Teiche. *Deutscher Gartenbau*, **11**, 694–697.
- Evert, K-J. (ed.) (2001). *Lexikon Landschafts- und Stadtplanung*. Springer, Berlin.
- Grime, J. P. (1974). Vegetation classification by reference to strategies. *Nature*, **250**, 26–31.
- Grime, J. P., Hodgson, J. G. and Hunt, R. *Comparative Plant Ecology*. Unwin Hyman, London.
- Hafner, C. and Eppel, J. (2002). Ist Algen im Teich vorzubeugen? *Deutscher Gartenbau*, **29**, 18–21.
- Hagen, P. (1995). *Teichbau und Teichtechnik*. Ulmer, Stuttgart.
- Kircher, W. (1994). Keimverhalten von Sumpfpflanzen. *Taspo-Gartenbaumagazin*, **11**, 22–24.
- Kircher, W. (1996). *Wasserpflanzen für den Garten*. Ulmer, Stuttgart.
- Maier, E. (2000). *Das Moor im eigenen Garten*. Parey, Berlin.
- Newman, J. (1997). *Control of Algae with Barley Straw. Information Sheet No. 3*. Institute of Arable Crops Research, Centre for Aquatic Plant Management, Berkshire.
- Niesel, A. (Hrsg.) (2002). *Bauen mit Grün. 3. Auflage*. Parey, Berlin.
- Schlüter, U. (1996). *Pflanze als Baustoff. 2. Auflage*. Patzer, Berlin, Hanover.
- Succow, M. and Jeschke, L. (1986). *Moore in der Landschaft*. Deutsch, Frankfurt/Main.
- Wachter, K. (1996). Verbal communication, Walderbach.
- Wachter, K. (1998). *Seerosen*. Ulmer, Stuttgart.
- Wissing, F. (1995). *Wasserreinigung mit Pflanzen*. Ulmer, Stuttgart.
- Ziepke, S. (1990). *Flor-Rekult-Logatainer-Pflanzen*. Information paper of Flor-Rekult, Bensheim, Germany.
- Ziepke, S. (1992). Ein Pflanzendach zur Wasserkühlung. *Landschaftsarchitektur*, **6**, 18–20.

Chapter 9

Communicating naturalistic plantings: plans and specifications

Nigel Dunnett, Wolfram Kircher and Noel Kingsbury

One of the major obstacles to the wider application of a more ecologically-informed approach to landscape and garden plantings is the gap between the vision of the designer and the actual practical implementation of that vision. Much has been made of the lack of appropriate knowledge and skills among maintenance personnel to enable the appropriate and subjective management decisions to be made over the short- and long-term development of naturalistic plantings, and the lack of resources to support this. But there is another important hurdle to overcome before maintenance is even considered: how can the designer's intentions (in the form of a plan or specification) be best translated into the actual vegetation on the ground. This is not so much of a problem if the person doing the designing is also the person who implements a planting (as might often be the case in a private garden), or if a designer works very closely with the client to realise the aims of a plan. But if a scheme is to be implemented by a contractor with little or no contact with the original designer, then how best might naturalistic plantings be communicated? Of course, it can be argued that the ideal situation is one in which the landscape architect or garden designer is able to supervise planting operations, or that a new type of horticulturist/designer provides specialist services to architects and landscape architects, controlling the whole process from planting design through to implementation, and that these models become the norm. However, at present, this is not a realistic option on a widespread scale and cost limitations mean that, in the great majority of public landscape contexts, contractors implement planting plans often without the direct involvement and supervision of the original designers.

In a survey of leading practitioners of new naturalistic perennial plantings in the UK, carried out by the Department of Landscape at the University of Sheffield in the late 1990s, it was found that 90% of those designers questioned implemented their schemes by laying out the plantings themselves on site, or directly supervising the laying out of plantings by contractors. The great majority of the schemes involved were located in private gardens or institutional gardens, such as botanical gardens or pay-for-entry educational or demonstration gardens – all situations where there is greater access to skilled maintenance, supervision against damage and controlled public access. When this is considered, it is perhaps not surprising that naturalistic plantings (particularly herbaceous plantings and non-native naturalistic plantings) have not yet been widely applied in urban public landscapes in the UK. A principal reason why the implemented schemes tend to be those in which the designer has a close association is because of the great complexity of the plans that are produced to depict naturalistic arrangements of plants. This is particularly true of the German naturalistic planting tradition that has had so much influence over contemporary ornamental naturalistic planting styles. Not only are these plans impossible for the uninitiated to understand, they are also time consuming to produce and are very labour-intensive to carry out.

This chapter presents a predominantly visual overview of the main strands of planting plan depiction before focusing specifically on how naturalistic plantings have been communicated. Finally, we attempt to chart a sensible way forward for the communication of naturalistic plantings, with the aim of widening their application.

The principle methods of drafting planting plans

The whole and only purpose of a technical planting plan is to enable whoever is to do the planting to make sure that the right plants are obtained for the scheme and that they go in the right places. It is the green equivalent of a technical construction drawing to enable the correct building of a structure made from hard materials. In terms of our discussions in this chapter, the crucial aspect here is the placing of plants: their distributions, arrangements, spacings and patterns. Now, this is relatively straightforward if one is dealing with individuals – the placing of individual feature plants in a bed or lawn, or the grouping of standard trees, for example, into an avenue. But things start to become more complicated when one is dealing with groups of plants that interact to give a particular desired effect. And it becomes very complicated when a strongly naturalistic outcome is desired. As discussed in the other chapters in this book, the defining characteristics of ecologically-informed and naturalistic plantings are that they do not follow rigid rules, plant groupings are complex and intermingled, and they have a very dynamic development in which plants do not necessarily stay in the same place over time. How can all this be communicated in a way that is relatively accessible?

Ornamental planting plans

Before moving on to discussing the specification and depiction of naturalistic plantings, we will first briefly mention the way that the grouping of plants in standard landscape and garden plantings are depicted. In order to do so, it is helpful to categorise such plans into three main types that form the basis of most standard approaches to producing planting plans: the monoculture, the block and the drift. These terms generally refer to layers of planting beneath tree level – shrub and herbaceous layers. Trees, being larger-scale units, are generally depicted

9.1
Monocultural planting – ground-cover shrub mass

9.2
The perennials and grasses in this scheme by the Oehme and Van Sweden partnership are planted in large blocks

as individuals, unless planting is on a woodland scale. An excellent overview of the composition of planting plans for landscape and garden plantings is given in Robinson (1992). It is not the intention of this chapter to provide an in-depth guide to the drafting of a planting plan, but rather to indicate different approaches to setting out a planting and how these might be communicated graphically.

Monocultural plantings (Figure 9.1) represent the antithesis of what much of this book is about, featuring extensive plantings of one or two species (usually cultivars), often filling up space alongside highways, in commercial developments or public landscapes. This type of planting is more commonly encountered on a large scale in continental Europe rather than Britain, and is essentially a modernist concept, treating planting in a purely functional sense, as 'green concrete'. Aesthetically, there is a certain simplicity, purity and sense of scale about monocultural planting that works well in certain contexts and, of course, in terms of drawing up planting plans, very little basic knowledge is required (because the same small pool of plants are used ubiquitously) and it is time-efficient because of the lack of complexity.

Block planting is essentially a more complex version of the above and is perhaps the most common approach to landscape planting. Rather than using extensive areas of the same species, smaller monocultural blocks are arranged adjacent to each other to fill a space with planting (Figure 9.2). However, this remains a relatively simple approach to putting together a planting that again draws, in the main, from a limited plant palette. In the context of landscape planting, limited aesthetic decisions are made: perhaps plants will be graded according to height or foliage colour but, generally, plants are again treated as green materials – tough space-fillers. Block planting does result in textural variety and a degree of diversity, but the rigid demarcation of groups in regular shapes and the predominance of evergreens makes for visually dull and undemanding landscape.

Of the planting types described earlier in this book, the perennial and grass plantings of the Oehme and Van Sweden partnership (see Chapter 3) come closest to this approach, but the greater use of contrasting forms, the softer nature of perennials and a higher degree of seasonal change, lift these plantings beyond the mundane.

Drift planting could be regarded as an extension of block planting. Plants are still used in demarcated monocultural groups, but groups are much more intimately arranged, with a range of group sizes and shapes, and groups are generally arranged to give a *direction* to the planting. Drift planting (Figure 9.3) has very much grown out of the British informal garden planting tradition, and owes much to the design style of Gertrude Jekyll who employed

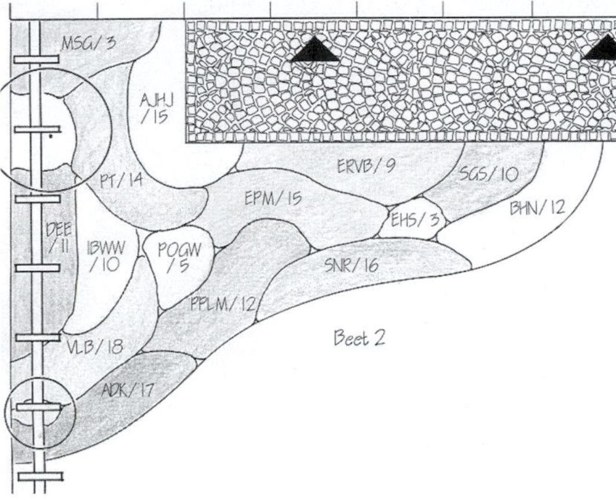

9.3
Ornamental drift planting – part of a scheme incorporating paving and a pergola (the plant names and quantities are not important). Plan by Gunther Rapp, HS Anhalt, Bernburg, Germany

colour-themed drifts of hardy and tender perennials arranged by height, with the main visual effect of the planting gained at an angle or along the length of the planting, rather than straight on, thereby increasing the sense of depth.

Drift planting was originally intended in the late 1800s to mirror the patterns of natural vegetation (Figure 9.4), giving a more naturalistic appearance than the more formal schemes common at the time, and also attempted to capture the effect of the somewhat chaotic vernacular cottage gardens that again were seen as an antidote to highly controlled geometric gardens

Despite being a century old, this style of planting remains the predominant style in British garden design, and the more studied of landscape schemes. The associations between plant groups are much more intimate in drift planting and, as a result, there is greater emphasis on both contrast and harmony in colour, form and texture between nearby plants.

Because drift planting has its roots in natural patterns, it is not surprising that strongly naturalistic schemes can be created using this technique, especially when free-growing or wild-character perennials are used. For example, Figure 9.5 shows spontaneous ruderal vegetation composed of interlocking strands of clonal perennials and grasses. A clear pattern of drifts and groups is apparent.

9.4
Drift planting – the natural model. Drifts and patches of buttercups in an agricultural field

Naturalistic planting design

Much naturalistic planting design is an abstraction of the patterns and groupings of plants to be found in wild or semi-natural vegetation. Although drift planting can achieve some of this effect if repeated over a sufficiently large area (as shown in Figure 9.5), there is a fundamental problem to this style that leaves many ecologically-minded designers less than satisfied: plants are growing in distinct groups with very little interactions between those groups. This is very different to the more natural situation where there is much greater merging between stands of different species, and where many species may not occur in well-defined groups at all. To many people it is the very intimate mixing of compatible species at the smaller scale that grades up into recognisable patterns at the larger scale that is particularly attractive. However, anyone who has studied a unit of diverse vegetation in any detail will realise that the arrangement of plants can be extremely complex. For example, Figure 9.6 shows a small-scale plan of a 1 × 1 m area of Central European steppe grassland, with the locations of each plant indicated by symbols. Each species has a different symbol. Where species occur in groupings where no clearly defined individuals can be identified, they are shown as patterned masses rather than as fixed points.

At first glance, the arrangement of the different plants in Figure 9.6 appears entirely random, but closer inspection reveals more distinct patterns. Whilst it is very difficult to distinguish monocultural groups, it is possible to detect clumpings and aggregations of the same species. In most cases, these aggregations are very closely mingled with aggregations of other species. These types of patterns are discussed in more detail in Chapter 4.

9.5
Spontaneous rudeal vegetation. *Calmagrostis epigejos, Solidago canadensis* and *Dipsacus fullonum* form individual groups. The emerging Dipsacus seedheads are rising bewteen lower growing drifts of perennials and grasses

Because of the complexity of the arrangement of the different species in this patch of vegetation, it is necessary to depict each different species with its own symbol – only in this way can an accurate depiction of the true distribution of the different plants be shown. This type of mapping of vegetation in sample units or quadrats, together with the collection of complete species lists from quadrats in the first half of the twentieth century, was a strong part of the Central European plant sociological approach to plant ecology. Plant sociology involved the classification of vegetation into recognisable plant community types that were deemed to occur wherever the same environmental conditions (e.g. soil type, water regime and pH) occurred within a geographical region. Although such a tradition has never been central to British plant ecology, it has relatively recently been given greater recognition through the publication of the National Vegetation Classification (Rodwell 1991). The crucial point here is that ecologically-leaning horticulturists in Germany were steeped in a tradition that suggested that plants formed repeatable assemblages according to their environments, and that there were distinct spatial patterns in the way that enabled these species to co-exist in any finite area of space. The merits of this proposition are discussed more fully in Chapter 4. In particular, the idea that these patterns, *in themselves*, automatically lead to ecologically-functioning vegetation is suggested to be based upon a false premise, ignoring ecological processes of competition and succession, and instead resulting in relatively short-term visual

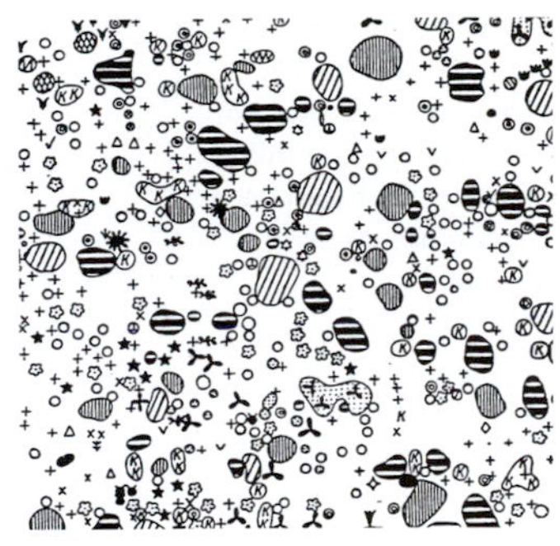

9.6
A plan of the location of individuals and groups of different species in a 1.0 ¥ 1.0 quadrant of steppe grassland vegetation. Each different species has its own symbol (from Braun-Blanquet, 1964)

compositions in the absence of ongoing maintenance. However, the pattern-influenced ideas lead directly to the German 'Garden Habitat' planting style.

Symbol-based plans – Garden Habitat planting

The background to the Garden Habitat style of planting – or the 'Hansen School' of planting as it has come to be known after its greatest proponent, Professor Richard Hansen – is given in Chapters 2 and 3. In essence, this approach aims to mimic the spatial patterns of plants in the wild, using species and cultivars that are very well adapted to prevailing site conditions, and with a strong aesthetic element thrown in. There is much less emphasis on the block or the drift, and a far greater emphasis on the individual plant and its placing. Whilst each species may show a degree of clumping or aggregation, it is the interactions between these aggregates that gives rise to the naturalistic effect, and much of the visual beauty of these plantings.

The philosophical basis to Garden Habitat planting arises partly from ecological fitness to site principles, but also partly from spatial factors that describe the typical degree of association or aggregation of that species in the wild. As discussed in Chapter 4, five degrees of aggregation or Plant Sociability are recognised, ranging from isolated scattered individuals through to species that form dense monocultural stands. Most Garden Habitat plantings contain a mix of these different types to achieve complete vegetation cover. Moreover, there is a clear structural component to the plantings, with species classified according to their size, form and dominance in the planting.

A variety of graphical representations have been used to depict these naturalistic plantings. At the basic level, plans can simply label each individual plant (Figure 9.7a), but this becomes very difficult to follow when applied to plantings of any considerable size. A particular problem is that this type of planting relies on the repetition of species across the space. In Figure 9.7a it is very difficult to tell which species are repeating, and where. Implementing a plan such as this is very time-consuming and the laying out of plants has to be done bit by bit as one advances across the area. Of course, it is possible to give each plant a different colour or shading, but most technical planting plans have to be produced in black and white, and there are a limited number of patterns that can be used to identify each circle from the others.

A more sophisticated approach, and one that is much more common, is to give each plant its own symbol. For example, Figure 9.8 shows a similar-sized area of planting to that depicted in Figure 9.7a,

a

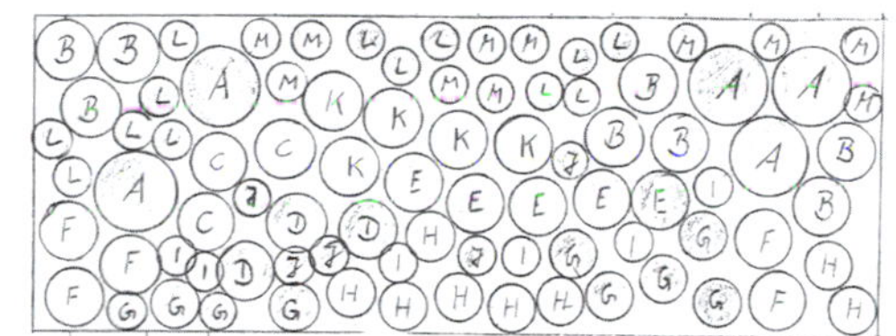

b

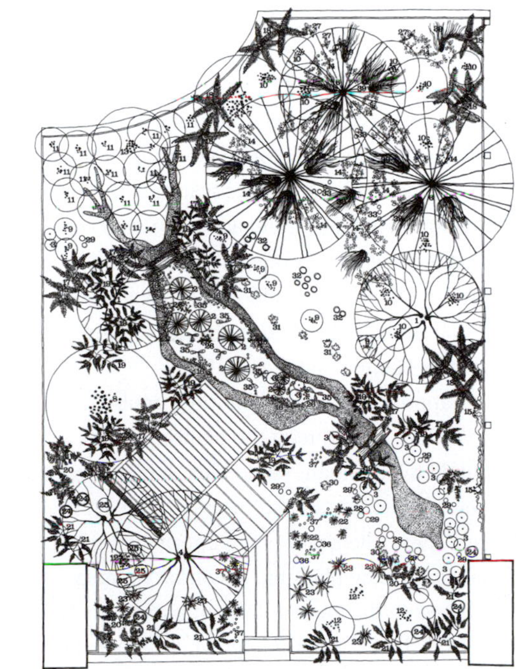

9.7
(a) A naturalistic planting plan showing the location of each individual plant
(b) Andropogon Associates Planting Plan – bog garden for Longwood Gardens. A naturalistic planting plan with all the plants individually located

9.8

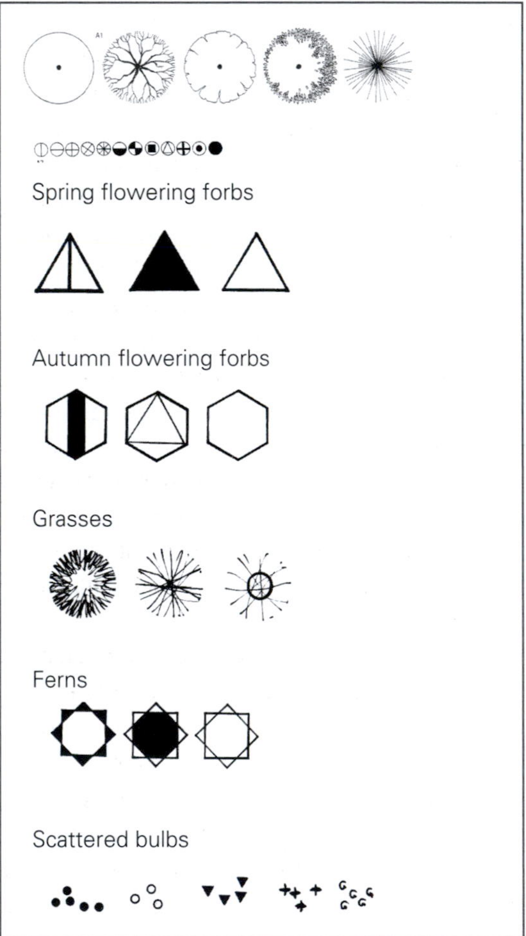

9.9

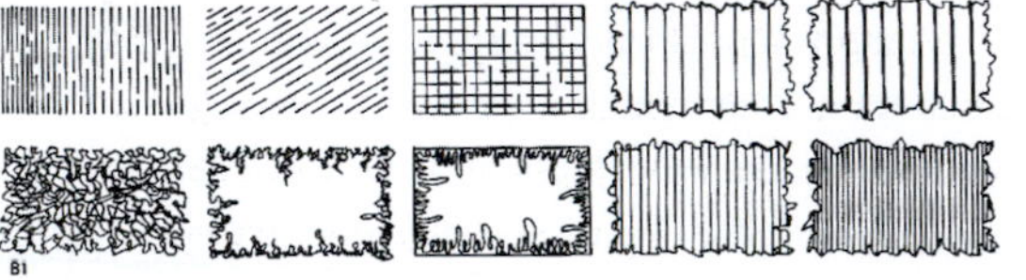

9.10

but this time symbols are used instead of named circles. The structure of the planting is immediately more obvious and, importantly, it is relatively easy to see where each species is repeated. Standardised symbols can be applied to represent different plant types – the plan shown in Figure 9.8 uses these symbols. Figure 9.9 shows some of the common symbols used in planting plans in Germany.

Close examination of Figure 9.8 indicates that, although each individual plant is shown, much of the arrangement of the plants is into single species blocks or drifts. For some groupings, there is actually little need to show where each plant goes – it would be more efficient to indicate the boundaries of the group. This is particularly true of ground-cover plants where individuals merge to form a mass where no single plant is indistinguishable from any other. In such situations, it makes sense to show these plants as a mass rather than as individuals. These can still be illustrated symbolically by giving each group its own graphic, as indicated in Figure 9.10.

Figure 9.11 illustrates two plans where these techniques have been combined. A strong structural impression is given by these plans, with the arrangements of different types of perennials being clearly shown. Aggregated clump-forming species arise out of lower-growing and ground-covering masses, with larger, more solitary species scattered throughout. This structural or architectural approach represents the most straightforward way of composing such naturalistic planting plans and has achieved wide recognition through the Garden Habitat planting promoted by Hansen and Stahl (1993).

This approach is most commonly applied to perennials. The structure of the planting is determined by dominant perennials that are scattered rhythmically throughout and impose order on the planting. These 'theme' or emergent plants determine the character of the planting. Secondary plants fill-in spaces between the more dominant plants, according to their 'sociability' (see Chapter 4), whether they be

9.8 (above, left)
A similar plan to 9.7, showing the location of each plant but, in this instance, each species or cultivar has its own symbol

9.9 (centre, left)
Typical symbols for different plant types as used in the German 'Garden Habitat' approach to planting. These symbols help the planner gain an impression of the flowering period of planting

9.10 (below, left)
Examples of graphic representation of ground-cover species

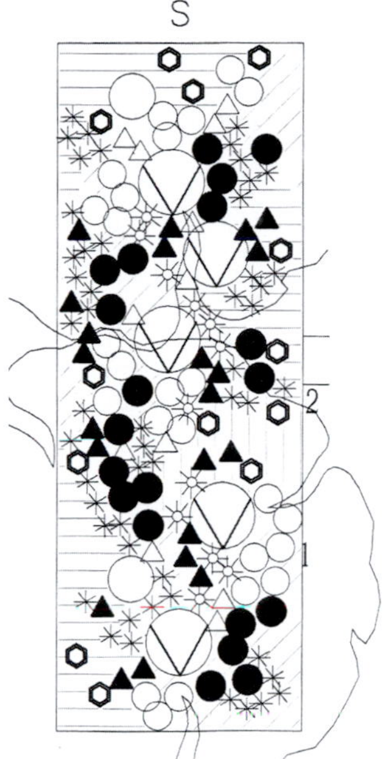

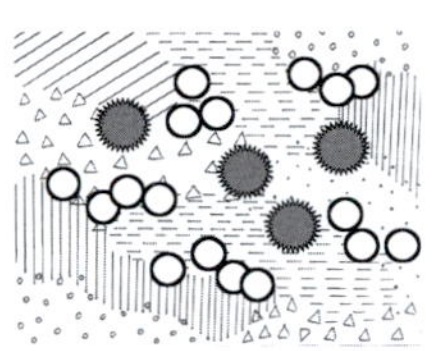

9.11 (above)
Some examples of combined symbol-based naturalistic planting plans

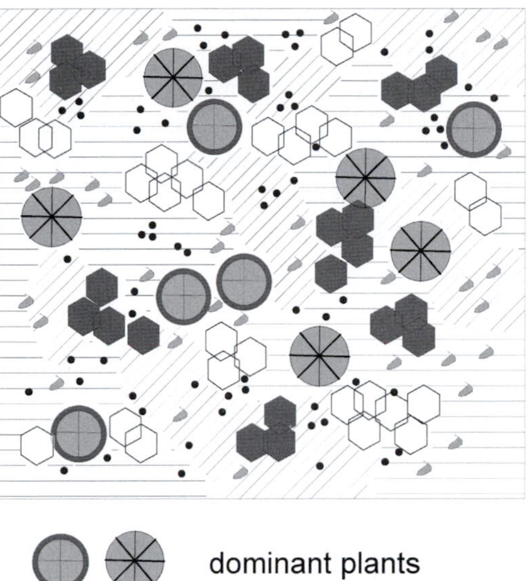

9.12 (right)
The basic components of 'Garden Habitat' planting

aggregated 'companion perennials', ground-covering perennials or scattered perennials (Figure 9.12).

Mixtures

Whilst the symbol-based planting plans discussed above undoubtedly achieve a naturalistic distribution of plants across an area, they are also complex and very time-consuming to lay out. It has already been noted that the majority of practitioners in this field either lay out the plantings themselves or supervise the layout of the plantings. It has also been noted in Chapter 2 that even in Germany, where this style of planting originated, examples in public landscapes are relatively rare and are generally restricted to former garden festival sites that have subsequently become public parks, demonstration sites or botanical gardens, as well as private gardens. Part of the explanation for this could be the technical difficulty in implementing the plans, but may also be partly related to maintenance. Ironically, laying out plantings with such a strong naturalistic pattern may require ongoing maintenance to maintain that pattern and to prevent dominance by more vigorous species or weedy invaders. And this maintenance must be skilled and knowledgeable to enable the desired balance of structural plant types to be maintained. This is perhaps the biggest difference between 'naturalistic' styles and 'ecological' styles – whilst the former are maintained to be nature-like in appearance, the latter are maintained to be nature-like in function. Of course, the natural patterns in wild or spontaneous vegetation from which the inspiration for nature-like plantings are derived are much more a result of chance – plant distributions are related both to the random chance that a particular species is available but also to whether that species is able to establish and persist under the precise set of environmental conditions operating on that site. Natural patterns develop over time and, as has been discussed elsewhere in this book, are not static entities but continually develop and change over the years.

For this reason, significant strands of naturalistic planting design have not relied on precise planting plans at all, but have rather been based upon the specification of mixtures of plants that are laid out with varying degrees of randomness. This has been most widely applied to woody plantings but there is now also increasing interest in the use of mixtures of perennial plants.

Woody plant mixes

The use of mixtures as the basis for setting out plantings is most commonly encountered in amenity or landscape settings as the basis for naturalistic native woodland planting. In particular in the UK, mixture-based techniques have been developed in recent decades for extensive new naturalistic 'community woodlands' on the urban fringe (Hodge 1995) and for new farm woodlands on surplus agricultural land. These woodlands are created using young trees (generally two-year-old 'transplants'), planted relatively closely to achieve quick canopy closure. Because planting has to be carried out simply and efficiently, detailed planting plans are rarely used. Instead, written specifications are followed that give the contractor all the necessary information to obtain the plants, lay them out and get them planted. At its most basic level, this information includes:

- plan showing the area the mix is to fill
- percentage composition of the mix – what proportion of the total number of plants does each species or cultivar make up?
- the size of each plant
- planting density, i.e. the number of plants per m^{-2}, or the distance between each plant
- group sizes – approximately how many individuals of each species or cultivar are to be planted together to form groups or clumps
- planting method, i.e. notch or pit planting.

In most situations it will be left to the contractor to randomly arrange groups of each species within the total planting area – rarely will the position of each group be shown on a plan. However, there may be specific instructions regarding the placing of certain species that, for example, may be congregated close to the edge of a plantation or around paths or entrances. In any given scheme there may be a range of mixes, the number of which will vary according to the complexity of the scheme, for example woodland-core mixes and woodland-edge mixes, edge mixes that respond to different aspects, or mixes of different species composition that respond to differences in soil type or aesthetic outcome. The main point here, however, is that drafting these planting plans is relatively quick and, importantly, the laying out and planting can be done through a series of instructions that do not require advanced horticultural knowledge to implement.

Within this model it is possible to have varying degrees of specificity in the placing of individuals and groups. Certain trees may be located individually if, for example, large material (standards or larger) are included among a mass planting of small material to give immediate structure. Again, larger material may be included as more formal elements along paths or edges. Perhaps ornamental species may be included at specific points in predominantly native plantings to produce enhanced aesthetic effects. Plant selection generally in these plantings is made on an ecological or habitat basis, choosing common native species that are suited to the site conditions.

Herbaceous plant mixes

There has, until recently, been little application of this approach in non-woody or herbaceous plantings, and virtually no application (be it with woody or non-woody plants) in ornamental plantings. However, in the late 1990s, a series of research projects, based primarily in Germany, Austria and Switzerland, began to explore random mixtures as a basis for setting out perennial plantings. The trials are now finding their way into public landscapes, supported enthusiastically by sectors of the nursery industry that see this approach as opening up potentially important new markets.

Essentially, the aim behind these mixes is to provide ecologically and aesthetically compatible mixtures of perennials that suit particular environmental conditions and which respond to simple 'extensive' maintenance techniques. One of their main selling points is that, compared to the standard planting design and implementation process, they are relatively cheap and straightforward to install. This is partly because there is no need for the drawing up of a detailed

Table 9.1. Properties of different structural types in random planting

Number: 100 m^2	Type
1–5	Emerging perennials
10–50	Companion perennials
30–80	Ground-covering perennials
30–300	Scattered perennials

planting plan: the plantings are established using a specification not dissimilar to that of the woody plant mixes discussed above. As a result, there is a design cost-saving and because the plantings do not necessarily require great skill and knowledge to set out, and because they are simple to maintain, they potentially offer much scope to extend the use of high-quality naturalistic plantings in public places.

Although different structural plant types might be planted at different distances from each other, in all other respects, planting in these mixture-based perennial systems is entirely random. It is purely a matter of chance whether one species or cultivar fills a particular planting position or another does. As such, mixture planting has been heavily criticised by some landscape designers and horticulturists as representing a diminution of the worth or value of the designer. True, the traditional skills of placing individuals or groups of different species in studied compositions or associations for aesthetic effect are no longer valid, but this is not to say that artistic or creative vision is not important in such plantings. On the contrary, there is still a great need for aesthetic considerations, but additional skills and knowledge are also important for such mixtures to be successful.

It is also necessary to go beyond Plant Sociability as the basis of the planting. Yes, this remains an important factor, but it is also necessary to have a stronger ecological basis for plant selection. Some of the factors to take into account in formulating perennial mixtures include:

- the *habitat requirements* of the component species
- *life history* – the inclusion of short-lived rapidly flowering ephemeral species as well as slower-growing longer-lived species ensures a dynamic development of the mixtures over the long-term, as well as flowering display *from the earliest stages*
- *ecological strategy* – matching species according to their competitive compatibility, for example through the use of Grime's plant strategy classification (see Chapter 4)
- *regeneration* – what might be the long-term dynamic characteristics of the planting and how will species persist and regenerate into the long term (if required)?
- *aesthetic characteristics* – working towards harmony or contrast in colour associations, for example
- *structural characteristics* – application of the principles of Garden Habitat planting in terms of the balance between different structural plant types
- *phenology* – ensuring a compatible mix of species in terms of flowering time and pattern of growth throughout the year
- *maintenance intensity* – are the species compatible with the anticipated intensity of maintenance?

Through repeated trials, one of the co-authors of this chapter (Wolfram Kircher) has found that the proportions in Table 9.1 of different structural types generally give satisfactory results in a random planting. The figures in Table 9.1 are for 100 m^2 of planting.

The mixture planting method can be used as the basis for the design of new and original plantings but, in Germany and Switzerland, it has also been used as the basis for planting 'recipes' that can be applied 'off the shelf' in any location, provided that soil conditions and climate are correct for that particular mixture. For example, the 'Silver Summer'

a

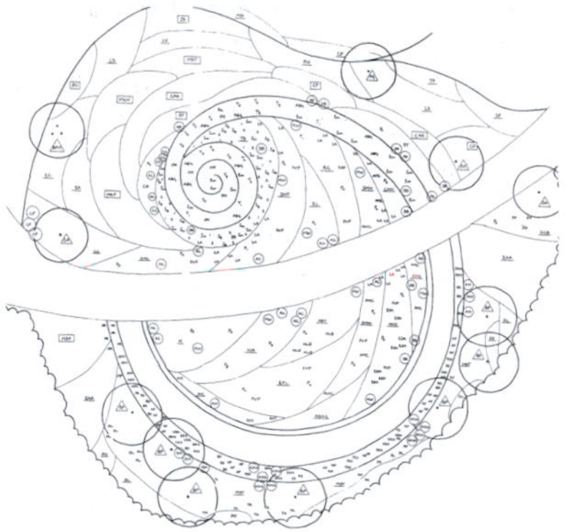

b

9.13
(a) A 'Silver Summer' planting, Bernberg, Germany; (b) A mixed planting by the landscape practice LandArt

mixture (Figure 9.13) is suited to sunny, warm conditions over free-draining soils.

Whilst in many cases it is true to assert that 'the arbitrary planting of a great many randomly chosen perennials can never lead to satisfactory results' (Hansen and Stahl 1993), if the above factors are considered it is likely that a well-chosen randomly planted mixture will not produce results that are greatly different from a carefully worked-out naturalistic scheme. Figure 9.14 shows the results of an independent visual assessment of the same group of perennial 'Silver Summer' species that have been either randomly planted in drift or blocks, or planted according to a 'garden habitat' scheme based upon their sociability characteristics. The randomly planted mixture receives higher average scores. The difference in summer scores hardly repays the extra effort in working out a detailed planting plan.

Seed mixes

The use of seed mixtures to create flowering wildflower meadows has always relied upon complete randomness to achieve its aims. The use of broadcast mixed seed to cover an area with vegetation not only produces a truly spontaneous effect but it also enables a very close 'fit' of that vegetation to site conditions: different species will respond to variations across a site in such factors as fertility and moisture in different ways and will, therefore, 'distribute' themselves accordingly.

The make-up of a seed mix can be based upon exactly the same factors as those outlined in the section above on randomly planted perennial mixtures. The use of seeding as a technique has been very well-developed in relation to the use of native species in meadow mixtures, but its application has been very limited outside of this field. There is, however, no reason why the use of seeding should be confined to native wildflowers. The majority of cultivated plants in temperate landscapes, for example, originate from grassland habitats, and exactly the same techniques can be used for producing meadow-like mixtures of non-natives as for natives. James Hitchmough's chapter on herbaceous vegetation in this book discusses the use of seed mixes for ornamental plantings in depth (Chapter 6).

Seeding can be combined with other types of establishment methods. For example, a combination of seeding and planting of perennials (if a framework of perennials is planted first at relatively low density and then a seed mix over-sown to fill the gaps between the plants) can give the advantage of a definite structure and provide guaranteed results from the planted species in the initial stages, combined with the truly naturalistic effect of the seed mix.

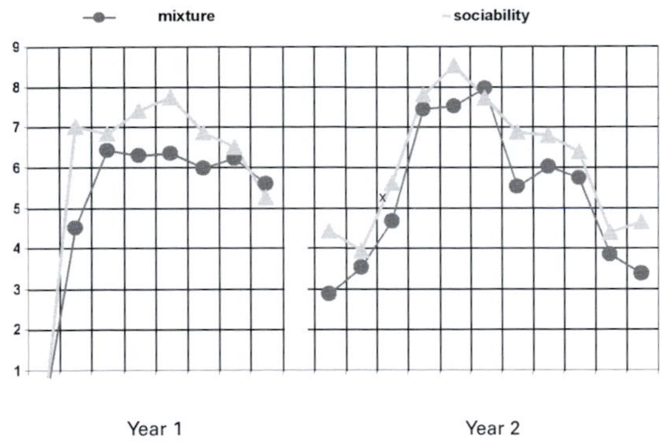

9.14
A visual comparison of the same mixture of species in the same proportions planted according to one of four different methods: random mixture, according to the sociability of each species, using drifts and using blocks. Visual scores are on a scale of 1 (no visual appeal) to 9 (highest visual appeal)

Conclusions

There are merits to all the approaches to specifying and designing plantings described in this chapter. A major conclusion, however, is that the standard method of depicting a detailed naturalistic planting plan (the Garden Habitat or Plant Sociability based method) has relatively little application on a wider scale outside of the private garden, the botanical institution or the well-resourced scheme where the designer can also be involved in plant placement and layout. This is because the sheer complexity of the plantings, where, in many cases, each plant has its own location, makes not only for a very time-consuming (and, therefore, expensive) process but also one which requires a good deal of skill and feeling for the naturalistic distribution of plants.

We propose that there is merit in relying much more heavily on a randomised, mixed approach to planting (whether from seed or through planting, or both), given that the evidence appears to support the idea that a completely randomised planting (if the balance of species and cultivars is correct) appears to lose little in aesthetic terms. Having said this, there is a role for varying degrees of plant placement within random plantings. It may be, for example, that the more structural species (the dominant or 'theme' plants of the Plant Sociability school) are shown on a plan scattered in their actual positions. In this way, a framework is developed within which all the other species are introduced as mixtures. It may be that, as with naturalistic woodland planting, each species is planted in groups of constant or varying sizes, rather than as individuals. And, of course, a variety of different mixes can be used within any given area. In this respect, a mixed planting plan may be quite similar to 'drift planting', only instead of each drift or group being composed of a single species, in this instance they may contain a mixture. Where a variety of mixes are being used, there may be some common components to the majority of the mixes to ensure some form of unity or coherence across a scheme, or they may be quite different from each other. And some drifts or blocks may indeed be monocultural, the effect might then be similar to the plot shown in figure 9.5.

What must be stressed when advocating the greater use of mixtures is the avoidance of a formulaic procedure, whereby the same mixtures are specified universally across a region or country. The specification of mixes (whether with plants or seed, or both) can be as creative as the formulation of traditional planting plans – it simply requires a different set of skills from the purely horticultural-based approach to planting.

References

- Borchardt, W. (1997). *Pflanzenverwendung in Garten und Landschaftsbau.* Ulmers, Stuttgart.
- Braun-Blanquet, J. (1964). *Pflanzensoziologie 3.* Auflage, Wien.
- Hansen, R. and Stahl, F. (1993). *Perennials and their Garden Habitats.* Cambridge University Press, Cambridge.
- Hodge, S. (1995). *Creating and Managing Woodland around Towns.* Forestry Commission, London.
- Robinson, N. (1992). *The Planting Design Handbook*. Gower, Aldershot.
- Rodwell, J. (1991). *British Plant Communities Volume 1. Woodlands and Scrub*. Cambridge University Press, Cambridge.

Chapter 10

Creative management

Hein Koningen

Things are not all as easily understood and expressed in words as one is often led to believe. Most events cannot be expressed in words at all; they occur in a space that has never been entered by any word. Even more difficult to express in words than everything else are works of art – those mysterious forms of existence that go on living whilst our lives perish.

Rainer Maria Rilke (1903)

Design and management – integral process direction

Principles

In the naturalistic parks or '*heemparks*' of Amstelveen (the Netherlands), ecology and design have been going hand-in-hand ever since the 1930s (Figure 10.1). The approach that is required to accomplish this has been found to differ greatly from the traditions of conventional design and management. Practice in Amstelveen illustrates a number of essential principles of what may be called an integral approach to design and management. Ecology and design, spontaneous process and human intervention are inextricably linked and are complementary. The time seems ripe to propose a

a

b

c

d

e

10.1

Woodland, wetland and grass habitats are used in the naturalistic '*heemparks*' of Amstelveen, the Netherlands, to create rich pictorial impressions

(a) A ribbon of *Caltha palustris* along a lake edge

(b) Wetland and wet meadow amongst housing

(c) A dramatic underplanting of *Primula elatior* amongst young birch

(d) Another young birch plantation

(e) Wet meadow vegetation

complement to existing design traditions, which are typically rather abstract and linear in nature. This can be accomplished by giving more attention, especially in landscape design and horticultural practice, to the development of a flexible, integral management process founded on tried and tested practical experience in the field. In this tradition, the disciplines of design and management, often rigidly separated, are organically united.

Static layout

After the construction phase of the first Amstelveen *heemparks*, a crucial difference was soon found to exist between plantings with horticultural cultivars as used in traditional parks, and the vegetation created in the new *heemparks*. Plantings of the former actually have a rather static character; appearance does not change very drastically. In essence, its management aims to maintain the image projected by the designer as closely as possible. The designer thus has a strong and often long-lasting influence upon the layout. The planting as a whole complies with a rather clearly circumscribed scheme, individual plant species are restricted to their original positions, whilst the soil used meets the average demands they have in common. It is usually a well-drained nutritious leaf-mould rich in humus, its acidity varying between slightly alkaline and slightly acidic.

Dynamic process

The vegetation of '*heemparks*' are part of a *dynamic process*, with patterns changing continuously in space and time. However conscious the choice for a certain vegetation or plant species may have been, the initial design can only be the start of a process that gains its momentum in time. Plant groups, and even individual plants, will change position and arrange themselves in new, often unforeseen, patterns. Instead of being considered as disturbing changes that require correction, the fluctuating, spontaneous elements in '*heempark*' vegetations of any type are seen as essential and explicitly valued characteristics. In as far as a design as such is applied, its principles are completely different from those used in traditional plantings. Firstly, the designer should possess a considerable amount of botanical and ecological knowledge and experience. Without this, the design will soon prove incompatible with the natural demands and opportunities of the environment and the plant material chosen. In practice, designers hardly ever possess this knowledge. Secondly, it is evident that a design formulated as a one-off cannot comply with the processes inherent in the character of '*heempark*' vegetation. Since it is generally impossible to maintain the initial image the designer constructed of a planting in perpetuity, neither is it possible to formulate any 'final' image. To demand this would be to apply a theoretical abstraction, which is incompatible with natural processes. It is exactly the process itself that unfolds through time and which will always, within the limits one sets or expects, keep surprising one to a certain extent. At best, all that can be done to maintain a desired image is to apply continuous watchful-management and, if necessary, adjustment of the vegetation in the hope that this will achieve the desired effect. In addition to the aforementioned botanical and ecological experience, a *lasting involvement* of the designer and the park manager with the management of the vegetation is often required. For the average designer this, in itself, is a highly atypical approach and requires a certain degree of restraint and even modesty which many traditional designers will find difficult to cope with. This type of process management does not allow the designer to put his own personal stamp on the design in the way he is used to. It will, rather, be a process consisting of careful, continuous and often subtle small-scale interventions at the right place and the right time, with the appropriate tools, in order to create intensely detailed and refined vegetation, a profound harmonious effect or an evocative landscape.

Interaction

In order to produce a '*heempark*' with a rich diversity of plants that offers a high degree of social experiences, human intervention is an obvious prerequisite. It is essential, however, that this intervention should not be strictly programmed and not be limited to an administrative timetable, but rather that it should be made when most appropriate to achieve the desired results. As a matter of fact there should be a subtle, almost intimate, *interaction* between the vegetation and its manager, in which the latter will apply his management techniques creatively, reacting to natural developments. Whenever valuable patterns or motifs appear, he will observe these carefully and, if possible, try to intensify them. A designer in the usual sense hardly feels an urge to engage himself as intensively and continuously in his design as the maintenance of a '*heempark*' requires. Very often he is too focused on the larger implications, the striking contours or his own particular, contemporary style for him to create his own impact on the timeless atmosphere of a '*heempark*'. After the construction phase, the images within a *heempark* actually evolve 'from within' rather than 'from the outside'. Not only is this evolution much more sedate, but it often also results in a mosaic that is spatially and visually more *implicitly interwoven* and delicately structured. It is these internal dynamics, cohesion and variety that can offer to its visitor – whose daily life typically proceeds at a terrific pace – the natural and creative breathing space his psyche needs to keep functioning adequately on a social level. Comparatively, a *heempark* provides the time and space that both nature and man require to develop their talents and qualities. Especially in the more mature and richly varied *heemparks*, this not only creates an all-encompassing aesthetic, sensory satisfaction, but it also emanates a soothing, often downright healing, effect.

Prerequisites

The realisation of a *heempark*, a naturalistic garden ('heemtuin') or any other vegetation of wild plants requires preparatory study. The first requirement is the knowledge of the plant material to be used, and the ecological conditions and environments suitable to them. In order to obtain such knowledge, one must study vegetation typology. Insight in this field can, however, only partially be gained by studying the theory of plant communities. Equally important, or more so, one needs to be thoroughly versed in ecological field-study. When developing plans for a *heemtuin* or *heempark*, one needs to start from the fact that the first stage will consist of the artificial construction of environments. This section will only deal with this subject briefly – it is described extensively in other chapters. The environments should, in principle, match the natural environments of the required vegetations or plant combinations, and thus provide a solid base for the envisaged result. During the maintenance phase, one can subsequently try to refine the vegetation by complete or partial elimination of undesirable competing plants.

Spontaneous and managed naturalism

When choosing the type of management, the manager will be led by the final results he envisages. He may thus discern between:

- vegetation with a spontaneous, self-regulating naturalism
- vegetation with a managed naturalism.

For the former, it is only the initial environment (especially the soil type), which decides the composition of the species in the vegetation. In later stages, the species themselves decide their spatial arrangement. The management type suited for these vegetations is extensive and consists of cutting and mowing, with as little influence or direction as possible on free competition between the species.

They will basically behave in the same manner as they do in nature. In the end, the environment is the dominant factor in the selection process.

In vegetation with a managed naturalism, the initial environment in itself is not the only decisive factor: the manager will be the one who decides which species are wanted and which are not. Competition between the species is greatly reduced by management practice to allow species that would otherwise be eliminated to persist. The species, only to a certain extent, decide their mutual arrangement themselves; the role of the manager also comes into play. Such vegetations will require an intensive to relatively extensive management, involving pruning and weeding.

Experience demonstrates how some species may show a different behaviour when competition is restricted or even completely eliminated. The influence of the soil type, for instance, is no longer decisive. Many species turn out to be able to survive on different soils and in different environments than they require in nature. They become less restricted to soil type and show a larger ecological amplitude. Some species, such as ferns, may also turn out to be tolerant to positions in full sun, provided that enough moisture is available, whereas they usually require shade. In fact, they are not strictly shadow-requiring, but are shadow-tolerant species. Less competition may also result in species reaching larger sizes, in width or in height, or flowering more freely with larger flowers.

This is a rather surprising phenomenon, offering equally surprising options to the manager. It implies that a purposeful management of cutting and weeding provides the opportunity to realise vegetation with much greater visual impact than shown in nature, which could otherwise not occur at all in garden or park situations. Heather and bog vegetation and woods with a matching, differentiated undergrowth, are outstanding examples of this phenomenon. The choice of management practices in such plant communities depends largely upon the specific aims one has in mind. 'Extensive' management techniques (cutting and mowing) can only be used to create and maintain meadows, roughs, and water and marsh vegetation, unless one has very specific soils at one's disposal. More intensive pruning and weeding types of management, i.e. the traditional horticultural techniques, allows one to realise many other vegetation types. And when both methods can be applied side-by-side and in combinations, with all possible shades, mixed forms and transitions, an extraordinarily rich variety and differentiation of vegetations may be achieved.

From young to old

Before having a look at the different vegetation and planting forms, it is necessary to ponder the meaning of *time* and *continuity* in *heempark* management. As soon as the soil has become available to the plants one wishes to use – i.e. immediately after groundworks have been completed and the plants have been sown or planted – the time factor comes into play. The clock of succession starts ticking immediately, independent of the construction or vegetation type. The manager cannot escape this factor and must take it into account very seriously. Many plant communities become more valuable as they grow older. It is not just the aesthetical and sensory values that increase, the ecological and natural values are also raised: 20, 30, 50 years or even longer may be required before they are at their most interesting. These types of vegetation are the result, so to speak, of a harmonious combination of evolutionary processes in combination with constant and careful human intervention across time. Of these elements, the continuity factor is decisive for the success of *heempark* management. The development and maintenance of a *heempark* is a long-term investment.

The early stages of *heemparks* are usually characterised by a fast, often spectacular, change in the vegetation. After sowing and planting, open soils are increasingly colonised by plants and reach full coverage. Shrubs may reach canopy closure after three years; ponds, lakes and canals see a rapid growth of pioneer plants; herbaceous plants produce colourful displays, especially in sunny spots, right from the start. Then, gradually, the vegetation will start to slow down in growth, environmental disturbances become less frequent and intense, and management is aimed towards reducing these as much as possible.

The first years

The annual maintenance routine consists of intensive weeding, frequent hoeing at certain spots, pruning, seed collecting and sowing, planting and replanting species, mowing as a regulatory measure, thinning and cutting back. It varies from the intensive management of vegetation with managed naturalism to the extensive management of vegetation with a spontaneous self-regulating naturalism. In other words, it varies from strict correction and regulation to global guidance and direction, in accordance with the images and effects one wishes to achieve. Recently cultivated soils in full light, with little to no competition from other individual plants, enable fast growth and change. Trees and shrubs increase in width and height, the open spots of soil becomes rarer and are increasingly covered, competition has become more intense. Meanwhile, mosses have spontaneously appeared everywhere, contributing to an increasingly naturalistic image and helping to refine the colour shades. The formation of leaf mould has commenced, soil erosion and humus formation are taking effect. The soil is developing, and under the trees and shrubs specialised species such as Wintergreen (*Pyrola)* are able to establish themselves. The first years thus display a wealth of growth and bloom, with colourful effects and abundance all around.

Youth to middle age

In this period, trees and shrubs reach maturity, and they attain their full height and width. Herbaceous vegetation has evolved into balanced compositions, combining with the tree and shrub canopy. Management will react to the changing situation, here and there species are inserted because the original ones have disappeared, or because a suitable environment for new species has come into being. Some species start decreasing in number, finally to disappear completely if suitable new growing spots are not provided. Others, such as ferns, can thrive at the same spot over a very long period and require little attention. The park manager therefore has to decide again and again what he wishes to retain and what can be let go, whether he wishes to intervene or not, and, if so, how and when exactly. This is one of the fascinating elements of the management of young and older *heemparks*. Caution, prudence and a feeling for planning in stages are essential. Instead of relying entirely on spontaneous regeneration for 'propagation', one can, in a way that is hardly noticeable to the visitor, insert different species into a spontaneous development of the vegetation. When exactly this stage is reached will usually be suggested by one's ecological intuition. In the course of time, one will keep intervening: patches may be dug over, replanted or re-sown; trees and shrubs pruned and thinned. On wet clay or peat soils, which are rich in nutrients, the woody plantings will already have reached full maturity after 30 years. On such soils they provide the layout with a mature aspect. The park has increased in age, creating new situations.

Rejuvenation

After the mould layer of organic debris under the older woods has formed and matured, all sorts of woody plants will appear spontaneously. These may be pioneers, such as alder, rowan, mespil and aronia, or species of mature woods, such as oak, ash, hawthorn, hornbeam, beech, field maple, holly, yew and ivy. Other non-indigenous species, such as crabtree, rhododendron, privet, barberry, horse chestnut and prunus species, are often imported from elsewhere. In this manner, rejuvenation is almost spontaneous. With the exception of the exotic species, which are removed when weeding, seedlings of indigenous species that fit into the image one has in mind are carefully retained. These seedlings contribute to a lively and dynamic appearance of the woodland areas. One treats these newcomers the same way one treats planted seedlings. One can, however, rarely allow the retained seedlings to over dominate the image. To avoid too great a disruption of the park's image, one will strive to replace woodland on a small scale, in stages if necessary. Depending on the situation, the herbaceous layer will be taken up and planted again on the spot. Sometimes skimming off the surface of the mould layer, containing seeds, bulbs and spores is a useful method. New young trees are then planted into this layer.

Herbaceous plants

In the old parks, the woody species exert their full influence on reducing the open, light, sunny spaces. This encourages the opportunities for woodland edge and fringe species, but diminishes the chances for the lovers of full sun and light. Their habitats decrease in size and become scarcer. All this has an influence on the flowering times and abundance within the different parts of the park. Shade inhabitants are usually spring flowering species. Under the trees and shrubs, a festive explosion of flowers and colour takes place over a relatively short period. During the rest of the year, the atmosphere is subdued and sober, shades of green and foliage and trunk shapes determine the image. The decline in the sun-loving species limits the abundance of summer flowering species, so characteristic for the younger *heemparks*. This is probably why, on the whole, visitors find the atmosphere of older parks more sedate, and far less colourful. For that reason, it is important to keep monitoring developments continuously, deliberating time and again if one has to intervene in order to maintain a balance between sun and shade vegetation. Sometimes deliberate non-intervention may be the right solution, allowing one vegetation type to gradually transform into the next. On other occasions, one will have to decide whether a more drastic intervention is called for in order not to lose too much of the park's attractive qualities.

Management practice: process direction

In the following sections the practice of detailed maintenance and management will be dealt with. A number of vegetation units are discussed:

- woody plantings, plantings with trees and shrubs and woodland planting
- herbaceous undergrowth
- open vegetations and herbaceous vegetations of open spaces
- cultivated flower fields, cultivated fields rich in flowers and annual flower fields
- meadows rich in flowers
- water and water bank vegetations
- heath and bog vegetations
- rocky substratums, rocky environments and shallow soils.

Tables 10.1 and 10.2 place these naturalistic vegetations in the context of gradients of maintenance intensity and 'naturalness'.
In order to understand and to gain insight into the maintenance of naturalistic vegetations, practical experience is required and this must be continually added to. Experience is the crucial factor. Theoretical knowledge is totally different from the experience gained in dealing with plants and vegetations. Moreover, this practical experience should cover the complete range of succession. Experience with young and middle-aged naturalistic parks is indispensable in learning to understand and to gain insight into the maintenance of older naturalistic gardens, parks and vegetations. This type of experience contains all stages and variations, it is, in a manner of speaking, a holistic instrument.

Table 10.1. Planting types with cultural and natural maintenance

Planting Category numbers	Planting categories/planting groupings
1	PLANTERS
2	BUSH ROSES
3	LAWN, MOW 26–28 TIMES
4	PERENNIALS
5	HERBACEOUS GROUND COVER
6	HAYLAWN, LAWNMEADOW
7 SHRUBS	INTENSIVE
	REGULAR
	EXTENSIVE
8 HEDGES	TRIMMING 2X PER YEAR
	TRIMMING 1X PER YEAR
9	STREET TREES
10	ANNUAL FLOWER MEADOW/–FIELD
11 GRASS-LANDS	MOWING 3X PER YEAR
	MOWING 2X PER YEAR
12 GRASSLANDS WITH FLOWERS	MOWING 2X PER YEAR
	MOWING 1X PER YEAR
13	WATERSIDE VEGETATIONS
14	INFERTILE LANDS
15	REEDLANDS
16 ROUGH WITH FLOWERS	MOWING 1X PER YEAR
	MOWING 2–5X PER YEAR
17	AQUATIC PLANT VEGETATIONS
18	SPECIMEN TREES
19 WOODLAND AREA HERBACEOUS LAYER	NORMAL
	EXTENSIVE
20	ROCKY SUBSTRATUMS
21	(SUB)SPONTANEOUS WOOD
22	SPONTANEOUS VEGETATIONS

	Range (categories 1 → 22)
A. Human intervention	← maximum — care maintenance — minimum →
B. Horticultural measures	← maximum → (TRADITIONAL ORNAMENTAL PLANTINGS; RESIDENTIAL AREA/PARKS) | ← → minimum →
C. Nature-cultural measures	MINIMAL |← ·········· |← →
D. Cultural elements	← maximal presence — minimal presence →
E. natural elements	← maximal presence — minimal presence →
F. Nature	← little — much →
Natural/ecological values	← low — high →

Table 10.2. Green management methods: the range from horticultural to natural

Planting Category numbers	1,2,7,8,9	10	3,4,5	5,6,11,12,13,14,15,16,17	18,19	20	21	22	nature
	maximal, such as:						minimal, i.e. hardly any/no action		
	irrigation	digging	intensive mowing	regular-extensive mowing	extensive weeding	extensive weeding			
	spraying hoeing	ploughing hoeing	intensive weeding	regular-extensive weeding	pruning/cutting	extensive mowing	extensive cutting		
	raking trimming					extensive cutting			
	pruning cutting fertilizing weeding covering								
	100 maximal ←						→	0 minimal	- - - - - -
	ornamental plantings ←→	← naturalistic plantings						→	nature - - - - - -
		intensive naturalistic plantings/parks effect driven/based on aesthetics				extensive naturalistic plantings			

Only a limited representation of our experiences can be given in the next few sections. Practice offers one an almost unlimited range of management options. In fact, practice is different from one moment to the next, and it is exactly this that makes it so extremely interesting. *Heempark* management always poses challenges to be inventive and creative, using all the experience, caution and patience one possesses. Tree and shrub plantings will almost always be present. At the same time, there are always options for a rich herbaceous understorey. Within these parameters, the possibilities and, consequently, the sort of images one may realise are practically unlimited.

Woody plants

As woody plants and especially trees form the backbone of a park, they always demand special attention and care. With them one maintains the defining green structure of a park or garden. Wherever possible they should be allowed to fully evolve into their own characteristic habit. This requires much space, which is not always available. Therefore, it remains necessary in many spots to apply rejuvenative pruning in order to achieve the preferred internal variation and composition.

Although woody vegetation may vary considerably, and thus may appear in many forms, they are all characterised by a forest or woodland-like image. Naturalistic woodland plantings could be categorised as comprising plantings of woody and herbaceous plants belonging to the indigenous flora, containing four to five vegetation layers:

- tree layer
- higher shrub layer, and/or
- lower shrub layer
- herbaceous layer
- moss/fungus layer.

Of the woody species, the tree-forming species are decisive for the main impact.

Woody plantings can be divided into categories with a high, average or low degree of refinement. This degree of refinement has a direct bearing on the manner in which they should be maintained. The higher the degree of refinement, the more intensive human intervention will be, implying a higher maintenance level. This is valid for both woody and herbaceous plants.

For the maintenance of woody plants one may discern:

- management during the initial phase; that is the period of planting and the following period of approximately four years
- management during the maintenance phase, that is the period following the initial phase.

Maintenance differs greatly during these two different periods.

Initial phase

Methods of management for herbaceous plants in newly planted woody plantings have often been described. Experiments have been carried out by many parties. Most of these experiments led to the conclusion that herbaceous plants can be planted in the initial phase without adverse effects on the young woody planting. Some have argued that this method is advantageous, if not in terms of the quality of the plantings at least in terms of cost. In the author's experience, however, one should not establish herbaceous plants during the construction phase of woody plantings. Contrary to allegedly positive experiences, practice shows that if one keeps the soil free of herbaceous growth during the initial phase, woody plantings will reach closure more rapidly. Herbaceous plants that were sown or introduced spontaneously will always exert a degree of competition with woody plantings. If one eliminates this competition, one allows tree plantings to grow quickly and achieve canopy closure. Another factor influencing time to canopy closure is the spacing of woody plantings. If spacing is not too wide – a minimum of 1.25 × 1.25m – the planting may reach closure as early as the third year after construction. After this, the main focus of maintenance will be on the edges, where weeds have to be removed.

The description above also makes it clear that it is very important to start construction on a clean soil that is free from weeds. If one needs to get rid of weeds on a terrain that will be planted in the future, one can do well by sowing vigorous herbaceous plant 'cover crops'. Once perennial weeds have been controlled, annuals, such as phacelia, lupins and such, will be beneficial since their dense coverage of the soil will prevent seedlings of many weed species from establishing. If, however, a decision is taken to establish herbaceous plants at the same time as trees and shrubs at planting distances greater than 1.25m, one should expect canopy closure to take six or eight years. During this prolonged period, a certain degree of maintenance will still be necessary if more competition-intolerant species are to persist. Only the woody species that are more or less resistant to competition – such as ash or field maple – can reliably hold their own against weeds such as sow thistle or bindweeds. This is especially valid on highly fertile soils. The costs involved in keeping a woody planting weed-free for three years usually match those of the longer period of maintenance involved in the latter example, whilst the quality of the result in the former is considerably higher.

Another important guideline for the initial phase is that one should start pruning early. By keeping the young planting completely free from weeds, results in quick growth. On rich soils this means that one has to start pruning at the end of the third growing season. It will mainly be limited to cutting back to the lateral shoots of a number of individuals of species that will later form part of the shrub layers. These may include hawthorn, hornbeam, field maple, oak, common maple, holly and yew. When these are cut back to laterals early on, they will start developing more strongly in a lateral direction. The prunings that are produced must, however, be removed. If they are left lying where they fell, this will make maintenance in later years more cumbersome. By the fourth year after the initial planting, one should also start thinning: full-scale maintenance pruning commences. So as to be able to develop well, every tree and shrub needs sufficient lateral growing space. By timely providing for this space, we can prevent the emergence of a planting of stakes or a forest of masts. Shrubs should not just be cut back hard, allowing re-growth after which it will reclaim its original space, but some of them should be removed completely. The space that is thus created can subsequently be filled by the remaining shrubs, allowing them to keep developing and growing in size.

In large-scale plantings – for instance, at town edges or in rural areas – one may also consider using the method of bark-ringing for thinning. It consists of locally removing a ring of bark, causing the tree to die on its trunk. Dying on the trunk has a number of advantages:

- no prunings are produced, resulting in much lower pruning costs and also because one does not incur costs for shredding and or removal
- gradual destruction of the wood that is produced, causing less disturbance
- an increase of the ecological variety – dead wood is an important environment for all kinds of plants and animals.

The method has some disadvantages as well:

- the need for careful execution; in young trees and shrubs, the bark should be removed just above the root neck, i.e. just above and below ground level, or else re-growth will occur – in older trees re-growth will not take place, even when the bark is ringed higher on the trunk
- in older, larger trees, the total decay process may take several years.

Maintenance phase

After the initial phase, a period follows in which the stand of the woody planting is very tight, and, although space is created by means of thinning and cutting back, this will, for some time, be restricted to the space needed by the trees and shrubs themselves. The trees and shrubs still have low branches, causing a very dense shade at ground level. Herbaceous plants have no chance of survival at this stage. Only years after the initial planting, when the trees and shrubs have gained height and when purposeful pruning has created more space within the woodland and more light has started to be admitted, can herbaceous plants start growing there. Purposeful maintenance pruning has thus created a variation that will be expanded in the time to come. It will be maintained throughout the complete lifecycle of the woodland planting. Slowly, an environment suitable for some species of herbaceous plants comes into being. The species of herbaceous plants best fitted to the developing woodland depends upon the habitat requirements – foremost the quantity of light – of the species to be used and the degree of refinement of the plantings. The insertion of the herbal layer, therefore, is not done at once but gradually.

Daily and periodical maintenance and overall management should be aimed at the woodland plantings *in its totality*. This management comprises the tree and shrub layers, the herbaceous layer, the moss and fungus layer, and the fauna pertaining to it. In practice, one's focus will mainly be on the management of woody and herbaceous plants. If maintenance and management are favourable to them, environments will result that enable the other elements of flora and fauna to spontaneously establish and maintain themselves and to expand. The most important maintenance measures are the pruning of woody plants and the regulation of the herbaceous layer. Although pruning has been dealt with to some degree before, some vital points need to be added. Its practical implications justify some more attention. In addition to maintenance pruning, adapted to the range of woody plants chosen and directed towards a spatial variety that is as large as possible, the frequency of pruning is also important. Thinning and cutting back are performed in the winter season. In the initial phase it is carried out once every two years and in the maintenance phase every three years. This may seem rather intensive, but it turns out that each pruning cycle involves relatively little work. In addition, the vegetation is disturbed less, and this is an important factor in creating a plant community that is well-composed, harmonious, aesthetically attractive and possesses a high quality.

If pruning is executed only once every five, six or more years, the intervention will be on a much larger scale; more work will be involved and much more prunings will be produced. The increase in light and large quantities of shredded wood all contribute to a large-scale disruption, leading to an explosion of mostly unwanted herbaceous species. Conversely, one may (in smaller planting strips) suppress the growth of unwanted herbs by enclosing its fringes to a large extent with a shrub layer. This, however, also impedes the growth of desirable herb species during the summer. In such situations, the main aspect of the herbaceous layer will consist of spring flowering plants, including bulbs and corms. If we do wish to see naturalistic herbaceous plantings at certain spots in these fringes, we will have to resort to intensive summer maintenance.

In older woodland plantings it is desirable, where possible, to leave dead wood where it is, standing after bark-ringing or lying on the ground after felling, with trunks and branches cut in pieces. This is possible where it does not conflict with existing rules and regulations (for example those associated with Dutch Elm Disease). The wood remaining in the system is very valuable to many plants and animals. As it will decay slowly, it can be completely reabsorbed by the system without causing disturbance. How far this is aesthetically acceptable will depend on the scale and the situation in which we apply this. In an older (±20 years) or mature woodland planting, a coverage percentage of 50% for the tree layer, 70% for the shrub layers and 30–90% for the herbaceous layer can result in a very attractive image. The coverage percentage of the herbaceous layer may increase with the nutrient level and the moisture content of the soil.

Wood prunings

How one should deal with wood prunings – removal to a different place or leaving it in the planting, with or without reducing its size or concentration – depends on the planting's type, character and atmosphere. In highly refined plantings, one will always remove the waste for aesthetic reasons. The rougher its character, the more wood waste one can leave on the spot. Removing organic material implies reduction of soil fertility. In the long run, the removal of wood waste may therefore exert an impoverishing influence on the vegetation. It will depend largely upon the nutrient situation of the soil and the period over which it takes place. Thus, rich soils will hardly be influenced by the removal of wood waste, as the period over which this takes place (the duration of our intervention) is too short to have any effect. Poor, dry soils, however, may undergo negative effects sooner. If desired or necessary, the wood waste may be brought back later to the spot in the shape of thoroughly composted material, applied with care on a small scale.

Leaving rough pieces of wood waste on the spot is, in most situations, less desirable for a number of practical reasons:

- it is unattractive and for this reason is unacceptable in most cases – this effect is stronger in small- as opposed to large-scale plantings
- maintenance will be bothersome if there are a lot of dead branches and twigs in the vegetation
- visitors may look at it as having an unkempt appearance, inviting illegal waste-dumping
- it may invite wood gathering for domestic fireplaces
- youthful visitors like dragging branches around.

A good alternative is shredding wood waste (the finer the shreds the better), which considerably reduces its volume: 10 m^3 wood waste = ±1 m^3 of shredded wood. Shredded wood waste can, in principle, be brought back into the vegetation from which it originated. It is only a matter of scale. If pruning has been performed with the aforementioned frequency, the quantity of shredded wood produced can be reabsorbed into the woodland planting's system without adverse effects. If, however, at a much lower pruning frequency, too much shredded material is produced, the surplus will have to be carried off, in order to prevent excessive blanketing of the surface.

When the shredded wood waste is brought back into the vegetation – often by ejecting it straight from the shredder into the planting that has just been pruned – the following points should be noted:

- the wood shreds should be applied in a thin layer (maximum 1–2 cm (0.4–0.8 inches)) and spread evenly over the total surface of the area
- the procedure must only take place during the winter season, i.e. when the vegetation is dormant – it should never be performed during the growing season! The herbaceous layer will be disturbed (e.g. through suffocation) and the visual aspect will be less attractive.

Another method for leaving wood waste in the vegetation is to concentrate it by creating branch stacks. Branches and thin trunks are stacked lengthwise in stacks that are narrow (40–50 cm (16–20 inches)) and not too high (0.8–1.0 m (2.5–3 feet)), kept together by straight branches stuck upright into the soil. Providing the vegetation's surface is not too small and the branch stacks are laid out in the aesthetically right places, using more or less curved or winding shapes, this will be a good solution for more extensive, less-refined situations. After each pruning round, the produced wood, after being somewhat shortened, is put on top of the existing stack. The lower, decaying branches in the stack can be pressed together, so as to keep the total height end width of the stack at its original size. If this method is applied with care, the necessity of carrying off wood waste will be eliminated. Branch stacks can provide elements of rest, both as cover for animals and as preventive boundaries against visitors and animals (dogs!) disturbing the vegetation.

Shredded wood from prunings may also be used to improve the soil structure (e.g. of heavy clay soils) or to encourage humus formation, thus creating better opportunities for the application of some naturalistic plantings. Application of an initial layer (15–20 cm (6–8 inches) thick) and yearly supplementary layers of 5–7 cm (2–3 inches) of wood shreds can help create a suitable humus layer.

In large woodland areas one may wish to create working paths especially for the purpose of pruning. Hauling out and shredding the produced wood waste can be performed using these paths, as well as its reintroduction into the vegetation. This may help to greatly decrease the workload. Such paths, when covered with shredded wood as a top layer, may also be made accessible to visitors.

Tree stands and composition

The variation in the composition of tree stands can be maintained by using a differentiated method of thinning, cutting back, pruning and leaving untouched. In older stands it is not always easy to keep this in hand: the older the trees, the more difficult it becomes. After trees and shrubs have reached their maximum height, growth tends to switch to an increase in width. Trunks and branches increase in girth and become heavier accordingly. On *heempark* soils with continuously high water-tables – sometimes as high as 30–35 cm below ground level – it is no less than a miracle how heavy willows, black and white poplars, ashes and oaks generally manage to stay upright. Mature specimens can become over-heavy for their habitat and may finally be toppled over by a storm. This calls for timely decisions, as they may inflict considerable damage in their immediate vicinity should this happen. These problems are far less likely to occur on soils with lower water-tables. Felling such trees is never easy on the manager; it often means having to say goodbye to beautiful old specimens, clad in mosses and lichens. It may sometimes be possible to remove a number of heavy main branches or to cut it back rigorously. In doing so one will choose shapes that may be artificial but still fit the atmosphere of the park.

Thinning and cutting back woodland trees and shrubs will remain necessary in order to keep sufficient gaps in the upper layer, providing enough light for the lower levels to grow in. This is a never-ending work, in keeping with the dynamic character of naturalistic plantings. That is why it is fiction to claim that it would be possible to reach a proper 'final image' by performing only a limited number of pruning rounds – six to seven times is sometimes mentioned. This is merely a forestry concept, based upon a permanent, static image only. Our parks and public gardens, with their limited scale, pose a problem in as far as one cannot go on thinning endlessly. This means one sometimes has to revert to artificial interventions, such as thinning the boles of hornbeam or field maple at a high level. This can be done in such a way that its effect is hardly noticeable from the ground level. Pruning trees in old parks has a similar workload to that of young and middle-aged parks. Although the total number of individuals to be thinned out or cut back decreases with age, the mass, girth and weight of the produced wood become greater, with the workload staying more or less equal. In naturalistic parks, as in other vegetations with high natural values, one notices as they get on in age how difficult it is to let plants do their own work as the scale of 'nature' in and around towns is so restricted. It is the knowledge and art of the manager that

10.2
(a) Mass flowering of Wood Anemones (*Anemone nemoralis*) in April.
(b) Summer Snowflake (Lencojum aestium) beneath birch trees.
(c) Flowering woodland edge herbaceous layer alongside a path.
(d) A wetland 'meadow' with Marsh Marigold (*Caltha Palustris*) and Primrose (*Primula vulgaris*)

a

b

c

d

allow him to exert his influence on the images and values, using larger or smaller interventions to compensate as best he can for the shortcomings caused by its small scale. He will primarily be led by the intended functions, such as the values for flora and fauna and its importance to the inhabitants, but especially by the continuity of achieving these goals.

The herbaceous layer

Herbaceous plants form a layer of their own in woodland plantings. In order to create opportunities for variety, it is desirable that:

- sufficient gaps are available within the woodland, allowing the light to reach down to ground level, with varying intensity
- the fringes of the plantings are open, in order to admit lateral light in varying intensities.

This implies that the shrub layers, both within the woodland and at its fringes, should not become fully closed. They should be managed to provide the space that is needed by the lower layers and so that it is aesthetically desirable. A method and frequency of pruning aimed towards this goal is essential in maintaining variation in woodland plantings. A changing play of light and shade is a prerequisite for a richly differentiated herbaceous layer.

Refined and intensive

In refined and intensive plantings, nursery grown herbs are planted out. This is done in a global fashion, using a design as a guide only: one plants out spontaneously and intuitively by hand. The species are planted in such a way that the planting matches the plants' natural growth patterns, that is to say, in large groups or swathes, in smaller units, a few together or as specimens. The patterns follow the images one has seen in the field or one's own ideas. A knowledge of vegetation structure, a feeling for naturalistic composition and personal creativity produce limitless variation. Choice of species, combinations and composition decide the degree of refinement, all matching the variation of the woody plants present. One always plants out in a wide to very wide spatial arrangement, never using equidistant or regular rows or symmetrical arrangements. Thus, one allows room for spontaneous evolution and differentiation.

In this manner one can obtain vegetations with a strong impact, composed of species with an abundance of conspicuously coloured flowers (e.g. *Anemone nemorosa, Corydalis solida* and *Corydalis bulbosa, Primula vulgaris* (syn. *P.acaulis*) and *Primula elatior*), as well as species with an attractive habit and foliage, or species whose aesthetic appeal lies in their ability to melt into a 'mass of green tapestries' (such as *Oxalis acetosella* combined with *Phyteuma nigrum, Arum maculatum* and *Blechnum spicant*, or *Chrysosplenium* spp. with *Primula elatior, Cardamine amara* and *Cardamine pratensis*).

Maintenance will range from very intensive for open vegetations with 'refined' species to less intensive for the more closed vegetations. Other species have their own place, from the lighter woodland fringes to the inner parts of the dark wood. The light-admitting crowns of a birch stand, supported by the fragile white trunks, combine extraordinarily well with the vivid tapestry of *Chelidonium majus* underneath. Where shade reigns during the summer, a white cover of *Asperula odorata* is perfected by the tender spring green of *Athyrium filix-femina*.

Along a forest path, single masses of *Aconitum lycoctonum* present to the visitor their pale yellow, fine flowers, with an astonishing natural generosity. Under the wood, where in spring plenty of growing opportunities exist for herbaceous plants, showing a massive bloom of *Pulmonaria, Primula* or *Viola reichenbachiana*, in summer the atmosphere is subdued and sober. Its strength now lies in species with strong foliage shapes, shades of green and variation in habit. Combinations with ferns are excellently suited to achieve this: *Blechnum, Dryopteris* spp. with *Convallaria majalis, Sanicula europaea, Maianthemum bifolium* or *Lamium maculatum*. Spots with dappled shade are the situations par excellence where filtered light, varied shades of colour and green, foliage shapes and habit contours can play a subtle game.

Woodland and water edges and fringes all offer their own opportunities for perennials. A wide variety of habitat elements that one can use meet at those points: light and shadow, moist and dry, cool and warm. They are the situations where lateral and back lighting are found in continuously changing strength and effect. *Petasites hybridus*, with its powerful habit, is very suitable for large-scale situations, it combines a spring flowering aspect with a long summer effect of great ornamental value. *Doronicum willdenowii* or *D.plantagineum*, on the other hand, are very colourful for a short period during spring, vanishing completely in summer, and, in doing so, giving space to other species such as *Campanula*.

The maintenance and management of refined, aesthetic vegetations such as these consists of weeding out spontaneously appearing, unwanted species, but, more importantly, of closely and carefully monitoring its evolution into more or less desirable forms. From this, the way to go ahead arises as by itself: leaving it alone or intervening and, in the latter case, how, when and into which direction, all depending on what one considers as desirable. The weather circumstances through the seasons and the years greatly influence these decisions, especially the quantity of rainfall and the occurrence of frost periods. Wet years, for instance, especially when a few of them occur in a row, show a dramatic increase of many species, not just through the strong growth of spontaneously germinated young plants, but also by the increased vegetative growth of existing plants as a result of greatly reduced moisture competition with woody plants. *Arum maculatum, Lamium galeobdolon, Viola* spp. and *Stellaria nemorum* are good examples. Conversely, dry years may have a positive influence upon the development of relatively drought-tolerant species. Within plantings, the compositions may now be dominated by one species, then by another, fluctuating between retraction and recovery. In this manner, *Anemone nemorosa* may dominate over *Maianthemum bifolium* in wet periods, whereas the latter will take over during very dry summers.

Suitable mixtures of indigenous species and cultivars

In certain spots a combination of indigenous vegetation in combination with horticultural cultivars may be applied. Traditional parks and public gardens, generally planted with cultivars, offer many situations to do so. Their atmosphere may lend itself perfectly to blend in with some wild-occuring indigenous species. Practical examples include: *Lamium galeobdolon* 'Florentinum' with *Campanula trachelium* and *Doronicum plantagineum*; *Onoclea sensibilis* with a cover of *Adoxa moschatellina*; *Matteucia struthiopteris* with *Convallaria majalis* or *Hyacinthoides non-scripta*. Genera such as *Primula, Vinca, Polygonatum multiflorum, Pulmonaria, Geum rivale, Asperula odorata* and *Galium sylvaticum*, ferns like *Blechnum, Polypodium vulgare* and *Dryopteris*, and many other species may effortlessly be combined with cultivars.

More rough and extensive

Woodland plantings with a rougher character and more extensive maintenance require a completely different management approach. How does one achieve an undergrowth that is rich in herbs in such plantings? The answer to this question is threefold: through spontaneous development, by deliberately inserting plants, or by using a combination of the two. When one lets nature run its course, the species appearing spontaneously will mainly be those that are characteristic for eutrophic habitats, strongly influenced by human activity and therefore common these days. Examples of this group of plants are lesser celandine, ground ivy, ground elder, cow parsley, several willowherb species and common nettle. Generally speaking, these are not the most spectacular plants. It may take a long time, if it happens at all, for species with more attractive flowers or fruits to find their way into these places spontaneously. If one wishes to achieve a more interesting vegetation rather more quickly, with high-impact naturalistic, differentiated woodland vegetations, one should resort to the insertion of the desired herbaceous species. In doing so, one can encourage natural developments, and with the right maintenance and management, many species will be able not only to assert themselves but even to proliferate. It goes without saying that the insertion of desired species should only be attempted when the habitats they require are available. In new plantings the time to start inserting plants will be ripe when, providing the woody plants have evolved favourably when the methods described above have been used, the vegetation is about eight years old. In other cases it may take longer. On the other hand, many existing and older parks are suitable for the application of herbaceous plant insertion right away.

Insertion method

The insertion of herbaceous species can be performed by either sowing or planting them. One usually sows clean seeds, but for some species freshly picked berries or seed heads with ripening seeds can be used as well. Both in sowing and in planting one should pay attention to the following points.

- Sow or plant out during the right period, for example right after seed or berry collection, in accordance with the seed's germination requirements. As a rule of thumb, one sows ripe seeds directly after collection. Many species' seeds require a certain dormancy period in the open air, germinating only when the circumstances are favourable. This applies especially to real woodland plants. Each species has its own germination period. Wet or cold periods are particularly influential: in very wet years one sees much more germination and young plants than in dry years. Vernal, spring-flowering species, such as *Corydalis cava* and *C.solida*, lords and ladies, early and common dog violet and Goldilocks buttercup, germinate solely in (early) spring, whereas cow parsley, herb Robert and rough chervil germinate both in late summer/autumn and in spring.
- After they have established themselves, it can be left to the plants themselves to proliferate and propagate.
- In small-scale situations – i.e. in gardens and parks – one often sows and plants out single species or combinations of a few species in individual spots. Besides creating a more naturalistic image, the visual and aesthetic effects are much better. Combining all species into one single mixture rules out the element of surprise. In large-scale situations. sowing one mixture may be more practical. For the more refined species, however, this is less desirable.
- Among the species that establish themselves spontaneously, there will be some that one may wish to keep. Species such as cow parsley, ground ivy or lesser celandine often do not warrant deliberate insertion.
- One should start from a preconceived plan, containing more or less detailed work routines, or leaving room for spontaneous deviation.

Maintenance during the growing season

The degree of maintenance intensity may vary from one place to the next. The main activities will consist of curtailing, pushing back or removing altogether the species that are too intrusive, thus helping to encourage the desired species. One can achieve this in a number of ways, on the understanding that maintenance as a whole may be (rather) extensive. The usual techniques, activities and work methods may be applied, sometimes adapted to the type of vegetation in question. Thus, one may sometimes have to pull out large weeds by hand and, on other occasions, cut them out with a hoe, onion hoe or spade. Particular spots may be mown with the traditional scythe or the brush cutter in order to prevent further spreading or to clean out high herbaceous plants after flowering.

A certain amount of creative 'dragging around', that is to say, sowing out, planting out and replanting, has an enriching effect: 'a little at a time, but a lot over the years'. Some examples include:

- common nettle (which is definitely not a taboo everywhere) may be kept short by cutting them once or more often per *growing* season – as such, they may be acceptable in certain places, even if they are the main aspect of the vegetation
- cow parsley, rose bay and hogweed may be mown out at certain spots immediately after flowering
- individuals of a coarse grass species, broad-leaved dock or common nettle appearing occasionally may be cut out to prevent further proliferation
- a spot where *Corydalis cava* is emerging may be protected by mowing out and thus weakening the surrounding ground elder that is threatening it
- ripening seed heads of wood ragwort, berries of lords and ladies, or seeds of rough chervil harvested on the spot may be directly sown out elsewhere in the same area or in suitable places in other areas
- large clumps of Solomon's seal, wood anemone and snowdrop may be divided and planted out in different spots.

This illustrates how maintenance has many different aspects which may be performed as part of each work cycle on a spontaneous basis, responding to the conditions as found. It is characteristic of the maintenance of naturalistic woodland plantings that tasks that present themselves in a rather random fashion.

The materials produced after cutting, mowing or weeding may be left in the area, provided that the quantities are not too large and that it does not produce viable seed. Very small quantities may be left on the spot, in other cases one can leave it in spots not covered by herbaceous plants, for example under shrubs or in slightly bare spots. It should, however, always be spread out thinly in order to encourage its decomposition. If larger quantities or more refined vegetations are concerned, carrying the material off is preferable. Fallen leaves of trees and shrubs are left on the spot. Leaves from other spots may only be applied in thin layers, just as wood shreds may be used to improve the soil structure. If, for the lack of a leaf-mould layer, it is impossible to obtain an undergrowth of herbaceous plants, one can create this layer by applying larger quantities of tree leaves over a number of years (preferably as a mixture of leaves from different species, with the exception of oak and plane).

Patience is a crucial element in achieving success with this type of management. All of one's efforts are part of a process that is characterised by its gradual course. One should not expect quick results. The gist of one's work is to 'graft' the suitable species onto an existing situation. With the aid of proper, deliberate maintenance and management, and before all the help offered by Mother Nature itself, will the plantings as a whole evolve. This takes time. Ramsons, to give but one more example, may start flowering only after a three-year period of favourable development. For these plants to provide the next generation of flowering offspring takes at least six years. Nevertheless, one may achieve a lot within a period of 10 years.

Vegetation of open (sunny) situations

Depending on the vegetation type or combinations of species, the high-impact herbaceous plantings in naturalistic parks may require more or less maintenance than woodland herbaceous communities. Changes in the soil, in mutual competition and in climate all exert their own particular influence over the years. Many species thrive during short peaks

10.3
(a) Royal Fern (*Osmunda regalis*) amongst heathland vegetation.
(b) Royal Fern and Bog Asphodel (*Nasthecium ossifragum*) in a woodland glade.
(c) Emerging Royal Fern fronds with clumps of Amenlanchier

a

b

c

and then decline, others may proliferate over large spaces and subsequently have to expand into new areas in order to maintain their population.

Variations in management

For this type of vegetation, daily care also consists mainly of removing unwanted species or intervening by allowing them to go to seed or not, or to proliferate, by planting and replanting and, last but not least, monitoring its development. Open grounds with refined species such as thyme, pinks, stonecrops, sundew, bog asphodel or *Viola calaminaria* require a lot of work. Less intensive is the maintenance of species with denser foliage and greater competition power, such as creeping jenny, bugle, yellow corydalis, meadow sage, marjoram and common rock rose. Requiring only extensive maintenance are densely leafy, vigorous species such as meadow cranesbill, common bistort, marsh marigold, purple loosestrife, crown vetch and dark mullein. In contrast to shade-tolerant field layers, which generally need little care, vegetations in full light require more maintenance. The limiting factor of shade obviously is an advantage for the park manager. When there is a shift of light-requiring species towards more shade-tolerant ones, the essence of daily maintenance changes as well. Weeding out unwanted species becomes less important, the workload shifts towards keeping in check desired plants trying to dominate the lighter, more open spaces. Lily of the valley, Solomon's seal and periwinkle have to be kept at bay in order to prevent them from pushing out the light-requiring species. The planting as a whole degenerates, foliage canopies intertwine and become less and less attractive.

Competition

Annuals and biennials such as centaury, trailing St John's wort, petrorhagia and Deptford pink require open spaces with bare soils, as they have little competitive power. It is necessary to remove *Sagina procumbens*, mosses and other low-growing species forming dense mats, in order for the former to find growing opportunities in specific spots. Scratching open the fringes of paths creates new opportunities for species such as pale St John's wort, purging flax and grass of Parnassus. By combining species of comparable competitive capacity, an acceptable balance can be maintained, making the vegetation stable for a long time. Plants with corms and rhizomes usually need to be able to move. If they are forced to stay in the same spot for long they will react by flowering less freely, and will show decreased vitality. In a flower meadow from which grasses are excluded, it is left to the competitive species to arrange themselves. The only weeding is of grasses and other species adjudged to be weeds. Great burnet, meadow cranesbill, agrimony, common ragwort, purple knapweed and ox-eye daisy may provide splendid displays with an abundance of flowers. Whenever necessary, the over-dominant species are restrained in places by surface cultivation, thus creating growing spots for other species. In this manner, one can maintain the flower meadow for many years. If, however, one does not intervene, the number of species will be reduced as a result of the dominance of one or just a few species.

Open spots with lots of light, especially those in full sun, offer many opportunities for herbaceous vegetations with many aspects. One can discern a number of main vegetation types:

- pioneer vegetation
- half-open vegetation
- closed vegetation
- woodland fringe vegetation.

The boundaries of these vegetation types, generally, are rather diffuse, with all sort of transitions and mixed forms. It is often a certain degree of interweaving that makes these communities attractive, it is a substantial element of their nature and atmosphere. Not only should the manager have a keen eye and sense for the meaning and the use of these vegetation types, he also needs to have an understanding of their evolution and progress. He needs to read, as it were, what is desirable and how he should act in the given circumstances, tuning his reactions to the development of a specific plant community. The manager also needs to be able to recognise the following stages and to act accordingly when necessary: a starting point, an optimum, continuing progress and, finally, decay.

Very refined and subtle combinations of species that are partly ground covering, partly of a more upright habit, may provide a perfect background for specimen plants such as ferns, small brooms or wild roses. A combination of early flowering *Lychnis flos-cuculi* with low-creeping plants like thyme, sedum, dianthus, Veronica – with *Pulsatilla vulgaris* or *Dactylorhiza praetermissa* as special elements – but also *Dianthus deltoides, Hypericum pulchrum* with *Arnica montana* and *Gentiana cruciata*, are a few examples. *Ajuga reptans* as a dark-green tapestry against which its own blue candles form a beautiful contrast, or *Lysimachia nummularia* in combination with the numerous blue button flowers of *Succisa pratensis*, reminding one of a swarm of insects. High-impact vegetations may also consist of species with conspicuously coloured flowers, carried in abundance – for example *Salvia verticillata* and *Helianthemum nummularium* or *Origanum vulgare*, with some solitary plants of *Verbascum nigrum.*

With more competitive species, strong effects can be obtained by using them en masse. *Polygonum bistorta, Geranium pratense, Agrimonia procera* and *Sanguisorba officinalis* are ideal for use in masses. Atmospheric effects may be obtained by bringing together species with related flower colours. Yellow and blue-purple-pink combinations provide strong contrasts. More harmonious contrasts can also be achieved, for example the yellow shades of *Hypericum perforatum, Verbascum nigrum, Senecio erucifollius* and *Genista germanica* blend into a splendid composition. The blue, purple and pink shades of *Campanula rapunculoides, Knautia arvensis, Scabiosa columbaria, Centaurea pratensis, Origanum vulgare, Coronilla varia* and *Malva moschata* have an equally splendid effect. One may increase the impact by letting the effects of the open spaces spread into the woodland verges, using, for example, *Senecio nemorensis, Aconitum lycoctonum* and *Aristolochia clematitis* for the yellow shades and *Campanula trachelium, Leonurus cardiaca* and *Malva alcea* for the blue, purple and pink shades.

Maintenance and management

Shortly after the planting of the desired species, maintenance commences. As the sown and planted species start growing, so do the unwanted species, in quite a range: *Poa annua, Cardamine hirsuta, Cerastium fontanum* spp. *vulgare, Cardamine pratensis, Epilobium* species and *Ranunculus repens* are but a few examples. As soon as they can be recognised, they are removed by weeding them out.

Weeding always causes some disturbance of the soil. One should therefore try to perform it in a manner that causes the least disturbance possible. The smaller the plants that one is weeding out, the better: this way the soil surface is least disturbed. In any case, one should take care to remove unwanted species – and unwanted individuals of desired species! – before they go to seed. This way one can make sure the workload does not get out of hand.

Meanwhile, the desired species are developing well, they are spreading out and increasingly occupying the open spaces. Their seeds will provide offspring, so as to cover all open spaces after a period of one to three years. In addition to weeding, maintenance consists of cutting and carrying off wilted and dead parts of the plants, collecting leaves that have been blown into the area, and distributing seeds of desired species at the spots one would like them to establish themselves in. One may transplant seedlings to more favourable spots and spread seeds of suitable new species that one expects to be successful. In the meantime, the vegetation starts closing and development continues. Certain species are becoming intrusive through self-seeding and strong growth, they will occupy more and more space, thus oppressing the slower or weaker species. In such cases, the hand of the manager will correct, lead and guide their development.

Whenever one needs to enter and tread on the vegetation, this needs to be done with the utmost care. It is essential to create as little disturbance and damage as possible. It follows that in rainy, wet periods it is preferable to stay out of the vegetations: treading on the soil will compact it and damage the soil structure. All maintenance activities are performed unobtrusively, making it seem to the visitor that there is no maintenance at all, as if it is all spontaneous development. In such a way one can have intact vegetation giving a strong, intense expression of naturalism. It also allows the spontaneous establishment of all kinds of mosses, their spores, leaflets and gemmae being introduced by the wind. Consistent weeding management may result in splendid moss vegetations, which create a supporting tapestry, lending a naturalistic image to the whole. In addition, it creates a favourable germination substratum for species such as orchids and helps tender species like *Wahlenbergia* to survive the winters.

On moist, often acidic soils, one may also see the spontaneous development of a plant with moss-like features: *Sagina procumbens*. In spots, it may grow into an attractive, evenly green soil-cover. Only where it becomes too thick, tending to suffocate everything else, should one keep it at bay.

Where the examples mentioned previously concern perennials only, one can also use vegetation composed of annuals and biennials to great effect. *Ornopordon acanthium* and *Isatis tinctoria, Melilotus species, Oenothera* species, *Reseda luteola, Echium vulgare, Verbascum* species, *Dipsacus sylvestris, Arctium tomentosum, Centaurea cyanus, Agrostemma githago* and *Papaver* species are some examples. They often have a ruderal character and require a relatively rich, sunny and dry, preferably calcicolous, habitat. Besides the weeding out of unwanted species, its management consists of keeping the soil open by intermittent digging, disturbing and, when necessary, additional sowing. Each species is sown on the 'spot of its own' that one has determined beforehand. In a later phase, when it has started self-seeding, one can, if one wishes, let more naturalistic patterns and compositions take shape. The guiding hand of the manager, here restraining and there stimulating developments, is the invisible means of control. In this manner, one can avoid the over-domination of strong over weak species, resulting in a more exciting vegetation.

Dead flower stalks and seed heads are left alone wherever possible. On one hand, they offer food and cover to many animals: goldfinch, linnet and greenfinch will eat the seeds of *Tragopogon pratensis* and *T.porrifolius, Dipsacus sylvestris, Carduus nutans* and *Arctium lappa*. The hardened dry stems offer hibernation and pupation places to many insects. This way these animals can be attracted into gardens and parks. On the other hand, dead plants can be very ornamental, especially when covered with snow or frost. In spring, all of the decayed parts of the plants are cut off and cleared away. During the same work rounds, blown-in leaves and such are removed. If one does not do so, the formation of humus is encouraged, leading to rougher vegetations, and decreasing the aesthetic quality.

Woodland edge and fringe species constitute the harmonious transitions between open and closed spaces, between sunny spots and woods. These transitions of light and shadow offer spaces to many plant species, for example: *Agrimonia procera, Aquilegia vulgaris, Digitalis purpurea, Vincetoxicum hirundinaria, Galium cruciata* and *G. sylvaticum, Geranium phaeum, Lathyrus sylvestris, Euphorbia amygdaloides, Campanula persicifolia, Geum rivale, Polygonatum multiflorum* and several fern species. Some other species are best used singly or with a few grouped together, sometimes in narrow ribbons or small groups. They may be used to create special accents, provide depth or place a few 'pearls' in the open field. A few examples are *Euphorbia palustris,*

Asparagus officinalis, Parietaria officinalis, Cirsium oleraceum and *Osmunda regalis*.

Annual plant communities associated with cereal fields

Most agricultural weeds germinate and thrive on bare or open soils. They are the species of disturbance habitats and real pioneers. As a result they can not survive in vegetations composed of perennials. As a rule they require relatively rich, (moderately) dry and warm soils. If one can provide these conditions, many species are available for application in urban gardens and parks. One must start, however, with a soil that is free from persistent unwanted weeds. These are usually biennials or perennials, such as *Tussilago farfara, Polygonum amphibium* (land form), *Elymus repens* and *Cirsium arvense*. It may be necessary not to start sowing the desired species in the first year, but to take this period to cultivate the plot repeatedly until it is thoroughly cleaned of unwanted weeds.

Although the desired species used to occur in fields with agricultural crops, such as cereals, they are not restricted to these. Therefore, it is not necessary to sow the crops as well. It is not so much the presence of the cultivated crop as the disturbance habitat the field presents that provides the precondition for their survival. Depending on what one wishes to achieve, one can, of course, sow the cereals as well; species like rye can be very beautiful and, for educational purposes, it is often indispensable. If one chooses to do so, a quantity of 40–50 kg/ha will suffice.

Sowing is done by hand, in a wide sweeping motion. Mixing the fine seeds with sand helps to distribute them more evenly over the sowing area. The required seed quantity is determined by the size of the plot. Larger plots require less seed per square metre than smaller ones, where low density is less visually acceptable. Another important factor is seed size: *Papaver* has very fine seeds, whilst *Agrostemma* has coarse and heavy seeds. As a general rule, one requires 1–3 g/m^2. After sowing the seeds they must be lightly worked into the soil with a rake or harrow, depending on the plot size. Subsequently, the soil is slightly compacted using treading boards or a roller.

One has the choice of either composing a seed mixture of different species, or sowing each species separately. This way one can create all sorts of compositions, for aesthetic or agricultural-historical or ecological reasons. If one prefers an aesthetic starting point, one could use, for example, *Papaver rhoeas* with *Matricaria recutita*, *Papaver rhoeas* with *Chrysanthemum segetum* or both combined with *Centaurea cyanus*, *Chrysanthemum segetum* with *Delphinium consolida*, or all species put together with *Agrostemma githago*. *Vaccaria pyramidata* is, especially in warm dry springs, a fast germinating and growing species whose flowering period usually precedes that of other species. By sowing a slightly larger quantity of this species, one obtains an early peak of flowering, followed by a second one when the other species are flowering.

Most species can be sown in spring, from the beginning of March until the end of May. March is preferable, since germination is less successful in later periods due to cold and dry spells caused by the April north winds. The seeds of unwanted species already present in the soil are less susceptible to these climatic disadvantages and thus get a head start on the others, causing aesthetically less acceptable results. Some species germinate better after an autumn sowing, for example *Legousia speculum-veneris* and *L.hybrida, Ranunculus arvensis, Galeopsis segetum* and *G.speciosa*, and *Scandix pecten-veneris*. If winter cereals are included, one obviously has to sow in autumn. The best way to go about this is to finish sowing before the middle of October. The grains must have germinated before the first frost arrives. Spring sowing is generally preferable for soils containing a lot of weeds. Since they germinate early, one can remove them by working the soil over before sowing the desired species.

Sowing each year or not?

Although one would expect species to develop and maintain themselves through self-seeding – when after a few years a sufficient seed reserve has been built up in the soil – practice shows us that one will need to sow additional seeds every year. On moist soils, some of the species in the composition one has sown turn out to start dominating through self-seeding. Other, less vigorous species will, as a result, decrease in numbers and may disappear completely. In this manner, one may, in the end, be left with only a few or even just one or two species. This is the case on highly fertile cultivated soils where, for instance, *Papaver rhoeas* and *Matricaria maritima* may gain the upper hand at the detriment of other species.

The more the soil type matches the type on which the species thrive under natural circumstances, the better the results of self-seeding. Generally, this is not the case. It is therefore preferable to apply additional sowings each year. One may reduce the quantity of seed sown initially, 0.5 g/m^2 will usually suffice. In addition, one may try to intervene in such a way that the desired species persist. After sowing, basically no maintenance is necessary until after flowering. Yet it may be wise to weed out obnoxious unwanted species as long as one can do so without visibly disturbing the vegetation. Aesthetically speaking, the results will be greatly improved. After the *main* flowering period is over, the flower field is mown. On soils susceptible to weed invasions, one should not wait with mowing until the last flower has faded, for one really needs to start battling the unwanted species in time. If one prefers to do so, one may leave the mown-off plants for a number of days, thus allowing the seeds to ripen and fall out. After carrying off the hay, the soil is worked over at a shallow depth, which is called 'stubbling' (working on the stubble, i.e. the remaining parts of the stem base), with the aid of hoe, onion hoe, hand cultivator or disk harrow, depending on the size of the plot. This technique is very important in battling the unwanted species; they are removed and do not get a chance for re-growth. It must be repeated as often as the plot starts 'greening'. One keeps repeating this until the plot is sown again. Obviously, during these activities and during the soil cultivation prior to sowing, one cannot avoid removing the seedlings of the desired species as well, unfortunate as it may be.

Maintenance generally mirrors traditional agricultural techniques; ploughing, harrowing, sowing, harrowing in and rolling the field in autumn or spring. On smaller plots, ploughing becomes digging, harrowing becomes raking, etcetera. All of the aforementioned activities are repeated each year.

Older flower fields may suffer from the development of noxious perennial weeds such as *Equisetum arvense*. Cultivation (i.e. removing their rhizomes completely) may be possible in small-scale situations. In larger plots, a year of letting it lie fallow, combined with repeated mechanical activity (hoeing, harrowing) may give good results. Biological measures, such as crop rotation with higher and denser crops over a period of some years, for example with *Phacelia*, may be effective as well. But as a rule, older flower fields are rather difficult to keep free from unwanted weeds, giving them a disturbed and less free-flowering aspect. Incidentally, one may prevent situations of too low soil fertility by spreading a bit of old manure or fresh soil.

Perennial meadows

After the preparation of the desired habitat (a subject dealt with elsewhere in this book) and planting and/or sowing, a period of waiting patiently and monitoring the coming developments starts. Slowly and gradually, the vegetation develops; as a rule, the more gradual it is, the better the results, typically due to the reduced influence of vigorous weedy competitors. The difference between poor and rich soils is visible immediately. Slow development with few germinating weeds is an indicator of poor soils. An explosion of seedlings on the other hand tells of richer soil conditions. In a poor, dry situation with a clean initial soil condition, few species will be obvious at first. The pioneers will generally consist of common species: *Poa annua, Cardamine hirsuta, Stellaria media, Chenopodium* and *Atriplex species, Lamium purpureum, Polygonum aviculare, Matricaria recutita* and *M.maritima*, to mention a few. Gradually, their part is taken over by perennial species, such as *Cirsium arvense, Rumex obtusifolius* and *R.crispus, Poa pratensis* and *P.trivialis, Plantago major* and *Trifolium pratense*. In wet situations, *Ranunculus repens, Alopecurus geniculatus, Typha latifolia* and *Juncus effusus* are counted among them. They all are characteristic species for pioneer and disturbance situations. Such vegetation during the first few years looks rather rough and shows little flowering. Patience is the word, one just has to sit it out. It is a phase that may sometimes take years, and it is part of the natural succession. By and by the rougher species make place for the more refined, more free-flowering ones. This is how a flower meadow evolves.

If one does not wish, or is not able, to wait for natural evolution to run its course, since it usually does not offer much in the way of rich species variety, one may additionally sow a mixture of flower seeds (with or without grass species mixed in) and plant out some other species. One can do this as soon as the initial groundwork is finished, and when weather conditions are favourable for germination and establishment. This method gives quicker results and, particularly when one also applies certain maintenance measures, the rough pioneer phase may be avoided. A slightly different pattern of succession during the first years will be the result. At first the field weeds appear, immediately followed by the biennials, such as *Berteroa incana, Dianthus armeria, Echium vulgare* and *Isatis tinctoria*. One cannot use these species on wet soils, they can be replaced by quick flowering species, such as *Lychnis flos-cuculi* and *Aster tripolium*. Soon after, the first perennial species will appear: *Geranium pratense, Dactylorhiza praetermissa, Cirsium dissectum, Anthyllis vulneraria, Astragalus glycyphyllos, Silene vulgaris, Hypericum perforatum, Prunella vulgaris, Centaurea pratensis* and *Galium mollugo* are some arbitrary examples. With spring sowing on poor soil there will generally be a thin, very open vegetation by the end of the first year. Mowing may sometimes not be required at this stage. Yet it is wise to start removing anything that should be removed. The next year, an increasing number of species will start to germinate, among which are the seeds produced during the first year. The vegetation gradually closes, the turf becomes more dense and the pioneers disappear.

Maintenance

However important it may be to start off with the right habitat, for the development and preservation of the desired vegetation appropriate maintenance and management methods are just as essential. The crucial point in the maintenance of flower meadows is mowing and carrying off the hay that is produced. This is absolutely vital not only to preserve the flower meadow, but also to keep it in good condition. A tight mowing schedule is important, especially to restrict the chances of unwanted species. If hay is left on the ground where cut, it does not only make the soil richer but it causes gaps to appear in the vegetation. If, during the pioneer phase, the less attractive, coarse species, which are unattractive especially in small-scale situations, are kept at bay by weeding, one will achieve a visually more refined or stable aspect sooner. This requires slightly more intensive maintenance, but this is balanced by the fact that the less attractive initial phase is less obvious. A number of species deserve special attention, since they may expand rapidly after they have established themselves, and may subsequently dominate for years. These include: *Equisetum* species, *Sonchus arvensis, Cirsium arvense,*

Polygonum amphibium (land form), *Elymus repens, Glyceria maxima, Tussilago farfara, Rumex obtusifolius* and *R.crispus*. As soon as they start establishing themselves – and therefore are still small in size and numbers – the best method is to remove them root and all, after which one stamps the soil down again. At this stage it is still a relatively easy job to remove them and, in doing so, one can prevent a situation that may be unattractive for years. Species of disturbed situations such as these will rarely establish themselves in older meadows where the turf is closed.

As a rule, mowing should take place once or twice a year. If the development of the vegetation indicates that mowing twice is not sufficient – the vegetation is very lush and high (70–120 cm (2–4 feet)) during the whole growing season, the grass species are mainly the coarser types and the vegetation falls over quickly – then one will have to revert to mowing three times a year: in the middle of May, the end of June and in September. In such cases, the soil is very rich, usually producing great quantities of biomass, and, in all probability, is not very well suited on which to develop a flower meadow.

Raking and carrying off

On larger plots one may use a 'raking machine' to rake the grass into stacks. Smaller raking machines may be coupled onto two-wheeled tractors, for the larger ones one needs to use a four-wheel tractor. The raking machine should be adjusted in such a way that it does not rake the soil open and damage the sod. It is possible, however, to adjust the raking machine to such a height that it rakes out the moss layers from moss-covered turf, creating new spots for desired species to establish themselves. Specific, small-scale disturbances of the sod must be created from time to time in order to present opportunities for the recruitment of existing and new species. Collecting and carrying off can be done mechanically if the soil can carry the machine's weight, as a powerful heavy tractor is required. These methods can therefore only be applied without causing damage under dry conditions. The likely type of damage is the formation of tracks, but also damage to plant buds and rosettes. On wet and peaty soil, heavy equipment will always result in the deterioration of the soil structure, both internal and superficial. The formation of tracks will make mowing and carrying off increasingly harder through the years. Manually performed maintenance work will always give the best results where this is economically feasible.

Making the turf less fertile

By spreading sand one can make a soil less fertile. In the winter period a small quantity of sand, i.e. 1–3 m^3 per 1,000 m^2, is sprinkled over the meadow, very finely distributed, creating a thin film of sand on its surface. After a few years of doing so, the sod will become less fertile. If this method is consistently applied, a very poor turf may be created, with a relatively open sod. Moderately rich to richer soils may thus be made less fertile without creating disturbances. It also makes the turf more able to be trafficked when wet, which is advantageous for maintenance work.

Manuring

On poor soils, where older meadows have been maintained for a long time with the methods for making the turf less fertile, a point may be reached when the fertility becomes so low as to result in less free-flowering vegetation. Uncommon and even rare species with less conspicuous flowers enter the scene. On wet peaty soils, for instance, one will see an increase of *Agrostis canina, Viola palustris, Ranunculus flammula* and *Carex nigra*, which will start to form the main aspect. This will be at the expense of *Lychnis flos-cuculi, Succisa pratensis, Ranunculus acris, Centaurea jacea, Lotus uliginosus, Briza media, Anthoxanthum odoratum* and *Rhinanthus angustifolius*. Although this shift may be very interesting in a botanical sense, leading up to the development of unusual vegetation of high ecological or curiosity value, the manager has to take other aspects into account as well. Public green space is there for the public and should therefore be attractive, especially in residential areas. At the same time, the natural values being as high as possible are appreciated. A differentiated type of management may be the solution here. If the free-flowering aspect diminishes, it is time to reduce the measures taken to decrease fertility, and it may even be necessary to start fertilisation. It may sound strange to vegetation experts, yet this is nothing new, farmers used to do this all the time. Since one is striving for differentiation, one will manure carefully chosen spots, at the same time refraining from manuring other spots that have been chosen with the same carefulness. The method of manuring should have a limited effect, adding only a small quantity of fertilising material. A good method is the application of mud from an adjacent pond or ditch. This is applied in a thin layer, allowing the plants to push through easily. The layer should be a few centimetres thick, measured when wet and applied before winter. In many cases, however, one will use well-decomposed farmyard manure. The quantity to be applied depends on the local situation, but one should stay on the safe side and start with a small dose, 0.25–0.5 m^3 per 100 m^2. The manure is thoroughly shaken loose and distributed over the selected spots as evenly as possible.

Manuring may be repeated periodically, for example once every few years. The vegetation will indicate when it is required. That is why one should monitor the results closely in order to be able to plan the next step deliberately: continuing manuring or not, finding the right dose and the correct frequency. There may be other circumstances inducing one to increase mowing frequency, for example in the case of flowery road verges. Exhaust fumes, litter and water 'spray' from the road may contribute to soil fertility considerably. Even on poor soils the quantity of nutrients available to the vegetation may reach such levels as to increase biomass production. This may lead one to bring the moment of mowing forward or even to increase its frequency. The November to December mowing round is brought forward to September, causing a greater reduction of soil fertility. Alternatively, one may change the single mowing round in September to two, one in July and one in October.

Development and change in the vegetation

The longer one monitors flower meadows, the more one will notice that species composition as well as vegetation patterns and composition are not static, but are in constant change. These changes do not occur abruptly but very gradually. It is one of the fascinating aspects of flower meadows.

One determining factor is climate. A very dry hot summer, for instance, may defoliate or occasionally even kill species in the sod and create open spots. Drought-resistant species will keep on flowering longest, for example *Silene vulgaris, Centaurea scabiosa, Malva moschata* and *Hypericum perforatum* will contrast strongly with the yellow-brown 'burnt' grasses. Others may not survive the drought and disappear as a plant but persist as a soil seed bank. Moist and wet summers not only encourage the development of grasses but also encourage the proliferation of flowering plants. Species like *Veronica austriaca* spp. *teucrium, Saxifraga granulata, Stachys officinalis, Agrimonia eupatoria, Polygonum bistorta* and *Geranium pratense* will seed themselves prolifically if there are a few wet summers in a row. *Lathyrus tuberosus* may proliferate along road verges.

The open spots in the vegetation caused by dry years will be colonised by other species, immediately after droughts by annuals – for example the well-known poppy-effect of dikes and road verges – later followed by perennials. A year after a drought period, wet meadows may suddenly be massively invaded by *Juncus conglomeratus* as an indicator of recent disturbance. Continuous shifts and changes in species composition are thus occurring, although causes are not always known. Animals may exert a

10.4
(a) Those areas where there is a heathland vegetation develop into a mosaic of different foliage colours and textures with purple Marsh Orchid (Dactylorhiza majalis) emerging through dwarf shrubs
(b) a heathland glade amongst oak woodland
(c) Lady's Smock (Cardamine pratensis) makes a dramatic display in this spring meadow alongside a canal

a

b

c

considerable influence, for example mice love to eat starchy rhizomes, bulbs and corms (*Crocus tommasinianus*, *Dactylorhiza* and *Orchis* species).

One aspect of managing flower meadows is to continuously ensure the availability of sufficient colonisation spots for plants. Natural causes have been discussed above, and human intervention can add some more. Some of these opportunities may be created involuntarily: slight, local damages to the sod caused by mowing, raking off hay and the like, offer new opportunities for plants to colonise. Light and very shallow tracks and scratches caused by the raking machine are examples of a mechanical nature. Translated into small-scale activities, it means that it is not a bad thing if every now and then the scythe is cutting through or under the sod when mowing. The local removal of less attractive species or spots through digging up or cutting the sod may have the same effect.

Flower meadows frequently require one's attention, the more so if one has the impression that a situation is ready for the introduction of specific species. One may try to speed up the process by sowing some seed of the species. This is a good method for introducing *Saxifraga granulata, Orchis species, Fritillaria meleagris* and even rarities like *Carum verticillatum* into the meadow. Planting out one or a few individuals of a species may work equally well. If one's intuition was right they will proliferate by themselves. Conversely, one may remove unwanted species appearing spontaneously by cutting them out completely or just below the soil surface as soon as they are noticed. One should always take care to cause as little damage to the sod as possible. By using such a method of 'guidance in the background', a very refined, harmonious and valuable flower meadow may evolve through the years.

Improving the flowering of existing meadows

If the soil condition lends itself to the purpose, existing meadows that are poor in species of flowering plants may be converted into more diverse ones without having to revert to intensive groundwork. The presence of a habitat suitable for desired species may be obscured but may be available nevertheless. The conditions may be changed by simply adjusting mowing frequencies and schedules. How exactly it should be adjusted depends on the situation itself. When the potential and the mowing regime are in tune, one can achieve amazing results within a relatively short period of time. In this manner, many meadows situated on poor sand, loam and silt soils can, within a few years, be transformed into real flower treasuries. *Hieracium* species, *Linaria vulgaris, Torilis japonica, Veronica chamaedrys, Tanacetum vulgare, Leucanthemum vulgare, Achillea millefolium, Campanula rotundifolia, Jasione montana* and *Sedum telephium* are examples of species with conspicuous flowers that may spontaneously (re)appear in potentially suitable habitats in the Netherlands.

Sowing hemi-parasites of the genus *Rhinanthus* on grasses offers different opportunities, as practical experience with *Rhinanthus angustifolius* shows. Once it has established itself, its development may be quite spectacular. Its massive appearance may strongly inhibit grasses in their growth, creating opportunities for different forbs to increase or appear. Even tall vigorous grass species, such as *Glyceria maxima* are subdued. One can profit from this effect by introducing specific desired species in weakened, more accessible spots through sowing, for example *Geranium pratense, Centaurea jacea, Dactylorhiza praetermissa, Primula vulgaris* (and *P. elatior*).

By mowing once or twice a year at the right moments only, using additional measures as described above, one can further increase species diversity and flowering display. It must, however, be made clear that *sowing and planting out in really rich meadows is completely useless.* The vegetation is too dense and too high to allow attractive species to develop. Seed sown in it will not germinate or the seedlings will soon perish. Planted out species suffer the same fate.

Spring meadow and hay lawn

The main flowering period of this type of meadow is April to May, after which little flowering is seen. Such meadows are mown shortly after flowering (end of May/early June), then again once or several times during summer. This way, one obtains a meadow that is free flowering in spring and a short-trimmed meadow or lawn in summer, which may be used for recreation without the vegetation being adversely influenced. It is therefore very suitable for application around housing or in smaller gardens. This method may also be applied to larger meadows. A spring meadow contains common species such as *Cardamine pratensis, Bellis perennis, Veronica filiformis* and *V.serpyllifolia, Taraxacum officinale, Cerastium arvense, Geranium molle* and *Luzula campestris*, but could equally accommodate species like *Veronica chamaedrys, Leucanthemum vulgare, Primula vulgaris* and *P.elatior*. It may also be suitable for bulbs and corms, such as *Galanthus nivalis, Crocus tommasinianus, Tulipa sylvestris, Corydalis bulbosa, C.cava, Narcisssus pseudonarcissus* spp. *pseudonarcissus, N.obvallaris* or *N.lobularis*. Mowing can commence when the foliage of bulbs and corms has begun to die back in late May, early June. Throughout the rest of the year the grass may be kept short. One may use the lawnmower to do this, setting the mowing height no lower than 4 cm. Depending on the extent to which the meadow is used, one may use more sensitive species, for example *Ajuga reptans, Fritillaria meleagris, Corydalis bulbosa* and *C.solida* and *Prunella vulgaris*. Under favourable conditions they may be self-seeding.

Flower meadows without grasses

A flower meadow without grasses might be regarded as a semi-natural wildflower border. With this type of meadow, the restrictions posed by highly fertile soils are greatly reduced, since species with a great competitive power, such as grasses (and also potentially dominat forbs such as *Rumex* species, and *Taraxacum officinale*), are removed by weeding. It is the method for obtaining and preserving a refined impact. The desired species mingle freely. *Geranium pratense, Centaurea jacea, Sanguisorba officinalis, Leucanthemum vulgare, Agrimonia eupatoria, Senecio jacobaea, S.erucifolius* and *S.aquaticus, Succisa pratensis, Stachys officinalis, Knautia arvensis, Scabiosa columbaria* and many others among the finest indigenous flowering plants can thus be combined in a high-impact flower meadow. Groupings of bulbs and corms may provide an attractive spring effect: *Crocus tommasinianus* and *C.vernus, Narcissus pseudonarcissus, Fritillaria meleagris, Ornithogalum nutans, Gagea pratensis* and *Leucojum aestivum*. The meadow is mown once during the summer, after the seed has set, and once more in autumn. It is weeded in early spring, shortly after mowing. In the course of time the more competitive species, for example *Sanguisorba officinalis, Campanula rapunculoides* or *Centaurea nigra*, may gain the upper hand and start pushing out other species. By digging over in spots and sowing or planting again, variety can be preserved. Maintained in this manner, such flower meadows, which lie outside the typical composition of semi-natural meadows, can be maintained for a relatively long period of time.

Vegetation of water and water margins

Aquatic vegetation types vary with the water type and quality. Generally speaking, they will do well in young parks where there are many opportunities, with new water conditions and usually a good water quality. During the first few years its development may be spectacular but, as the park ages, restrictions on water plants will often arise.

Unfavourable influences

Many people are familiar with the rich young vegetation of *Ceratophyllum, Elodea, Potamogeton,*

Nymphoides peltata, Butomus umbellatus, Scirpus and *Typha*. In the long run, they are strongly reduced by increasing shade on the water, degradation of banks through erosion, increasing quantities of mud, strong development of thread algae caused by eutrophic water, and a generally decreasing water quality. As the park grows older, one is confronted with these developments. *Nymphoides peltata* will no longer grow in muddy water bottoms. Embankments with *Caltha palustris* and *Senecio paludosus* that are in decline, as a result of increasing shade, may be replaced with more shade-tolerant species, such as *Filipendula ulmaria, Angelica sylvestris* and *Lysimachia vulgaris*.

By reconstructing shallow banks using underwater reinforcements, one may create new opportunities. Generally speaking, the bottom of water bodies are held together by the roots of emergent species such as *Typha, Butomus* and *Phragmites*. Where they are not present, the bottom of water bodies erode, with shallow spots becoming deeper again. One can raise them with mud produced by erosion and decayed waterplants from elsewhere in the park. The phenomena of now rich and then poor years of *Lemna, Spirodella* and *Azolla*, the increase or decrease of species such as *Ranunculus, Nymphaea* and *Nuphar* are hard to explain. They may be connected to climatic factors, which seem to influence water habitats more strongly than others.

A subtle balance

Yearly maintenance activities, such as the removal of thread algae, *Lemna* and detritus, in addition to periodical dredging, keep ponds and waterways and their vegetations in reasonable shape. One must, however, be very careful. Reducing vigorous, abundant populations of *Stratiotes aloides, Menyanthes trifoliata, Calla palustris* or *Potentilla palustris* may cause a sudden decrease in vitality or even their complete disappearance. The subtle balance of such vegetation appears to be easily disrupted. A gradual development and seemingly unrestrained proliferation over a period of years may deflate when it is interfered with unwisely, never to regain its previous vigour.

Banks and pond edges

Banks and pond edges are the preferred sites for species of moist and wet soils. Many marsh and bank plants are among the most beautiful and free-flowering of the wild flora: *Caltha palustris, Leucojum aestivum, Iris pseudacorus, Filipendula ulmaria* and *Lythrum salicaria* create spectacular combinations, as do *Valeriana officinalis, Euphorbia palustris, Osmunda regalis, Senecio paludosus* and *S.fluviatilis,* and *Eupatorium cannabinum*. Whether planted as individual species or in combinations, they offer many opportunities. In very wet soil or shallow water (i.e. with waterlevels up to 10cm, or with the water table up to 30cm below soil level), one may create transitional vegetation between land and water. Species such as *Caltha palustris, Veronica beccabunga, Calla palustris, Thelyptera palustris* and *Potentilla palustris* are excellently suited for this purpose. Additional species include *Alisma plantago-aquatica* and *A.lanceolata*, *Gratiola officinalis* and *Myosotis palustris*. The latter should be used with caution, since it may spread quickly through seeding and the rooting of loose stems. *Galium palustre* and *G.uliginosum*, with their lacey, romantic flowers, may lend a very nice, airy effect to marsh vegetations, but one should take care! They do not look like it, but they may grow rampant, self-seeding profusely and their roots, thin as gossamer, colonising mosses and all other kinds of other plants. Once they have thus established themselves, they become almost impossible to restrain or weed out. The fine roots break off easily, making it easy for the plants to regrow into flowering, seeding plants. Rampant growth is the reason for caution in the use of species like *Mentha* and *Scutellaria galericulata* as well. If one can provide them with a spot of their own – where they may proliferate without causing trouble – they may certainly be applied. If not, one does better to apply it only in vegetation subjected to a mowing regime.

Maintenance

Maintenance of the more subtle, highly detailed marsh vegetations is none too easy. Unwanted species are weeded out. Depending on the soil, more or fewer weeds will come up. Peat soils always have an abundant weed seed bank, ranging from *Typha* to *Salix*. In order to reduce disturbance, the unwanted species are weeded when they are still small. This implies having to make frequent weeding rounds – approximately once per three to four weeks. Since wet soils are very susceptible to damage by trampling, one has to use boards, 20 × 30 cm, tied underneath one's boots to spread your weight. They can be useful in shallow water as well. Another option is to work standing on long boards resting on supports, which are moved when one moves on to the next spot. Plants are not cut in autumn, the dead foliage and stems are removed in spring.

Marsh vegetations in shallow water may develop fast and reach their climax in a few years. Fast development often means early decay. The frequent cutting back of vigorous species in favour of slower ones, or taking the vegetation up completely and planting back young parts, may help to preserve it for many years. In contrast, other species may occupy the same spots without requiring substantial (rejuvenating) maintenance, for example *Calla palustris, Menyanthes trifoliata* or *Acorus calamus*. In rougher, more extensive vegetation – where one allows or encourages the growth of grasses, sedges and rushes – a mowing regime is applied. Mowing once or twice a year during summer and/or autumn is usually sufficient. In addition, one may sometimes wish to remove spontaneously appearing species that are considered too rough. Such vegetation are, for practical and sometimes aesthetic reasons, best combined with wet meadows. They may offer desirable transitions to reedland and real water plants.

Water birds and fish

Both water birds – such as coots, ducks, geese and swans – and fish have a negative influence on water and marsh plants. This does not mean that a single *Carp* (*Cyprinus carpio*) does any harm, but larger numbers may stir up the bottom to such an extent that vegetation cannot develop or existing valuable ones are destroyed. Owing to its strong 'grazing' and fertilising capacities, the grass carp (*Ctenopharyngodon idella*) should be completely banned. Indigenous fish species – excepting bream (*Abramis brama*) and carp – should not pose any problem.

Coots, ducks, geese and swans can cause real destruction. In small-scale situations they should not be encouraged. Coots (*Fulica atra*) will create problems even in small numbers. They manage to destroy older and deep-rooting white water lilies (*Nymphaea alba*) and yellow water lilies (*Nuphar luteum*) within a few years. The plants often do not succeed in rejuvenation by seeding, as erosion has often made the shallow banks they require for germination too deep. Chasing the coots away generally is of no use, since the water body will immediately be filled by other individuals from the too often overcrowded populations in urban areas. As with most noxious animals, the presence of coots has a positive side as well. They keep their territories free from wild city mallards who spend their days sleeping and defaecating on the banks, causing damage with their highly saline manure. Where flower meadows border on banks, the fertilising effect is serious but other vegetations may be influenced as well. Ericaceae and species such as *Thelypteris palustris, Cochlearia* spp. or *Caltha palustris* may suffer severely.

Reedlands

One of the best-known marsh vegetations is reedland. In shallow (20–60 cm) water and on rich soils, reed (*Phragmites australis*) may provide simple but very characteristic and, on a larger scale, attractive vegetation with its own atmosphere and beauty. Creating a suitable habitat for reed is done as follows: the soil is dug down until, or slightly under, the water table. On bare soil one does best to plant out reed cuttings. Since reed germinates under special conditions only – for example in wet, muddy situations on soils that have gone dry shortly before, in spring or summer – and as one usually cannot meet these requirements, planting out cuttings is the most successful approach. The best time for planting reed is the first half of May, as it likes the heat, therefore being a slow-starter, with two to five cuttings per m^2. It is also possible to plant reed on reclaimed land. In water that is too deep for reed to grow in, one delineates the future border of the reedland with poles, laying it out in a naturalistic shape; the distance between the poles is approximately 50 cm and the heads are at the summer water level. This area is then filled with tree prunings in such a manner that a more or less passable floor is created. One may well use bundles of branches, packed tightly and weighed down with thicker pieces of trunks and branches, reaching up to the water level or just under it. As an occlusive layer, which should prevent the next layer of mud or soil to run off, one tops this off with a layer of finer material, such as heather, bracken, old reed stem cuttings or course mown material, hay etc., to a thickness of 10 cm. A layer of 15–20 cm of mud is the last layer to be applied. Owing to its weight and the compression of the lower layers, it will, in the end, be at about water level. After the mud layer has solidified, one can plant out the reed cuttings at the beginning of May. In order not to trample the mud, one uses treading boards. This is also a suitable situation for sowing reed seed that was collected in the previous winter months. For seeding to be successful, one should make sure that the mud does not dry out. In order to obtain a more naturalistic reedland border, one may also plant out typical species such as *Carex pseudocyparis, C.riparia* and *C.paniculata, Iris pseudacorus, Cicuta virosa* and so on. In the course of time, other species will find their way into this vegetation, for example *Epilobium hirsutum, Typha angustifolia, Stachys palustris, Sium angustifolium* and *S.latifolium*.

Maintenance

Reed vegetations growing in water do not require yearly mowing in order to remain in good shape. Especially in deeper water, they may survive for a long time without human intervention. Its charm and its natural value as a habitat for birds, mammals, etc., lies mainly in the rough, naturalistic impression it evokes. This is valid even more in larger expanses, and its aesthetic value during winter can be considerable. Yet it may be advisable to now and then mow 'over the ice' when the ice floor allows this, and to carry off the reed produced. It cleans the vegetation up and improves the aesthetics.

The maintenance of reed vegetations on land consists of the yearly mowing in November to January. Less valuable reedlands may be mown as late as the end of March. This is useful to prevent the rougher plants from establishing and to prevent young shrubs and trees from taking over.

The mown reed stubble should remain high enough so as to be about 10 cm (4 inches) above water, as it needs to be able to breathe. Reed that is constantly mown underwater will become less vital and will decline. The mown-off reed is carried off and should definitely not be burnt at the spot. This will kill the moss and herbaceous cover, and will encourage rougher vegetations to appear. Mowing should preferably be carried out by hand (scythe, brush cutter); machines on wheels will give less favourable results because of track formation and other damage done to the soil.

Sufficiently wet reedlands on acid soil are suitable for starting *Sphagnum* vegetations by sprinkling a thin layer (a few centimetres (an inch or so)) of *Sphagnum* species between the reed stubble after mowing and removing the reed. One may need to repeat this for some years. After some time,

Sphagnum reedland may be the result. If reed vegetations start to degenerate – the plants staying lower, the vegetation thinning – a thin layer of mud (approximately 5 cm (2 inches) measured when wet) is applied. It has a fertilising effect that will revitalise its condition. By doing so, one may preserve reedland for many years.

Low-fertility grassland

Reedland that does not receive a steady supply of nutrients will display an increasingly thinner vegetation and will lose shape, with the vegetation becoming more open. Only at the waterside will the vegetation keep its height, since nutrients are provided via the water. Mowing in the long run has such a fertility reducing effect that the reed vegetation will be transformed into low-fertility grassland. One may then switch to summer mowing, as in wet flower meadows. In *Sphagnum* reedland turning into low-fertility grassland, one should be mowing through the *Sphagnum* layer, just above the substratum. In this manner, the *Sphagnum* layer stays in good condition, and at the same time it prevents the mosses (*Polytrichum* spp.) present in this layer from dominating. As a result of the conditions becoming increasingly poorer in nutrients and more acidic, species characteristic for this situation will gradually start to appear, for example *Eriophorum angustifolium, Potentilla erecta, Drosera rotundifolia* and *Juncus subnodulosus*.

'Peat heath'

When this type of maintenance by mowing with a scythe is carefully and strictly adhered to, the reed will, in the long run, disappear completely, with the *Sphagnum-Polytrichum* vegetation, including the aforementioned species, transforming into a vegetation of dwarf shrubs from the heather family (*Ericaceae*). This anthropogenic vegetation is called '*veenheide*'. Its formation may be encouraged by sowing *Vaccinium oxycoccus* and *V.macrocarpus, Erica tetralix, Calluna vulgaris, Vaccinium vitis-idaea* and *Empetrum nigrum*. As soon as they appear, one should start mowing at a slightly higher level to encourage their proliferation and further development. In general, it will not be feasible to stop mowing altogether. It would be the next logical step in creating a bog-like vegetation, but since the environment and the vegetation are generally too rich in nutrients (and partially dependent on the groundwater), this will rarely be feasible. One may, however, leave a number of dwarf shrubs unmown, causing them to attain larger sizes or clumps evoking a strong naturalistic aspect. Incidentally, one may treat moss vegetations in the same manner. In addition to providing the right environment, a carefully and consistently maintained maintenance and management schedule (40–50 times per year is not an exception!) is vital in preserving a vegetation such as this – in fact, a miniature bog – which is a unique result.

In older and poorer (*Sphagnum*) reedlands, young trees and shrubs may appear spontaneously, for example *Betula pubescens, Sorbus aucuparia, Frangula alnus, Salix aurita* and *Aronia x prunifolia*. The vegetation tends to develop into marsh woodland, which is, in fact, the next natural succession phase. By cutting at, or under, ground level – and, when necessary, cutting out older stubs too thick for mowing off – one can keep trees and shrubs at bay, thus allowing anthropogenic succession to continue.

Heath and bog vegetations

Species of the heather family (*Ericaceae*) lend themselves perfectly to the creation of heath vegetations, which are more or less closed vegetations of dwarf shrubs taking on the role of the herbaceous layer, with a strong spatial impact in open areas. In it, members of the heather and crowberry (*Empetraceae*) families may be combined with fine low shrubs, such as *Salix repens, Genista* spp., and somewhat taller species, such as *Ulex, Sarothamnus, Myrica* and *Juniperus*. In addition, one may establish some of the most refined and subtle herbaceous indigenous species. A number of vegetation forms may be discerned, with the characteristics and the atmosphere of:

- dry heath
- wet heath
- bog.

Heath and bog vegetations are best realised on poor acidic soils: sand, poor loam or peat. The initial conditions are rarely sufficiently stable and poor in nutrients to create these vegetation types through more or less spontaneous and natural processes. The latter is possible only on moist to wet loam and sand soils still in their 'original' state. In this case, one may use extensive maintenance and management methods, consisting of cutting, mowing, etc. Grazing is feasible on very large areas only. When gardens and parks are concerned, the initial conditions will usually be severely disturbed or non-existent, necessitating the creation of those conditions by artificial methods. The management measures described in the following sections refer primarily to artificially induced and guided heath and bog vegetations using the pruning-weeding method. In daily practice, this method combined with the cutting-weeding method has proven to be equally successful for vegetations with a spontaneous naturalism.

Starting phase

After suitable initial conditions have been created, one starts with a soil that is free from vegetative weeds – as usual, but even more important, in this particular case. *Calluna vulgaris* and *Erica tetralix* can be sown or planted out. Using a mixed method is generally successful, i.e. planting out a few plants that are allowed to self-seed, thus creating a gradually closing vegetation. The seed of *Calluna* is ripe by November, *Erica tetralix* seed a little earlier. When it is preferred to start by sowing a dry heath vegetation, the trimmed-off heather heads containing the ripe seeds are distributed over the plot immediately, allowing the seed to fall out on the spot. The woody heads themselves are left in place, since they offer some protection during germination and provide a favourable microclimate to the young seedlings. In addition, they protect the soil against dehydration, strong winds and washing off, etc. As the young plants develop, the heads are gradually carried off in late spring and early summer. All other shrubs are planted out, for example *Arctostaphylos uva-ursi, Genista pilosa, G.anglica, G.germanica, Sarothamnus, Ulex*. Herbaceous plants are either planted or sown: *Viola canina, Campanula rotundifolia, Antennaria dioica* and *Gentiana cruciata* are planted, whereas *Jasione, Centaurium, Arnica, Dianthus armeria* and *Petrorhagia prolifera* are sown. Wet heath and bog vegetation are started on *permanently* wet soils, generally with a high water-table level, approximately 10–15 cm under the surface. In wet heath vegetation, combinations can be made of typical, characteristic pioneer vegetations of the 'wet heath habitat' with the species described for vegetations on open plots. After planting out *Erica tetralix* possibly combined with *Salix repens, Genista anglica, Vaccinium vitis-idaea* and *V.uliginosum*, accompanying species such as *Gentiana pneumonanthe, Narthecium ossifragum, Drosera rotundifolia* and *D.intermedia*, and *Hypericum elodes* are immediately sown. Autumn sowing is preferable as germination is stimulated by frost. Pseudo-grasses, such as *Eriophorum, Scirpus cespitosus, Carex* or *Rhynchophora*, are not used as they are too vigorous. *Sphagnum* spp. may also be brought in as sprinkled or planted heads.

Bog vegetations may be started by planting out *Andromeda polifolia, Vaccinium uliginosum* and *V.macrocarpus, Erica tetralix* and *Sphagnum* heads, and by sowing typical pioneer species (see the previous paragraph). One may prefer to create species vegetation types, such as Bog Rosemary- or Bog Bilberry heath, etc., or create species compositions. Species such as *Salix repens* may be added in places.

It should be noted that one chooses in the initial stage – in fact, in the designing phase – whether one wishes to create wet heath or bog vegetations. In a later phase, wet heath vegetations, especially the *Sphagnum* component, may be transformed into vegetation types characteristic of bog vegetations. These two vegetation types are, in fact, closely related. Vegetations of *Vaccinium oxycoccus*, for instance, have the best chance of succeeding when the species is inserted as pre-raised plants into young maturing *Sphagnum* cushions. After planting it out in the subsoil in-between the *Sphagnum*, it will develop well if it grows into the *Sphagnum* cushions. Species growing in separate spots elsewhere in the same area may also sub-spontaneously establish themselves in bog vegetations, for example *Vaccinium vitis-idaea, V.myrtillus* and *Empetrum nigrum*.

Vaccinium vitis-idaea, V.myrtillus and *Empetrum nigrum* are also perfect species for using along the edges of heath and bog vegetations, in transitional situations with woodland for example.

As separate vegetation types, *Vaccinium vitis-idaea* and *Empetrum nigrum* are particularly well-suited to create aspects with a very special atmosphere, the so-called bilberry and crowberry heaths. Combined with ferns such as *Blechnum spicant, Polypodium vulgare* and *Dryopteris cristata*, very subtle and strongly evocative images may be created.

The king fern (*Osmunda regalis*) plays a part of its own. As it is utterly ornamental and full of character and grows to a very large size over the years, it provides strong images and accents like no other. Its majestic shape and appearance throughout the year makes it suitable for application everywhere, but it fits in best in the atmosphere of marsh, heath and bog. If it is applied correctly, in larger numbers and repetitively, it lends a definite air of grandeur to the area.

Maintenance

Plants belonging to the heather family may be kept in good shape for years by the two elementary maintenance measures of weeding and trimming. In addition to weeding out unwanted species, annual trimming will keep the vegetation vigorous and will extend its vitality to a very long period. Without such maintenance measures, however, vegetation types like these may rarely be preserved.

The same is valid for ground covers composed of crowberry or billberry (*Empetrum* or *Vaccinium* spp.), but since trimming is, in this case, not required or tolerated, it will only rarely be necessary. When its vitality is reduced as a result of old age, frost or if a snow cover was trampled, *Vaccinium vitis-idaea* and *V.myrtillus* are cut back to the ground completely, after which a sprinkling of fresh peat applied in spring will provide new nutrients and will bring revitalisation. Small areas of heath and bog may thus last and remain in an attractive condition for many years. It is exactly their age that gives them their own special character and atmosphere. In these times of volatility and haste, these are remarkable forms of green, demonstrating how plantings on the one hand and natural growth on the other blend into a perfectly harmonious whole. They provide clear examples of the succession of vegetations, which is at the same time occurring elsewhere in the park as well.

In the formation of the mould layer of heath vegetations, mosses play an important role. Together they create a whole new growing environment on the substratum of, for example, poor peat or loamy soils: mats of roots, stalks and mosses, growing increasingly thicker as the vegetation ages. It provides an excellent environment for species such as *Empetrum nigrum, Calluna vulgaris, Vaccinium myrtillus* and *V.macrocarpus*. If the vegetation is not disturbed as it is growing older, these species will establish themselves spontaneously if they are found elsewhere in the park. In this manner, succession occurs, but, as in the other plant combinations in the park, in a manner that is different from the succession as it is seen in nature.

Gradual shifts

In other locations, vegetations of *Calluna vulgaris, Erica tetralix* or *Andromeda polifolia* that have become increasingly shaded are taken over by *Empetrum nigrum, Vaccinium vitis-idaea* or *V.myrtillus*. One vegetation aspect silently transforms into the next. On a spot where *Vaccinium macrocarpus* has been growing for over 30 years, with a mat of mosses and stems as thick as 10 cm, *Gentiana pneumonanthe*, which formerly flowered there by the thousands, is gradually disappearing completely. It does not tolerate the competition of the thickening moss-and-stem mat and is pushed out. Long before this stage is reached, *Empetrum nigrum, Erica tetralix* and *Calluna vulgaris* have established themselves, in addition to the usual unwanted species. It is hard to remove them from the vegetation mat: deep mowing in early spring, which is tolerated well by *Vaccinium macrocarpus*, removes *Empetrum nigrum* but not the other two species. A phased combination of weeding and mowing may offer a solution.

Climatic influences are very important for a vegetation of *Ericaceae*. Wet years with a high humidity favour its development, whereas dry hot years impede it. This obviously applies to other vegetation types in a similar way. One therefore discerns '*Ericaceae* years' and '*Rosaceae* years', the former being the wet years and the latter years with little rain and low humidity. In dry years, the development of *Vaccinium vitis-idaea* stagnates; it withdraws, the vegetation's size decreases. The resulting open spots may be left to other suitable species, self-seeding there because they are more drought-tolerant, for example *Genista germanica, Arnica montana, Campanula rotundifolia* and *Jasione montana*. When wetter times arrive, *Vaccinium vitis-idaea* reclaims these spaces by sending out its shoots. This may be stimulated by trimming and cutting back its competitors.

As long as the park's aspects with its vegetation remain attractive, one may continue working in the same vein. If not, one has to renovate parts of the park completely, with measures consisting of lifting, digging, applying fresh sand or peat where required, planting out pre-raised plants and sowing out others. Another round starts, the clock of succession has been turned back as an element of dynamic creative management.

Rocky substrates – walls, dry walls and shallow soils

Whereas vegetation of organic and mineral soils have been dealt with in the preceding sections, this section is about more unusual substratums and soils, such as inorganic materials, like bricks or rocks that are found in many shapes – walls, broken rubble, lava, minestone and slate – and very shallow soils situated or created with the former as its base. With these rocky materials, all sorts of habitats and substratums may be created. They will initially look very artificial and barely natural, but they may lead to very special, unusual and surprising results. The most interesting characteristic of these materials is their suitability for creating special reliefs and gradients, impossible to achieve with normal soils. In the wild flora, many species prove to adapt to these conditions quite well. The results one may obtain are not only unusual, their variety of designs and shapes may also be very attractive, both in an aesthetic and an ecological respect.

The situations dealt with in these paragraphs concern the sunny, artificial ones; conditions that are stony or rocky by nature are left out. The most familiar rocky habitat or substrate for plants are walls – mortared or dry – and the artificial arrangements of rocks called rock gardens. Less well-known is the fact that demolition products, such as old or used bricks, roof tiles, shingles, paving stones, curb stones, tombstones and the such, have great potential for being used in rocky substrates.

During the last few decades, many fine examples of these have been created in the Netherlands, both on a small and a large scale. One of the materials' special advantages is that they are perfectly suited for working in relief, especially in height or three-dimensionally. This makes it possible to create a lot of growing and living space for plants on a small surface. In addition, these constructions are less susceptible to damage caused by trampling or by animals such as cats and dogs. Wherever little space is available and much 'human pressure' is present, rocky substrates offer many opportunities.

Rocky materials of very small sizes offer further opportunities. Lava, crushed rock, brick and rock split in 0–40 mm (0–1.5 inch) fractions are excellently suited for creating typical habitats. The finer fractions (0–5 mm) provide water retention and a root penetrable substratum. In addition, material rich in lime results in the most diverse vegetation.

Thin soil layers on top of stones, bricks or paved surfaces (e.g. 5–10 cm) and layers of sand or sandy clay are called shallow soils. A special type of shallow soils are roofs covered with gravel and roof covers specially constructed for growing plants on them, known as green or *Sedum* roofs, the latter after the genus usually grown on them.

Rocky habitats are situations in which large differences in temperature are present within short periods of time and, consequently, large differences in humidity. Drought and low soil fertility are its common traits. In the more extreme conditions, only plants that are very well adapted to these can survive.

The application of rocky materials starts with a preconceived plan or design, worked out in detail or in broad outline. In the latter case, one may work largely intuitively. Using the materials in a construction requires knowledge of its qualities. The design, the material and its utilisation determine the final visual result to a much larger degree when compared to the usual soils. The chances for plant growth will increase with the quantity of soil applied or mixed in. As the quantity of nutrients and moisture are increased, more species will be able to grow on the substratum. These quantities and the composition of the added soil allow one to create different habitats and opportunities for plants. One may thus provide living space for high-impact species, such as *Salvia verticillata, S.pratensis, Malva moschata, M.alcea, Coronilla varia, Verbascum* spp., *Galium verum, Ononis spinosa, Silene nutans, Silene cucubalus, Campanula rapunculus, C.rapunculoides, Centaurea scabiosa, Genista germanica, G.anglica*, etc. A final important factor is the exposure to sunlight. Northern and southern expositions each have their own possibilities, caused by the presence or absence of shade, sunlight, heat, light and moisture. Where it is necessary to use a certain quantity of soil for moisture and nutrient provision, soils such as clay, sandy clay or loam are preferable. Peaty soils are reduced by oxidation and are therefore unsuitable. For shallow soils, sandy types are useful as well.

First stages

When openings have been left in walls, these are filled with soil, offering immediate growing opportunities for plants. On built walls without openings, the start for plants is slowest. The mortar has to be weathered to a certain extent before it is ready for plants, a process that may take many years. Once the environment is amenable to it, fern spores can be blown in or seeds can be smeared on the surface using some clay or old manure. On dry walls or in flat situations, sowing or planting is obviously much easier. When a number of desired individuals have been established they will usually propagate and distribute themselves, for example species such as *Linaria cymbalaria, Corydalis lutea* and *C.ochroleuca, Cheiranthus cheirii, Hieracium amplexicaule, Phyllitis scolopendrium, Asplenium ruta-muraria* and *A.trichomanes*.

Maintenance

Vegetations on rocky substratums are largely maintained by weeding out unwanted species and cutting off wilted and dead parts. Blown in leaves are removed. With increasing nutrient and moisture quantities in rocky substratums, plant growth will become more abundant and, consequently, weeding will become more time-consuming. As a rule, maintenance will vary between very little in dry poor walls and relatively intensive in flatter, richer and moister situations and shallow soils. For the latter, one may choose either the mowing or the weeding maintenance method, corresponding to spontaneous or guided naturalism. In the former, grass species will be part of the desired plant community, resulting in a (free-flowering) low-fertility meadow vegetation. Mowing once a year and carrying off the hay will suffice. If the weeding method is preferred, entailing more direction and guidance, a great variety of vegetations is possible. One may freely choose from a variety of compositions and combinations, ranging from vegetations with a more ecological layout and impact to artificial vegetations aimed at an aesthetic impact.

The timely weeding of trees and shrubs appearing spontaneously is of special importance in keeping built and dry walls in good condition. Trees such as *Acer pseudoplatanus, Fraxinus excelsior* and *Ulmus* spp., and shrubs such as *Sambucus nigra, Crataegus monogyna, Viburnum lantana, Rubus fruticosus* and *Hedera helix* may cause severe damage to the construction. These unwanted species are weeded out as young as possible; larger individuals are hard to remove without damage. In doing so, one should obviously use one's own judgement: rare or special species may be spared in places, only trimming them back when they grow too large, for example *Ficus carica, Buddleja davidii, Rubus uva-crispa* and the such. On weak slopes and flat situations, weeding in rocky substratums may cause painful fingertips. A useful method for preventing this is to apply a layer of sand (a few centimetres (an inch) or so in thickness) immediately after planting and supplementing it as required. An important aspect of built and dry walls is the correct spatial and visual balance between subtratum and vegetation, since it determines the charm and beauty of such environments. Walls that are largely or completely overgrown are less adventurous and are aesthetically less appealing. By weeding out or cutting back parts of the vegetation – i.e. of the desired species! – one may maintain this balance.

Professional skills of staff and managers

The development of vegetations within a *heempark* must be considered as a sliding scale, from simple to complex, and from young to old. In the same way, daily maintenance is, in many respects, done on a sliding scale. As such, we work within the laws of nature. Natural processes are not only cyclic but also gradual. As stated before, the management of a *heempark* is characterised by the attentive and empathic guiding and following of processes, and for one to be able to do so a broad and open consciousness of *context* – in time and space – is of vital importance. For instance, the practice of rejuvenating vegetations is, in fact, setting back the clock of natural succession, and to be able to do this in the right way one should truly know the whole range of succession phases. Such dynamic movements are considered by the manager as being 'a game of to and fro', of 'now this, then that'. He takes all this into account, moving with the current, as experience has taught him that it is useless to go against it, but that going with the flow gives the best results with the least exertion. Thus, he learns the game of playing chess with nature: now it is his move, now his opponent's.

For this reason, it is also crucial that staff are skilled not only in extensive, mechanical management, but also in a wide range of traditional, small-scale horticultural techniques. This will enable them to apply these skills in a versatile, discriminating way, adapting to its complete gradient, from more global and large-scale management up to selective and individual small-scale maintenance –

depending on the character of the vegetation at hand and the intentions of a planting scheme. Often among laymen, the idea seems to persist that ecological management would generally and principally imply overall extensiveness, global management and a certain spontaneous disorder. It cannot be stressed enough that, in such general and absolute terms, this is a serious misunderstanding.

Besides lacking ecological insight, fixation upon theoretical standards and unilateral management considerably reduces the range of possibilities for natural differentiation. As a principle, the apparatus should embrace the complete gradient from vegetation management up to a refined and individually adapted species maintenance.

From the above it may be clear that maintenance of high-quality naturalistic green space requires even more continuity than high-quality green in general. The process character of naturalistic vegetations requires expert personnel, both on the levels of specialised staff and management. It is of crucial importance that gardeners with appropriate craftsmanship are employed. To date, it has been difficult to find them. Horticultural training institutes provide no specialised courses, necessitating one to instruct new staff oneself. In general, it takes five to six years to form a fully skilled quality *heempark* gardener. Most of the required craftsmanship is learned in daily practice. Just as the park itself, practical knowledge in this field can only be accumulated over the years. Training of this kind requires an in-depth investment.

At first sight, and looking from the outside, what has been explained in the preceding paragraphs may seem complicated and even out of reach. In this respect, it is like nature itself. It may be a reassuring thought that the Amstelveen *heempark*s were also started small and simple. *Practice* will, in time, and even much sooner than one might expect at the outset, bring knowledge and expertise, as well as promising results. One has to start small, but *starting* is the operative. In a way, the process is like sowing seeds. One finds oneself engaged in a process that keeps on generating new and inspiring perspectives. Perspectives which, precisely because of their highly natural inspiration, can express the quality of a living culture!

> Nothing of importance can be created in an instant, just as grapes or figs cannot. If you tell me that you wish to have a fig, my answer is that it takes time. The tree has to flower and bear fruit first, and the fruit has to ripen.
>
> Epictetus

Chapter 11

The social and cultural context of ecological plantings

Anna Jorgensen

11.1
Wild-looking vegetation in an urban setting

What would the world be, once bereft
Of wet and of wildness? Let them be left,
O let them be left, wildness and wet;
Long live the weeds and the wilderness yet.
(Manley Hopkins, 1948)

Introduction

At the beginning of the twenty-first century many urban-dwellers' experience of naturalistic or wild-looking vegetation in towns and cities is restricted to specific settings: remnants of ancient woodland on land deemed unsuitable for development, natural succession taking over on derelict or brownfield sites, abandoned allotments, vegetation beside rivers or other water bodies and urban nature-reserves.

11.2
Parkland in the style of the English Landscape movement

11.3
A mix of sown meadow and shrubs provides a visually and ecologically complex landscape that requires a fraction of the input and maintenance of conventional urban landscape

These settings usually have one thing in common: they are often associated with abandonment and decay (Figure 11.1). In most maintained public open spaces the predominant landscape is parkland in the style of the English Landscape movement, combined with floral displays inspired by the Victorian gardenesque, a style as far removed from ecological planting design as it is possible to be (Figure 11.2). Given these polarities, it is not surprising that people may find the idea of deliberate ecological plantings in public spaces difficult to appreciate (Figure 11.3).

Whilst much of this book is about the technical,

aesthetic and design issues related to ecologically-informed planting, it is equally important to consider the social and cultural context. Although designers and managers may believe in the inherent benefits of a naturalistic approach, and may appreciate its aesthetic qualities, if it is not accepted by those that have to live, work and play in such a setting, then these plantings can never be truly sustainable. This is perhaps particularly true of 'nearby nature' – the areas and patches of public green close to people's homes which, to some extent, urban dwellers have no choice as to whether they use or not. Helford (2000) has noted (in the context of urban habitat restoration):

> Making nature is inevitably the making of social relationships. And this is why land-managers, volunteer restorationists, and ecologists, to name a few, might want to listen to what social scientists have to say about nature, conservation practice, and in particular, public conflict over these natures and practices.

There are perhaps two great conundrums that must be addressed in any discussion of public acceptance of ecological landscapes in towns and cities. Firstly, for some time, mainstream landscape preference research has found that most humans prefer landscapes that resemble the previously referred to English Landscape style parkland (wide open spaces with trees scattered singly and in clumps). This landscape was adopted wholesale by the designers and planners of many towns and cities in the twentieth century: in particular, by the designers of post-war, high-rise, high-density housing in open parkland, based upon the 'Radiant City' of Le Corbusier (1923). Yet, this type of landscape has been criticised by many commentators for its uniformity, lack of human scale and inadequacy as a setting for a variety of human activity (Newman 1972; Coleman 1985; Jacobs 1994). Do people really prefer this bland landscape, or could it be that this mainstream research has limitations, or have designers missed the full potential and richness of a naturalistic 'urban savannah' style? Secondly, does the widely held view that structurally more complex, ecological, nature-like landscapes in urban areas are unsafe, mean that any attempt to introduce naturalistic vegetation on a wider scale is doomed to failure, or could it be that much of this negativity is founded on little evidence and, again, a failure by designers to create appropriate contexts and types of naturalistic vegetation in different settings?

In an attempt to answer some of these questions, this chapter reviews research findings relevant to the issue of public perception of urban ecological plantings, by considering, firstly, the theoretical basis of landscape preference and perception, and, secondly, public perception of specific ecological vegetation types in designed settings. It is helpful to have a definition of the broad concept of 'ecological plantings' at the outset. In this book, 'ecological plantings' describes plantings that are structured around natural processes, or natural plant communities, or both, and which may also have a naturalistic appearance. It does not entail the exclusive use of native species, though many plantings that fall within the definition are very natural to look at and may consist mainly or entirely of plants of native origin.

Theories of landscape perception

There are two basic explanations for the way in which we react to different landscapes: (i) we have an innate or biological response to landscape; and (ii) responses to landscape are acquired through cultural background and personal development, to a greater or lesser degree.

Historically, many of the proponents of the innate explanation have concentrated on landscape preference research in an attempt to discover what kind of landscape humans prefer. Although it is obviously useful to gauge public preference for different types of landscape, the nature of this type of research sometimes obscures the complexity of people's attitudes. These issues are particularly relevant to people's responses to ecological plantings because such plantings arouse particularly strong and sometimes conflicting responses. It can be argued that landscape preference research simply does not access the full spectrum of people's reactions to landscape in general, and ecological plantings in particular. This may lead to conclusions that are incomplete and, in some cases, downright misleading.

Adherents of the view that responses to landscape are acquired believe that human aesthetic preference is not an abstract or static concept, but rather a process that is deeply embedded in changing cultural values and individual experience: thus, any examination of public attitudes towards urban ecological plantings must also examine these wider issues.

Innate responses to landscape

The innate theories propose that we derive our aesthetic responses to landscape from an earlier evolutionary phase of *Homo sapiens*. It is argued that evolution favoured individuals who had the ability to evaluate their environment successfully in terms of its capacity to fulfil their need for shelter, safety and nourishment. Because human civilisations have been in existence for only a fraction of the time that it has taken our species to evolve, we still retain a strong and instinctive inbuilt preference for landscapes that display the characteristics necessary to meet these needs. Orians and Heerwagen (1992) have claimed that we have an inbuilt preference for landscapes resembling the savannah because the crucial phase of human evolutionary development took place there. Ulrich (1993) has proposed that the English Landscape style, found in so many Western parks and open spaces, is highly preferred because it resembles the savannah.

Jay Appleton's prospect/refuge theory (1975) also relies on an innate or biological explanation, but goes on to develop a landscape typology based on this foundation. Appleton believes that during human evolution the overriding need favouring survival was the ability to see without being seen. He classifies landscapes according to their ability to meet this need either as 'prospects' or 'refuges'. Hence, we retain a preference for landscapes that clearly display features that bear the characteristics of prospects or refuges. The examples given by Appleton are frequently derived from landscape paintings, such as the idealised classical landscapes of Claude Lorraine and Nicholas Poussin: paintings that were often the inspiration for the original practitioners of the English Landscape movement.

Another innate approach that is sometimes described as 'psycho-evolutionary', because of the strong psychological overlay to the evolutionary basis, is the Kaplan's 'preference matrix', (Kaplan and Kaplan 1989), though the Kaplans also went on to examine the impact of different cultural and personal factors. The Kaplan's approach is, in some ways, similar to Appleton's, in that they introduce a series of factors that explain our preference for certain landscapes. However, the Kaplan's factors are more abstract (see Table 11.1).

In the 'preference matrix', the four critical factors of coherence, complexity, legibility and mystery are defined by reference to the different ways in which humans obtain information about their environment – 'understanding' and 'exploration' – and how accessible that information is: whether it is 'immediate' or 'inferred/predicted'.

Table 11.1. The Kaplan's 'preference matrix'

	Understanding	**Exploration**
Immediate	Coherence	Complexity
Inferred/predicted	Legibility	Mystery

Through extensive studies of human reactions to different landscapes, usually depicted in photographic representations, the Kaplans found that these four factors had the greatest explanatory power. Individually, coherence and mystery were found to be the most powerful but combinations of factors were also significant.

In terms of its practical application, the Kaplans found that the preference matrix explained preference for natural scenes that contain views or vistas, plus elements such as curving sightlines that suggest that there is more to discover just around the corner: all qualities that are inherent in the English Landscape style.

There are, in fact, a large number of persuasive authorities that support the view that Westerners' favourite landscape is English Landscape style parkland and that this preference is derived from our evolutionary bias in favour of savannah landscapes. Yet, to return to the first of the two questions posed at the start of this chapter – how can this evidence be reconciled with the many critiques of the twentieth-century interpretations of these landscapes? – one explanation for this apparent contradiction is that the style of the English Landscape movement has been adopted as a generalised solution and has become oversimplified in the process. Many urban landscapes that seek to imitate this style lack the subtlety of the historic landscapes, with their manipulation of landform, variations in vegetation type and structure, water bodies and associated water's edge vegetation, and far more sophisticated management techniques and regimes.

A further explanation is that the 'urban savannah' style is essentially a paradigm for large-scale landscapes that has been monotonously applied without differentiation to both large- and small-scale landscapes. Rather than being seen as a universal solution, this approach could be seen as a way of creating a larger-scale landscape framework, with the potential for introducing greater complexity and ecological richness into the elements of that structure – open space, glades, woodland, woodland edge, landform, water and water's edge.

There may also be some limitations inherent in the landscape preference research. To date, most of this research has concentrated on visual preference. Whilst this may be a perfectly valid way of evaluating preference for what kinds of landscapes people want to look at, it may not tell us anything about the suitability of landscapes for other activities, for example playing games, exploring, socialising, or just being alone. Nor does it tell us anything about the different types of landscape that people might prefer in different settings, say on their way to the shops, to sit out in close to home, or to visit at the weekends with their families.

The major strength of the preference research based on innate theories of preference is that it has enabled us to identify the generic qualities of landscapes that the majority of Westerners consistently express visual preference for. The Kaplans (1989) have come the closest to defining these qualities in their preference matrix. Up to the time of press, the type of landscape that seems to have displayed these characteristics most fully is parkland in the English Landscape style. However, there may be other types of landscape that could meet these requirements. As stated above, one weakness of the innate approach is that it does not take account of the richness and diversity of human needs and experience. Nor does it explain why people might hold views that differ from the norm, or how tastes in landscape change, other than on a strictly evolutionary basis.

Cultural and personal responses to landscape

The existence of other factors differentiating landscape preference has been acknowledged for some time: factors relating to the individual as opposed to the landscape. Lyons (1983), for example, found that age, gender, place of residence and familiarity affected landscape preference. Further, she concluded that if variables such as age, place of residence and familiarity influence landscape preference, then preference must have a dynamic quality, changing over an individual lifespan. Thus, landscape preference is not based solely on innate characteristics acquired during human evolution.

Bourassa (1991) postulated that, as well as a biological component (genetic acquired through evolution), the aesthetics of landscape also has strong cultural and personal components. According to Bourassa, the cultural component is derived from the process by which different groups in society ascribe different symbolic meanings to landscape – meanings that reinforce group identities – whilst the personal component is an individual's personal interpretation of the biological (innate) and cultural rules. Further, he argues that every individual has the ability to transcend and alter these rules through creativity.

Thus, the cultural and personal characteristics of the individual may also determine their reaction to landscape. Furthermore, the different strands may sometimes conflict or compete with each other. Ongoing research in Warrington New Town, in the United Kingdom, one of the first British New Towns to be developed within a setting of woodland ecological planting, suggests that some residents preferred specific places in their locality whilst simultaneously finding those same places the most unsafe (Jorgensen *et al.*, in press). These findings cannot be accounted for satisfactorily by a purely biological explanation of human reaction to landscape. Arguably, two or more of the strands or components determining preference are conflicting here: on the one hand, the biological strand is producing a sense of aesthetic preference, based on notions of personal survival, whilst, on the other hand, the cultural or personal elements are contradicting this, or vice versa. In evaluating public perception of ecological plantings, there is therefore the likelihood that public attitudes to them are complex (made up of different layers or strands) conflicting and multi-dimensional.

Bourassa also argues that there are fashions in theories of landscape aesthetics as well as public preferences for landscape. Secondly, he argues that the aesthetic appreciation of landscape is not something that should be, or can be, divorced from the rest of our experience: the relationship between humans and landscape is essentially an interaction that can take place in many different ways.

These two points have important consequences for a study of public attitudes to particular landscapes. Firstly, if landscape preference can change, we should be suspicious of any theory of landscape preference that consistently returns a particular type of landscape as the most universally preferred landscape. Secondly, if we adopt Bourassa's interactive definition of landscape aesthetics, then it becomes impossible to say that one type of landscape is the best for all interactions or purposes. Instead, we can allow that landscapes and our reactions to them can, and should, be complex.

All of the innate theories outlined earlier attempt to explain an aesthetic preference for landscape, but offer an incomplete picture. We also need to look at people's perception of landscape in a broader sense: to understand how and why people value, use and abuse landscapes within their various cultural contexts and personal perspectives.

The impact of cultural factors

Rohde and Kendle (1994) describe the different views of human relationships with nature held by Dutch, French and Japanese people. The French view of nature is said to be characterised by a desire for order and control, whereas the Japanese are said to view humankind and nature as part of an integrated whole. Clearly, these are sweeping generalisations and all cultures contain sub-cultures and individuals who may hold entirely different

11.4
Battlemented laurels – an example of a military approach to shrub maintenance from the public frontage of a hotel in Grange-over-Sands in Cumbria

views, but, nevertheless, such overarching cultural influences clearly do play an important role in forming attitudes.

In their account of the history and development of ecological landscape styles, Forbes *et al.* (1997) identify changes in human perception of nature as one of the key factors influencing the development of landscape styles, such as the English Landscape movement, the open space movement and the Victorian gardenesque.

It may be that our view of this fundamental relationship is also capable of influencing our taste in planting styles. In her social history of gardens and gardening, *The Pursuit of Paradise*, Jane Brown (2000) devotes an entire chapter to what she calls 'the military garden', surely the ultimate emblem of human domination over nature (Figure 11.4). She writes:

> It is in the small gardens of Britain that traditional military neatness has been retained. In allotments with their miniature parade ground proportions, everything in impeccable rows. In the immaculate trenching, ridging and earthing up of potatoes or celery, in the line of guardsmen-red salvias marching beside a path, in the tiny but precise forty-five degree angles and ditches where the well-kept lawn edges meet the weedless soil.

It is easy to recognise aspects of this approach in the horticultural plantings that still form the backbone of many public landscapes as well as private gardens.

It seems plausible that there is a relationship between individual perception of the appropriate human relationship with nature and individual perception of different types of landscape: would individuals with an ecocentric view of the human-nature relationship be more attracted by natural or wild landscapes? Van den Born *et al.* (2001) propose a model of human relationships with nature ranging from 'man the technocrat adventurer' to 'oneness with nature' (Table 11.2). Research suggests that the majority of Westerners now have a non-anthropocentric view of the human-nature relationship when asked to express their views in the abstract (Catton and Dunlap 1980; Van den Berg 1999; Van den Born *et al.* 2001). In the latter study, in the Netherlands, 76% of respondents preferred the statement that 'humans are part of nature and hence should bear responsibility for it'. It would clearly be unwise to assume that, because of the high prevalence of these ecocentric views, there is likely to be a generalised preference for more ecological styles of planting. It may in fact be the case that, whereas the majority of Westerners have broadly ecocentric views in the abstract, many hold different views in concrete instances closer to home. The only reported research on this issue was carried out in Norway by Kaltenborn and Bjerke (2002), who found that respondents with ecocentric views preferred wilderness landscapes, whilst those with anthropocentric views preferred farm environments. Their sample was drawn from the inhabitants of Røros, a sparsely populated mountain region in Norway, so it is difficult to generalise from their findings. This is an area that merits further investigation.

As will become apparent later in this chapter, context has a crucial bearing on the public acceptance of naturalistic ecological plantings. Even people who are supportive of nature conservation may have very different ideas about what measures are to be taken in their locality. A case in point is the recent bitter controversy over plans to restore prairie landscapes in Chicago. Despite the fact that the plans were drawn up by a broad network consisting of volunteer groups, public agencies and non-governmental organisations, the implementation of the plans involving large-scale tree clearing met with vehement opposition from large and disparate

Table 11.2. Possible relationships between humans and nature (adapted from Van den Born *et al.* (2001))

Anthropentric	Man the technocrat adventurer
	Man the manager-engineer
	Man the steward of nature
Ecocentric	Man the guardian of nature
	Man and nature as partners
	Man as participant with nature
	Oneness with nature ('*unio mystica*')

sectors of the public, such that much of the programme came to a standstill. The controversy centred around whose vision of nature (prairie or woodland?) should prevail, and what constituted nature conservation expertise (Helford 2000).

Some of these social and political issues were examined in a Dutch study of the impact of planned change context on landscape evaluations (Van den Berg and Vlek 1998). Two groups of respondents were shown a set of five digitally manipulated images of an agrarian landscape and four other landscapes showing lesser degrees of human influence. One group of respondents was told that the five images represented 'five existing Dutch landscapes', whereas the other group were told that the images represented 'one existing landscape and four plans for nature development from this landscape'. Generally speaking, the four more natural landscapes were judged less beautiful when they were presented as planned changes than when they were presented as existing landscapes. On closer investigation it was found that the planned change context affected beauty ratings only if two conditions were met, firstly, when planned changes involved the development of natural landscapes with a low degree of human influence, and, secondly, where planned changes were evaluated from a user as opposed to a non-user perspective.

There are many possible explanations for this resistance by users to the development of more natural landscapes, and far more research is needed in this area (Van den Berg and Vlek 1998). However, what seems clear is that the strength of local users' personal investment in their local green-spaces should not be underestimated, and that this is a factor to be taken into account in design using large-scale ecological plantings that are naturalistic in appearance.

As well as having their own ideas about the appropriate relationship between man and nature, Westerners also use the concepts of 'nature' and 'naturalness' to classify landscape. The Kaplans were among the first to articulate that a fundamental method of categorising visual images incorporating natural and built elements was according to the degree of human influence (Kaplan and Kaplan 1989).

In an Australian study, people were also found to be able to discriminate between different vegetation types and densities, and to detect structural changes in vegetation of a non-natural origin, on the basis of 'naturalness' alone (Lamb and Purcell 1990). Respondents were asked to rate slides of a number of naturally occurring vegetation forms according to how natural they thought they were. Taller and denser vegetation was considered most natural, and respondents were able to detect structural changes in the vegetation of a non-natural origin. Lamb and Purcell concluded that expected vegetation structure was the main criterion of naturalness used by the respondents in the study. Significantly, they also concluded that there is no straightforward relationship between perceived naturalness and preference in landscape.

A further complication is that people have different interpretations of naturalness and human influence in landscape. Lutz *et al.* (1999) found that Canadian urban and rural dwellers' perception of what constitutes wilderness differed significantly,

with urban dwellers being far more ready to classify scenes as wilderness, despite clear evidence of human intrusion in the form of agriculture or structures such as a hydro-electric dam. This has implications for our reactions to particular landscape types, but also for the question of what constitutes a natural or wilderness landscape, and the role and location of such landscapes. For urban dwellers, the idea of having natural or semi-natural landscapes in public urban settings may well seem inappropriate if such landscapes have connotations of 'wilderness'.

Our attitudes to certain landscapes have changed a great deal, illustrating how much the cultural constructs underpinning landscape perception can change (Thomas 1983). An example that is often given is the change in Westerner's attitudes towards mountains. Until relatively recently, mountains and mountain ranges were regarded literally with horror. Referring to the modest hills of the Yorkshire Dales at the beginning of the eighteenth century, Daniel Defoe wrote:

> Nor were these Hills high and formidable only, but they had a kind of an unhospitable Terror in them. Here were no rich pleasant Valleys between them, as among the Alps; no Lead mines and Veins of rich Oar, as in the Peak; no Coal pits, as in the Hills about Hallifax, much less Gold, as in the Andes, but all barren and wild, of no use or advantage either to man or beast.
>
> (Defoe 1727)

What is striking about this extract is not only the 'unhospitable terror' that these hills evidently inspired in Defoe but also his palpable disgust for the fact that they cannot be used to human advantage: what amounts to a very anthropocentric view of the relationship between nature and humans. There is a marked contrast between the views expressed by Defoe and the fact that many millions of people now visit the Yorkshire Dales National Park for pleasure and recreation, attracted by the same landscape that Defoe found so repugnant. There has, therefore, been a major shift in our attitudes towards wilder natural landscapes, possibly because humans are now more capable of controlling nature, which is therefore seen as less threatening.

Thus, whilst views of the appropriate human/nature relationship may vary between different cultures, there is evidence to suggest that it is this cultural construct that underlies and informs our perception of different landscapes. Furthermore, far from being fixed and immutable, such constructs are susceptible to change. The evidence also indicates that, although there is some disagreement about the meaning of 'naturalness' and 'human influence', these notions are used by humans to classify landscape and to decide what kind of landscape may be appropriate in a given setting. Lastly, these concepts seem to be particularly pertinent in places that people are familiar with and have a personal investment in.

The impact of personal factors

Education, income and occupation

Although in the early 1970s research reported that environmental agendas were primarily supported by the middle or upper-middle class, this notion was rebutted by Buttel and Flinn (1978) who found that age and place of residence were better predictors of awareness of environmental problems and support for environmental programmes than education, income and occupation: what they called 'the three major indicators of social class'. Of these three, education was the most significant.

Two of the main factors accounting for differences in landscape perception are occupation and expertise. Farmers have been found to react differently to nature development plans compared to other residents of an area and visitors to that area (Van den Berg *et al.* 1998). In this study, respondents were presented with a photograph of an existing agrarian landscape and five digitally manipulated versions of the same landscape incorporating changes that represented different kinds of nature restoration (rough field, open swamp, half-open swamp, forest and stretch of water). The farmers differed significantly from both the residents and the visitors in rating the existing agrarian landscape as the most beautiful. Interestingly, the six images were also rated for biodiversity by a panel of experts. The expert ratings of biodiversity were positively related to the beauty ratings of the residents and the visitors; but not to the farmers. Thus, it would be reasonable to assume that farmers (certainly in the Netherlands and possibly elsewhere) might also react less favourably to naturalistic ecological plantings in public urban settings, given their apparent preference for ordered landscapes.

Not surprisingly there is also evidence indicating that members of environmental groups have particular preferences for wild landscapes and vegetation (Dearden 1984; Kaplan and Herbert 1987).

However, the relationship between expertise and preference for particular types of landscape is not always straightforward. In his recent study of the values held by British Landscape architects, Ian Thompson (2000) found that most of the practitioners he interviewed thought that ecological values in the practice of landscape architecture were no more important than aesthetic or social ones, and some thought they were less important. Furthermore, Thompson encountered a number of critiques of an ecological approach to design, including accusations of superficiality and tokenism, and the belief that ecology is anti-design. Whilst these findings do not relate exclusively to planting design, it seems safe to assume that many landscape architects may be somewhat wary of introducing ecological plantings in public urban settings. This may, in part, be a legacy of the backlash against what is known as 'the ecological approach', pioneered in Warrington New Town in the 1970s.

Age

Lyons' study (1983) confirmed that age was an important factor in landscape perception. This study found that young children expressed the highest landscape preferences and elderly people expressed the lowest. However, there was also a significant dip in preference around the teenage years. Similar findings were reported by Herzog *et al.* (2000). Interestingly, they also found that, although the adults had lower preference than the young children (but higher than the teenagers), the adult scores were more variable, suggesting that by the time people reach adulthood other factors have come into play. They also suggested that young children display higher landscape preference because of their tendency to view landscape as a good playscape, whereas teenagers are more preoccupied with social and other concerns. It is difficult to know how age would influence preference for ecological plantings. Balling and Falk (1982) found that young children had a preference for savannah scenes, even though they were not familiar with them. However, there is a dearth of evidence about how children and young people view landscapes generally, and this is certainly an interesting area for further research.

Familiarity

Research has also confirmed that residence or familiarity can have a significant affect on landscape preference. 'Residence' is really just another way of evaluating familiarity because living in a particular environment means that we become familiar with it. Broadly speaking, the findings suggest that familiarity increases preference (Kaplan and Kaplan 1989; Herzog *et al.* 2000). The latter study compared Australians' and Americans' preference for Australian natural landscapes. The Australians gave their own landscape higher preference scores than the Americans. Within the Australian group, the Aboriginal respondents showed the highest overall preference, a finding perhaps explained by their greater familiarity with the landscapes in question.

The research into familiarity also suggests how this issue might influence the perception of different types of vegetation. An early study by Rachel Kaplan (1977a) compared preference and familiarity in relation to different views of a stormwater drain, ranging from very natural to highly engineered. An interesting finding emerged in relation to one very natural view of the drain: this view was low in preference for all except those respondents who indicated that it was similar to their own view of the drain. In Lyons' study (1983), respondents showed higher preference for their own home 'biomes' (climatic zones with their own distinctive vegetation, for example northern coniferous forest). Thus, all respondents from the deciduous forest biome preferred this one to all others. Desert dwellers did not prefer the desert biome overall, but exhibited a higher preference for it than any other group. Dearden found that residents of low-density predominantly natural housing developments expressed higher preference for more natural scenes and vice versa (1984). So it seems that familiarity with more natural landscapes does enhance preference for these landscapes, and it is therefore logical to assume that familiarity with natural vegetation would produce an enhanced preference for more naturalistic ecological planting styles.

However, a word of warning should be sounded here. Not all the research into the effects of familiarity has produced straightforward or consistent results. Another early study by Kaplan (1977b) found that local people displayed lower preferences for roadside scenes from their region than visitors. The locals also preferred open forest to dense forest, whereas the visitors preferred forest to flat farmland without discriminating on the grounds of forest density. These findings may not necessarily contradict those suggesting a positive relationship between familiarity and preference. It may simply be that the relationship is more complex than first appears. There are a number of possible explanations for the findings but these are outside the scope of this chapter.

Gender

Lyons' study (1983) did not find gender to be significant. However, gender has been found to be very significant in studies of perception of safety in urban landscapes, with women being far more fearful than men (Valentine 1989; Madge 1997; Jorgensen *et al.* 2002). Given the connection between landscape preference and perception of safety referred to earlier in the discussion of innate theories of landscape preference, it seems likely that gender does play a significant role in landscape perception but this may well be far more complex than a simple correlation between gender and preference for particular views or types of landscape (Rohde and Kendle 1994). However, given that women have been found to be more fearful in urban public landscapes, it seems likely that they would be more resistant than men to the introduction of ecological plantings in the form of tall woody vegetation.

Cultural background and ethnicity

Cultural background and ethnicity have been found to play a similarly complex role in landscape perception. Cross-cultural comparisons have consistently shown that differences in landscape preference, at least between the inhabitants of different Western and 'Westernised' cultures, are surprisingly small (Bourassa 1991; Van den Berg 1999; Herzog *et al.* 2000). Research on the question of whether people prefer their own familiar landscapes as opposed to exotic, unfamiliar landscapes seems fairly evenly divided (Rishbeth

2001). However, research does suggest that some ethnic minorities in the USA and in Britain prefer public urban landscapes characterised by openness and visibility (Rohde and Kendle 1994; Rishbeth research in progress). There is also evidence to suggest that members of ethnic minorities use public open spaces less than their white British counterparts, and that people with different cultural and ethnic backgrounds use open spaces in different ways, and value them for different reasons (Rishbeth 2001). Personal safety has been found to be a major factor restraining the use of public open spaces for members of some ethnic minorities (Madge 1997). Research on the impact of ethnicity in landscape perception is still fairly limited and it may in fact be the case (just as in the previous example of social class) that some aspects of landscape perception that appear to be correlated with ethnicity actually relate more to other factors, such as the impact on an individual of recent immigration or residence (Rohde and Kendle 1994; Rishbeth 2001).

Thus, it appears that personal factors can have a powerful effect on landscape preference, and, by inference, preference for different types of vegetation and ecological plantings. However, not enough is known about these differences and more research needs to be done to determine the nature of these variations.

Potential benefits of ecological plantings

There is a large body of evidence suggesting that contact with nature in various different forms has a beneficial effect on human beings, physically, psychologically and socially. Most of this research is outside the scope of this chapter, as it does not relate exclusively to ecological plantings: in most cases it would be impossible to assert that ecological plantings do more good than any other type of planting.

However, there are some notable exceptions to this. The first relates to the benefits sustained by people as a result of wilderness experiences. Kaplan and Kaplan (1989) summarised the results of a decade of research into the effects of participation in outward-bound programmes. They found that the participants gained certain physical crafts and skills, as well as an improved self-image: feeling more self-confident and having a more positive outlook. They also found that after a fairly rapid period of acclimatisation, participants experienced a sense of self-discovery, wholeness, well-being, renewal and restoration, as well as what Kaplan and Kaplan described as 'the recovery of aspects of mental functioning that had become less effective through overuse.' They concluded that:

> The role of the natural environment is inherent to these experiences. Not only did participants notice more aspects of that environment, but they came to realise that they lived differently and felt differently during their immersion in this setting. The coexistence with other creatures and growing things gave them a new perspective on themselves. The existence of the wilderness became a comforting thought.

Yet there is also evidence that some young people particularly have very different and negative reactions to exposure to nature as part of wilderness experiences (Bixler and Floyd 1997). It is interesting that *The Blair Witch Project*, a film by Eduardo Sanchez and Daniel Myrick about a group of young people lost in the woods, who become prey to supernatural forces, should have a dense woodland of young trees and saplings for its setting. These polarisations are likely to become even more extreme given the nature of contemporary childhood, with outdoor play competing with virtual reality and being further restricted by parental concerns about safety.

Tartaglia-Kershaw (1980) found that, as well as

11.5
Two views of a lake in Central Park, New York – they indicate that rich naturalistic wetland planting is fully compatible with the recreational use of an urban park

valuing local woodland for aesthetic and functional reasons, urban dwellers valued them for bringing a sense of continuity to their lives: they had played in them as children and now their children and grandchildren were playing in them. Bussey's (1996) research has confirmed that, as well as having restorative benefits, urban woodlands are rich in cultural and symbolic meanings for urban dwellers. Respondents valued their woodland visits for their ability to relieve stress and for their spiritual qualities. The woodlands were found to have a range of meanings, including acting as a woodland garden, doorstep recreational area, symbol of the pastoral idyll, wildlife sanctuary and gateway to the natural world.

As Rohde and Kendle (1994) have pointed out, it is difficult to draw firm conclusions from the findings to date, particularly as to the implications for the design of urban public open spaces let alone ecological plantings. They have questioned whether the value of wilderness experiences may derive partly from the perceived scarcity of these environments: if wilderness was commonplace then its perceived value and consequent benefits might diminish. Arguably, this concern has been allayed by Bussey's research, which strongly suggests that natural areas that are closely integrated with an urban setting are no less valued for being accessible.

Another exception relates to the developmental benefits to children of growing up in natural environments. A number of Scandinavian studies indicate that playing in complex natural environments has a positive impact on children's social play, concentration and motor ability (Bang *et al.* 1989; Grahn 1991; Fjortoft 1995, 1998, 1999; Grahn *et al.* 1997). Diversity in vegetation and topography enhances the ability of the natural playscape to improve motor ability (Fjortoft and Sageie 2000). Clearly, vegetation is just one component of complex natural environments. Nevertheless, this research does suggest that an urban setting containing robust naturalistic woody and herbaceous vegetation is likely to be a more stimulating environment for children than some of the more conventional alternatives. Given these findings, it is interesting that people with no knowledge of this research often support urban nature on the basis that it is beneficial to children, relying on their own childhood experiences to support their beliefs (Tartaglia-Kershaw 1980; Burgess *et al.* 1988).

Thus, we can say that there is clear evidence suggesting that natural or semi-natural landscapes in urban settings have distinct benefits in terms of their restorative qualities, cultural meanings, and their beneficial role in many aspects of children's development. It seems logical that naturalistic ecological plantings would form part of these landscapes (Figure 11.5). There is evidence that some people may have equivocal or even negative feelings about such landscapes but it is suggested that in many cases this can be overcome through sensitive planning and design, and public involvement.

There is no consensus yet as to the precise nature of the relationship between our visions of nature and our preference for different landscapes. Ulrich (1986) and Kaplan and Kaplan (1989) found that people generally seem to prefer urban landscapes with a natural content over those consisting of predominantly built form; though in these studies the so-called natural content was often limited to small quantities of vegetation without any ecological value. The question remains as to what form the natural content of urban landscapes should take. To date, preferred landscapes have been exemplified by parkland in the English Landscape style. However, it may be that other types of landscape bearing these basic characteristics would be considered equally attractive. The challenge for designers is to find out what these alternatives are. One option would be to adopt the savannah style as a large-scale framework, which then becomes the setting for a number of more diverse, complex and ecologically-rich smaller-scale landscapes.

Public preference for ecological vegetation types

For reasons of time and space, this review of the available research about public attitudes to ecological plantings in public open spaces concentrates predominantly on the UK, but comments are also made about Europe and the US, where evidence is available.

Different countries and cultures have very different planting traditions in their public landscapes and this needs to be borne in mind when interpreting the literature. It is noteworthy that, whilst theorists and practitioners such as William Robinson in the UK and Herman Jäger in Germany, were writing about how to establish naturalistic meadow-style plantings from the late nineteenth century onwards (Woudstra and Hitchmough 2000), these ideas appear to have had little impact in, for example, southern Europe. Naturalistic plantings began to be used in the Netherlands from the 1930s onwards in the Amsterdam bos and the gardens and parks of Jacques P. Thijsse (Ruff 1979), and from the 1920s in Germany in the work of A. D. Heicke in Frankfurt am Main (Woudstra and Hitchmough 2000). In the UK, on the other hand, ecological plantings in public open spaces did not begin until the later half of the twentieth century in the ecological woodland plantings of the new towns. Whereas naturalistic landscapes and an ecological approach to green-space management are widespread in Germany and the Netherlands, they are still the exception rather than the norm in the UK. This strongly suggests that these variations are cultural in origin, rather than being due to an absence of awareness or expertise. The basis of these differences may well lie in fundamental differences in the way these different cultures see the relationship between humans and nature.

Predicting how people might react to ecological plantings in public urban settings is a difficult task because both plantings and context can differ so widely. For example, ecological plantings of herbaceous vegetation can take the form of a meadow comprising only native species, but can also become a formal herbaceous border, comprising mainly exotic species. Both can be described as 'ecological', but the whole style and context is different.

Given the diversity of possible approaches, it is impossible to come up with one universal formula to predict public reaction. As 'naturalness' and 'degree of human influence' are a fundamental basis for discriminating between landscapes, it seems reasonable to draw a dividing line between naturalistic and non-naturalistic plantings when considering public attitudes towards ecological plantings. A further useful division is between woody and herbaceous vegetation, though clearly there are many plantings that include both.

Ecological woodland plantings

Naturalistic ecological woodland plantings

The key distinguishing feature of ecological plantings of trees and other woody species is the presence of one or more layers of understorey vegetation. Conversely, conventional urban parkland in the English Landscape style consists of mature trees limbed up to several metres above ground level in a setting of mown grass.

From the earliest days of landscape preference research in the 1960s, there have been a number of lines of research that have consistently found that images depicting multi-layered woody vegetation of the kind one would expect to find within ancient woodland or along a woodland edge in a state of natural succession attract lower preference scores than images of parkland in the style of the English Landscape movement (Ulrich 1977; Kaplan 1985). Based on these studies, the assumption has grown that multi-layered woody vegetation itself is lower in preference than mature trees set in mown grass:

> Thick undergrowth and dense stands of trees detract from the scenic beauty of forested environments. In particular, recent research suggests that humans may have a biologically prepared predisposition to associate negative consequences with spatially restricted natural environments.
>
> (Ulrich *et al.* (1993) quoted in Parsons (1995))

Some of these studies are open to criticism. For example, it can be argued that that the images depicted simply do not compare like with like: a close-up of a woodland edge is quite different from a long view of an open woodland glade – one is an image of the structure of the vegetation itself, the second is an image of the spaces defined by the vegetation. This is the case in the study by Ulrich cited above (1977). In a later paper (1986), Ulrich refers to two sample images from the high and low preference groups in the earlier study. The first is a typical parkland landscape in the English Landscape style. The second example is a much closer view of roadside scrubland. In the first image, the vegetation consists of mature trees limbed up to several metres from the ground, combined with what appears to be mown grass; in the second the vegetation consists of young trees with a dense understorey of thorny scrub and herbs. In the first image the vegetation appears healthy but in the second there are several leafless trees or shrubs that appear to be dead or dying. The topology in the two images is also completely different. In the first image the ground is predominantly level, whereas in the second the ground rises markedly away from the viewer, thus further reducing the visual permeability of the scene. There are in fact a number of variables that differ between the two scenes, variables that are not controlled for in the study.

In terms of aesthetic preference for the two different landscapes, it is arguable that most people would choose the long view for the simple reason that it is more interesting, because the image itself contains more. It is rather like comparing a photograph of a strip of wallpaper with a photograph of an entire room papered with different wallpaper. Whilst people may prefer scenes that contain long view distances over close views when comparing visual images of landscapes, such studies certainly do not support the hypothesis that certain kinds of vegetation are inherently lower in preference.

In one study focusing exclusively on near-view forest scenes, the degree of visual penetration was found to be a significant predictor of scenic beauty (Ruddell *et al.* 1989). However, visual penetration is not associated exclusively with certain kinds of vegetation. Visual penetration is also dependent on the spatial arrangement of vegetation and view distance. The relationship between view distance and vegetation density was explored by Purcell and Lamb (1998) who found an interesting interaction. They found that whereas sparser vegetation was preferred to denser vegetation in close views, the reverse applied in wide views. Here preference was related to view distance and not solely to the qualities of the vegetation itself.

Further, the bulk of the research relied upon by commentators such as Parsons (1995) was carried out in American forests, many of which were planted and managed for commercial purposes. The levels of tree density encountered during some of these studies (in excess of 1,000 trees per acre) (Hull *et al.* 1987) are far higher than one would normally expect to encounter in an urban public situation. Schroeder and Green (1985) investigated public perception of optimum tree density in American public parks and found that the preferred density varied from 40 to

65 trees per acre depending on whether the background was dense or open. Hence, the research carried out in American forests has to be viewed with some caution. Further, many of the findings from this research relate to coniferous rather than deciduous forests. In at least one of the studies relied upon by Parsons in support of his contention that 'thick undergrowth and dense stands of trees detract from the scenic beauty of forested environments', there was no significant relationship either way between understorey vegetation density and perception of scenic beauty, although the impact of this variable may have been represented by other stand characteristics in the study (Hull *et al.* 1987).

To some extent, however, these studies miss the point, because, as we have already seen, landscape aesthetics should not focus solely on preference for different views of landscapes rather they should embrace a whole gamut of different approaches, ranging from how we perceive landscapes in terms of their utility to the feelings they evoke in us. Further, we do not experience landscape solely from a series of static viewpoints. A great deal of our experience of landscape is dynamic: we get to know landscapes as we move through and interact with them, seeing them from different perspectives and experiencing them in different ways at different times.

From the 1960s onwards there has been a large tranche of research into forest landscapes, particularly in Scandinavia and the USA. This research has generally taken the form of collecting public responses to photographs depicting different forest conditions. Participants are shown a series of photographs of different forest scenes and are then asked to rate them for scenic beauty. The ratings are then compared to the content of the photographs to determine the relative preference for different factors: an approach known as the 'psychophysical' approach. A review by Ribe (1989) made the following findings. Comparisons of preference for managed as opposed to unmanaged or natural forests have yielded contradictory results (presumably because these definitions are fairly loose: managed and natural forests come in many different forms). High tree-density, particularly of young trees, is considered less attractive than medium densities (though one study found the optimum number of trees per acre to be 1,150 (Buyhoff *et al.* 1986). Vegetation structures that permit visual penetration are preferred to those that do not. The presence of a shrub or sapling understorey has been found both to enhance and detract from a scene (again, this may be because of the many different characteristics a woodland understorey can have in terms of variation in vegetation type and structure). A variety of species is preferred to a monoculture where it gives rise to visual diversity. The presence of large trees enhances preference as does a ground cover of grasses, ferns, forbs or seedlings. Slash (the stumps and offcuts that are the aftermath of tree-felling) is strongly disliked.

Thus, it would appear that multi-layered woody vegetation is not disliked *per se* but that public perception of it depends largely on other factors, such as view distance and visual penetration.

In the UK there has been a growing movement in favour of habitat creation schemes in urban settings since the 1970s. This has led to the conservation and creation of natural or semi-natural vegetation, including woodland, in discrete locations

11.6
The full aesthetic potential of urban woodlands is rarely realised – how often do the trees and ground flora come together to produce a rich display in a designed woodland?

in these settings. These initiatives are often led or supported by the community, and anecdotal evidence suggests that they are, on the whole, popular. However, because urban nature reserves or habitat creation schemes are popular, it does not follow that all naturalistic woodland ecological plantings in urban settings will automatically secure public acceptance. The urban nature conservation movement often builds on existing ecological capital so there is frequently a perceived need to protect what is already there: public support frequently rallies around such issues. Further, the overriding aim is to create or repair habitats for wildlife: also an objective that attracts popular support. These schemes are often restricted to distinct locations with recognisable qualities of their own, and constitute a small proportion of urban green-space overall, so that most urban dwellers have a clear choice about whether to visit them. There are major differences between these initiatives and using ecological woodland plantings in public urban landscapes for structural or aesthetic purposes (Figure 11.6).

The idea of using woodland ecological plantings in designed landscapes in public urban settings first emerged in the 1970s in the UK. One of the first pioneering examples was Oakwood in Warrington New Town. Oakwood was remarkable not only for the way in which the naturalistic woodland belts, landform and open spaces were used to structure the whole development, but also for the manner in which the vegetation and other landscape elements were skilfully and closely integrated with the built development. Oakwood marked a sea change that had come about in the minds of many landscape professionals.

The naturalistic landscapes created at Oakwood were seen as beneficial for its future residents for many reasons. Adults could enjoy nature on their doorstep in the form of vegetation and green spaces that were robust enough to withstand regular use. Children would have many opportunities for adventurous and creative play amongst the vegetation. For all age groups there were opportunities to interact with nature whilst carrying out the daily activities of living: going to school, work or to the shops (Tregay and Gustavsson 1983). There was a desire to enable residents to actively experience the interior of woodland rather than just looking at it from the outside (Figure 11.7). The designers of this new landscape were passionate and committed, and were strongly influenced by similar developments that were already taking place in Europe, particularly in Sweden and in the Netherlands. Under the circumstances, it is perhaps hardly surprising that public involvement or consultation was not considered to be an important part of the design process. In any event, this would have been difficult logistically, as most of Oakwood's residents came from far away, from Manchester and Liverpool.

11.7
In Oakwood naturalistic woodland is closely integrated with the built development

By the 1980s there was a growing awareness of the desire to incorporate more natural landscapes into towns and cities. The approach first used at Warrington became known as 'the ecological approach' and passed into mainstream thinking among the planners and designers of local authorities and New Town Corporations. One of the first evaluations of the validity of this approach, in terms of public perception, when compared to more traditional approaches to green-space planning, design and management, was the study of Tartaglia-Kershaw (1980) into the role of urban woodland in residents' daily life. Tartaglia-Kershaw carried out a detailed study of the Gleadless area of Sheffield, a housing area planned around an existing mature woodland. Although the woodland in Gleadless was generally within 500 m of the housing, and often considerably closer, it was not closely integrated with the housing as in Warrington. In Gleadless, the woodland and the housing formed two distinct and separate areas. 72% of the sample in the study said that the woods were important to them. An overwhelming 90% liked living on the estate, and 94% said that they liked the way the area had been planned. However, Tartaglia-Kershaw (1980) concluded that the overall findings did not support the approach used in Warrington:

> The residents do not want woodland to the door as many figures in the 'Nature in Cities' movement suggest, and which is happening in New Towns based on woodland structure planning [sic].

In another early study responding to the need for research on the impact of the nature and character of urban green-space, Burgess *et al.* (1988) examined the views of urban dwellers about their local green-spaces. They found that traditionally managed urban green-spaces characterised by isolated trees and mown grass were not valued as much as natural or semi-natural urban landscapes characterised by woodland, multiple layers of vegetation and an un-mown grass/herb layer. However, they also found that many people had ambivalent feelings about the landscapes they most valued: these landscapes were also the ones that aroused the most fear. They concluded that what people really want is a range of opportunities provided simultaneously in as many different green spaces as possible, and not zoned between different parks and green spaces.

Burgess' findings about the value that people place on natural or semi-natural urban landscapes were confirmed and explored in more detail by Bussey (1996) in another landmark study. Bussey carried out an extensive study of urban-dwellers' attitudes and feelings towards their local woods in Redditch, England, and found that woods were ranked above parks and were second only to open countryside as the preferred landscape for informal recreation. These findings are mirrored in an extremely large Dutch study of 3,118 respondents throughout the Netherlands. In this study, 57% of respondents said they would prefer small areas of nature and green-space close to home as opposed to a large nature area further away (Reneman *et al.* 1999).

The studies of Tartaglia-Kershaw (1980), Burgess *et al.* (1988) and Bussey (1996) were unusual and pioneering within the genre that can be loosely called landscape perception research. Through their mixture of qualitative and quantitative techniques, they were able to examine the ambivalent and sometimes conflicting feelings that we hold towards naturalistic landscapes in urban settings: such landscapes inspire negative as well as positive feelings.

Despite the innovative work done by researchers such as Burgess and Bussey, the idea that 'woodland structure planting' is regarded as unsafe by members of the general public, and is therefore unsuitable for use in urban situations, has persisted among local authorities (Thompson 2000):

> Fear of crime can be as disabling as crime itself. One of the most unfortunate results of this widespread apprehensiveness is that vegetation has come to be regarded with mistrust by many urban residents. It is seen as providing hiding places for potential

> assailants. Landscape architects have had to take account of this fear. Some local authorities have actually been taking shrubberies out of parks and residential areas, and when considering new plantings designers are urged to use low-growing shrubs and to keep shrub beds back from the edges of paths. This defensive approach is in many ways the antithesis of the ecological ideals which were being imported from Holland in the 1970s. These called for mass plantings, more relaxed plantings, and an altogether shaggier, more naturalistic style of landscape design.

There is clearly a danger that, in seeking to reassure the general public by the removal of shrubby vegetation, local authorities are also destroying the landscapes that people most value, despite their understandable fears. However, it may also be the case that the 'ecological approach' was too wholesale, in that naturalistic vegetation was used too indiscriminately and too close to people's homes, as predicted by Tartaglia-Kershaw (1980). There may well be an appropriate gradient of planting styles, ranging from more formal and manicured to 'shaggier' and naturalistic, corresponding roughly with distance from people's homes and the places they have to visit daily. Arguably what is needed is an element of choice, as proposed by Burgess. People may well tolerate or even welcome more naturalistic treatments provided they can choose when to interact with them. These issues are explored in more detail in the final section.

A more recent study (Jorgensen *et al.* 2002) examined the impact of the spatial arrangement of woodland and the nature of the woodland edge on public perception of safety and preference in an urban park. Several different naturalistic edge treatments (flowering herb layer, dense understorey, flowering herb layer combined with dense understorey and, finally, native woodland edge) were contrasted with a more conventional parkland vegetation of specimen trees and mown grass in three different spatial arrangements (full enclosure, partial enclosure and no enclosure). Respondents were asked to rate digital images of the 15 combinations of edge treatment and spatial arrangement for safety and then preference. Although the respondents found the native woodland edge to be the least safe of all the edge treatments, there were some interesting findings in relation to the interaction between edge treatment and spatial arrangement. Reactions to the three different spatial arrangements of the woodland varied dramatically according to the nature of the woodland edge in the case of the spatial arrangements known as full enclosure and no enclosure, but not in the case of partial enclosure, when all edge treatments received similar ratings for safety and preference. The most dramatic variation was in the case of the dense understorey edge treatment: rated most unsafe in the full enclosure spatial arrangement but most safe in the no enclosure spatial arrangement. These findings suggest that, whilst safety issues are undoubtedly an important issue when working with naturalistic woody vegetation, design can play an important role in mitigating these issues.

There seems to be something particularly powerful, if not shocking, about a certain kind of urban nature, namely the kind of nature that takes over when an urban building or plot has been abandoned. Perhaps it is the speed with which the transformation takes place or perhaps it has something to do with the palpable power of nature to invade and even destroy man-made structures, splitting concrete and rapidly colonising seemingly inhospitable horizontal and vertical habitats. In Germany, this kind of nature has been given its own name: 'industrial nature'. Up until recently, industrial nature was not tolerated. In the UK, where funds were available, industrial sites were dismantled, carefully graded and levelled, covered with topsoil and replanted with what came to be known as 'woodland structure planting'. Evidence of this approach can be found on the outskirts of many of our towns and cities in the form of the Country Park. In Germany, an appreciation of the special qualities of these post-industrial sites has led to a whole new design approach:

> The visitor first has to set aside his preconceptions, his knowledge that the land was once a workplace full of labour and toil, and is now nothing more than a devastated polluted site. Only then will he be able to appreciate its peculiar attraction, its atmosphere of decay, disorder, wilderness and chaos in a basically urban setting.
>
> (Dettmar 1999)

These properties have been exploited to the full in the Ruhr district of Germany, in Emscher Park, other woodlands in the Ruhr District, and in the Südgelände nature park in Berlin. These woodlands are all the effect of natural succession on derelict industrial sites. At some point during the late twentieth century, various public authorities in Germany came to the conclusion that these areas of industrial dereliction combined with spontaneously occurring vegetation had special qualities of their own worth preserving. In the case of Emscher Park, they conceived the idea of retaining the existing industrial structures and working with the spontaneously generated vegetation to create a framework for a large number of different recreational activities, as opposed to razing the entire site to the ground and starting again from a tabula rasa (Figure 11.8). An even more radical approach has been taken in other parts of the Ruhr where the 'wild industrial woods', as they are now known, are simply left to their own devices, subject only to a fairly minimal management regime (Dettmar 1999). There has been no attempt so far to evaluate the success of these projects in terms of public attitudes but the very fact that such measures are taking place on such a vast scale (Emscher Park

11.8
An example of 'industrial nature' – derelict industrial structures combined with spontaneously occurring vegetation in Emscher Park, Germany

alone covers 300 km^2) must surely indicate a degree of public acceptance?

The use of the former power station at Bankside to house the Tate Gallery's collection of modern art in the gallery known as Tate Modern, and the reincarnation of the former steel plant at Rotherham as Magna, a new interactive centre for recreation, suggests that former industrial structures are being re-evaluated in the UK. So far, however, these developments have focused on the built form, rather than the surrounding landscape, and it remains to be seen whether the radical approach to industrial nature exemplified by Emscher Park would find favour in Britain, given the differences in outlook referred to above.

Non-naturalistic ecological woodland plantings

These might involve using a multi-layered vegetation structure typical of natural wood or scrub whilst imparting formality through context and layout. Arguably, the deployment of flamboyant exotic species can also make a multi-layered woodland planting look more designed; but this approach depends on the viewer's ability to recognise the species as exotic. Ecological planting using woody vegetation arrayed in a formal as opposed to informal spatial arrangement is rarely seen, but is likely to be equally valuable as wildlife habitat. This approach is largely untested in recent years but certainly provides interesting possibilities for innovative new designs. There are, however, numerous historic instances, for example at Versailles, Schönbrun and the Boboli gardens in Florence, where the great vistas are carved out of straight-edged blocks of woodland. The interior spaces within these woodlands could well have had a very naturalistic feel to them.

Given our lack of experience with these types of plantings in contemporary urban landscapes one cannot predict public reaction with any certainty. Woody vegetation has a potentially large physical presence in the landscape and a corresponding ability to conceal potential attackers. Thus, it seems likely that formal layout and context, and the use of exotic species, may not necessarily make such plantings feel any safer than their naturalistic counterparts, though it may render them more appropriate in an urban setting.

Ecological herbaceous plantings

Dividing herbaceous ecological plantings into the two categories of naturalistic or wild-looking and non-naturalistic is an artificial exercise in one sense, suggesting that such plantings fall into one category or the other. In reality, there is a continuum from wild-looking to highly-designed, with many intermediate points. Naturalistic or wild-looking herbaceous planting tends to rely for its effect on the overall appearance of the plant communities, whereas non-naturalistic planting tends to rely more on the properties of individual species. However, although it is usually the nature of the planting that defines the perceived degree of naturalness, this is not always the case. The context of the planting can also play a very important role. For example, the meadow plantings by the charity Landlife in Knowsley, Liverpool, on empty urban spaces within public housing developments, clearly have a completely different context and function to naturalistic prairie-style planting in a private garden.

However, given that one of the main methods by which people categorise landscape is the degree of naturalness, the basic dichotomy of naturalistic and non-naturalistic is still a convenient way of structuring a discussion of public attitudes to these kinds of plantings (Kaplan and Kaplan 1989).

Naturalistic ecological herbaceous plantings

Whilst research into public preference for natural and natural-looking woodland landscapes has been continuing since the 1960s, interest in the public

11.9
Rosemary Weiss's pioneering steppe planting in the West Park, Munich, Germany

11.10
A wildflower meadow created by the charity Landlife in Knowsley, Liverpool

perception of ecological plantings of herbaceous vegetation in urban landscapes in the West is relatively recent; a reflection of the fact that such vegetation has never been common in public settings, even in Germany, where such vegetation has long been admired. One of the first contemporary examples was Rosemary Weisse's steppe planting in the West Park, Munich, carried out in 1979 (Figure 11.9).

Although there is considerable anecdotal evidence, particularly about public reactions to the mass meadow style plantings, there is very little published research about the public perception of any of these different approaches.

The anecdotal evidence suggests that many people react extremely positively to meadow-style plantings whilst they are in flower. For example, a local resident made the following comments about one of these plantings by the charity Landlife, in Knowsley, Liverpool (Figure 11.10):

> It has been my good fortune to live opposite what was once a derelict site, full of rubbish and ugly to behold ... It has now been transformed to an attractive open space. From spring onwards you could see the start of young growth plus lots of wildlife. Midsummer, the colours of different flowers with a background of mown grass plus walkways. It would be very heart warming if the same could be done for the lots of ex-building sites all over the country.
>
> (Extract from questionnaire research carried out by Landlife (1994))

A recent study examined public preference for flowering as opposed to green herbaceous vegetation (Dai 2000). The impact of vegetation height (low, medium and tall), colour (yellow or multi-coloured), and pattern of colour distribution (spots or patches) was examined. Again, respondents were asked to rate digital images depicting different combinations of the variables. The variations were inserted into an urban scene including people and a number of residential buildings. The respondents liked the colourful vegetation (both yellow and multi-coloured) distributed in patches as opposed to spots regardless of whether it was low, medium or tall. They disliked the exclusively green herbaceous vegetation, particularly when it was tall. In the study by Jorgensen *et al.* (2002), referred to earlier, the flowering herb layer edge treatment was preferred to every other woodland edge treatment, including the conventional parkland vegetation of specimen trees and mown grass. This evidence clearly supports the use of naturalistic herbaceous vegetation as an alternative to mown grass in urban green-space. There is also considerable anecdotal evidence indicating that colour, and plenty of it, enhances the public appeal of naturalistic herbaceous vegetation; which Dai's research (2000) confirms.

Approval for such vegetation is thought to decline outside of the flowering period and especially in winter, when the dried out plants and seed heads are brown. However, recent unpublished research within the Landscape Department of the University of Sheffield (Dunnett, N. and Mynott, L., unpublished) suggests that familiarity with the seasonal changes in such plantings mitigates their negative impact. This seasonal variation in public approval for such plantings can also be diminished by careful species selection to extend the flowering period.

Research has been carried out in Germany regarding public reaction to a new perennial planting mix known as '*Silbersommer*', developed by the 'Arbeitskreis Pflanzenverwendung' to deal with a number of issues, including ease of maintenance and public approval. The concept behind *Silbersommer* is a robust, ecologically inspired planting, with appeal over at least three seasons, characterised by a preponderance of plants with silver foliage (Bitter and Huettenmoser 2001). This mix has been trialled along streets, plazas and pedestrian zones in several German cities. A survey of public attitudes towards these plantings found that most people did not find its appearance untidy, and valued its naturalistic appearance and perceived ecological value. 75% of those questioned thought that there was a need for more such ecological plantings in the city. The only negative findings were that people would have liked to see a greater variety of colours and plants.

The *Silbersommer* plantings are very clearly at the horticultural end of the naturalistic continuum, which may well explain why they elicited such a positive response. Public opinion in Germany is not always so positive regarding naturalistic vegetation in urban settings. As far back as 1992, de la Chevallerie was critical about the role of wilderness in the city, claiming that it was unsuitable for an urban setting (de la Chevallerie 1992). In his opinion, urban green-spaces should meet the need for urban development, and social and cultural functionalism. As you cannot play football in a herbaceous meadow, such a planting does not meet his criteria. Kuehn (2000) concluded that an attempt to establish ruderal, naturalistic vegetation in a park was considered weedy, disordered and inappropriate in an urban setting, though this particular brand of ruderal vegetation may have been very different in terms of species selection from what is more commonly thought of as herbaceous meadow. Milchert (2001), another German commentator, has stated that the majority of the German public consider naturalistic plantings to be 'weedy' or a 'neglected occurrence', and therefore not aesthetically desirable, and has stressed a greater need for public consultation and information.

Because of the differences between cultures referred to earlier, it should not be assumed that any of these German findings are representative of public opinion throughout the rest of Europe, let alone the Western world as a whole. Public opinion may in fact be much more tolerant of the appearance of naturalistic herbaceous vegetation in Germany as a result of legislation forbidding the use of herbicides in public landscapes, which has permitted the development of ruderal vegetation in many urban settings.

There is anecdotal evidence suggesting that, in the UK, in some settings, meadow-style plantings are viewed as a safety hazard. Plans to introduce a wildflower meadow as part of the King's Cross Estates Action strategy in London had to be abandoned because of residents' fears that the tall vegetation might conceal drug-users' discarded hypodermic syringes (Landscape Design Trust 2001).

Whilst concerns of untidiness and lack of aesthetic appeal outside the flowering season can, to some extent, be dealt with by means of design techniques, and careful species selection, the fundamental question of the appropriateness or seemliness of these kinds of plantings in an urban situation remains. This is connected to the debate highlighted earlier in this chapter about the place for wild nature in our lives. For people who view the appropriate human/nature paradigm as humans in control of nature, there is no problem as long as wild nature is out there, outside the city, but if wild nature appears in the city then are humans still in control? And what if wild nature appears in places traditionally reserved for floral declarations of civic pride, such as urban squares, the focal points of parks or even just roundabouts at busy intersections? Does this mean that the traditional values of human order and control are being abandoned in favour of the anarchy of the wilderness? And what if some parts of the city, perhaps the more prosperous parts, are seen to retain the order and control whilst others are apparently abandoned to the chaos? Does this mean that the powers that be, or even society in general, is abandoning some of its members to the back of beyond?

This might seem to be an exaggerated view of public fears in relation to naturalistic plantings in urban situations but such ideas are encapsulated in the comments by de la Chevallerie and Kuehn, and also in the following statement by Michel Corajoud about the planting in his 1996 park design for Park Gerland in Lyon, France:

> Nature in its wild state is not a place for civilised life ... With reference to the city I am interested in presenting a fertile kind of nature brought under control, worked on by human hands, and more likely to correspond with the specific nature of urban places.
>
> (Quoted in Davoine (2001))

To summarise, there may well be considerable public resistance to naturalistic herbaceous ecological plantings in public urban spaces, but there is also evidence to suggest that people derive intense pleasure from such plantings, appreciating them for their aesthetic appearance as well as their ecological value. Important considerations are safety, tidiness, length of flowering period, colourfulness, context, and, last but not least, public awareness and consultation.

Non-naturalistic ecological herbaceous plantings

As previously indicated, changes in the context or the nature of the planting, particularly in plant density and spatial organisation, can determine whether an ecological herbaceous planting appears designed as opposed to natural. So, on the one hand, there is the Garden of Movement in Parc André Citroen in Paris, and, at the other extreme, are some of the designs of Piet Oudolf, such as his planting design for the ABN/AMRO Bank in Amsterdam.

If there is little research regarding public attitudes to wild-looking herbaceous ecological plantings in urban public settings, there is even less about its non-naturalistic equivalent. Consequently, in order to try to evaluate public opinion, we have to examine current fashions in planting design and the views expressed by commentators.

For the last two years a number of the gardens at the Chelsea Flower show have included large-scale ecological herbaceous plantings in a context of high design that is quite unlike the folk or conservation ethic that has frequently accompanied the use of wildflowers or meadows in the show in the past. A similar design language can be found on a much larger scale in Gilles Vexlard's design for the new park at Messerstadt Riem, near Munich, Germany. The park services the residents and employees of the new settlement at Messerstadt Riem. Both the park and the new settlement are being built on a brownfield site, a former airport. Here wild-looking herbaceous vegetation is used in meadow-style plantings, but these are firmly contained and held by formal tree planting in blocks and strips.

The question is whether such examples of ecological plantings in a formal context are just another fashion or whether they are a sign of a more fundamental sea-change – perhaps the reflection of a more generalised ecocentric world-view that is becoming prevalent in the West. Penelope Hill argues convincingly for the latter view:

> The idea of the garden as a purely aesthetic creation is old-fashioned nowadays – the most important factor is consideration for the environment, linked with the well-being of the plants worked out according to where and in what conditions they grow naturally.
> (Hill 2001)

In support of her argument, Hill cites the work of a number of designers and horticulturalists, such as Beth Chatto in her garden near Colchester.

Further examples can also be given, such as the work of the late Derek Jarman in his garden on the shingle at Dungeness. Jarman produced a garden that was extraordinarily beautiful and visually appropriate because of its reliance on species that were either native or naturalised locally, such as sea kale (*Crambe maritima*) and the yellow horned poppy (*Glaucium flavum*), supplemented by species that were well-adapted to the particularly harsh conditions on the shingle at Dungeness, for example giant sea kale (*Crambe cordifolia*) and the Californian poppy (Figure 11.11). Another example is the garden created by Dan Pearson at Home Farm. This garden relies partly on a more flamboyant and overtly exotic species selection, but these are frequently combined in a naturalistic fashion. There is, moreover, an overriding concern to blend the garden seamlessly into the surrounding landscape by a gentle transition from the more formal areas to the more natural ones. There is, for example, the slender path that creates a line of vision through the hummocky carpet of thyme and across the lake to the woods and countryside beyond.

11.11
The garden created by the late Derek Jarman at Dungeness

It is doubtless possible to think of numerous further examples, but perhaps the ultimate example, given by Hill herself, is that of the garden designed by Beth Galí for a private house in Girona, Spain. As Hill describes, this garden relies exclusively on 'the relationship between the spontaneous evolution of plants and the changes due to human intervention'. The human intervention was limited to careful site preparation and an irrigation system providing differential watering. It was then just a case of standing back and waiting to see what appeared.

An indication that a more naturalistic visual aesthetic has taken hold is the fact that some of its visual characteristics are being copied even by designers with very different agendas. For example, there is the planting in Park Gerland in Lyon, France, designed by Gabriel Chauvel and Yannick Salliot. The planting is in highly formalised monocultural strips and blocks, separated by paths, that are intended to resemble agricultural plantings. A wild, uncultivated look is deliberately avoided, as emphasised by one of the project managers, Michel Corajoud (Davoine 2001). Nevertheless, despite these clear intentions, the great swathes of herbaceous material and grasses are quite naturalistic in appearance. It is as if these designers have adopted the aesthetic visions of designers using ecological plantings without the ecological baggage that go with them.

It is difficult to predict how members of the general public would react to naturalistic herbaceous planting presented in a formal context in public urban situations. However, it seems plausible that such an approach would allay many of the concerns that are thought to exist in relation to naturalistic or wild-looking herbaceous plantings, namely untidiness, dislike of seasonal variation, incongruity in an urban situation and safety issues.

There are, of course, many ecological approaches to herbaceous planting that would fall either wholly or partly within the definition at the beginning of this chapter but which do not look at all naturalistic or wild either because of the structural way in which the plants are used or because of the exoticism of the species. Examples of these two different non-naturalistic approaches are, respectively, some of Piet Oudolf's more formal designs, such as the planting in his own garden at Hummelo, in the Netherlands, and some of the plantings pioneered by Richard Hansen at Weihenstephan, Germany (Figure 11.12). Neither of these approaches is likely to be rejected by the public on the basis of the concerns that seem to exist in relation to ecological plantings that are more naturalistic in appearance. If such plantings turn out to be unpopular, it is more likely to be because they are simply different from more traditional approaches. Like other forms of artistic expression, they will have to stand or fall on their own merits.

To summarise, whilst it seems that many urban dwellers in the UK may have a positive regard for naturalistic herbaceous vegetation in public urban settings, there seems to be concern over issues of safety, tidiness, seasonal variation and appropriateness. The challenge inherent in designing with this type of vegetation is how to overcome these concerns through design, species selection, technical expertise, and public consultation and involvement. For the reasons explained earlier, it seems unlikely that the more overtly designed herbaceous ecological plantings will be subject to these concerns.

11.12
An example of an 'exotic' ecological planting from the trial gardens at Weihenstephan, Munich, Germany

Future focus

This final section does not seek to lay down hard and fast rules for the social dimensions of planning or designing with ecological plantings, naturalistic or otherwise. This chapter has shown that the state of knowledge about public attitudes to ecological plantings in public urban settings is patchy and much more research is needed to fill in the gaps. More importantly, it shows that the perception goal posts are always moving, and that we must constantly re-evaluate public attitudes. Setting out rules would be repeating the mistakes of the past by suggesting that one solution fits all, once and for all. Instead, this section summarises the most important contemporary issues or problems, and suggests possible solutions in relation to naturalistic ecological planting. Kaplan *et al.* (1988) have already addressed many of these issues in their comprehensive text *With People in Mind*.

Aiming for diversity

As has already been discussed, one of the shortcomings of the so-called green deserts of the second half of the twentieth century was their monotony: the fact that they did not afford opportunities for the different experiences and activities that are such a valued part of more natural landscapes (Burgess *et al.* 1988). Monotony was possibly also one of the shortcomings of some of the applications of 'the ecological approach' in British New Towns, and may partly explain the adverse reactions to some of these plantings. Whilst large areas of flowering herbaceous vegetation may have a dramatic impact that justifies a uniform approach, the same cannot always be said of large-scale ecological plantings of woody vegetation. Thus in the case of woody vegetation particularly, the emphasis should be on creating landscapes with the maximum amount of diversity in terms of the character of the plantings, the nature of the spaces and the uses and activities they accommodate. The planting itself could be varied by the use of colour, exotic species, varying the species selection along a continuum from a monoculture to a species mix, varying the rhythm and pattern of the planting, the vegetation structure (one or more layers), combining with herbaceous vegetation, application of differing management techniques (coppicing, pollarding, standards) and generally by applying many of the techniques that are normally associated with conventional planting design.

Public involvement in relation to naturalistic ecological planting

It seems likely that a clear consensus as to the appearance and characteristics of ecological planting will be uncommon among the general public. Sharing information is therefore likely to be an important part of the involvement process (though not the only part). Realistic photomontages showing the anticipated appearance of the new plantings may be a helpful means of both giving information and getting feedback about people's reactions to the proposals. Visits to sites where successful ecological planting has been employed may also be useful. Information giving should not be restricted to issues such as appearance, form and siting, but should include more fundamental issues, such as the whole raison d'être of ecological plantings, and there should be an emphasis on consensus building.

Pilot projects are also likely to be a useful means of demonstrating what can be achieved, as well as introducing people to some of the seasonal variations in ecological plantings.

Ecological plantings, unlike some other forms of planned change in the urban environment, are unique in that the public can play a significant role in their creation, and possibly also their maintenance (Lickorish *et al.* 1997). There is therefore real scope for ongoing public involvement in the creation and maintenance of ecological planting projects.

Safety and freedom to choose

Safety is the single most important issue relating to all kinds of naturalistic ecological planting in public urban settings, but particularly to woody vegetation. Whilst both anecdotal evidence and research suggest that thoughtful design can contribute to a sense of safety (Jorgensen *et al.* 2002), it seems clear that there are many people who will remain wary of naturalistic ecological plantings. Equally, there is evidence that such people might value the existence of such plantings whilst not wanting to interact with them (Tartaglia-Kershaw 1980; Kaplan and Kaplan 1989). Ways of addressing these concerns are suggested below.

– One method is to provide a gradient from

intensive and overtly designed landscapes to extensive and naturalistic ones (Manning 1982; Dowse 1987). The intensive and overtly designed landscapes should be located close to buildings and centres of activity. This enables users to make choices about whether and when to visit the more naturalistic landscapes, and gives them a range of possible activities and settings.

- Another approach, which can be used either on its own or in tandem with the gradient suggested above, is to incorporate route choices into public urban green-spaces and to make these options legible (Luymes and Tamminga 1995). This means always giving people realistic choices between routes that are open, well-lit and hard-surfaced, and routes that do not necessarily have all of these characteristics and are more integrated with the vegetation, with a more adventurous feel to them. An essential feature of this approach is to make the differences between the routes consistent and clear, implicitly by design and explicitly through signage.
- A further method of mitigating concerns about safety, tidiness and appropriateness is to place naturalistic ecological planting within a very formal context, as previously mentioned. This can clearly be done on a small scale, but also on a larger scale, as in the Parc des Poteries in Strasbourg, France (Figure 11.13). Here the naturalistic meadow-style planting is contained within an area demarcated by a grid of trees in circular concrete 'planters'. The meadow can be viewed or entered from the ground but can also be traversed by a boardwalk passing above ground level.

11.13
An urban meadow in a formal context – Parc des Poteries in Strasbourg, France

Character and location of urban woodland

In her study of public perception of urban woodland in Redditch, Bussey (1996) came to certain conclusions regarding the character and location of urban woodland that are relevant to large scale ecological plantings of woody vegetation. Bussey found that people have a surprising need for woodland close to their home:

> A woodland visit is not an 'occasional event' that has to be planned and prepared for. Where the resource is locally available, it is an important part of everyday urban life. This highlights how important it is, that in order that they function as people require them, the woods should be conveniently located on the doorstep, within the urban fabric, not on the urban fringe or in the open countryside.

Bussey went on to make certain specific recommendations based on her findings.

- Urban woods should be readily accessible to a wide range of people and the journey to the wood should be considered part of the recreation experience and should therefore be made as enjoyable as possible.
- Provision should be made for access to a choice of woodlands within 300–650 m of the home.
- Woodlands of 7 ha generally appear to be satisfactory in terms of size. Smaller woodlands should be configured so as to maximise depth to give sufficient enclosure, variety and complexity.
- Most respondents preferred mixed woodland with a canopy density around 65%. Interestingly, the study did not support the conventional wisdom that large mature trees are preferred – people derived as much pleasure from relatively young plantations as they did from the ancient woodland sites.
- Hard-surfaced paths with lighting are welcomed, as are car parks, sign-posted walks and nature trails, and information leaflets.

An important but unresolved issue is to what extent woodland should be integrated with built development, and particularly with people's dwellings. In parts of Warrington New Town, the woodland forms part of the street landscape and is extremely closely integrated – in some cases no more than a couple of metres away from the dwellings themselves. Further work needs to be done to establish whether this degree of proximity is considered satisfactory. However, for woodland that does not form part of the streetscape, Bussey's findings are clearly important indicators.

Conclusions

This chapter has attempted to explore current attitudes towards the use of both naturalistic and formal ecological plantings in public urban settings, and some of the cultural and social meanings underlying those attitudes. It has shown that public perceptions and expectations of urban landscapes are far more diverse and complex than some of the research would have us believe. It has also shown that there is room for natural and even wild-looking landscapes in towns and cities. It is not suggesting that such landscapes should replace more formal approaches to planting, ecological or otherwise. What is clear is that a greater understanding of the social issues involved in dealing with urban nature and nature-like landscape is required if the undoubted environmental and social benefits of a more ecologically-informed approach to landscape design and management in towns and cities are to be realised.

Acknowledgements

-- With many thanks to Judith Bachmeier and Kerstin Kähler for their generous and invaluable help with researching the European sources.

References

-- Appleton, J. (1975). *The Experience of Landscape*. Wiley, London.
-- Balling, J. D. and Falk, J. H. (1982). Development of visual preference for natural environments. *Environment and Behaviour*, **14**, No. 1, 5–28.
-- Bang, C., Braute, J. and Kohen, B. (1989). *Naturleikplassen. Ein Stad for Leik og Laering*. Universitetsforlaget, Oslo, Norway.
-- Bitter, R. and Huettenmoser, B. (2001). Bestimmende faktoren für staudenpflanzungen im offentlichen gruen. *Stadt und Gruen*, **9**, 636–640.
-- Bixler, R. D. and Floyd, M. F. (1997). Nature is scary, disgusting, and uncomfortable. *Environment and Behaviour*, **29**, No. 4, 443–467.

-- Bourassa, S. (1991). *The Aesthetics of Landscape*. Belhaven Press, London and New York.

-- Brown, J. (2000). *The Pursuit of Paradise – A Social History of Gardens and Gardening*. Harper Collins, London.

-- Buhyoff, G. J., Hull IV, R. B., Lien, J. N., and Cordell, H. K. (1986) *Prediction of Scenic Quality for Southern Pine Stands*, Forest Science 32: 769–778.

-- Burgess, J., Harrison, C. M. and Limb, M. (1988). People, parks and the urban green: a study of popular meanings and values for open spaces in the city. *Urban Studies*, **25**, 455–473.

-- Bussey, S. (1996). *Public use, perceptions and preferences for urban woodlands in Redditch*. PhD thesis. University of Central England, Birmingham.

-- Buttel, F. H. and Flinn, W. L. (1978). Social class and mass environmental beliefs. A reconsideration. *Environment and Behaviour*, **10**, No. 3, 433–450.

-- Catton, W. R. and Dunlap, R. E. (1980). A new ecological paradigm for post-exhuberant society. *American Sociologist*, **13**, 41–49.

-- Coleman, A. (1985). *Utopia on Trial. Vision and Reality in Planned Housing*. Hilary Shipman Ltd, London.

-- Dai, L. (2000). *Public Perception of Naturalistic Herbaceous Vegetation in Urban Landscape and Key Elements that Determine Response*. Master's dissertation. Department of Landscape, University of Sheffield.

-- Davoine, G. (2001). Agriculture in the middle of town. *Topos*, **37**, 43–47.

-- Dearden, P. (1984). Factors influencing landscape preferences; an empirical investigation. *Landscape Planning*, **11**, 293–306.

-- Defoe, D. (1727). *A Tour thro' the Whole island of Great Britain*. Peter Davies, London.

-- de la Chevallerie, H. (1992). Freiraeume in der Stadt. *Schriftenreihe des Deutchen Rates für Landespflege*, **61**, No. 5.

-- Dettmar, J. (1999). Wildnis Statt Park? *Topos*, **27**, 31–42.

-- Dowse, S. (1987). *Landscape design guidelines for recreational woodlands in the urban fringe*. Master's dissertation. University of Manchester.

-- Fjortoft, I. (1995). Fysisk miljo og sansemotorisk stimulering. Forsknings og udviklingsarbeid med barn i naturen. *Kroppsoving* 1 s, 2–5.

-- Fjortoft, I. (1998). Ut i skoven- opp i traerne! Naturen- et sted for lek og laering. *Konferensrapport,* Barn og Friluftliv, Friluftsframjandet.

-- Fjortoft, I. (1999). The natural environment as a playground for children. The impact of outdoor play activities in pre-primary school children. *Proceedings of OMEP's 22nd World Congress and 50th Anniversary on the child's right to care, play and education*, Copenhagen, Denmark.

-- Fjortoft, I. and Sageie, J. (2000). The natural environment as a playground for children. Landscape description and analyses of a natural playscape. *Landscape and Urban Planning*, **48**, 83–97.

-- Forbes, S., Cooper, D. and Kendle, A. D. (1997). The history and development of ecological landscape styles. Kendle, T. and Forbes, S. (eds) *Urban Nature Conservation- Landscape Management in the Urban Countryside*. E. & F. N. Spon, London.

-- Grahn, P. (1991). Om Parkers Betydelse. *Stad & Land*, **93**. Sveriges Landbruksuniversitet, Alnarp, Sweden.

-- Grahn, P., Martensson, F., Lindblad, B., Nilsson, P. and Ekman, A. (1997). Ute pa Dagis. *Stad & Land*, **45**, Sveriges Landbruksuniversitet, Alnarp, Sweden.

-- Helford, R. M. (2000). Constructing nature as constructing science: expertise, activist science, and public conflict in the Chicago Wilderness. In Gobster, P. H. and Bruce Hull, R. (eds) *Restoring Nature – Perspectives from the Social Sciences and Humanities*. Island Press, Washington, DC.

-- Herzog, T. R., Herbert, E. J., Kaplan, R. and Crooks, C. L. (2000). Cultural and developmental comparisons of landscape perceptions and preferences. *Environment and Behaviour*, **33**, No. 3, 323–346.

-- Hill, P. (2001). The planting revolution in the modern garden. *Topos*, **37**, 48–57.

-- Hopkins, G. M. (1948) *Poems of Gerard Manley Hopkins.* Oxford University Press, Oxford.

-- Hull, R. B. IV, Buyhoff, G. J. and Cordell, H. K. (1987). Psychophysical models: an example with scenic beauty perceptions of roadside pine forests. *Landscape Journal*, **6**, 113–122.

-- Jacobs, J. (1994). *The Death and Life of Great American Cities*. Penguin in association with Jonathan Cape, Harmondsworth.

-- Jorgensen, A., Hitchmough, J. and Calvert, T. (2002). Woodland spaces and edges: their impact on perception of safety and preference. *Landscape and Urban Planning*, **60**, No. 3, 135–150.

-- Jorgensen, A., Hitchmough, J. and Dunnett, N. (in press). Living in the urban wildwoods – myth and reality in Warrington New Town, UK. In Kowarik, I. and Körner, S. (Eds) *Urban Wild Woodlands*. Springer, Berlin.

-- Kaltenborn, B. P. and Bjerke, T. (2002). Associations between environmental value orientations and landscape preferences. *Landscape and Urban Planning*, **59**, 1–11.

-- Kaplan, R. (1977a). Preference and everyday nature: method and application (Swift River drain study). In Stokols, D. (ed.) *Perspectives on Environment and Behaviour: Theory, Research and Applications*. Plenum, New York.

-- Kaplan, R. (1977b). Preference and everyday nature: method and application (Alternative strategies in the study of roadside preference). In Stokols, D. (ed.) *Perspectives on Environment and Behaviour: Theory, Research and Applications*. Plenum, New York.

- Kaplan, R. (1985). Nature at the doorstep: residential satisfaction and the nearby environment. *Journal of Architectural and Planning Research*, **2**, 115–127.
- Kaplan, R. and Herbert, E. J. (1987). Cultural and sub-cultural comparisons in preference for natural settings. *Landscape and Urban Planning*, **14**, 281–293.
- Kaplan, R. and Kaplan, S. (1989). *The Experience of Nature. A Psychological Perspective*. Cambridge University Press, New York.
- Kaplan, R. and Kaplan, S. and Ryan, R. L. (1988). *With People in Mind: Design and manufacture of everyday nature*. Island Press, Washington, DC.
- Kuehn, N. (2000). Spontane Pflanzen für urbane Freiflaechen. *Garten und Landschaft*, **4**, 11–14.
- Lamb, R. J. and Purcell, A. T. (1990). Perception of naturalness in landscape and its relation to vegetation structure. *Landscape and Urban Planning*, **19**, 333–352.
- Landscape Design Trust (2001). *King's Cross Estates Action Public Realm Strategy. Landscape Institute Awards Brochure*. Landscape Design Trust, London.
- Le Corbusier (Jeanneret, C.E.) (1923). *Vers une Architecture*. Translated into English by Etchells, F. (1974). Architectural Press.
- Lickorish, S., Luscombe, G. and Scott, R. (1997). *Wildflowers Work*. Landlife, Liverpool.
- Lutz, A. R., Simpson-Housley, P. and de Man, A. F. (1999). Wilderness. Rural and urban attitudes and perceptions. *Environment and Behaviour,* **31**, No. 2, 259–266.
- Luymes, D. T. and Tamminga, K. (1995). Integrating public safety and use into planning urban greenways. *Landscape and Urban Planning*, **33**, Nos 1–3, 391–400.
- Lyons, E. (1983). Demographic correlates of landscape preference. *Environment and Behaviour,* **15**, 487–511.
- Madge, C. (1997). Public parks and the geography of fear. *Econ. Soc. Geogr.*, **88**, No. 3, 237–250.
- Manning, O. (1982). Designing for man and nature. *Landscape Design,* **140**, 31–32.
- Milchert, J. (1998). Von der neuen poesie der industriel landschaft. *Stadt und Gruen*, **11**, 800–804.
- Milchert, J. (2001). Ein modell für den stadtpark des 21.jahrhunderts. *Stadt und Gruen*, **12**, 867–876.
- Newman, O. (1972). *Defensible Space: Crime Prevention Through Urban Design*. Macmillan, New York.
- Orians, G. H. and Heerwagen, J. H. (1992). Evolved responses to landscapes. In Barkow, J. H., Cosmides, L. and Tooby, J. (eds) *The Adapted Mind – Evolutionary Psychology and the Generation of Culture*. Oxford University Press, New York and Oxford.
- Parsons, R. (1995). Conflict between ecological sustainability and environmental aesthetics: conundrum, canärd or curiosity. *Landscape and Urban Planning*, **32**, 227–244.
- Purcell, A. T. and Lamb, R. J. (1998). Preference and naturalness: An ecological approach. *Landscape and Urban Planning*, **42**, 57–66.
- Reneman, D., Visser, M., Edelmann, E. and Mors, B. (1999). Mensenwensen. De Wensen van Nederlanders ten aanzien van Natuur en groen in de Leefomgeving. Reeks Operatie Boomhut nummer 6. Intomart, Hilversum. Ministerie van Landbouw, Natuurbeheer en Visserij, Den Haag.
- Ribe, R. (1989). The aesthetics of forestry: what has empirical preference research taught us? *Environmental Management*, **13**, No. 1, 55–74.
- Rishbeth, C. (2001). Ethnic minority groups and the design of public open space: an inclusive landscape? *Landscape Research*, **26**, No. 4, 351–366.
- Rohde, C. L. E. and Kendle, A. D. (1994). *Human Well-being, Natural Landscapes and Wildlife in Urban Areas. A Review*. English Nature, Peterborough.
- Ruddell, E. J., Gramann, J. H., Rudis, V. A. and Westphal, J. M. (1989). The psychological utility of visual penetration in near-view forest scenic beauty models. *Environment and Behaviour*, **21**, No. 4, 393–412.
- Ruff, A. R. (1979). *Holland and the Ecological Landscapes*. Deanwater Press Limited, Stockport.
- Schroeder, H. W. and Green, T. L. (1985). Public preference for tree density in municipal parks. *Journal of Arboriculture*, **11**, 272–277.
- Tartaglia-Kershaw, M. (1980). *Urban Woodlands: Their Role in Daily Life*. Master's dissertation. Department of Landscape, Sheffield University.
- Thomas, K. (1983). *Man and the Natural World. Changing Attitudes in England 1500–1800*. Allen Lane, London.
- Thompson, I. H. (2000). *Ecology, Community and Delight – Sources of Values in Landscape Architecture*. E. and F. N. Spon, London.
- Tregay, R. and Gustavsson, R. (1983). *Oakwood's New Landscape – Designing for Nature in the Residential Environment*. Sveriges Lantbruksuniversitet and Warrington and Runcorn Development Corporation. Stad och land/Rapport No. 15, Alnarp No. 15.
- Ulrich, R. S. (1977). Visual landscape preference: a model and application. *Man-Environ. Syst.*, **7**, 279–293.
- Ulrich, R. S. (1986). Human responses to vegetation and landscapes. *Landscape and Urban Planning*, **13**, 29–44.
- Ulrich, R. S. (1993). Biophilia, biophobia and natural landscapes. In Kellert, S. R. and Wilson, E. O. (eds) *The Biophilia Hypothesis*. Island Press/Shearwater Books, Washington, DC.
- Valentine, G. (1989). The geography of women's fear. *Area*, **21**, No. 4, 385–390.

-- Van den Berg, A. E. (1999). Nature images, environmental beliefs, and group differences in the evaluation of natural landscapes. *Individual Differences in the Aesthetic Evaluation of Natural Landscapes*. Doctoral dissertation. University of Groningen, the Netherlands.

-- Van den Berg, A. E. and Vlek, C. A. J. (1998). The influence of planned change context on the evaluation of natural landscapes. *Landscape and Urban Planning*, **43**, Nos 1–3, 1–10.

-- Van den Berg, A. E., Vlek, C. A. J. and Coeterier, J. F. (1998). Group differences in the aesthetic evaluation of nature development plans: a multilevel approach. *Journal of Environmental Psychology*, **18**, 147–157.

-- Van den Born, R. J. G., Lenders, R. H. J., De Groot, W. and Huijsman, E. (2001). The new biophilia: an exploration of visions of nature in Western countries. *Environmental Conservation*, **28**, No. 1, 65–75.

-- Woudstra, J. and Hitchmough, J. (2000). The enamelled mead: history and practice of exotic perennials grown in grassy swards. *Landscape Research*, **25**, No. 1, 29–47.

Index

Page references for figures are in *italics*.